READING HERZL IN BEIRUT

Reading Herzl in Beirut

THE PLO EFFORT TO KNOW THE ENEMY

JONATHAN MARC GRIBETZ

PRINCETON UNIVERSITY PRESS

PRINCETON & OXFORD

Published by Princeton University Press
41 William Street, Princeton, New Jersey 08540
99 Banbury Road, Oxford OX2 6JX

press.princeton.edu

Library of Congress Cataloging-in-Publication Data

Names: Gribetz, Jonathan Marc, 1980– author.
Title: Reading Herzl in Beirut : the PLO effort to know the enemy / Jonathan Marc Gribetz.
Description: Princeton : Princeton University Press, 2024. | Includes bibliographical references and index.
Identifiers: LCCN 2023044587 (print) | LCCN 2023044588 (ebook) | ISBN 9780691260525 (hardback) | ISBN 9780691176802 (paperback) | ISBN 9780691255637 (ebook)
Subjects: LCSH: Munaẓẓamat al-Taḥrīr al-Filasṭīnīyah. Markaz al-Abḥāth. | Zionism—Study and teaching—Lebanon—Beirut. | Judaism—Study and teaching—Lebanon—Beirut. | Israel—Study and teaching—Lebanon—Beirut. | BISAC: SOCIAL SCIENCE / Jewish Studies | HISTORY / Middle East / Israel & Palestine
Classification: LCC DS115.95 .G75 2024 (print) | LCC DS115.95 (ebook) | DDC 320.54095694071—dc23/eng/20240109
LC record available at https://lccn.loc.gov/2023044587
LC ebook record available at https://lccn.loc.gov/2023044588

British Library Cataloging-in-Publication Data is available
Editorial: Fred Appel and James Collier
Production Editorial: Terri O'Prey
Cover Design: Heather Hansen
Production: Erin Suydam
Publicity: William Pagdatoon

Cover Credit: PLO Research Center stamp from private collection

This book has been composed in Arno

Printed on acid-free paper. ∞

Printed in the United States of America

10 9 8 7 6 5 4 3 2 1

For Sarit,
Daniela, Sophie, and Max

CONTENTS

vii

NOTE ON TRANSLATION AND TRANSLITERATION

I FOLLOW here a simplified version of the *International Journal of Middle East Studies* transliteration system for Arabic and a simplified version of the Library of Congress system for Hebrew, generally avoiding diacritics. In rendering names of individuals—in the text, notes, and works cited—I adopt the spelling they used if they ever published in Latin script (e.g., Assʿad Razzouk for Asʿad Razzuq, Shukairy for Shuqayri, Asaʾd Abdul-Rahman for Asʿad ʿAbd al- Rahman, Khairieh Kasmieh for Khayria Qasimiyya, al-Abid and al-Abed for Ibrahim and Lutfi al-ʿAbid, respectively) or the common Latin spelling of their names if they were well known in English; for those unknown in Latin script, I have rendered their names with simple transliteration. Most of the PLO Research Center publications studied in this book were written first in Arabic; in some cases, the Center also published versions of these books in English. I generally refer to the Center's books by an English translation of the titles, whether my own or that of the Center itself. In all cases, I italicize the titles to indicate that they refer to books. When quoting from books produced in both Arabic and English, I generally follow the published translation, except when there are substantive differences, which I address in my analysis. As the Hebrew newspaper *ha-Arets* is recognized widely today by the transliteration *ha-Aretz*, I follow the latter for the Hebrew version. The English publication is named *Haaretz* (no hyphen).

PREFACE

DURING A FELLOWSHIP at the University of Toronto, where I was finishing a book on Zionists and Arabs in Late Ottoman Palestine, I took a stroll through the library stacks. I found myself among shelves packed with books on modern Jewish history. Alongside those written in English, Hebrew, and various European languages was another volume that grabbed my attention. The spine read, in Arabic script, *al-Fikra al-Sahyuniyya*.

The Zionist Idea, as the title translates to English, was a book I knew well—an anthology of classic Zionist texts. I had even had the opportunity to meet the book's cantankerous compiler, Rabbi Dr. Arthur Hertzberg, who welcomed me as a college student into his New Jersey home some five years before his passing in 2006.

What an interesting coincidence, I thought as I opened *al-Fikra al-Sahyuniyya*—an Arabic book with the same title as Hertzberg's English one. A glance at the first pages revealed, however, that the books shared more than a title. The structure of the Arabic volume was identical to that of Hertzberg's book: thirty-seven chapters dedicated to the same thirty-seven proto-Zionist and Zionist thinkers. The Arabic was a translation, it seemed, of Hertzberg's compendium. Curious, I thought: had Hertzberg decided to translate his book into Arabic?

As I examined the title page, though, I realized that Hertzberg probably had not known about the Arabic translation of his work. His name did not appear in the book. Instead, there were six other names listed: Anis Sayegh, Lutfi al-Abed, Musa ʿAnaz, Assʿad Razzouk, Hilda Shaʿban Sayegh, and Ibrahim al-Abid. I was startled. Had I discovered a bootleg version of *The Zionist Idea*? Who would have produced such a work? My eyes turned to the publisher's name:

Munazzamat al-Tahrir al-Filastiniyya
Markaz al-Abhath
Shariʿ Kulumbani al-mutafariʿ min Shariʿ al-Sadat

This Arabic version of Hertzberg's *The Zionist Idea* was published in 1970 by the Palestine Liberation Organization's Research Center, housed on Colombani Street just off Sadat Street, an intersection in the heart of Beirut, the capital of Lebanon.

In this way, I stumbled upon the PLO Research Center. But I needed to stay focused on the task at hand, finishing my first book, *Defining Neighbors: Religion, Race, and Early Zionist-Arab Encounter.*

Once *Defining Neighbors* was published, I felt myself drawn back to the Arabic *Zionist Idea* and to the institution that had produced it. I was captivated by the idea that a branch of the PLO had deemed it worthwhile to dedicate human and financial resources to bringing to the Arabic-reading public the writings of Zionists such as rabbis Yehuda Alkalai (d. 1878), Zvi Hirsch Kalischer (d. 1874), Samuel Mohilever (d. 1898), Abraham Isaac Kook (d. 1935), Judah Magnes (d. 1948), and Solomon Schechter (d. 1915), or lay luminaries such as Moses Hess (d. 1875), Eliezer Ben-Yehuda (d. 1922), Leo Pinsker (d. 1891), Asher Ginzburg (d. 1927), Hayyim Nahman Bialik (d. 1934), Micha Berdyczewski (d. 1934), Joseph Hayyim Brenner (d. 1921), and Dov Ber Borochov (d. 1917).

Why, I wondered, was the PLO interested in Zionist intellectual history that most Zionists had long forgotten? Who was behind this Research Center and what were they doing when they weren't translating early Zionist works? What tools and means were at their disposal? And what was in it for the PLO? This book, *Reading Herzl in Beirut*, is the fruit of my decade-long quest to answer these questions.

In certain respects, *Reading Herzl in Beirut* is a continuation of the work I began in *Defining Neighbors*. There, I studied how Arabs and Zionists in Palestine and the broader region conceived of one another in the final decades of Ottoman rule. I found that those who left us written evidence of their perceptions of their neighbors often defined them through the categories of religion and race, with unexpected implications from the vantage point of the present day. For example, a prominent Muslim Arab of Jerusalem concluded that the belief in the return to Zion was central to the Jewish religious tradition and, therefore, Zionism should not be viewed as a marginal or insignificant threat to Palestine's Arabs or to the Ottoman Empire. Meanwhile, recognizing the close similarities between Judaism and Islam and the long history of generally amicable relations between Jews and Muslims in the Levant, Zionists were often surprised that Palestine's Muslims opposed Jewish immigration, and many blamed the local Christian Arabs for spreading their religiously moti-

vated anti-Judaism and spoiling Muslim good will. At the same time, employing the dominant race-thinking of the age, certain Arab intellectuals in the
region argued that the economic, social, and cultural success of Jews in Europe
demonstrated that Semites were no less capable than European races and thus,
that as the Jews' racial relatives, Arabs were equally able to excel in these areas,
and would do so in less oppressive political circumstances. Also utilizing early
twentieth-century race-thinking, key Zionists including David Ben-Gurion,
the man who would become Israel's founding prime minister, believed that
Palestine's Arab peasants were not merely the Jews' racial relatives but themselves bona fide Jews in racial terms. After the Balfour Declaration, the British
Mandate, and the rise of a zero-sum nationalist, territorial conflict, Zionist-
Arab perceptions rigidified, but these early, forgotten assessments of the Other
reveal that the conceptions and dynamics of the Zionist-Arab conflict have
been neither timeless nor immutable.

In this book, I focus on a later period, the mid-1960s through the early
1980s, in Beirut, a city 150 miles north of Jerusalem, the primary setting of
my first book. During the half-century-plus after the collapse of the Ottoman
Empire, dramatic changes took place in the lives of Palestine's Arabs and
Zionists—transformations that, among other consequences, renamed these
communities "Palestinians" and "Israelis." Consider just a few of these developments. The British conquered Palestine from the Ottomans, ruled the region for three decades, and then sailed home, having failed to deliver on their
League of Nations mandate to establish in Palestine a "national home" for the
Jewish people without prejudicing the "civil and religious rights of existing
non-Jewish communities." The British decided to abandon the Palestine Mandate two years after the end of World War II, in which the Nazis and their allies
murdered six million Jews in Europe and left a trail of devastation in their
wake. When the British departed, Palestine was violently divided between the
newly founded State of Israel and two other former British-governed states,
Jordan and Egypt. Hundreds of thousands of Palestinians were exiled from the
territories Israel ruled by the end of the 1948 war, settling mainly in refugee
camps in historic Palestine and neighboring countries, and hundreds of thousands of Jewish refugees from Europe and the Arab world flocked to Israel.
Thus, by the time the Palestine Liberation Organization established its Research Center in 1965, the political encounter between Zionists and Arabs was
profoundly different, almost unrecognizably so, from the one I had studied in
the Late Ottoman period. Two years later, after the 1967 war, the differences
were even more dramatic, as those parts of Palestine that Arab regimes had

ruled for nineteen years were seized by Israel, leaving all of Mandate Palestine, including the iconic Old City of Jerusalem, in Israeli hands.

And yet, while the language of "enemy" perforce replaced that of "neighbor," the compulsion to comprehend the Other persisted. In fact, it became ever more urgent. On the Palestinian side, the PLO Research Center sought to fill this need. Similar to my study of perceptions in the Late Ottoman period, this book assesses how the Center's intellectuals conceived of Zionists. However, in contrast to *Defining Neighbors*, in which I studied mutual perceptions, here I take a mostly unidirectional focus on PLO perceptions of Israel. While part of the challenge in my first book was unearthing enough relevant evidence, in this case the problem was choosing from among the plethora of written material that the PLO Research Center published in its eighteen years in Beirut.

As in *Defining Neighbors*, I rely in this book mainly on written materials, especially the vast corpus of texts that the Center produced, primarily in Arabic but also in English and other languages. I conducted much of the research for this book in Jerusalem, as the National Library of Israel holds one of the world's most complete collections of the PLO Research Center's publications. Raquel Ukeles and Yaniv Levi-Korem of the NLI located library acquisition records that allowed me to solve one of this story's many puzzles—namely, whether Israel actually returned everything the Israel Defense Forces had taken from the Center in Beirut. In Jerusalem, I received generous support from the Fulbright Scholar Program and the National Endowment for the Humanities, and a warm welcome from Hillel Cohen, Manuela Consonni, Abigail Jacobson, and other colleagues at the Hebrew University. I wrote substantial portions of the book in the spacious library of the Van Leer Jerusalem Institute, which hosted me as a fellow for two years.

Archival materials also proved ample and essential for this project. The documents that the Israel State Archives has made available online are rich and revealing. That these sources are accessible only digitally remains frustrating, but digital access has proven its advantages in recent years, especially as those who have been unable, or have not been permitted, to enter Israel have been able to study these archives from their computers abroad.

I benefited from access to other archival documents thanks to the kindness of scholars who believed in this project. Yigal Sheffy assisted me in locating and declassifying a key document in the IDF Archives, which I had initially been told did not exist. Geoffrey Levin shared scanned files from the archives of Fayez Sayegh, housed at the University of Utah, and from the personal files of Don Peretz that he collected from the home of Peretz's widow Maya. Sheffy's and Levin's generosity allowed me to tell parts of this story I would otherwise not have been able to write.

Beyond written sources, there were other types of material accessible to me as I examined the story of the PLO Research Center that had been unavailable for my studies of the Late Ottoman period. This difference first struck me as I tried to find an obituary upon which I could rely for the basic biographical details of the last director of the PLO Research Center in Beirut, Sabri Jiryis. I failed to track down any death announcements and learned why when I discovered Jiryis's personal website and blog, which appeared to be active. From the "About Me" page, I retrieved Jiryis's contact information and within hours I was in close contact with another principal player in this story. On the heels of my previous project, which studied events from a century prior, I was at first startled by the ability I now had to speak with the story's main protagonists. These opportunities turned out to be a most rewarding aspect of this project. Gracious and gregarious, Jiryis permitted me to interview him by phone and in his home, again and again, answered my questions by email and text message, and even shared with me a draft of his still-unpublished memoirs.

Nearly forty years had passed since the end of the PLO Research Center's term in Beirut, so I found myself racing against the clock to locate people who could enlighten me from their personal experiences. I interviewed Walid Khalidi in his Massachusetts home about the relationship between the PLO Research Center and the Institute for Palestine Studies that he had cofounded. I met with Yezid Sayigh, scholar of the Palestinian national movement, whose uncles founded and ran the Center for over a decade and whose father published research for the Center. I spoke with Anan Ameri, who had served on the Center's research staff, and with Philip Mattar, who had briefly conducted research in the Center's library. Reading the Peretz files Levin had shared with me led me to correspond with author Cynthia Ozick and historian Stuart Schaar, both of whom responded helpfully. I also had the privilege of meeting with two fascinating figures who have since passed away. In 2016, I flew to Berlin to interview the Syrian philosopher Sadik al-Azm, who had worked at the Center in Beirut; we spent a full, captivating day together. Al-Azm died six months later. In 2018, I drove with my friend and guide Salah Ghannem to Ramallah to meet with Samih Shabeeb, who had also worked at the Center in Beirut and was then directing the new Center in Ramallah. Shabeeb died the following year.

During my time in Jerusalem, I also met with Israeli military and intelligence officials who had analyzed the Center's activities, confiscated and studied the Center's library during the 1982 war, and subsequently returned much of the seized material. I learned about Israel's fraught interest in the Center from conversations with, among others, Mike Herzog, Amos Gilead, Elyakim Rubinstein, Yigal Sheffy, Baruch Spiegel, Amos Yaron, Gadi Zohar, and especially Matti Steinberg, who spent hours answering my questions about his intelligence assessments of the Center. In most cases, I sought out these individuals upon hearing or reading about their roles in Israel's side of the Research Center saga. My introduction to Yigal Sheffy, however, was more personal. Following a lecture that I had delivered at Tel Aviv University, Sheffy raised his hand and recounted an assignment he had been given relating to the PLO Research Center in November 1983.[1]

Together, these diverse sources—published, archival, and oral—permitted me to tell the story of the PLO Research Center in Beirut from its establishment through years of prolific activity in Beirut to the ultimate wartime confiscation of its library, its surprising return, and its mysterious subsequent disappearance.

As an American Jewish professor of Near Eastern Studies, I was able, in writing this book, to visit Jerusalem, Fassuta, Ramallah, and Berlin; to interview Palestinians, Israelis, Lebanese, and Syrians and to persuade Israeli archives and the National Library of Israel to open records for me—privileges that might not have been accessible to others from different backgrounds. Even as my personal profile opened many doors, it kept others, including those of Lebanon, closed.[2] Ultimately, as is always the case, the sources upon which this book is based reflect the political realities in which it was written.

In engaging with my textual and living sources—whether PLO intellectuals, activists, militants, or Israeli intellectuals, intelligence officers, and government and military officials—I saw as my task not to judge but to understand. Readers will no doubt judge the actions and ideologies of those they meet in this book. I invite them to join me first on a journey to better understanding.

READING HERZL IN BEIRUT

Introduction

IN MID-SEPTEMBER 1982, as they invaded West Beirut, Israeli forces raided a high-rise on Colombani Street in the Lebanese capital. Though the building belonged to the Palestine Liberation Organization, it contained neither militants nor weapons. Instead, the Israeli soldiers discovered, and quickly seized, a library—a library teeming with books about Jews, Zionism, and Israel.

This library was the jewel of the Palestine Liberation Organization Research Center, an arm of the PLO founded in Beirut in February 1965, just months after the establishment of the organization itself. Over its nearly two decades of activity in Beirut, the Research Center's mission was to study *al-qadiyya al-filastiniyya,* the "Palestine question," and to increase knowledge about "the enemy."[1] It did so through the concerted efforts of researchers who produced hundreds of books, pamphlets, and journal issues in Arabic and other languages. Through books the Center published with titles such as *The Zionist Idea, State and Religion in Israel, The Kibbutz, The Moshav, The Histadrut, Mapai, Mapam, Israel and World Jewry, David Ben-Gurion, The Talmud and Zionism,* and *Discrimination against Eastern Jews in Israel,* the Center's leaders provided intellectual resources for Palestinian and other Arab readers to better understand Israel's history and ideological underpinnings.[2] The Center investigated other matters as well, but one of its prime areas of focus comprised Jews, Judaism, Zionism, and Israel.

The story of the PLO Research Center did not end with its library's confiscation in September 1982. Unlike the thousands of books Israel seized from Arab libraries in the 1948 war that sit until today in the National Library of Israel,[3] the PLO Research Center's library was, by all accounts, mostly returned. And quickly. In November 1983, Israel and the PLO negotiated a prisoner swap through the International Committee of the Red Cross. In exchange for the PLO's release of six Israeli soldiers it held captive in Lebanon, Israel agreed to free more than four thousand Arab prisoners—and the PLO Research Center library. Air France planes arrived at Ben-Gurion Airport to transport one thousand of the freed Arab prisoners to Algeria and, as they boarded the planes, the IDF loaded crates filled with books into the cargo sections beneath.

Reading Herzl in Beirut tells the story of the institution that created this library, the researchers who used it, the scholarship they produced in it, and the events that led to its confiscation and return. In telling this story, the book explores the role played by knowledge in the development of politics and by politics in the production and distribution of knowledge in the Palestinian-Israeli conflict.

Israel's seizure of the PLO Research Center was—and in historical memory remains—overshadowed by other events that transpired contemporaneously as Israel invaded West Beirut. Israel captured the PLO Research Center during the very days in September 1982 when a Lebanese Christian militia allied with Israel massacred hundreds of Palestinian civilians in the Sabra and Shatila refugee camps, a massacre for which Israel's own commission of inquiry declared Israeli officials "indirectly responsible."[4] In a week when hundreds of people, including many women and children, are slaughtered, it is hard to notice, much less to recall, anything else.

Beyond the particular timing of these events, there is a broader reason why many in the West have never heard of the Center and its research output: the Center does not fit neatly into any of the dominant perceptions of the PLO. Among those who remember the organization in its heyday, common associations with the PLO might range from freedom fighters, embattled nationalist heroes, bold or ambivalent peacemakers to corrupt bureaucrats, gun-toting hijackers, or merciless terrorists. The variety of associations is wide, but would not typically include prolific researchers of Judaism, Zionism, and Israel. Yet, one official wing of the PLO consisted of precisely such individuals. If today, four decades after its period of intensive activity in Beirut, the PLO Research Center is largely forgotten, it may be because few have a political interest in remembering it.

Leaving aside such interests, however, the PLO Research Center, from its founding through its conquest and beyond, merits our attention. The war that Palestinians and their allies were waging against Israel had many fronts. Arab state militaries and Palestinian guerrillas, no doubt, played key roles in the broad effort to defeat Israel but the pen joined the sword in this war—and considering Israel's increasingly clear military superiority over the Arab states, Palestinian activists and supporters took very seriously the potential power of the pen. If the chances of defeating Israel on the battlefield were slim, perhaps Israel could be undermined through rhetorical and intellectual challenges to its legitimacy. To undertake such challenges, some believed, one had first to develop a deeper understanding of the object of the challenge. The PLO Research Center's studies of Jews, Judaism, Zionism, and Israel thus proved crucial for Palestinian nationalist endeavors.

As the PLO Research Center's motivation in studying Jewish and Zionist history was to "know the enemy," it is not surprising that the authors generally related in an antagonistic way to the subjects of their research. But, as we shall see, there are also subtle hints in the Center's publications of an interest not only in combatting but also in emulating certain aspects of their objects of study. In any case, the Center's scholars took their jobs seriously. Whether in their writings for an internal Palestinian and Arab audience or in those for an external Western audience, these university-educated researchers employed scholarly sources and academic methods. In this sense, the story of the PLO Research Center constitutes an important chapter in Palestinian intellectual history.

Odd as it may sound, the PLO Research Center may be regarded as having been a pioneer in the field of Israel studies. The founding of the Center preceded by a full two decades that of the Association for Israel Studies (AIS). If Israel studies is defined as the study of the State of Israel and its origins, and "is open to all individuals who are engaged in, or share an interest in, scholarly inquiry about the State and society of Israel," regardless of "citizenship, nationality, religion, or political orientation,"[5] much of what the PLO Research Center did in its years in Beirut qualifies. In fact, many of the research questions that the Center asked—for example, about the relationship between Judaism and Zionism, ethnicity and gender in Israel, or colonialism and violence—participated in the scholarly discourse on these matters. Some of the conclusions that the Center's authors drew heralded future trends in the field of Israel studies.

An examination of the PLO Research Center is thus not only a study in Palestinian intellectual history but also in Jewish and Israeli history. Moreover, Jews from Israel and abroad were at various times and in different ways connected to the work of the Center (and ultimately, to its demise). Jewish authors appear prominently in the footnotes and bibliographies of the Center's publications and, in certain instances, Jewish scholars and activists were part of the

Center's intellectual life not only as subjects but also participants. Like the story of the Palestinian people since the rise of Zionism, the Center's story is deeply intertwined with that of Jews and Zionism. (The reverse is no less true, of course, as the history of the Jews and Israel has been, since the rise of Zionism, profoundly enmeshed with that of the Palestinians.) This book, then, is also a story of intellectual and personal encounter—generally adversarial though occasionally collaborative—among Palestinians and Israelis, Arabs and Jews.

The PLO Research Center also presents us with a fascinating case study of the fraught relationship between scholarship and politics. The Center was at once an official arm of a militant nationalist organization with a clear political agenda and an institution dedicated to objective research. Notably, while the PLO was not, in principle, opposed to propagandistic efforts, its propaganda was meant to be conducted by other entities within the organization.[6] In this book, I explore the bidirectionality of influence between the Center's ideology and its research.

Though this book focuses on an institution run by a handful of local intellectuals housed in an ordinary building in a medium-sized city in a small Middle Eastern country, it also tells a global story. The PLO Research Center was founded by the PLO, itself the creation of the Arab League, and it continued to be funded by the Palestine National Fund, the Arab League, and individual Arab governments. From its inception, the Center was implicated in a regional network of states and interests, which themselves evolved over the course of the Center's lifetime in Beirut. In addition, the Center's intended audience was both local and global, and included Arabic and non-Arabic readers alike. This book thus considers the broader intellectual community and interlocutors who shaped the scholarship of the Center. It also reflects on the Center's impact on the PLO political leadership's decision to engage in global diplomacy.[7]

While the story of the Research Center has been largely forgotten, as I was writing this book, I learned of several fellow scholars who have also become interested in different aspects of the Center. These scholars of archives, libraries, and film have made important contributions from which my own research has benefited. Digital humanities scholar Jacqueline Bader Husary, in her thesis "Recovering the PLO Research Center: Limits and Potential for Digital Methods to Retrieve Dispersed Archives," used technological tools to mine online library catalogues to "locat[e] the Research Center traces that survive in libraries across the world." Through this sophisticated research, Husary pro-

duced a fifteen-page bibliography of the Research Center's publications in its
Beirut years.[8] Two other scholars have been particularly interested in the episode of Israel's wartime capture of the Center's collections. In an article entitled "The Paper Trail of a Liberation Movement," archivist and historian
Hana Sleiman argued that Israel's seizure of the PLO's institutional archives
held by the PLO Research Center constituted neither the first nor the last
period of "captivity" of these archival materials. Rather, Sleiman contended
provocatively, the archive's "first captor" was the PLO Research Center itself
while, after Israel returned the materials in 1983, "the Palestinian state-
building enterprise" became "its current captor."[9] Rona Sela, a scholar of art
history, portrayed the 1982 conquest of the Research Center, as well as the
films from the PLO's Cultural Arts Section, as examples of "colonial plunder-
ing/looting of cultural and historical treasures and archives and their administration and dominance in military colonial archives."[10] Two documentaries,
Looted and Hidden by Sela and *Shalal—A Reel War* by Karnit Mandel, have
recently been released, focusing especially on the films the Research Center
had collected.[11] This book thus joins in a budding rediscovery of the PLO
Research Center in Beirut.

The chapters that follow are divided into three parts, each motivated by certain
driving questions. In part 1, as I recount the history and work of the Research
Center between 1965 and 1982, I ask what led the PLO to devote substantial
resources and talent to an in-depth investigation and presentation of Judaism,
Zionism, and Israel, and what drew the Center's leadership to this enterprise.
In part 2, I analyze in detail a number of publications on a variety of topics that
the PLO Research Center produced, and I ask how the Center's researchers
undertook their work and what conclusions they drew. In part 3, I inquire into
what happened to the Center and its library after its confiscation in 1982 and
ask whether we might be able to discern the Center's impact on the development of the Palestinian-Israeli conflict.

   The PLO Research Center played an important role in the history of the
PLO, in Palestinian intellectual history, and in the history of the Palestinian-
Israeli conflict and its global perceptions. Studying the Center's research yields
insights about the PLO, its intellectuals, and its perspectives on Judaism, Zionism, and Israel. The story of the PLO Research Center in Beirut is thus a crucial piece of Palestinian history, Israeli history, and the history of the
conflict.

PART I

The PLO Research Center between Academics and Politics

1

Why Did the PLO Need
a Research Center?

Founding the PLO

To understand why the Palestine Liberation Organization created a research center, we must first consider the aims of the PLO itself. Beginning with the establishment of Israel in May 1948, the surrounding Arab states regarded themselves, and were regarded by their populations, as responsible for undoing the historic injustice perpetrated upon Palestine and the Palestinians. Those Arab states, however, were plainly unsuccessful in their efforts to liberate Palestine, as they phrased it. The failures were obvious. In the war of 1948, the Arab states failed to thwart the establishment of Israel, to prevent the exile of some 700,000 Palestinian refugees, or even to limit Israel's territorial boundaries to those delineated in the United Nations' partition plan (General Assembly Resolution 181 of 1947). In 1956, in Israel's secretly coordinated assault with England and France, Egypt lost still more territory to Israel, and Israel only withdrew from the Sinai Peninsula due to pressure not from the Arab states but from the US and the Soviet Union.

By the late 1950s, Palestinian refugees had grown increasingly skeptical of the Arab states' capacity to defeat Israel—and some wondered whether the Arab states even cared to do so. Jaded by the Arab states' repeated promises and disappointments, Palestinians asked: were Arab states conspiring with Israel? Were they controlled by Western powers? Did the fate of the Palestinians truly matter to the Arab states? Whether in the Jordanian-annexed West Bank, the Egyptian-ruled Gaza Strip, or outside the borders of British Mandate Palestine in Egypt, Jordan, Syria, Lebanon, and beyond, many Palestinians decided that the time had come to take matters into their own hands. For some, it was a matter of principle, arguing that even if Palestinians lacked the ability to liberate their homeland, they were dutybound to try. For others, this was part of a broader strategy known as "entanglement" (*tawrit* in Arabic). The idea was to attack Israel from bases in Arab states so as to provoke Israeli reprisals against those states. Such Israeli attacks would in turn compel the Arab states to engage Israel militarily out of concern for their own dignity, if not for that of the Palestinians.[1]

A number of Palestinian militant groups were thus founded in the 1950s to fight Israel and to force the Arab host states to join them on the Palestinian militants' own terms.[2] These groups emerged from Muslim or Arab organizations, especially the Muslim Brotherhood and the Arab Nationalist Movement (ANM), when Palestinian members of these groups grew frustrated with their subordination to the interests and authority of Arab states. The tension between addressing broad Arab and Muslim interests, on the one hand, and addressing particularistic Palestinian interests, on the other, ultimately animated the formation of both the Palestinian National Liberation Movement (Fateh) and the Popular Front for the Liberation of Palestine.[3]

Fateh was created mainly by Palestinian refugees who first reached political consciousness as youths and young adults in the Muslim Brotherhood in Gaza. In 1957, Ramleh refugee Khalil al-Wazir demanded of the Muslim Brotherhood's leadership to establish "a special organization . . . that would not appear outwardly as Islamist, but rather promote the slogan of liberating Palestine through armed struggle."[4] When the Brotherhood's leadership refused, al-Wazir and fellow Brotherhood activists met in Kuwait and created a new organization: Fateh (a reverse acronym for the Arabic words Palestinian National Liberation Movement). At that founding meeting in Kuwait, al-Wazir was joined by another former Muslim Brotherhood member, Yasser Arafat, and four others. Yezid Sayigh, the preeminent scholar of Palestinian nationalist organizational history, highlighted that Fateh's founding program proclaimed "two cardinal principles: the absolute independence of Palestinian organization and decision making from the Arab governments, and the primacy of armed struggle as the sole means of liberating Palestine."[5] Fateh's founders demanded independence from Arab governments not merely because those governments had proven themselves ineffective in liberating Palestine, but because, as they asserted, the Arab states were actively and deliberately thwarting the Palestinians' effort.[6] In the view of the Fateh founders, Palestinian liberation was not a victim simply of the Arab states' neglect or incompetence but of calculated, even conspiratorial, obstruction.

While Palestinian disillusionment with the ANM was initially more ambivalent than the Fateh founders' frustrations with the Muslim Brotherhood,
the two stories contain notable parallels emerging from the same tension between broader regional interests and particularistic Palestinian concerns. The
ANM was founded in 1951 by a group of students at the American University
of Beirut. The leading early personalities in the ANM group were George Habash, a medical student who came from a wealthy Christian Palestinian family
that had been expelled from Lydda during the 1948 war, and Hani al-Hindi,
scion of an important Damascene family.[7] Soon they were joined by student
groups from Lebanon, Syria, and Jordan. Though the organization was principally committed to the goal of Palestinian liberation, it argued that this long-
term aim could only be achieved after the Arab states were free from Western
colonial control. As Wadie Haddad, a Palestinian Christian refugee from
Safed, explained to ANM recruits, "the road to Tel Aviv passes through Damascus, Baghdad, Amman, and Cairo."[8] In its aim for Arab independence from
foreign powers and for Arab unity, the ANM was inspired by the rise of Gamal
Abdel Nasser, the charismatic Egyptian president who sought to lead the Arab
world in combatting colonialism.

But as time passed, some Palestinian ANM members sensed that the
organization's goal of Arab unity would indefinitely take precedence over Palestinian liberation. The Palestinian break from the ANM was slow and tortu-
ous. First, in 1959, the ANM established a "Palestine Committee"; then, in
1963, Palestinian ANM members founded their own autonomous Palestinian
branches of the movement.[9] Finally, after the 1967 war debacle, Habash merged
a portion of the ANM with other Palestinian-oriented groups to form the
Popular Front for the Liberation of Palestine (PFLP).[10] The new organization's
name reflects the shift in emphasis and the decision to no longer defer the
cause of Palestine until after Arab unity was achieved.

At times, various Arab states supported and encouraged Fateh, PFLP, and
other fedayeen, those willing to sacrifice themselves for the sake of freedom,
as the militants who undertook cross-border assaults on Israeli targets from
bases in neighboring Arab countries came to be known. Over time, however,
the governments of those neighboring countries learned that these groups
could, and in fact intended to, provoke damaging Israeli retaliation, which
might then demand a reaction for which their militaries were not prepared or
in which the state had no interest.

The leaders of the Arab states, represented by the Arab League with Nasser
at the helm, found a creative solution to the problem: the establishment of an

organization dedicated to the liberation of Palestine that would be beholden to the Arab League. In January 1964, at the first Arab summit conference, the Arab leaders called upon Ahmad Shukairy (1908–1980), the representative of Palestine to the League of Arab States, "to continue his consultations with member states and Palestinian people with the aim of arriving at the setting up of sound foundations for organizing the Palestinian people and enabling it to play its role in liberating its homeland and determining its destiny."[11] With Nasser's blessing, over the course of the following four months, Shukairy planned the founding meeting of the Palestine National Council (PNC), the leadership body of the new Palestine Liberation Organization.[12]

The inaugural session of the PNC opened on May 28, 1964, in Jordanian-annexed Jerusalem. That the ruler of Jordan would permit this meeting to be hosted in Jerusalem was not a foregone conclusion. King Hussein had good reason to fear Palestinian nationalism as the majority of citizens in his kingdom were themselves originally Palestinian, and he had annexed most of the territory that the UN partition plan had allotted to the Arab State in Palestine (i.e., the West Bank). Ultimately, however, both to strengthen relations with Nasser and to exercise maximal control over the meeting and the future organization, Hussein approved the Intercontinental Hotel on the Mount of Olives as the site of the meeting. The hotel offered a clear view of the iconic Dome of the Rock, Jerusalem's Old City, and, just beyond, Israeli-controlled West Jerusalem. As the host, Hussein selected most of the 422 Palestinian invitees, and the king's intelligence services carefully monitored the sessions.[13]

The delegates' first task was to define the new organization's goals and structure. To that end, Shukairy presented his proposed drafts of what would soon become the two founding documents of the Palestine Liberation Organization.

One was the Palestinian National covenant or charter (*al-mithaq al-watani al-filastini*—hereafter, "the Covenant"), which laid out the core principles of the PLO.[14] In its original form (it would be revised four years later, in 1968), the Covenant was primarily concerned with three issues.[15] First, and most important for the PLO's Arab League patrons, the Covenant emphasized that Palestinian nationalism and Arabism were not contradictory, but rather mutually reinforcing movements. The very first article of the Covenant reads: "Palestine is an Arab homeland bound by strong national ties to the rest of the Arab countries and which together form the large Arab homeland." Nasser wished ultimately to unite Arab countries into a single unit (as he had attempted to do through the short-lived unification of Egypt and Syria between 1958 and 1961 in the United Arab Republic). For those who worried that a particular focus on Palestine might harm the goal of broader Arab national unity, Shukairy's Covenant meant to allay such fears. "The Palestinian people firmly believe in Arab unity," he wrote, but, he continued, the Palestinian people "must, at this stage of its struggle, preserve its Palestinian personality and all its constituents." The Covenant's next articles assert, however, that "Arab unity and the liberation of Palestine are two complementary goals" and that "the destiny of the Arab Nation and even the essence of Arab existence are firmly tied to the destiny of the Palestine question." For those readers who wanted to be sure that Palestinian nationalism would be subordinate to Arab unity, the Covenant offered reassurance ("at this stage"), while also aiming to please readers who regarded Palestinian national liberation as an independent value.

Nasser was not the only Arab leader whose sensibilities the PLO had to take into account. The rulers of both Jordan and Syria expected assurances that the PLO would accept their countries' respective claims to Palestine's West Bank and the Himmah region. Hence, the Covenant also contains an article declaring that "this organization does not exercise any regional sovereignty over the West Bank in the Hashemite Kingdom of Jordan, on the Gaza Strip or the Himmah area." The implication was that the PLO would limit its sights to those parts of historic Palestine that Israel now ruled.

Second, the Covenant sought to define Palestinian nationalism in the broadest possible terms and to defer any internal debate or tension until after Palestine's liberation. Palestinians, the Covenant declares, "are those Arab citizens who were living regularly in Palestine up to 1947, whether they remained or were expelled, as well as those born after this date to a Palestinian father within or beyond Palestine." Patrilineal descent, not ideology, defined Palestinian identity. Recognizing that Palestinian nationalism included socialist, communist, conservative, and religious factions, Shukairy stressed that "doctrines, whether political, social, or economic," will not distract the people of Palestine from "the primary duty of liberating their homeland." The precise nature of the political entity that would emerge upon the liberation of Palestine was a matter to be settled in the indefinitely deferred future, after the Palestinian people "completes the liberation of its homeland in accordance with its own wishes, free will, and choice."

The third concern of the Covenant was to articulate a Palestinian nationalist consensus on Jews and Zionism. The term "Zionism" appears first in the second paragraph of the preamble, which asserts that "the forces of global Zionism and colonialism conspired and worked to displace" the Palestinian Arab people. From the start, Zionism was regarded as a foreign colonial movement that aimed to uproot the native population. An article in the Covenant elaborates on this point: "Zionism is a colonialist movement in its inception, aggressive and expansionist in its goals, racist and segregationist in its configurations and fascist in its means and aims."

Shukairy was, of course, aware that there were Jews who were native to Palestine. If Palestinians were defined ethnically and as "Arab citizens," as we saw above, where did these Jews fit in? "Jews of Palestinian origin," the Covenant explained, "are considered Palestinians if they are willing to live peacefully and loyally in Palestine." Left aside was the question of which Jews ought to be regarded as being "of Palestinian origin," another ambiguity that Shukairy presumably regarded as necessary for the purposes of satisfying his organization's diverse constituents and the Covenant's global audience. If the PLO Covenant was vague on its definition of Palestinian identity, it was abundantly clear on its definition of Judaism. Judaism is "a divine religion," the Covenant asserts unequivocally, and "not a nationality with independent existence."

The other document that the PLO delegates approved at their inaugural meeting has been subject to far less scrutiny than the Covenant, but it is essential for understanding the birth of the PLO Research Center. The text, *al-nizam al-asasi*, alternatively rendered as the Constitution or the Basic or Fundamental Law, lays out the organizational structure and procedural systems of the PLO. Article 18 of the Constitution calls upon the Executive Committee of the Palestine National Council to establish a number of departments, including a military department, a department for political and information affairs, a Palestine National Fund department, a department for research and specialized institutes, and a department for administrative affairs, each with its own director general and staff.[16] It was this call for "a department for research and specialized institutes" (*da'irat al-buhuth wa-l-mu'assasat al-mukhtassa*) that sanctioned the creation of the PLO Research Center.

Founding the PLO Research Center

While in this first meeting in May 1964, the Executive Committee of the Palestine National Council declared the need for a department of research within the PLO, its scope and organization were not spelled out. What subjects would this entity be expected to study? Should the PLO build its own research department from scratch or could it absorb an existing institution under its auspices? Could the responsibility of studying the Palestine problem and learning about the enemy have been assigned to a separate group of sympathetic researchers? These were pressing questions for Shukairy because, when he established the PLO, an Arab think tank to study the question of Palestine already existed: the Institute for Palestine Studies (IPS).[17]

IPS, established in Beirut in 1963, a year before the founding of the PLO, was the brainchild of three pan-Arabist intellectuals: Constantine Zurayk, a Syrian of Greek Orthodox background; Walid Khalidi, a Palestinian from a prominent Sunni family of Jerusalem; and Burhan Dajani, a Palestinian Muslim born in Jaffa.[18] In its founding license, IPS defined its mission as "scientific research concerning various aspects of the life of Palestine and the Palestine issue [al-qadiyya], keeping distant from all political activity, governmental association, or party affiliation."[19]

Shukairy knew all about IPS. In fact, on his 1964 tour through the Middle East promoting the new PLO, he had tried to persuade Khalidi and Zurayk to incorporate IPS into the PLO. In return, Shukairy offered to make sure that the institute stayed financially afloat. This offer, Khalidi later recalled, was enticing indeed.[20] The burdens of fundraising for IPS had already begun to wear on him. Nonetheless, Khalidi and Zurayk declined, explaining that subsuming IPS into the PLO would violate an IPS founding principle, namely, its commitment to independence.[21] Remaining faithful to this pillar prevented the institute from becoming the PLO Research Center.

But a separate ideological issue was at stake as well. For IPS, the Palestine question was "a question of the entire Arab homeland."[22] Accordingly, IPS refused to become a specifically *Palestinian* institute. True, as we have seen, the early PLO indeed espoused elements of pan-Arabism. Nonetheless, for Khalidi, at least in retrospect, had IPS agreed to become integrated into the PLO, it could no longer have regarded itself as a broad-based Arab organization. It would perforce have become Palestinian.

The question arises: what was really happening in the Zurayk-Khalidi-Shukairy encounter? Were the actors indeed motivated by principle, or alternatively, by power struggle? This question, which is of course impossible to answer with certainty, brings into focus the issues of intellectual independence, political ideology, personalities, and also money—all of which are key elements in tracing the birth of the PLO Research Center.

Having failed in his meeting with Zurayk and Khalidi, Shukairy turned to Fayez Sayegh, a rising star in the movement for Palestinian liberation. Sayegh was born in 1922 in Syria to a Syrian father and a Palestinian-Lebanese mother. He grew up in Tiberias in British Mandate Palestine, where his father was a

Presbyterian minister.[23] A graduate of the American University of Beirut, Sayegh earned a PhD from Georgetown University in Washington, DC, in 1949.[24] As Yoav Di-Capua noted, for much of the 1950s and 1960s, Sayegh "persistently deployed an existentialist perspective in order to elucidate the impact of the colonial condition on the Arab subject." Di-Capua highlights that Sayegh was "staunchly committed to individual freedom and a just solution in Palestine," and "was one of the most courageous and clearheaded observers of decolonization."[25] Sayegh had proven himself to be a passionate, articulate, and gifted advocate of the Palestinian cause, which he defended frequently on English-language radio and television.[26] He had recently moved back to Beirut to join the faculty of the American University of Beirut's Political Science and Public Administration (PSPA) department, the same department with which Khalidi was affiliated.[27]

Shukairy found in Sayegh a receptive audience.[28] By December 1964, Sayegh had submitted a plan to establish a PLO-affiliated research center in Beirut and at the January 3 meeting of the PLO, the proposal was accepted. In that meeting, the Executive Committee appointed Sayegh to serve as a "specialist advisor" who would supervise the establishment and administration of the new center.[29] Within weeks, Sayegh became the founding director of the PLO Research Center. Shortly thereafter, Shukairy sent Sayegh a letter written on PLO Executive Committee stationery from "Jerusalem-Jordan," in which he thanked Sayegh for agreeing to supervise the establishment of the Center through June 1965.[30]

As we have seen, the PLO Constitution did not specify what sort of research the "department of research" was meant to perform. Sayegh was the first to articulate its agenda. In an internal PLO report Sayegh prepared while he worked to establish the Center, Sayegh described the mission and purpose of the Center as "researching the detailed facts about everything connected to the Palestinian issue [al-qadiyya al-filastiniyya][31] from all sides." Special focus, he said, would be given to

(1) Facts that are connected to the Palestinian issue as an issue—historically, legally, politically—which the adversary strives to erase or distort.
(2) Facts that are connected to the current situation, and to the present conditions in occupied Palestine—economical, social, political, and so on—that are not available to the average citizen without serious research and careful investigation.[32]

In Sayegh's vision, the newly founded PLO Research Center would offer critical information for the Palestinians to know both themselves ("the Palestinian issue") and the enemy ("occupied Palestine"). The following year, Sayegh would write in a foreword to a volume on Israel in the international arena that "knowing the enemy is a parallel process to knowing the self."[33]

What did Sayegh imagine the Palestinians and their new organization, the PLO, would do with the information that the Research Center would gather? The Center's research, Sayegh explained in the memo, would serve as raw material for other bodies of the PLO or institutions beyond the PLO engaged in what he regarded as an information battle. The research could be used, for example, by foreign media "to refute the enemy's arguments, to provide information about the roots of the issue, or to demonstrate Arab rights." The research could be employed by Arab media to "strengthen consciousness and faith." Political institutions might use the research "for political and practical planning." The information gathered could also prove beneficial to the Arab states and the Arab League.

As Sayegh imagined it, the Research Center would not be a "center for pure theoretical work," nor was it created to "pursue knowledge for the sake of knowledge or to satisfy curiosity." At the same time, though, the Center was not "an institution of action and performance." It was "not a department for writing and publication, not a communications department, and not a planning unit." As Sayegh defined the purpose of the Research Center in these early months, it was meant to be an institution that would stand behind and support the work of others, providing them "the material and content that they need!"[34] The Center's role was to be limited but absolutely crucial.

It is instructive to consider how Sayegh conceived the relationship between the PLO and its Research Center. In the same internal report from the first few months after the Center's founding, Sayegh wrote that the Research Center had an "independent identity"[35] and the "necessary administrative independence to define the best path that conforms with the nature of its work." Nonetheless, Sayegh explained that in choosing the topics of research and prioritizing among them, the Center would be guided by "the needs of the Organization [the PLO] as a whole." According to the report, the Center's director would submit a proposed research program and priorities list to the PLO Executive Committee, which would then decide upon it in consultation with him.[36] In theory, at least, the research agenda would be set in consultation with the political leadership but, once the agenda was set, the researchers would have the freedom to undertake their research as they deemed fit.

These foundational decisions—the IPS decision to maintain its independence, and Shukairy's decision to establish the PLO Research Center in the same Lebanese city where IPS was based—were only the beginning of the fraught relationship between the research entities. An internal report that Fayez Sayegh issued on May 13, 1965, concerning the first three months of the PLO Research Center's activities included an extended appendix called "Special Report on the Coordination between the Research Center and the Institute for Palestine Studies." Sayegh recalled that at the end of April 1965, Zurayk invited him to a private meeting to discuss coordination between the Research Center and IPS. Sayegh wrote that he confirmed to Zurayk what he had told the PLO Executive Committee the previous December—namely, that the two institutes must "coordinate as much possible . . . so as to avoid redundancy and squandering limited resources, first of all, and, secondarily, so as to avoid creating 'rivalry' between two bodies that share one goal." Three days later, on April 30, 1965, Sayegh held a "serious and amicable" coordination meeting with Zurayk, Khalidi, Dajani, and Said Himadeh, a former professor of economics at AUB. By the end of the meeting, the participants had developed a "general agreement on the principles of coordination and on many of its details." For instance, the two institutes would share with each other the lists of books in their libraries to avoid duplication and instead devote resources to expanding the joint collection.[37] They also decided to share their research plans with one another to prevent redundancy. Public lectures and programs would be the domain of IPS. The PLO Research Center would collect and print excerpts from the press as well as chronologies of events related to Palestine, while IPS would focus on translations and publishing historical documents.[38] The PLO Research Center had no plans at the time (this would change in subsequent years, as we shall see) to publish a quarterly magazine or a yearbook, so those projects would remain exclusively in the domain of IPS. The representatives of the two institutes also discussed the possibility of not merely coordinating but also collaborating, "undertaking joint projects" such as cofunding research projects, coorganizing seminars, and cofacilitating scholarly grants, but no immediate decisions were made in this regard.

In the course of the meeting, Sayegh attempted to correct a misconception held by IPS leaders about what some imagined to be a fundamental distinction between their institute and the PLO Research Center. As the group sought to identify areas of specialization for each institute, "it became clear to me," wrote Sayegh, "that some of the representatives of the Institute [IPS] hold an idea that may be mistaken about the job of the [PLO] Research Center and the line dividing it" from IPS. The mistake, Sayegh explained, began with the idea that IPS "was a body that had a purely scientific function while the Research Center had a political and propagandistic mission emanating from the nature of the Palestine Liberation Organization."

According to this report, Sayegh argued that this belief "comprised a twofold mistake." On the one hand, Sayegh challenged the view of IPS as a nonpartisan academic institute. "The commitment to the Palestinian cause [al-qadiyya al-filastiniyya]" that was shared by the directors, founders, and donors of the institute "invalidates the claim that it has a purely scientific function, serving knowledge for the sake of knowledge, regarding as equal from a scientific perspective that which benefits the cause of Palestine and that which damages it." Given the IPS leadership's evident sympathy for and alignment with the Palestinian cause, painting IPS as interested solely in advancing knowledge was, Sayegh asserted, plainly absurd. On the other hand, Sayegh challenged the view of the PLO Research Center as a political and propaganda tool. He insisted that the Center was rather a tool for scientific research, which "might benefit (and we hope that it benefits) the political and propaganda wings" of the PLO. Sayegh reported that most of the IPS representatives came to understand "that the dividing line that some of them had believed existed between the two bodies was a relative line and that both bodies in reality are scientific in their function and committed in their goals toward benefiting the Palestinian cause."[39]

Sayegh implied that one IPS member refused to accept this argument and continued to insist on the fundamental distinction between the two research units. Sayegh did not name the person but it may well have been Khalidi. When I met with him, Khalidi emphasized that, in contrast to the PLO Research Center, his institution was "not therapeutic" and "not flamboyant." Rather, IPS was meant to "create a discipline," namely, the study of Israel and the Palestine issue.[40] Apparently, more than fifty years after Sayegh had tried to persuade him of the core similarity between the two research units, and after watching the PLO Research Center in action, Khalidi remained unconvinced.

Sayegh was clearly aware of the challenges inherent in politically engaged research. He acknowledged, at least in his internal report if not publicly, that not all facts were of equal interest to the politically committed researcher. Facts that advanced the political cause were preferred to those that harmed the cause. If Khalidi believed that the same was not the case at IPS, it could only be due to willful self-delusion, Sayegh contended. As Sayegh saw it, a scholar's political agenda always informed the scholar's analysis of a political issue—whether the scholar was employed by an organization that was formally affiliated with a political party or rather by an independent organization with its own political sympathies. To think otherwise was nothing short of naïve.

Anis Sayegh

After founding the Center and directing it for its first year, Fayez Sayegh stepped down to return to his academic position at the American University of Beirut. Anis Sayegh, Fayez's younger brother, succeeded him as the Center's director general.[41] Unlike Fayez, who had been born when the family was in Syria, Anis, the youngest of the family's seven surviving children, was a native of Palestine, having been born in Tiberias in 1931, the year after the family moved there.[42] At the age of sixteen, in April 1948, in the midst of the war in Palestine, Anis fled with his family north to Sidon, Lebanon. After completing high school in Sidon, Anis earned a bachelor's degree in political science and history from AUB. He then worked as a journalist and author in Lebanon before moving to England, in 1959, to pursue a doctorate at the University of Cambridge. Sayegh returned to Lebanon in 1964 and became the editor in chief of an English-Arabic dictionary, a project funded by the Franklin Foundation. In 1966, Sayegh resigned from the dictionary team, a move he explained was a response to the Foundation's attempt to silence his criticism of American foreign policy in the Middle East.[43]

Shortly thereafter, Sayegh's brother Fayez invited him to meet with Shukairy to discuss the creation of a Palestinian encyclopedia, a project in which Anis had previously expressed interest. In that meeting, according to Anis's memoirs, Fayez announced his resignation as director general of the PLO Research Center. Shukairy accepted the resignation and offered Anis the job. When Anis accepted the position, Shukairy offered the following advice: "Take over the Center and put into it all your abilities, knowledge, and dreams, then lay the foundations of the work of preparing the Palestinian encyclopedia of which you dream within the framework of the Center."[44] Anis ran the PLO Research Center for a decade.

Anis maintained the approach that Fayez had taken regarding the relationship between the PLO and the Center. According to the entry on the PLO Research Center in *al-Mawsu'a al-Filastiniyya* (The Palestinian Encyclopedia) that Anis ultimately edited and published in 1984, "in fulfilling its goals, the Center followed the general policy of the [Palestine] Liberation Organization, and was guided by the plans and programs that were decided by the organization's institutions." However, aside from this institutional oversight, the encyclopedia entry emphasized, "the Center itself set its work and production plans and its internal organization," enjoying "a great deal of freedom of action, opinion, conversation, and expression of various positions and different points of view in the Palestinian arena." Moreover, the Center "enjoyed freedom in studying the activities of opponents of the Liberation Organization and their positions and points of view." In all of its work, Sayegh wrote as he looked back on an institution he led for a decade, "the Center follows the accepted methods of scientific research and does not subject itself to any political or propaganda factors that may conflict with all of this."[45]

The Curious Redundancy of IPS and the PLO Research Center

If we are to accept Fayez Sayegh's assertion that there was no substantial distinction between the Research Center's and IPS's respective raisons d'etre, we might still wonder if there were nevertheless ideological or other fault lines dividing them. Of course, the Research Center, as an arm of the PLO, was not in the business of criticizing the PLO, but then again neither was IPS in the early years. Moreover, the PLO Research Center was, as we shall see, willing to publish diverse and contrarian views within its journal *Shuʾun Filastiniyya* (Palestinian Affairs). In other words, neither institution held monolithic views on the Palestine question, the conflict, or the PLO. In addition, as the two institutes developed, both published materials that were explicitly polemical or what might be regarded as propagandistic and both also published materials that were highly sophisticated pieces of academic, if engaged, research.[46]

What about the principal players at IPS and the PLO Research Center? Did the two groups divide along demographic lines? While Muslims and Christians were involved in both institutes, all but one of the directors of the PLO Research Center were Palestinian Christians (Fayez Sayegh, Anis Sayegh, and Sabri Jiryis—the exception was the poet Mahmoud Darwish, a Muslim Palestinian citizen of Israel who served in this role for one year). There were Palestinians and non-Palestinians involved in both institutes, with all of the Research Center's directors exclusively Palestinian by origin. One prolific writer for the PLO Research Center, Assʿad Razzouk, was a native of Marjayoun, Lebanon, while several of the founders and leaders of IPS were Lebanese or, like Zurayk, Syrian.[47] Finally, it is worth mentioning that in some cases, the very same people were involved with both institutes. For example, the final director general of the PLO Research Center in Beirut, Sabri Jiryis—who hailed from the Catholic Palestinian village of Fassuta in northern Israel—started off working for IPS when he arrived in Beirut in 1970 before moving to the PLO Research Center in 1974.[48] The circumstances surrounding Jiryis's shift, discussed later in this book, may be instructive. In conversations I had with Jiryis and Khalidi in 2016, Jiryis regarded IPS as "aristocratic" and "elitist" while, as we have seen, Khalidi suggested that the PLO Research Center served "therapeutic" or "propagandistic" ends.[49] Hence, at least in retrospect for those who had been at the helm, the two institutes were fundamentally different.

Curiously, Walid Khalidi did not regard the PLO's research center as superfluous, even as it was created in Beirut, right alongside IPS. Sitting with the Palestinian intellectual in his home in Cambridge, Massachusetts, I asked him why the PLO needed a research center. "Every national movement needs a research center," Khalidi responded. "Can you imagine the Zionist Organization without a research center?" For Khalidi, Shukairy's insistence on a research center under the auspices of the PLO was perfectly reasonable. Khalidi had simply refused to permit IPS to become that entity.

Khalidi's motivation appears to have been a wish to avoid tension between researchers' ideas and those of the political organization's leadership.[50] During the lifetime of the PLO Research Center, tensions certainly arose between the PLO's political leadership and the intellectuals who ran the Center. We see this, for example, in the memoirs of Anis Sayegh. In his *Anis Sayigh 'an Anis Sayigh*, Sayegh complained that PLO chairman Yasser Arafat lacked respect for free intellectual inquiry.[51]

Funding the Research Center and Its Placement in Beirut

The PLO Research Center, like the PLO's other departments, did not need to raise its own funds. It was supported entirely by the central organization. According to Anis Sayegh's 1984 *al-Mawsuʿa al-Filastiniyya*, the Research Center's finances were covered by the Palestine National Fund (another wing of the PLO established in the *nizam al-asasi*). The Palestine National Fund was in turn funded by the Arab League. Over time, further subsidies paid directly by the Arab League to the Research Center supplemented the funds the Center received from the National Fund.[52] Some of the Center's books name the specific Arab government that funded their publication. For instance, the front matter of a 1970 book titled *An Examination of Documents on Which the State of Israel Is Based* indicates that "this book was published at the expense of the Kuwait Ministry of Guidance and Information."[53] Khalidi did not want IPS to be financially beholden to the PLO. Sayegh, by contrast, welcomed such support in the context of a commitment on the part of the PLO Executive Committee to the institute's research independence.

It was expensive to run the Center. According to a draft found in Fayez Sayegh's archive, the budget for the first year (when the Center was still quite small) was 102,000 Lebanese lira (about US $315,000 in today's currency).[54] About 65 percent was designated for salaries of researchers and staff; 12 percent for rent; 11 percent for office furnishings; 10 percent for library acquisitions; and 2 percent for telephone, electricity, and other office expenses.[55] This archive includes only the first year's budget, as this was the only year in which Fayez Sayegh ran the Center. While we do not have subsequent annual budgets, the needs grew exponentially as the number of researchers and staff expanded from a handful to more than eighty.

Beyond the budget issues in establishing the Research Center, we might also wonder why it was located specifically in Beirut. After all, the PLO was conceived of in Cairo, founded in Jordan's West Bank, and, after the 1967 war, led from Jordan's East Bank (until it was expelled to Lebanon in 1970). Why, then, did Shukairy choose Beirut over these locations? Would not the placement of the PLO Research Center in the same city as IPS have emphasized the perception of redundance?

One possibility is that Shukairy believed that the PLO Research Center would ultimately put the independently funded IPS out of business. When this happened, Shukairy may well have imagined, the Center would absorb IPS researchers and library.[56] Or perhaps Shukairy thought—and in this sense he would have been correct—that researchers at IPS would also participate in the life of the Center and vice versa, and that their colocality in Beirut would prove symbiotic rather than merely competitive.

In any case, even though the military and political efforts were initially centered elsewhere, the Lebanese capital proved to be a propitious site for the work of the Research Center. At the time, Beirut was a major academic and intellectual hub. The city housed an impressive number of major institutions of higher learning, including Université Saint-Joseph, the Beirut College for Women (renamed, after it became coeducational in the 1970s, Beirut University College and later renamed again, Lebanese American University), the Lebanese Academy of the Fine Arts, Haigazian College, Beirut Arab University, and the

American University of Beirut. The last of these, AUB, became, in the words of Samir Kassir, "the leading university in the entire Near East."[57]

The Beirut region was also home to a large population of Palestinians. In the course of the 1948 war, more than 100,000 Palestinians fled or were expelled to Lebanon from the region that became Israel—and the population grew dramatically over the following decades.[58] Most were denied Lebanese citizenship and lived in refugee camps under what were initially severe restrictions on employment, housing, movement, and expression, though over the ensuing three decades, between forty and fifty thousand Palestinians in the country managed to attain Lebanese citizenship.[59]

While they were surely the minority among the Palestinian refugee population in Lebanon, Palestinians who were sufficiently advantaged to pursue and earn degrees from Beirut's universities would play a key role in the PLO Research Center enterprise. Support for Palestinian resistance and for the various Palestinian militant groups was widespread among Beirut's university students. In October 1970, *Newsweek* dubbed AUB "Guerrilla U" and observed that "politics at AUB today is tied directly to the Palestine guerrilla movement." While AUB had previously supplied "Mideastern countries with a steady stream of presidents, prime ministers, ambassadors, doctors, lawyers, and businessmen," there were now "two striking new categories: aerial hijackers and guerrillas." Among the university's former students, the article observed, were PFLP leaders George Habash and Wadie Haddad as well as the famed hijacker Leila Khaled. Many AUB students "belong to one of the guerrilla groups, mainly the PFLP and Al Fatah," *Newsweek* explained, "and often spend their summers and weekends in commando training camps."[60]

Bordering Israel, Lebanon was an excellent combination of a neighboring "confrontation state" that also lacked centralized power strong enough to tightly monitor and control the PLO's efforts there.[61] Thus in Beirut, the PLO researchers could work without fear of government interference. In fact, shortly after the PLO Research Center's establishment—still several years before the November 1969 Cairo Agreement that "effectively legitimized the Palestinian armed presence in Lebanon"—the Lebanese government granted the Center the status of a diplomatic body and provided it the immunities offered to foreign diplomatic delegations.[62] Together, these qualities made mid-1960s Beirut an ideal city in which to establish the PLO Research Center, even as the Palestinian political and militant leadership sat elsewhere.

The Center's precise placement within Beirut was also no accident. It was housed in a building on Colombani Street at the corner of Sadat Street, near the famous Rue Hamra,[63] less than a ten-minute walk from the AUB campus in the West Beirut neighborhood known as Ras Beirut.[64] This neighborhood, though popularly imagined as a den of debauchery for its nightlife, was an intellectual and cultural center, filled with bookstores, cafes, and cinemas, and a modern business center. Ras Beirut was also the neighborhood where many Palestinian bourgeois refugees settled after they fled or were expelled from Palestine in the 1948 war.[65]

With this understanding of the origins of the PLO Research Center in Beirut, we next try to assess how the Center functioned in a practical sense, and what sorts of research took place within its walls.

2

The PLO Research Center at Work

WITHIN A DECADE after Fayez Sayegh established the PLO Research Center, it had grown into a large and vibrant institution, occupying six floors of the Colombani Street building.[1] By the mid-1970s, the Center had over sixty employees[2] and, at its height in the late 1970s, it employed more than eighty.[3] In this chapter, I explore who worked at the PLO Research Center, what sorts of topics the researchers studied, and for whom they were writing.

Over time, the Center developed ten different departments or units. Anis Sayegh outlined the respective foci of all ten in the entry he prepared about the Center for his *Palestinian Encyclopedia* project. They were (1) a library department, which was responsible for maintaining the two-story library facility[4] with more than 20,000 volumes (just over half in English, a quarter in Arabic, the rest in Hebrew) along with encyclopedias, dictionaries, atlases, other reference works, and periodicals in English, Arabic, Hebrew, and French;[5] (2) an archive unit, comprising mainly published documents, relating to the conflict, which the Research Center sought either to reissue or to copy on microfilm, and also current newspapers from abroad that the researchers translated and summarized in Arabic (more in part 3); (3) a unit devoted to a semiannual publication series called *al-Yawmiyyat al-Filastiniyya* (Palestine Chronology), which listed events relating to Palestinians (23 volumes by 1981); (4) a unit devoted to translating Israeli radio broadcasts and preparing a daily bulletin (producing more than 2,500 bulletins between 1971 and 1981); (5) a unit dedicated to the publication of the Research Center's monthly newspaper *Shu'un Filastiniyya* (Palestinian Affairs, 121 issues of which appeared in its first decade, beginning in 1971); (6) a technical department; (7) a unit for distribution of the Center's publications and for registering subscriptions; (8) a financial department, responsible for managing the Center's annual budget; (9) a department of administrative affairs, tasked with ensuring compliance with PLO and Center regulations; and finally,

(10) the core unit of the Center, namely, the Research Department. Over the Center's Beirut years, research units had different configurations but eventually there were three primary divisions: Palestinian studies, Israeli studies, and international studies. The greatest emphasis in the research department was on Israeli studies.[6]

A Publishing Spree

Immediately upon founding the Center in February 1965, Fayez Sayegh began publishing books and pamphlets under its auspices. On the back cover of the first publications, he ambitiously presented a list of seven different series that the Center would issue: Palestine Chronology, Facts and Figures, Palestine Essays, Palestine Monographs, Palestine Books, Palestine Maps and Pictures, and Special Publications.[7] While in Beirut, the Center published some 340 books, the majority of which were in Arabic. In addition to the Arabic books, the Center published eighty-seven works in English, twenty-one in French, and still others in languages such as German, Danish, Spanish, and Japanese.[8]

Initially, Sayegh was the Center's primary author, writing three of the four works published by the Center in 1965. Two of the books were Arabic and English versions of his short book *Zionist Colonialism in Palestine*, which was the first in the Palestine Monographs series (discussed in detail in chapter 4).[9] The other two publications were in the Facts and Figures series: an anonymously authored *Do You Know? 20 Basic Facts about the Palestine Problem* and Sayegh's analysis of the role of the United Nations in dealing with the question of Palestine from 1947 until 1965.[10]

The following year, the Center's publishing spree began in earnest. In 1966, the Center published nineteen books—twelve in Arabic, five in English, one in French, and another in Spanish. Again, several of the books published that year were written by Fayez Sayegh (a harsh Arabic critique of Tunisian president Habib Bourguiba's openness to normalizing relations with Israel, an English book on discrimination in the education of Arabs in Israel, and French and Spanish translations of two of Sayegh's books from the previous year). Another 1966 book was a collection of speeches by Shukairy, the man who had appointed Sayegh to lead the Center.[11]

Shortly thereafter, the Center began publishing expositions about topics in Israel's past and present. For instance, in 1966, it published an Arabic book on the Israeli economy written by Sayegh's economist brother Yusif Sayigh, along with several Arabic books on Israeli politics and political parties, including Rafiq Mutlaq's *Political Life in Israel*, Ass'ad Razzouk's overview of the parties, Ibrahim al-Abid's monograph on the ruling Mapai party, and Bassam Abu Ghazala on the opposition party Herut (and its roots in terrorism).[12] The Center also began offering its readers primers on other major Israeli institutions, such as Abd al-Wahab al-Kayali's book on the kibbutz, and on what it considered to be central features of Zionism (e.g., territorial expansionism, as in al-Kayali's other book that year, *Zionist Expansionist Ambitions*). In addition, the Center published books that year on Zionist and Israeli international relations (Leila Salim Kadi's Arabic edited compilation of figures and tables in *Israel in the International Arena* and Asa'd Abdul-Rahman's *United States and West German Aid to Israel* in both Arabic and English).[13] The Center was also interested in the treatment of the Palestinian cause by Arab states, as evidenced by its publication of Leila Kadi's English-language historical study of the Palestine issue at Arab summit conferences.

In the year in which the Center was under his direction, Fayez Sayegh also initiated the Palestine Chronology series that would run through 1982, the dedicated focus of one of the Center's ten units that Anis Sayegh had enumerated. This series was meant to document and record significant events in and for Palestinian history. It was designed, according to Sayegh, "for students and researchers of the Palestinian issue," to facilitate their access to information about relevant day-to-day developments. The first issue of the series was published in September 1966 and, in over 400 pages including three detailed indexes, covered the first six months of 1965. Along with events specifically associated with Palestine and Palestinians, the chronology also tracked three other categories of events that, Sayegh explained, could later prove relevant to Palestinian history: (1) inter-Arab conflicts, which divert Arab energies from the Palestinian cause, (2) Arab states' and Israel's relations with foreign countries, and (3) Zionist activities of Jews abroad as well as anti-Jewish and pro-Jewish events abroad, and their consequences.[14]

When, in December 1966, the second volume of the *Chronology* (July to December 1965, 368 pages in length) was published, Anis Sayegh had already taken over the reins of the Center. In his introduction to the volume, along with quoting from his older brother's explanation of the purpose of the series, Anis elaborated that this and other projects of the Research Center were "not only meant to contribute to raising the awareness of the Arab reader and increasing his knowledge about the Palestinian issue, but also to facilitate the work of professors, writers, historians, and specialists in nationalist issues in discussing the Palestinian issue and in treating the subject in the desired objective and precise way."[15]

The Research Center's publishing productivity generally persisted through 1975. The Center published twenty-seven books and pamphlets in 1967, forty in 1968, forty-eight in 1969, forty-two in 1970, twenty-one in 1971, six (only) in 1972, thirty-two in 1973, twenty-six in 1974, and eighteen in 1975.

Beginning with the publications of 1967, several broad areas and themes of the Center's research emerged. One such area of focus was Zionism and Israel. Examples in this category include Ghassan Kanafani's *On Zionist Literature*; Asa'd Abdul-Rahman's book on the World Zionist Organization; Leila Kadi's study of the Histadrut trade union; Angelina Helou's *Interaction of Political, Military, and Economic Factors in Israel*, Fayez Sayegh's brief pamphlet "Do Jews Have a 'Divine Right' to Palestine?"; a coauthored review of Israeli scientific, cultural, and artistic organizations; and Ibrahim al-Abid's *Violence and Peace: A Study in Zionist Strategy*.[16] Another focus, like that of Palestine Chronology, was on Zionist and Israeli relations with other countries and regions. In this category we find, for instance, Fayez Sayegh's *Zionist Diplomacy*; Asa'd Abdul-Rahman's *Israeli Infiltration in Asia: India and Israel*; and 'Aqil Hashim and Sa'id al-'Azm's *Israel in Western Europe*.[17] A third category was the history of Palestinians and the Palestinian resistance in Palestine, in Israel, and in exile. Here, for instance, we might place the Arabic translation of Sabri Jiryis's *The Arabs in Israel* (though this book, focused as it is on the system of Israeli military rule over Israel's Arab citizens, also fits in the first category); Naji Alloush's *The Arab Resistance in Palestine, 1917–1948*; Muhammad al-Sha'ir's *The Feda'i War in Palestine in Light of the Experiences of the Peoples in Guerrilla Fighting*; and Amira Habibi's study of "the second displacement" of the Palestinians in the Six-Day War that had just taken place.[18] Finally, there were books about the Arab states and their involvement in the Palestinian cause, such as Shukairy's book on the project to create a united Arab state; Hani Ahmad Faris's *Arab Diplomatic Representation*; and 'Abd Allah al-Tariqi's *Arab Oil as a Weapon in Battle*.[19]

Along with these four broad categories of research, the Center's publications developed along an additional axis. On one end of this spectrum, there were the more scholarly expositions while, on the other, there were the more overtly polemical works—though most books generally fell somewhere between the poles or included elements of each. Among the more polemical works, we might place *Zionism and Racism*, the second item published in the Palestine Essays series. In this brief work (a mere thirty-four pages), Hasan

Saʿb opened by asserting that "the essential claim of Zionism is the existence of a race, **a chosen race,** which has not been and should not be assimilated by other races, and which can fulfill its historic destiny only through the assertion of its unique nationhood and the establishment of its particular statehood in Palestine."[20] Saʿb continued by insisting that "the concept of a 'chosen race,' in Zionism, differs from the concept of a 'chosen race,' in Nazism, only in the identity of that race."[21] For Nazism, Aryans; for Zionism, Jews. Otherwise, the two are indistinguishable. The essay's epilogue begins thus:

> The Israelis have introduced racism to the Middle East under a new name: Zionism. The authentic traditions and ideals of the peoples of the area, as expressed in Judaism, Christianity and Islam, are anti-racial. Palestine was the cradle of Monotheism, which stands for the unity of all mankind under One God, One Truth,[22] One Justice, and One Peace for all. The Zionists advocate one justice for the victims of Nazi persecution in Europe and another for the victims of Zionist persecution in Palestine.[23]

This essay is meticulously footnoted, with citations of, among other works, Chaim Weizmann's *Trial and Error*; Moses Hess's *Rome and Jerusalem*; Leo Pinsker's *Auto-Emancipation*; S. D. Goitein's *Jews and Arabs*; and Naomi Wiener Cohen's *The Reaction of Reform Judaism in America to Political Zionism*. But the tone, as we sense in the quotations offered above, is that of a polemic. The Palestine Essays series seems to have been especially open to this genre of writing.

In contrast, 1968 also saw the Center's publication of more scholarly, less polemical works such as Ilyas Saʿd's *Israel and Tourism* and *Israel and Unemployment*; Yusuf Ahmad Shibl's *Monetary Policy in Israel*; Ibrahim al-Abid's *The Moshav: The Cooperative Village in Israel*; and Hilda Shaʿban Sayegh's Arabic translation of parts of Theodor Herzl's diaries.[24] To be sure, these works generally opened with polemical forewords and introductions (which we address in the coming chapters), emphasizing their place in the broader project of "knowing the enemy." It is not difficult to discern that their subjects were indeed "the enemy" in the eyes of the authors. The broad contents of many of these works, however, are generally presented in a relatively dispassionate fashion.

The Center also published other genres during its years in Beirut. For instance, it published a collection of political cartoons by Imad Shehadeh— *David and Goliath, in Nine Easy Lessons* (1970)—and works of poetry by the Palestinian poet Mahmoud Darwish: *Diary of Normal Sadness* (1973), *Goodbye*

War, Goodbye Peace (1974), and *That Is Her Image and This Is the Lover's Suicide* (1975).[25] Along with cartoons and poetry, the Center began to collect and publish the notes and papers of prominent Palestinian figures who had recently passed away. In 1973, the Center began publishing a collection of twelve volumes of reports and papers belonging to ʿArif al-ʿArif (1892–1973), the Palestinian journalist and historian, who also served as mayor of Jordanian Jerusalem.[26] The following year, in June 1974, the Center published the papers of the Nablus-born ʿAwni ʿAbd al-Hadi (1889–1970), who had served, among other important roles in his lengthy political career, as secretary to King Faysal in the short-lived state he established in Syria, and as Hajj Amin al-Husseini's secretary in the Arab Higher Committee.[27] These genres were the exception, however. Most of the Center's hundreds of books and pamphlets belonged to the other categories of publications detailed above.

Along with the Palestine Chronology series, which the Center established in its first year, the Center initiated several other periodicals in the ensuing years. The most important of these was *Shuʾun Filastiniyya* (Palestinian Affairs), the Center's Arabic-language journal launched in March 1971. When Anis Sayegh introduced its first issue, he explained that the journal would "specialize in Palestinian affairs in the most precise sense of specialization and in the widest sense of affairs: affairs of the Palestinian people, affairs of the Palestinian issue, affairs of the Palestinian struggle, affairs of the land of Palestine, of the society of Palestine, and of the culture of Palestine—past, present, and future." Sayegh noted that the journal would be a forum in which "divergent opinions meet, hosting all persuasions and ideas." However, not all views were given voice. Sayegh explained that the journal would welcome "multiple opinions, positions, and voices united in the belief in the complete right to all of Palestine [*al-ayman bi-haq kamil fi filastin kamila*]."[28]

Sayegh also served as the journal's first editor in chief. In July of 1973, Mahmoud Darwish (who had left Israel in 1970) joined Sayegh in editing the journal and, in May 1977, Darwish succeeded Sayegh in the role of chief editor. Elias Khoury served as Darwish's editorial secretary through October 1979 and was later succeeded by Faysal Hourani.[29] Darwish left his position at the helm of the journal in June 1981 and was replaced by Bilal al-Hassan, who continued in this role until Faysal Hourani took over in January 1983 and continued in this position during the Center's final months in Beirut and even beyond.

For its first year, *Shuʾun* ran every other month. Beginning in March 1972, the journal became a monthly, often exceeding 250 pages per issue. In 1975, however, the consistent publication of *Shuʾun* fell victim to the civil war that engulfed Lebanon and in which the Palestinian presence and PLO activities in the country were among the many casus belli. Numerous times over the ensuing eight years, two or even three months of the journal were joined in a single or double issue.[30]

As a result of Lebanon's civil war, the PLO Research Center's activities were significantly restricted. In contrast to the Center's first decade of spectacular productivity, the remaining years in Beirut were far less prolific, even though the Center continued to employ a large number of researchers during the civil war. Fearing attacks by the Christian Lebanese Phalange party or the Israelis, the Center's leadership had much of its staff work from home during certain periods of the war.[31] In 1976 and 1977, the Center published just one book each year; from 1978 through 1980, three a year; in 1981, six; and in 1982, the last year of the Center's full-fledged existence in Beirut, three.

Working at the PLO Research Center

To understand how the PLO Research Center achieved this remarkable level of productivity during its eighteen years in Beirut (especially in the years before the outbreak of the civil war in Lebanon), we turn now to the research staff employed by the Center. If in its first year or so, the Center's publications suggested something of a "one-man show" for Fayez Sayegh, in the years that followed, the names of many researchers and writers graced the title pages of the Center's publications and its journal—not to mention the support staff that stood behind the research. The Center was a collective effort.

The researchers that the Center employed generally joined the organization after attaining a master's or doctoral degree from a university in the US, Europe, or Lebanon (particularly the American University of Beirut). Given their advanced education, these native Arabic speakers generally also knew English and usually one or several additional European languages. Only some had a facility with Hebrew, though knowledge of this language came to play an increasingly important role in the work of the Center.[32]

Consider the case of Anan Ameri.[33] Ameri was born in Damascus in 1944 to a Jerusalemite Palestinian father and a Damascene Syrian mother. She recalled being drawn into politics in her early twenties when the 1967 war erupted the summer before the final year of her bachelor's degree at the University of Jordan. Shortly after the war, the Syrian-born author and University of Michigan–trained social psychologist Halim Barakat came to Jordan to study Palestinian refugees.[34] Ameri joined Barakat, then on the faculty of AUB, as an intern. This was Ameri's first significant research experience, and it was to have a lasting impact on the course of her career. After graduating from the University of Jordan, Ameri moved from Amman to Egypt to pursue a master's degree in sociology at Cairo University, which she earned in 1971.

The events known by Palestinians as "Black September," in which Jordan's Hashemite Kingdom violently routed and expelled the PLO in 1970–71, pushed the PLO to Lebanon and attracted young Palestinian and other Arab activists to join them in Beirut. Ameri was one such young person to follow the PLO to Lebanon. In 1972, she joined the staff of the PLO Research Center. Ameri recalled being, at the age of twenty-eight, among the youngest of the researchers. Alongside volunteering as a teacher at the Palestinian refugee camps of Sabra and Shatila, she worked for the PLO Research Center until she left Beirut to pursue a PhD in the US.

It was Beirut's "political and cultural vibrancy" that attracted her to the city, Ameri explained, as this was a time when many Arab writers and artists from the broader region settled in the Lebanese capital. Moreover, once the PLO's headquarters moved to Beirut after 1970, not only Arabs but "many revolutionaries from around the world" descended upon the city. And, for Ameri, the PLO Research Center was at the heart of this exciting city, drawing together an electrifying community of young, creative intellectuals, and "progressive Arab researchers and scholars . . . the legendary Palestinian poet Mahmoud Darwish and Lebanese novelist Elias Khoury."[35]

Ameri's memories offer crucial insights into the Center's work, culture, and productivity. Idealism was assumed; even full-time researchers like Ameri were paid only minimally. "As radicals," she wrote, "we were supposed to shun materialism and live on very little."[36] And a strong work ethic was equally taken for granted. Sayegh, Ameri noted in her conversation with me, was a demanding boss who expected a great deal from his workers. The six-day work week began each day at 8 A.M. in a Center that was so quiet, it "felt like a library." Anis Sayegh was "a very strict, disciplinary administrator" such that "if you came at 8:05," Ameri recalled, "Anis would insist that you work five minutes late" at the end of the day.[37] At 10:30, there was a half-hour coffee break. Work resumed at 11 A.M. and ended for the day at 2 P.M., except on Wednesdays, on which the staff worked an additional three hours, from 3 P.M. to 6 P.M. Aside from during the coffee break and the Wednesday lunch hour, researchers were not permitted to drink coffee, and newspaper reading was confined to research needs. According to Ameri, this sort of workplace environment was far from the norm at that time in Beirut.

During her time at the Center, Ameri recalled, the research department was divided into two units: one dedicated to studying Zionism and Israel and the other focused on Palestinian society before and after 1948. Socially, the two sections mixed and, when their research demanded it, members of one section would collaborate with members of the other, but they were distinct sections. Those who had a knowledge of Hebrew and of Israeli society, especially Palestinians who had lived previously in Israel, were typically assigned to the Zionism and Israel unit.

Ameri was placed in the Palestinian section. While working in this unit, which had its own small library, Ameri used statistical methods to analyze Palestinian agriculture and industry. In 1974, she published this work in an Arabic-language book called *Palestinian Agricultural Industrial Development, 1900–1970*.[38] Ameri worked alongside seven researchers in the unit focused on Palestinian society. Bilal al-Hassan (b. 1944), a Palestinian, headed the unit.[39] The other members were Palestinians Jamil Hilal (b. 1940), Daoud Talhami (b. 1943), and Nazih Qurah, an Iraqi named Said Jawad, and the Lebanese Elias Khoury (b. 1948) and Hani Mandes.[40]

A glance at the biographies of those in Ameri's research unit gives us a sense of the people who were active during these years at the PLO Research Center. They were mainly individuals in their twenties and thirties, including not only Palestinians but also allies from elsewhere in the Arab world, and both Muslims and Christians. Concerning religion, Ameri contended that "no one observed religion" at the PLO Research Center. "Maybe people would fast Ramadan," she elaborated, "but that's it." Christians would celebrate Christmas, but simply as a cultural day, Ameri insisted in our conversation. "Political affiliation mattered . . . religious affiliation did not matter." I return to the topic of the researchers' religious affiliation in subsequent chapters.

That the researchers and staff were conscious of one another's political affiliation is not to say that the researchers were politically homogeneous. On the contrary, within Ameri's small department of eight, there were members of at least five political parties: Fateh, the Popular Front for the Liberation of Palestine, the Democratic Front for the Liberation of Palestine, the Iraqi Communist Party, and the Lebanese Communist Party. According to Ameri, the various political party affiliations of her coresearchers were indicative of the political diversity that characterized the Research Center as a whole. The coexistence of divergent political views in a single institution was not to be taken for granted. In those days in Beirut, members of these parties would often have bitter disputes that, on occasion, could even turn violent. At the

PLO Research Center, however, they managed to work together. Indeed, the Palestinian department staff sat together in the same room, with their desks facing the center of the room; they spent all day looking at each other.

While most of the authors of the Center's publications were men, there were prominent and prolific women among the Center's staff. These included Hilda Shaʿban Sayegh, Hanneh Shahin Jiryis, Leila Salim Kadi, Angelina Helou, and Khairieh Kasmieh. In addition, women served as librarians and administrators at the Center. Ameri did not recall being treated any differently because she was a woman—"other than some flirtation." At the time, she said, the PLO was very inclusive of women; she often heard the line that "women are 50% of society."[41] This inclusiveness was in accordance with a more general "egalitarian attitude among the staff," even between the researchers and the unit directors, who would all socialize together. "The only boss was Anis," she concluded.

The staff at the PLO Research Center, according to Ameri, believed their work to be important and impactful. There was a strong sense of intellectual vibrancy in Beirut and elsewhere in the Arab world at this time, recalled Ameri, and the Center's books and journals were read and discussed in book clubs, political gatherings, and among various leftist groups. Though when he had founded the Research Center, Fayez Sayegh suggested that the task of organizing and hosting seminars would be left to the Institute for Palestine Studies, the Center did not maintain this position for long. In his memoirs, PLO Executive Committee member Shafiq al-Hout wrote of a seminar held by the PLO Research Center in July 1975 "to discuss Palestinian-Lebanese relations in order to avert a total breakdown." The first of the speakers was Kamal Jumblatt, the Druze leader of the Progressive Socialist Party, "who attributed the crisis to various factors, the first and most important of which, according to him, was the paranoia of the Lebanese Christians."[42] The Research Center had become a place where intellectual and political discussion and debate could be held on matters even as weighty as how to stop the descent into chaos and civil war in Lebanon.

Danger at the Center

Though the PLO Research Center was granted diplomatic immunity by the Lebanese government, when tensions flared between Israelis and Palestinians, the researchers at the Center were not immune from the danger. Consider the summer of 1972. On May 8, 1972, members of the Palestinian guerrilla organization Black September hijacked a Belgian airplane en route to Lod Airport and demanded that Israel release hundreds of Palestinian prisoners. Disguised Israeli paratroopers killed two of the hijackers and freed the hostages.[43] Later that same month, on May 30, Japanese Army of the Red Star members, working in coordination with the Popular Front for the Liberation of Palestine, landed at Lod Airport and opened fire on passengers gathered in the waiting area, ultimately killing two dozen individuals and wounding scores more.[44] On July 9, Ghassan Kanafani, the famed Palestinian writer who was a PFLP leader and spokesman—and the author of *On Zionist Literature*, published by the PLO Research Center in 1967—was killed in a Beirut suburb by a bomb planted in his car. Israeli agents were presumed responsible for his assassination.[45] Ten days later, Anis Sayegh received a letter bomb that exploded in his hands.[46] Sayegh survived the attack, but the bomb permanently impaired his hearing and vision and led to the amputation of several fingers. For Shafiq al-Hout, who had headed the PLO office in Beirut and would soon represent the PLO at the United Nations, the killing of Kanafani and the apparent attempted killing of Sayegh were of a piece, both part of Israel's "terrorist operations" against PLO institutions and people.[47] Less than two months later, in September 1972, Black September members killed two Israeli athletes and held nine as hostages at the Munich Olympics, demanding the release of Palestinian prisoners. All nine hostages were killed, along with several of the militants, in the West German police attempt to rescue them.[48] The cycle of attack and counterattack did not start or end with the PLO Research Center, but the fact that participants in, and even the director of, the Research Center were implicated in it reflects the importance of the Center not only in the minds of Palestinians but also in the minds of Israeli political and military decision-makers.[49]

Anan Ameri recalled that attacks involving the Center, especially the one targeting Sayegh—attributed to but never claimed by Israel—had a significant impact on life at the Center. She explained that there was a great deal of anxiety that resulted from these attacks and that precautions were taken, including not permitting all researchers to be in the building at once and, at times, requiring researchers to work at home rather than to assemble at the Center.[50]

The violence continued shortly after Ameri left the Research Center in 1974. On December 10, 1974, three different PLO offices—the main PLO Beirut office, the office of the Western Sector Bureau (responsible for militant activities in Israel), and the PLO Research Center—"suffered heavy damages," according to contemporary reports from the Associated Press, "in a series of sophisticated rocket attacks that Lebanon and the PLO blamed on Israel." This time, rockets were launched from the roofs of cars parked near the PLO buildings. Lebanese police at the time argued that "the nature of the attack, which involved sophisticated planning, careful timing and high technology," suggested that it had been organized by Israel. Israeli military officials denied involvement and, according to the AP, others "speculated that the attack was carried out by Palestinian dissidents opposed to the PLO and its leader Yasser Arafat on the ground that they are not pressing the fight against Israel vigorously enough." While five people were injured in these attacks, the assault on the PLO Research Center caused no human casualties. The attack did inflict significant damage to the Center's library. At the time, the AP reported that the rockets "ripped to shreds the library of the PLO's Palestine Research Center at the end of Beirut's fashionable Hamra Street." This appears to have been an overstatement, as the library resumed functioning soon after the attack.[51] Nonetheless, the Research Center staff was left shaken to its core.

For Whom Did the Center Write?

This book is focused mainly on the production of the Center's research rather than on its reception.[52] Nonetheless, at least preliminarily, we necessarily wonder: who was the intended audience of the PLO Research Center publications? While *Shu'un Filastiniyya* succeeded in attaining a broad reach, the books the Center was producing (the primary topic of part 2 of this book) were obviously not meant to be bestsellers. Works with titles such as *The Armistice in International Law* or *The Kibbutz: Collective Farms in Israel* or *Mapai: The Ruling Party in Israel* or *On Zionist Literature* or *The Jewish Woman in Occupied Palestine* or *Israel and Unemployment* were clearly aimed at political leaders and intellectuals engaged in the conflict with Israel. As most of the titles were produced only in Arabic, those books were not expected to have a direct impact on European, American, or Russian political positions vis-à-vis the conflict. Rather, they were meant for domestic consumption, that is, for Palestinian and Arab readers.

Some of the books, however, did appear in other languages, especially English and French. In part, this can be explained by the education and abilities of the researchers. Lebanon had been under French cultural dominance since the nineteenth century (and under French mandatory rule in the interwar period) and many of the intellectuals involved in the Center were educated in Anglophone schools and universities, whether in England, the US, or even in Beirut itself at the American University of Beirut. Thus, most of the researchers employed by the Center were competent and often fluent in English, French, or both.

With these non-Arabic publications, the PLO Research Center aimed to reach a broader audience, though not always a distant one. In 1969, the Center published a book in its Facts and Figures series called *The American Community in Lebanon and the Palestine Problem: A Study in Changing Attitudes.* The book was a report on a study that the Research Center had conducted on the attitudes of Americans residing in Lebanon toward the Arab-Israeli conflict. Anis Sayegh, in his preface, noted that "only one American [surveyed] attributed the change in his view . . . to Arab mass media" that he encountered during his time in Lebanon. "The rest of those who changed their views attributed the change to their acquaintances: Palestinian Arabs, and non-Palestinian Arabs," he wrote. Sayegh cautioned readers that "this important fact should make us take great care of personal relationships with foreigners, because personal contact seems closer to success than the ordinary mass media apparatus like the broadcasting system and the press."[53]

For Sayegh, then, it was imperative to persuade people of the justice of the Palestinian cause. Even Americans living in Lebanon, he lamented, needed to be convinced:

> Less than 25 per cent of them believe, after being acquainted with our point of view, that we are completely right in the conflict. The rest of them do not completely agree with our view of the conflict. They agree with some of what we see as our right and, at the same time, they believe some Zionist claims. Hence they give the Zionists support and sympathy which is more or less equal to that which they grant us.[54]

Fewer than a quarter of the surveyed Americans in Lebanon regarded the Palestinian-Israeli conflict as a binary, with Palestinians in the right and Israelis in the wrong. Palestinian advocates, it was clear to Sayegh, had much work to do.

Where did the PLO Research Center fit in? In the survey the Center conducted, respondents were asked "Did you know of the existence of the PLO Research Center before receiving this questionnaire?" Sayegh reported that "60 per cent of the Americans in Lebanon did know of the existence of the Center and that 50 per cent of them have read publications by the Center." Though encouraged, Sayegh noted, he was also "disturbed because half of the Americans in Lebanon did not read any publications [including, by that point twenty-five books in English] by the Center, which is quite a loss."[55] Sayegh concluded that "we must invest more efforts in trying to reach the maximum number of foreigners, including those who live among us and who probably are the closest to us, not only geographically, but mentally and psychologically."[56]

Sayegh's expression, in 1969, of the need for his Center to reach a non-Arab audience did not radically shift the Center's approach, though it did encourage the researchers to continue to publish some pamphlets in English and other European languages. The primary language of the Center's publications remained Arabic and, as we have seen, when the Center established its own monthly magazine, it did so in Arabic in the form of *Shu'un Filastiniyya*. The language choice for the monthly is especially noteworthy because the Center's collaborating/competing institution, the Institute for Palestine Studies, established its flagship journal the same year, 1971, not in Arabic but in English (the *Journal of Palestine Studies*). In these journals, then, the target audiences were distinct: the PLO aimed at the Arab world while IPS aimed beyond. Still, the PLO Research Center's gaze was also on the global community, both through shaping PLO leaders' relationship with Israel and the Great Powers and through directly reaching readers who followed their English-language publications.

In 1969, just four years into the Center's history, an American newspaper reported on "anti-Israel diatribes bombard[ing] Congress." According to the *Philadelphia Inquirer Public Ledger*, the Kuwaiti embassy in the US had recently been sending "packets of anti-Israel propaganda" to members of Congress and other government officials. The recipients were purposefully chosen, including four members of the Senate Foreign Relations Committee, J. W. Fulbright, George D. Aiken, Stuart Symington, and, "in a gesture that must be counted as supreme optimism," the newspaper quipped, Jacob K. Javits, a Jewish senator from New York. The packet that these officials received, shipped by the Fifth of June Society,[57] contained a collection of texts prepared by multiple institutions in Beirut. Among these texts about politics, religion, and international law in Palestine and Israel, according to this report, was a question-and-answer booklet distributed by the PLO Research Center that "charged Israel with aggression, with 'constantly attacking neighboring Arab states,' political assassination, [and] harassment of the United Nations' observers."[58] The text referred to here was surely Ibrahim al-Abid's *Handbook to the Palestine Question: Questions and Answers* (discussed in detail below).[59] Also included in the package was the Research Center's book *Palestine in Focus*,[60] by Sami Hadawi who, the reporter noted, said Israeli forces "terrorized more than half of the

Arab population into an Arab exodus." Along with the PLO Research Center publications were a brochure called "The Arabs under Israeli Occupation," prepared by the Arab Women's Information Committee;[61] William Holladay's "Is the Old Testament Zionist?" published by the University Christian Center Forum;[62] and several other texts published by the Institute for Palestine Studies, the common theme of which was, according to the newspaper, "that the founding and existence of the state of Israel are illegal."[63] A Kuwaiti embassy official, Jamil al-Hassani, acknowledged that his office had distributed these packets, arguing that only "one point of view has been put forward (in the U.S.) for the last 20 years" whereas "this material we are distributing gives the Arab point of view."[64]

While the Research Center generally provided the raw materials for others to use in their arguments against Zionism and Israel—as per Fayez Sayegh's stated purpose when he established the Center—at times, representatives of the Center used their work to advocate on behalf of the Palestinian cause more directly than Sayegh had imagined. In August 1969, for instance, Ibrahim al-Abid, compiler of the Center's *Handbook to the Palestine Question*, presented a report to a United Nations panel investigating the use of torture by Israel against Palestinian prisoners. The report, written in English, was apparently based on articles the Center had found in Israeli newspapers that indicated that torture had been employed against Palestinians.[65] Later, in 1975, during the debate over the United Nations General Assembly resolution declaring Zionism to be a form of racism, the Center (along with IPS) participated in the effort to persuade those not yet convinced to support the resolution.[66] In general, though, the Center tended to focus on supplying others with the basic information they believed was necessary for understanding the enemy.

Unintended Readers and Forbidden Readers

In addition to Palestinian and other Arab readers and policy-makers in the West, there was another PLO Research Center readership, one that may have been more committed than any other to following the Center's output: Israeli intelligence analysts. In part 3 of this book, I discuss the case of one such analyst, Matti Steinberg. As we shall see, Steinberg was especially interested in what the work of the Research Center revealed about developments in Palestinian political thought vis-à-vis Israel.

However, the output of the PLO Research Center was not available to all. One notable example of a community denied access to the Center's work were the Palestinians in the Israeli-occupied West Bank. On January 18, 1977, the official censor of the Israel Defense Forces, Yehoshuʿa Bar David, issued an "Order concerning forbidden publications." The order read:

> Under my authority according to Regulation 88(1) of the Defense (State of Emergency) Regulation 1945 and clause 8 of the "Order concerning the banning of hostile activity and propaganda (Judea and Samaria) (no. 101) 1967" and since I believe that the matter is necessary for the security of the region and public order, I hereby order:
>
> 1. The importing, printing, or advertising of the publications listed in the appendix of this order is forbidden . . .

The original list that Bar David issued in 1977 included numerous Arabic books published by the PLO Research Center, such as *Herzl's Diaries*, *State and Religion in Israel*, *Greater Israel*, *Israel and Oil*, *Israeli Militarism*, *Lights on the Israeli Media*, and *On the Parties of Israel*.[67]

Between January 1977 and July 1982, in fifty-four successive appendixes, Israel's West Bank censor supplemented this original list with additional books that were either newly discovered or newly published. On March 29, 1981, five of the Center's books were added; the following month, another fourteen Center-published works joined the list.[68] Between June and September 1981, the censor added another seven of the Center's publications.[69] The following summer, in June and July 1982, as Israel was in the midst of its invasion of Lebanon, the censor banned yet another eleven books published by the Center.[70] The final book added to this censor list, on August 4, 1982, was the Center's *Haganah, Etzel, Lehi: Relations between the Zionist Armed Organizations, 1936–1948*.[71] In 1985, the military censor issued a new list of 350 books to be banned from the West Bank, replacing the 1977 list and its fifty-plus appendixes.[72] Eighty-six of the books on the new list, roughly a quarter of the total, were published by the PLO in Beirut, nearly all by the PLO Research Center.

While the Israeli military censors no doubt regarded as "hostile propaganda" many of the scores of PLO Research Center books they banned in the 1970s and 1980s, the censor appears to have added to the list *any* book published by the PLO Research Center encountered by his staff—without regard to its specific content. Whether doing so was indeed "necessary for the security of the region and public order," as the censor claimed, is a matter of opinion, but what is clear is that Israeli officials were aware of the PLO Research

Center and its publications and sought to prevent these from reaching the West Bank Palestinian population.

The lists of censored publications tell us something else, as well. When the Israeli military raided the PLO Research Center in September 1982 and began shipping its library south to Israel (discussed in part 3 of this book), Israeli intelligence officials could hardly have been surprised by what they found. They had been seeing those same titles in the footnotes and bibliographies of the PLO Research Center publications for years.

3

From the Hebrew University to the PLO Research Center

The End of the Sayegh Era

Two years after the rocket attack on the Research Center, Anis Sayegh decided to resign his position there. His resignation, tendered in 1977, seems to have been connected to Anis's conflictual relationship with Yasser Arafat. It is possible that the Sayegh brothers may have felt more of a kinship with Shukairy (b. 1908), a fellow intellectual who was their senior (Fayez b. 1922; Anis b. 1931), than they did with Arafat (b. 1929), a contemporary whom they regarded as an anti-intellectual. Shafiq al-Hout, a friend of Anis Sayegh since their university days in the 1950s, wrote that he tried multiple times to make peace between Arafat and Sayegh, to no avail.[1]

Sayegh was replaced briefly by the renowned Palestinian poet Mahmoud Darwish (b. 1941).[2] Darwish was born in the Palestinian village of Birwa during the British Mandate. In the course of the 1948 war, he and his family fled to Lebanon. The following year, the family violated Israeli law by crossing back into what was now the State of Israel. He could not return to his native village, however, as it had been destroyed by the Israelis. Darwish thus experienced his adolescence and early adulthood as an internally displaced refugee within Israel. He was active in the Communist Party of Israel (Maki, then Rakah), but in 1971, he went to the Soviet Union for academic studies and chose not to return to Israel. Instead, he made his way to Beirut, where he joined the PLO and served as an editor of the PLO Research Center's newly established journal *Shu'un Filastiniyya*. His work as an editor was apparently successful but, by all accounts, Darwish was not a good match for a bureaucratic leadership position at the PLO Research Center. As Anan Ameri put it, this was "not his cup of tea. He was a poet, perhaps the greatest Palestinian poet, but not an administrator."[3] Another researcher at the Center, Sabri Jiryis agreed, reporting that Darwish "did not do anything" in his time as director of the Research Center. "A poet," Jiryis told me, "cannot lead a research center."[4] In 1978, Jiryis was appointed the new director general of the Center.[5]

Sabri Jiryis from Fassuta

Jiryis was born in 1938 in Fassuta, a small Greek Catholic Melkite Arab village in the north of British Mandate Palestine. In 1947, when the UN General Assembly voted to partition Palestine, Fassuta was designated to be within Palestine's Arab State. However, during Israel's Operation Hiram, in October 1948, Fassuta fell to Israeli forces. This village, like the rest of the Galilee, would remain under Israeli sovereignty.

As Jiryis recalled in the memoirs he shared with me, and in conversations we had in his home, the Zionist forces who entered Fassuta in October 1948, when Jiryis was just nine years old, were the first Jews he had ever encountered. When he saw them, he reminisced with a smile, he was surprised to discover that they did not have tails. As Jiryis tells it, he has been trying to understand Jews and Israelis ever since that fateful conquest of Fassuta in the autumn of 1948, and he has devoted much of his life to teaching his fellow Palestinians and Arabs about them.

How did a Palestinian Arab citizen of Israel from the Galilee become the director general of the PLO Research Center in Beirut? An analysis of Jiryis's path from Fassuta to Beirut may shed light on Palestinian politics in Israel and beyond in the few decades after the establishment of the State of Israel.

Jiryis studied in the local elementary school in Fassuta headed by a Melkite priest from the village. When it came time to choose a high school, he and four friends decided against the two local options and boarded at the Franciscan Terra Santa Gymnasium in Nazareth, adjacent to the Church of the Annunciation. With the help of a local village leader, Jiryis and his friends received a permit from the military government to travel between Fassuta and Nazareth. As he recalled in his memoirs, this was his first encounter with Israel's military administration regime that governed Arab-majority areas in the country from 1949 until it was officially disbanded in 1966. Jiryis began his studies at Terra Santa in September 1953, under the instruction of the school's staff of priests and monks. At Terra Santa, which followed the British educational curriculum, the primary language of instruction was English, though students also learned Arabic, Hebrew, French, and Latin. Notwithstanding the fact that the teachers were religious functionaries, the school, as Jiryis described it in his memoirs, was not overly religious and, so he claimed, actually strengthened his own secular perspective.[6]

In 1957, at the age of eighteen, Jiryis was admitted to the Hebrew University of Jerusalem on the new Givat Ram campus on the Israeli side of the divided city. There, according to a count he and his friends conducted at the time, he was one of forty-eight Arab students.[7] Jiryis undertook the study of law, the first step in the process of entering the Israel legal bar. In 1959, a few years into his legal studies, Jiryis joined in spearheading the creation of al-Ard ("The Land"), a political activist movement of Palestinian citizens of Israel.[8]

Al-Ard between Equality and Liberation

The Ard movement had splintered off from another organization of Arabs in Israel, the Arab Front, which had been founded the previous year.[9] The Front's aims were focused primarily on matters pertaining to the Arabs of Israel, including the efforts "to abolish the military government, to end the expropriation of Arab land, to abolish racial discrimination, [and] to introduce the use of Arabic in all government departments," but the Front also advocated for Palestinians outside of Israel in its call "to work toward the return of all refugees to their homes." The Front included both Communists and pan-Arab nationalists, Jiryis explained in a book he later wrote, and eventually the ideological tensions between these two groups led the nationalists to form their own organization, Usrat al-Ard (Family of the Land) or simply al-Ard.[10]

In its founding communique, al-Ard's members began by identifying themselves, and Israel's Arab citizens broadly, as "a part of the Palestinian people, who are in turn a part of the Arab nation." The group not only demanded "within this country . . . full equality between Arab and Jew" but also insisted that the Israeli government (1) recognize the Arab nationalist movement as "the established movement of the region," (2) discard "Zionist thought and the Zionist movement," (3) "pursue a policy of positive neutrality and peaceful coexistence," and (4) assist the Palestinians in claiming their "right to self-determination" and allow the Palestinian refugees to return.[11]

The organization began publishing a newspaper under various titles—each a different variation on the theme Ard—because the Israeli authorities would not grant its application to establish a permanent newspaper. In the four months of October 1959 through January 1960, al-Ard published a dozen issues. Notwithstanding their creative attempt to circumvent the legal process for registering a newspaper, al-Ard's activists and their political goals outlined in their newspaper caught the eye, and ire, of Israeli authorities.[12] As Jiryis wrote in his memoirs, "Al-Ard was not warmly received, to say the least, by any official in Israel."[13]

The following year, at the age of twenty-one, Jiryis was elected to Hebrew University's Arab student council. Israeli newspapers that reported these elections in February 1960 noted Jiryis's affiliation with al-Ard.[14] Just days after the Arab student council election, Jiryis was interrogated by the Jerusalem police because of his role as an editor of the movement's newspaper.[15] Al-Ard's newspaper was regarded by some in the Israeli press as "no different in spirit from the propaganda of Radio Cairo," considering its various political positions and its open admiration for Egyptian president Gamal Abdel Nasser.[16] Defending the government's attempt to shut down al-Ard's publication, the Histadrut's newspaper *Davar* reported, in March 1960, that officials recently "decided that even in the democratic regime of Israel it is impossible to tolerate the publication of unbridled incitement of this sort, and activity that has encompassed Nazareth, Haifa, Jerusalem, and the Triangle." The government actively cracked down on the organization,[17] such that by June 1960, Jiryis was among six al-Ard activists who were each fined 1,000 Israeli liras and sentenced to three months of probation for having published an unlicensed newspaper. All issues of the paper were banned.[18] Though it failed to attain permission to publish a newspaper, al-Ard fought and won a battle in the Israeli Supreme Court, between 1961 and 1962, to register as a limited, incorporated company.[19]

In 1962, Jiryis completed his law degree and began an internship at the Naqara law firm in Haifa. The firm's founder, Hanna Naqara (1912–1984), achieved prominence through efforts to protect the rights and property of the Arab minority in Israel.[20] In this new role, Jiryis began to represent Arabs in Israeli courts, challenging the various forms of legal discrimination Israel's Arabs experienced during these years of Israeli military rule over the state's Arab population.[21]

Even as he represented Naqara's clients as a legal intern, Jiryis continued his own political activism. In 1964, the year before he officially received his law license,[22] Jiryis led the effort to revive al-Ard as a fully-fledged political movement and party in Israel in advance of the 1965 Knesset elections.[23] When the Israeli government denied al-Ard's application for official status,[24] the group composed a twelve-page memorandum addressed to U Thant, secretary-general of the United Nations, in which al-Ard decried Israeli persecution of its Arab minority and articulated the organization's aspirations for the future of Palestine.

The June 1964 "Memorandum on the Arabs in Israel" asserted that Israel's Arabs "suffer from a dedicated policy of oppression, discrimination and persecution that the Israeli government wages against them."[25] The document highlighted four broad areas of Israeli policy in which discrimination against Arabs was evident: expropriation of Arab-owned lands; military (rather than civilian) rule over Arab citizens; suppression of Arab culture and education; and what was termed "racial discrimination" against Arabs in areas including public services, health services, local authorities, and freedoms of speech and expression. This last issue was of particular concern for al-Ard because the Israeli government was denying the organization the right to operate. "The government fiercely opposes all attempts to establish a free and independent Arab political movement which can really represent the Arab minorities," the memo asserted. "The government also denies the Arabs their basic right to publish their own newspaper, which can express their feelings and aspirations and claims their rights," Al-Ard noted after the government repeatedly denied the group a license to publish a newspaper.

The memo's reference to Israeli authorities' forbidding the publication of an Arab nationalist newspaper served as the segue to its discussion of al-Ard. "Amid this unhealthy atmosphere of persecution and discrimination, racism and chauvinism," the memo asserted, "a proud Arab voice rose urging for all the Arabs in Israel, their legitimate rights and proper place in Society and respect for their feelings and traditions." This group of young Arab men, who united under the slogan of "Justice" and with the motto "al-Ard," continued the memo, "stand[s] for equality, justice, respect, dignity and freedom."

The document then outlined al-Ard's beliefs and aspirations. As in al-Ard's founding communiqué, the authors of this memorandum also identified the Arabs in Israel as "part of the Palestinian Arabs who are an integral part of the whole Arab Nation." Next, the memo offered four broad goals and a commitment to cooperate with groups in Israel that shared any or all of them.

1. Total equality for all citizens with full right to the basic natural freedoms, and an end to discrimination and oppression.
2. The acceptance on the part of Israel of the U.N. Resolutions of November 29, 1947 on the Partition of Palestine—a just solution which safeguards the interests of the Arab and Jewish people and affirms stability and peace in the Middle East.

3. The adoption, by Israel, of a policy of non-alignment, positive neutrality and peaceful coexistence.

4. Israel's recognition of the Arab national movement, which calls for unity and socialism, as the most progressive and reliable force on which the future of this region depends—an outlook on which the future of Israel herself depends.

Notably, in this communiqué, al-Ard had dropped its earlier demand that Israel abandon "Zionist thought" as such. In addition, instead of calling for a Palestinian "right to self-determination," now al-Ard framed Palestinian statehood in terms of the UN's 1947 decision to partition Palestine. In this text, al-Ard accepted partition not merely as a fait accompli, or as an unjust solution that was the best the Palestinians could hope for; rather, al-Ard positively endorsed the partition of Palestine as "just."

This categorical embrace of UN General Assembly Resolution 181 stood in stark contrast to the PLO's complete rejection of partition, which the PLO expressed in its original covenant in May 1964, just one month before al-Ard sent its memorandum to the UN secretary-general. The PLO Covenant declared that "the partition of Palestine in 1947 and the establishment of Israel are fundamentally null and void [*batil min asasihi*] regardless of the time that has passed, because they were contrary to the wish of the Palestinian people and its natural right to its homeland, and in violation of the basic principles embodied in the charter of the United Nations, foremost among which is the right to self-determination."[26]

Why might al-Ard's position on partition have differed so markedly from the PLO's? Context and audience may help explain the difference. Al-Ard's leaders wrote under the military rule of Israel, a state formed upon the partition of Palestine, and they addressed their memo to the UN secretary-general, who could not be expected to be receptive to a message that denied the legitimacy of a UN resolution. Al-Ard's decision—not merely grudgingly to accept partition but rather to honor it as "a just solution which safeguards the interests of the Arab and Jewish people and affirms stability and peace in the Middle East"—suggests a degree of understanding of Zionism and the idea of a "Jewish people" that was categorically absent from the PLO Covenant.[27] "What was good for Israel after World War II and now," the al-Ard memo concluded—implicitly acknowledging the centrality of the persecution of Jews in the argument for creating a Jewish state—"is also good for the minorities living inside her boundaries." In his memoirs, Jiryis acknowledged that al-Ard effectively accepted the two-state solution a decade before the PLO "stammeringly" (*be-gimgum*) did so in the 1974 Ten Points Program and nearly thirty years before the Oslo Accords.[28]

One assumes that this memorandum reached Secretary-General U Thant, whether directly or through the international press that reported on it, but we have no record of a response.[29] In any case, the United Nations did not accede to al-Ard's request; it did not directly intervene on behalf of al-Ard. The movement's legal wrangling within the Israeli court system thus persisted over the following months.[30] In the meantime, Jiryis continued his activism, aiming to challenge the legitimacy of the military rule under which Israel's Arabs lived. On a Friday evening in August 1964, Jiryis participated in a "public trial" in the Moghrabi Theater in Tel Aviv. The "defendant" was an Israeli Arab student named Ali Rafa, sentenced for having violated the military government's confinement order when he traveled to Jerusalem to sit for his final exam at the Hebrew University. Jiryis was called as a witness in the mock trial.[31]

The concurrence of al-Ard's renewed activism in Israel and the birth of the PLO just across the Green Line in Jordan did not go unnoticed in Israel. The presumed coordination between Palestinian nationalists inside and outside Israel's borders alarmed the Israeli government. In September 1964, the Foreign Ministry's Research Department sent a memo to Yaakov Herzog, the assistant director general of the ministry, on the topic "The Palestinian Liberation Organization and the Arabs of Israel." In the memo, Naim Sofer, an Iraqi Israeli in the Research Department, began by noting that at the founding session of the PLO in May, "Shukeiry turned also to the Arabs of Israel and declared that they are part of the Palestinian nation and that they would eventually meet again." Since then, wrote Sofer, "the Arab newspapers have dedicated greater attention to this aspect, and all the more so because at the same time the Ard organization has renewed its activities, which have been cited in the Arabic press." Sofer referenced recent articles from the Lebanese paper *al-Anwar* in August and from the Jordanian *Filastin* in September that highlighted the activities of al-Ard and Israel's attempts to suppress them. According to Sofer, *Filastin* portrayed al-Ard as "the first spark in the Palestinian rebellion inside the occupied homeland." *Filastin* also stressed that al-Ard should be assisted "at all costs and in all ways" and should be integrated into the unified Palestinian command established through the PLO.[32] Al-Ard had insisted that they and the Arab citizens of Israel were part of the broader Palestinian national movement, and the Israeli authorities considered them to be just that.

At the same time, Israeli officials became increasingly anxious about cross-border attempts at militant coordination. It was in this context, in mid-November 1964, that Jiryis made the news again. The Israeli authorities announced that they had captured three Syrian-Lebanese spy squads that had entered Israel. Some of the captured spies allegedly divulged, under interrogation, that one of their aims in crossing into Israel was to establish contacts with the leaders of al-Ard. As a result, Jiryis and two of his fellow al-Ard leaders were arrested.[33]

While under arrest, Jiryis issued an appeal to the High Court of Justice in which he offered a clause-by-clause commentary on and defense of al-Ard's platform.[34] Concerning internal Israeli matters, Jiryis emphasized that the organization sought the end of discrimination against Israel's Arabs through, for example, "cancelling the military administration, ceasing to expropriate Arab lands and returning expropriated lands to their owners to the extent possible, improving the conditions of Arab laborers, Arab education, [public] services in Arab communities, etc." However, the "primary cause of instability and the absence of peace in the Middle East," he said, was the Palestinian problem—namely, the Palestinians' loss of "their political existence and their legal rights." Jiryis explained that the organization's call for "a just solution" meant one that resolved all aspects of the problem, including refugees, borders, abandoned property, Jordan River waters, and so on.

In his appeal to the Supreme Court, Jiryis juxtaposed the situation of the "Jewish nation" with that of the "Palestinian Arab nation." Al-Ard's founders believed, wrote Jiryis, that the problem of "the Jewish nation has been solved, as it has determined its fate, realized its sovereignty, and established a state of its own." Zionism had succeeded in resolving the challenges facing the Jews. By contrast, Jiryis asserted, none of these conditions "have been fulfilled for the Palestinian Arab nation." Again, Jiryis's acknowledgment, if only rhetorically, of Jewish nationhood stood in stark contrast with the Covenant the PLO issued just months earlier.

In interpreting the subsequent clauses of al-Ard's mission, Jiryis emphasized that the movement's goals were consistent with what he believed were Israel's ambitions for peace with its neighbors. For instance, were Israel to support the movement for "liberation, unity, and socialism in the Arab world," as al-Ard demanded, this would solve all related problems and would "bring peace to the region and secure the future of the state [of Israel]." Moreover, al-Ard's call for "working toward peace in the Middle East in particular and in the world in general" meant "working toward peace between Israel, on the one hand, and the Arab states, on the other." Al-Ard, argued Jiryis, could not be regarded as an organization hostile to the existence of the State of Israel; on the contrary, the State of Israel would only benefit were it to follow the organization's demands.[35]

A panel of three Supreme Court justices—Moshe Landau, Zvi Berenson, and Alfred Witkon—decided the case against Jiryis. Witkon, who was born in 1910 in Berlin, earned his law degree at the University of Freiberg, and immigrated to Palestine in 1935, wrote the lengthiest opinion. He argued that the court's primary source must be the text of the group's platform, to which its members declared commitment, rather than any individual leader's unofficial interpretation of the text. Al-Ard's purpose, as openly declared in its platform, "fully and completely denies the existence of the State of Israel in general, and the existence of the state in its present borders in particular," argued Witkon. After all, wrote Witkon citing the organization's platform, al-Ard called for "a solution to the Palestinian problem—viewed as an indivisible entity—in accordance with the will of the Palestinian Arab nation . . . which has the primary right to determine its fate within the framework of the supreme ambitions of the Arab nation." For Witkon, the central issue was that "in a portion of Palestine the State of Israel was established and this fact does not merit here [in Al-Ard's platform] any recognition." There was no discussion of "coexistence," wrote Witkon, "nor of equal rights of two nations." The "Jewish factor does not exist in this worldview," he concluded, adding that only a fool would believe that this program "could be carried out peacefully and through persuasion" since it was clear that it ultimately demanded "underground, hostile activities."[36]

Despite the importance Witkon saw in the democratic right to freedom of association, he argued that "no free regime would give its hand and its recognition to a movement that rejects the regime itself." He concluded with a reference to his own experience in Germany: "More than once in the history of states with proper democratic regimes, fascistic and totalitarian movements have arisen against them and used all the freedoms of speech, press, and association that the state provides them in order to undertake destructive acts under their cover. Whoever saw this in the days of the Weimar Republic will not forget the lesson."[37]

With this, Witkon voted to reject Jiryis's petition. Landau and Berenson concurred with Witkon. Landau asserted that "it is a fundamental right of every state to protect its freedom and its existence against enemies from abroad and those who follow [the foreign enemies] at home." No regime can be expected to permit the establishment of a "fifth column within its borders" simply for the sake of preserving freedom of association, he ruled.[38]

The editors of *al-Ittihad*, the Arabic newspaper of the Israeli Communist Party, blasted the High Court of Justice's decision.[39] Notwithstanding the Communists' disagreements with al-Ard, they wrote that "it is not the job of courts to decide the legality of political movements." Moreover, wrote the editors, the claim that al-Ard did not recognize the State of Israel was controverted by the group's platform (which called for "full equality and social justice between all groups of the nation in Israel"), its petition to the UN (which sought a solution to the Palestinian problem "based on the resolutions of the United Nations"), and the very fact that the group applied for legal status in Israel. The court's decision was thus plainly political and therefore, in the minds of *al-Ittihad*'s editorial board, illegitimate.

Notwithstanding *al-Ittihad*'s opposition, less than a week after the High Court of Justice's ruling was announced on November 11, 1964, Prime Minister and Defense Minister Levi Eshkol decreed that al-Ard in all of its manifestations was illegal on the basis of the still-enforced British emergency laws of 1945 and of Israeli law from 1948.[40] In informing his government of this decision, on November 22, 1964, Eshkol reminded his colleagues that the previous July they had agreed that he should use his powers to stop the activities of al-Ard.[41] "I assume you all heard of the High Court of Justice decision," wrote Eshkol, which "established that the organization's goals are illegal and that they completely deny the existence of the State of Israel in general and the existence of the state in its current borders in particular." Eshkol concluded that "there is an urgent security need to stop this group's activities" and added, suggestively, that the security services "have a lot of material" on al-Ard's "subversive activities."[42] Jiryis was arrested along with Mansour Qardush, Habib Qahwaji, and Salih Baransi, and their homes were searched for illegal materials.[43]

The Supreme Court's ruling and Eshkol's ban on al-Ard did not end the group's saga. In March 1965, house arrest orders against Qardush, Qahwaji, and Jiryis were extended. Jiryis threatened to appeal once again to the United Nations.[44] A few months later, in July, Jiryis returned to the Supreme Court to demand that the military administration's district commander cancel the police surveillance order against him. The district commander's order was motivated, Jiryis alleged, by political factors rather than security interests.[45] In September 1965, Jiryis was arrested again—this time for twenty days for violating his exile in Safed and returning to Haifa.[46]

Writing *The Arabs in Israel* in Hebrew

At the same time, Jiryis undertook a book-length study of the legal status of Arab citizens living under military rule in Israel. In April 1965, Jiryis wrote to Nathan Yellin-Mor (1913–1980), a former fighter in the right-wing Lehi militia who subsequently became an advocate for a Palestinian state and for Jewish-Arab equality inside Israel.[47] Apparently, Yellin-Mor tried to help Jiryis get his manuscript published. "I intend to publish the book in Tel Aviv," wrote Jiryis to Yellin-Mor. "However, because it is not possible for me to travel freely to Tel Aviv," Jiryis explained, referencing both the general restrictions on Arab movement and the particular limitations that the military government had placed upon him personally, "I will request of you to contact again the publisher you had contacted earlier and to confirm that they are prepared to publish the book."[48] It would seem that Yellin-Mor's interventions on Jiryis's behalf were unsuccessful as *The Arabs in Israel* was published the following year not in Tel Aviv but in Haifa by the Communist Party's *Ittihad* press.

Jiryis's *The Arabs in Israel* was written and published first in Hebrew but within a year it was translated into Arabic. The publisher this time was the Arab League office in Jordanian East Jerusalem. The original, politically neutral title of the book was transformed into one that left little question about its political perspective: *The Arab Compatriots [al-muwatinun] in the Hell [jahim] of Israel: A Precise Presentation and Depiction of the Issue of Arabs in the Occupied Region in Which the Grave Features of This Issue Become Clear.*[49] In May 1967, one month before the outbreak of the 1967 war, the newspaper *'Al ha-Mishmar* described Jiryis's book as "a most extreme indictment against the state of Israel" and contended that "the author's extremism distorted the picture, though this is precisely what the propaganda of the Arab League in Israel appreciated."[50] In December 1968, Jiryis's book was awarded the Honorary Prize at an Arab regional conference on human rights in Beirut.[51]

In 1968 and 1969, Jiryis participated in the defense of Arab Israeli citizens accused of various violent plots inside Israel, such as planting explosives around Jerusalem in "the Night of Grenades"[52] or bombs in a Tel Aviv movie theater,[53] or forming an armed, militant organization of Arab citizens of Israel.[54] In July 1969, Jiryis represented two residents of Jerusalem's Old City, Isma'il 'Aql and Muhammad Suleiman, in their appeal to Israel's Supreme Court against the confiscation of their homes.[55] In April and May 1970, Jiryis himself was placed under administrative detention in the Damon prison in northern Israel near Haifa; he represented himself and fellow prisoners in their appeals to Israel's Supreme Court.[56]

From Fassuta to Beirut

This experience in prison appears to have been the last straw for Jiryis. A few months later, on the ninth of September (the month Palestinians remember as "Black September"), Jiryis decided to leave Israel and, after a short stay in Greece, embarked on a self-imposed exile in Beirut.[57] Jiryis had good reason to be confident that he would be welcomed warmly in Beirut. Both the PLO Research Center in Beirut and the Institute for Palestine Studies in Beirut had published translations of his Hebrew-language *The Arabs in Israel*, the former in Arabic in 1967, and the latter in English a year later.[58] In 1968, Walid Khalidi had sent copies of the Arabic and English translations with a British tourist visiting Israel to pass along to Jiryis, "together with a message that if it ever occurred to me to leave Israel and come to Lebanon, he had work for me." In Beirut, Jiryis took Khalidi up on his offer. He became a researcher in IPS's "Israeli Department."[59]

The Israeli press's interest in Jiryis was undiminished by his departure from the country. Early in January 1971, *Ma'ariv* printed an article titled "A Palestinian Weekly in Beirut, an Arab-Israeli to Edit." The piece reported that "the Palestinian institute for researching the Israeli-Arab conflict, based in Beirut, which has published hundreds of books about the Land of Israel problem, is, in the coming days, about to publish a weekly that will deal exclusively with articles in the Israeli press about the conflict with the Arabs." This publication, wrote *Ma'ariv*'s correspondent for Arab affairs, would be edited by "the Arab-Israeli Sabri Jiryis, lawyer and author of the book *The Arabs in Israel*." The article noted Jiryis's links to al-Ard, his various periods of detention, and the fact that "he willingly went into exile." Now, the article reported, he was in Beirut and had "joined the activities of the Palestinian Research Center." Remarking on his education and qualifications to undertake this project, the article noted that "Jiryis is a graduate of the Hebrew University in Jerusalem and has a fine command of the Hebrew language." Of his book *The Arabs in Israel*, the article added that it "was translated by terrorist organizations into English and French and is distributed now among different groups in the world to prove 'just how oppressed the Arabs are under the Israeli regime.'" Jiryis's new place of employment, *Ma'ariv* claimed, is "managed in Beirut by Professor Sayegh and is funded by Kuwait and the other petroleum principalities in the Persian Gulf."[60]

A week later, the newspaper *Davar* also announced that Jiryis, "one of the most prominent Arab nationalist-communist characters," was set to begin editing a new weekly publication on the Arab-Israeli conflict focused on perspectives found in the Israeli press.[61] If the Israeli authors of these Hebrew press articles were conscious of—or amused by—the irony of the Israeli press reporting on a Palestinian who was planning an Arabic journal presenting Israeli press perspectives on the conflict, they chose to keep this to themselves.

Within weeks, Jiryis's voluntary departure from Israel was perceived as fitting into a broader pattern of young activist Palestinian citizens of Israel fleeing the country to take up residence and political activity in a supportive environment beyond Israel's borders. *Ma'ariv* reported in February 1971 that after the poet Mahmoud Darwish went to study in the Soviet Union several months earlier, he chose not to return to Israel but rather sought refuge in Cairo. Darwish's decision, the Israeli newspaper contended, "was made with the encouragement of the Soviets who wished to take advantage of him in the Soviet-Arab propaganda effort against Israel." Similarly, the newspaper reported that Rashid Hussein, poet and translator of Hayyim Nahman Bialik's Hebrew poetry into Arabic, lived in New York and worked on behalf of "an Arab anti-Zionist organization"[62] (which was, in fact, the PLO's New York office).[63]

The following month, in March 1971 in Cairo, Jiryis was officially welcomed as a member of the Palestine National Council. *Ma'ariv* commented at the time that "one of the most interesting decisions" made by the Council at this meeting was its vote to add "three Arab Israelis to its ranks." These were Mahmoud Darwish (whose poetry criticizing Israel's military administration and its expropriation of land, *Ma'ariv* noted, had been translated into French in *Le Monde*), Habib Qahwaji (a cofounder of al-Ard who, after landing in Israeli prisons several times, emigrated to Damascus), and Sabri Jiryis. A leader of al-Ard, *Ma'ariv* highlighted, Jiryis was "now serving as editor of a periodical dedicated to analyzing Israel's various problems."[64]

By the summer of 1971, Jiryis was no longer presented in the Israeli press merely as an author and a former political activist in al-Ard; rather, he was now regarded as an organizer of a Fateh cell inside Israel before he defected to Lebanon. In July, *Ma'ariv* reported that a network of Arabs suspected of terrorism was "a cell in the organization al-Fateh, which was organized previously by the lawyer Sabri Elias Jiryis, a former resident of Haifa, who after administrative detention emigrated to Lebanon and is active there in the terror organizations."[65]

According to Jiryis's daughter Fida, these allegations were not unwarranted. In her recent family memoir, *Stranger in My Own Land*, Fida wrote that during his final three years in Israel before emigrating to Lebanon, "Sabri continued to practice law and work with the resistance at the same time." She continued by explaining that her father "made contact with Khalil al-Wazir (Abu Jihad), the commander of al-Asifa, Fatah's military wing," who was "in charge of Fatah's Western Sector and was in contact with all the fedayeen groups." Fida recounted that "Sabri joined this sector, which operated in Israel and the occupied territory."[66] She remained circumspect about the nature of her father's activities, but she noted that Sabri's brother, Geris, engaged in "underground work" that included transporting illicit arms.[67] She also contended that Sabri left Israel in 1970 upon the urging of Abu Jihad, who had supposedly received word via Russian intelligence that the Israeli authorities were surveilling her father and planning to imprison him for a lengthy period of time.[68]

Jiryis's experiences over his twenty-two years living in Israel thus help us understand how a Palestinian Israeli from a small Catholic village in the Galilee became the director general of the PLO Research Center. From the age of ten through twenty-eight, he lived under Israeli military rule. He became active in Palestinian nationalist politics as a law student at the Hebrew University and discovered quickly, especially through his work in al-Ard, the degree to which the Israeli government sought to suppress such activism within its borders. He caught the attention of Palestinians and other Arabs outside Israel particularly after he published his monograph critically assessing the treatment of Arab citizens of Israel. Having failed to secure any meaningful political achievements through his activism in Israel, and having been detained, confined, and imprisoned for various lengths of time, Jiryis came to believe that he could accomplish more outside the borders of Israel than he could within them. He therefore decided to move north to Beirut to join the PLO.

Zionism Expertise Born in Israeli Detention

It is one thing for a Palestinian citizen of Israel to become an expert in the treatment of Palestinian citizens of Israel; it is another matter entirely for him to become the PLO's resident expert on Zionism and Israel. According to Jiryis's own narration, this transformation began when he was arrested, along with three other al-Ard leaders, during their effort to have the movement compete in the Knesset elections in 1965. Each detainee was required to live under house arrest in a distant Jewish city for a period of three months. Jiryis was sent from Haifa, where he had been residing, to Safed.[69] As he wrote in his memoirs, he brought with him to Safed several Arabic books on the 1948 war. He quickly finished those books and, bored out of his wits, during the limited hours he was permitted to leave his new quarters, he went searching for a local bookstore. He soon found one. "In this store," Jiryis wrote, "I did not find the sorts of new books I was seeking, about the Arab-Israeli conflict. However, while looking around I reached a treasure: a full shelf of books on Zionism." Jiryis recalls purchasing one book from the shelf and devouring its contents. He returned to buy a second book, and then a third. "The old storekeeper noticed my frequent visits," Jiryis recounted, and proposed to sell the whole shelf to him at a steep discount. And that was how an entire collection of Zionist literature came into his hands.

"I read these books—many of which were written by the fathers of the Zionist idea, such as Herzl, Hess, Kalischer, Lilienblum, Pinsker, and others—carefully and thoroughly," Jiryis explained to me. He was fascinated by what he read but, in his memoirs, he nonetheless insisted that "this reading did not bring it [the Zionist idea] closer to me and did not in the slightest make me fond of it." Jiryis elaborated:

> The influence of the colonial idea, the creation of the European nations, on the Zionist idea, which was so clear and obvious, amazed me. After all, they, the old colonialists, worked from the assumption that it was their "right" to rule over the nations and lands of Asia and Africa and to establish colonies for their countries, while the new ones, the Zionists, spoke in a very similar spirit about their "right" to establish a Jewish state, and some did not necessarily mean Palestine or, at least, were not certain about this.

Every Zionist leader or thinker among those whose writings he read, Jiryis asserted, related in some way to this comparison between Zionism and colonialism. In their political plans and ideas, he contended, colonialism's influence was apparent "in one way or another."

The one distinction that Jiryis drew between colonialism and Zionism concerned the issue of self-justification. In typical European colonialism, wrote Jiryis, "'the nobles,' spoke of 'the white race's burden' and 'its duty' to provide 'culture' to the 'natives'" as the reason that the Europeans must rule over them and their lands. The Zionists, on the other hand, "used religion—Judaism, of course—as the basis for their claims to a state of their own." With this conclusion, based on his reading of Zionist sources, Jiryis suddenly "realized that we 'the Arabs of the Land of Israel' (not Palestine, of course), are the 'natives' vis-à-vis the Zionists and later the Israelis."[70] Jiryis added wryly, "I also thought to myself that it had not been advisable of the military authorities to expel me."[71] Doing so, after all, had unintentionally provided him a golden opportunity to immerse himself in Zionist thought and to develop a perspective on the movement that the Israeli authorities would come to not appreciate.[72]

In his first years in Beirut, Jiryis was mainly involved with the Institute of Palestine Studies, which was eager to exploit his knowledge of Zionist ideology and Israeli society, and his fluency in Hebrew. Soon, however, Jiryis found himself at odds with Walid Khalidi. After the 1973 war, Jiryis published an article in the Lebanese newspaper *al-Nahar*. According to Jiryis's memoirs, Khalidi summoned him to a meeting with the IPS leadership where he expressed his displeasure that Jiryis had not submitted the article to an IPS publication. Had he done so, Jiryis recalled saying, the editors would have rejected the article as insufficiently academic, or sanitized it "so as not, heaven forbid, to offend any Arab leader." Khalidi then informed Jiryis that as long as he wished to work at IPS, he would be permitted to publish in IPS publications only. Finally, Khalidi demanded "that I choose between my work at the Institute [for Palestine Studies] and my Fatah-PLO activities," Jiryis recalled.[73]

Jiryis at the PLO Research Center

This episode marked the end of Jiryis's stint at IPS. He resigned, and Anis Sayegh recruited him to the PLO Research Center. Sayegh was "surprised," wrote Jiryis, "that someone like me, a man of al-Ard and Fateh, had found it appropriate to work with the 'aristocrats'" at IPS, when his natural place, as Sayegh described it, was at the Research Center. Jiryis would soon assume the leadership of the Center's research department and become deputy director of the whole Center.[74] After Sayegh's resignation and Darwish's short tenure as director, Jiryis would ultimately become, in 1978, the director general of the Research Center. He was selected for this position by PLO chairman Yasser Arafat.[75]

Even before he achieved the top position, Jiryis was recognized both within and beyond the Center as its resident expert on Jewish, Zionist, and Israeli affairs. When a researcher wished to publish about these topics in *Shu'un Filastiniyya*, Jiryis would be asked to review the articles.

Consider an exposition in the February 1976 issue of *Shu'un Filastiniyya* on the relationship between Zionism and Hasidism (the mystical Jewish revival movement born in Eastern Europe in the eighteenth century), written by

Egyptian-born and Columbia and Rutgers University–educated Abdelwa-hab Elmessiri (1938–2008).[76] In the article, "Hasidism: One of the Secret Zionist Tributaries," Elmessiri analyzed, inter alia, Hasidism's particular form of messianism. "If the traditional messianic vision is an apocalyptic vision that happens *suddenly*," he wrote, "the Hasidic messianism is *gradual*, such that messianism became not simply the arrival of the messiah but rather a slow, rising movement in which all members of [the people of] Is-rael participate." Through Hasidism, Elmessiri argued, "it became messian-ism without a messiah [*mashihaniyya dun mashih*]—a messianism that is based principally on the Jewish collective self."[77]

Elmessiri contended that many Zionist thinkers and leaders "were raised in the Hasidic environment or were influenced by Hasidic ideas consciously or unconsciously." Zionism, suggested Elmessiri, "is a kind of 'non-religious Hasidism,' so to speak." He presented a series of arguments about the similari-ties of Hasidism and Zionism, relying heavily on contemporary Jewish his-torical and theoretical scholarship, and noted that the "Hasidic idea that God is in everything is not dissimilar to the Zionist idea that God is embodied in the Zionist state and the Holy Land." He pointed to Hasidic immigration to Palestine as setting the stage for broader Zionist immigration. Elmessiri fur-ther argued that Zionism was informed not only by Hasidism's "messianism without a messiah" but also by "the special Hasidic idea that the messianic period will only come in stages and by means of acts of the Jews themselves." This, Elmessiri wrote, "is the religious-philosophical basis upon which Zion-ism relies, not to wait for the return of the messiah but rather to return itself to settle Palestine with force [or, more precisely, 'violence'—*bi-l-'unf*]." The Hasid and the Halutz (i.e., the Zionist settler in Palestine), Elmessiri wrote, "both participate in aspiring toward constructing the Kingdom of God on earth." Elmessiri concluded that "there is no doubt that Hasidism participated in preparing some sectors of the communities in Eastern Europe to accept the metaphysical ideas of Zionism, [and] in separating them from the civiliza-tions among which they lived and from the various progressive intellectual movements."[78]

Because Elmessiri's article concerned contemporary Jewish and Israeli so-ciety, the editors consulted with Jiryis about its arguments. In prefatory com-ments to the article, the editors wrote: "*Shu'un Filastiniyya* is publishing this study on a topic that is only rarely written about in Arabic. Because of the sensitivity of the topic, *Shu'un Filastiniyya* presented it to Brother Sabri Jiryis, who is responsible for [the journal's] Israeli and Zionist studies."

Jiryis was, to put it mildly, unpersuaded, and offered a devastating assessment of Elmessiri's article. First, Jiryis asserted that "Hasidism is a pure Jewish religious movement, founded and crystallized long before any 'bud' of Zionism had appeared. It has no relationship to Zionism, positive or negative." Further, Jiryis noted, most Hasidim live in the United States and "do not demonstrate noticeable interest in Zionism or Israel." Ultimately, Jiryis concluded, considering Hasidism's concern with "religion and metaphysical truths," it is a grave historical error to imagine that it played an important role in the rise of Zionism.

Jiryis's severe critique of Elmessiri's arguments did not lead the journal editors to reject Elmessiri's contribution. Instead, they printed both. Thus, on the very same pages of *Shu'un Filastiniyya*, the PLO Research Center published both an article asserting the deep theoretical interconnectedness of Hasidism and Zionism and a blunt advisory note to the effect that the author had gotten things entirely wrong.

Jiryis and the PLO in Washington, DC

From the perspective of Israeli officials, Jiryis was one of the most important members not merely of the PLO Research Center but within the PLO broadly. At the end of February 1977, a classified document was prepared by Israeli officials listing the forty most prominent members of the PLO. The anonymous compiler of the list divided the group into the various parties within the broader organization.[79] The list of fifteen Fateh leaders included Sabri Jiryis after top-ranking Yasser Arafat, Salah Khalaf, and Khalil al-Wazir, along with Faruq al-Qaddumi, Khaled al-Hassan, Hani al-Hassan, and Mahmoud Abbas.[80]

Why was Jiryis considered notable in the minds of Israelis? In part, he was already prominent from his time as an al-Ard activist and lawyer—long before he left Israel for Beirut and before he joined the PLO. And his status as the PLO's resident expert on Jewish, Zionist, and Israeli affairs surely piqued the interest of Israel's intelligence officers who were among the most loyal readers of *Shu'un Filastiniyya* and perceived his influence on its pages.

But Jiryis was on the Israeli radar for another reason as well. Having studied English during his childhood in British Mandate Palestine, he was tasked with leading the PLO effort to open an office in Washington, DC. In October 1976, Jiryis traveled to the US, entering on a Sudanese passport. By November, the *New York Times* reported that Jiryis had formally registered the office with the Justice Department with himself as a foreign agent. This move caused a significant stir in the US and in Israel, whose officials worried of an end to the American position of refusing to engage with the PLO until it accepted the existence of Israel and UN resolutions calling for a negotiated settlement. At least for the time being, however, the US held fast to this policy and declined Jiryis's requests to meet with government officials.[81]

While he was in the US, Jiryis, along with his colleague Issam Sartawi, met with a number of prominent American Jews, most of whom attended the meetings as private individuals. An article titled "American Jewish Leaders Are Split Over Issue of Meeting with P.L.O." ran on the front page of the *New York Times* in December 1976. Of the ten Jews who attended one of these meetings in New York, one acknowledged having done so to the press: George Gruen, an international affairs expert for the American Jewish Committee. In an interview with the *Times*, Gruen explained his rationale for participating. "It was useful," he reportedly told the journalist, "'to know your enemy' and to find out whether even remotely there was a change in the P.L.O. attitude."[82] One wonders if Gruen and Jiryis had any sense whatsoever of their parallel motivations.

In November 1976, Jiryis and Sartawi met again with a small group of five current and former American Jewish institutional leaders and staff: Herman Edelstein, the former director of the B'nai Brith International Council; David Goren of the American Jewish Congress; Olya Margolin of the National Council of Jewish Women; Rabbi Max Ticktin of B'nai Brith Hillel Foundations; and Arthur Waskow of the Institute for Policy Studies. Ticktin and Waskow were also among the leadership of Breira, an American Jewish organization that was critical of Israeli government policies and advocated for the creation of a Palestinian state alongside Israel.[83] The following month, Waskow published an op-ed in the *New York Times* in which he described the encounter and his thoughts about it. Waskow recounted that Jiryis and Sartawi told their interlocutors that the PLO was ready to accept the existence of "two sovereign states on the territory of Palestine—a Palestinian state and a Jewish state." Waskow related: "I thought to myself: The formulas of 'Jewish state' and 'sovereign state' have never before been used by the P.L.O. in private or public." While Waskow had previously heard Palestinians privately consider the possibility of accepting "'a de-Zionized Israel' or even just 'Israel,'" wrote Waskow, "it is new to suggest accepting that Israel is, and will be, chiefly Jewish in outlook and connections throughout the world." Moreover, the fact that Jiryis and Sartawi used the phrase "sovereign state," Waskow explained, "suggests that the P.L.O. would abandon its claim that Israel is not a legitimate state in international law." According to Waskow's account, Jiryis and Sartawi presented this statement of willingness to accept a sovereign Jewish state in Palestine not as their own personal view but as "official P.L.O. policy," even as it was then too controversial within the PLO "to lay out as its formal official position." Jiryis and Sartawi suggested, though, that the PLO would, in the future, issue "official public statements about the acceptance of a two-state settlement" that were far clearer than those the organization had made previously, wrote Waskow.

In relating his thoughts about the meeting, Waskow posed a number of questions. The first concerned the value of unofficial statements made in private. He observed that as "the private statements of P.L.O doves have become more conciliatory, the official ones do, too—but on a slower track." As a result, private statements mattered because they were "an advance signal" of official policy changes to come. Waskow also wondered whether the PLO's presentation to this group of American Jews was simply "a propaganda ploy." Perhaps it was, Waskow concluded, "but it is hard for a government or political leadership to carry out such a ploy unless there is a lot of political support within its ranks." Without this internal support, the group's "constituents would be outraged by the propaganda statements and would topple the leaders who said them." Thus, Waskow asserted, "even if the P.L.O. is seeking gains from propaganda, many of its home folks must now want a peace of Palestine-alongside-Israel." By engaging with and embracing those who articulate this position, Israel could "strengthen the Palestinian doves."[84]

Waskow's colleagues pressed Jiryis and Sartawi on why the PLO continued to attack Zionism, such as in the UN General Assembly resolution of the previous year declaring Zionism a form of racism and racial discrimination. One of the two—Waskow did not mention whether it was Jiryis or Sartawi—exclaimed, "Yes, the U.N. resolution against Zionism was our resolution. We are against Zionism. We believe Zionism is our enemy. But you make peace only with your enemy, not with your friend." At that point, as Waskow narrated the dramatic scene, the speaker "paused, looked around the room, and with great intensity said again, 'We are ready to make peace with our enemy.'"[85]

Notwithstanding the message Jiryis attempted to deliver while in the US, his presence and especially his effort to open a PLO office in Washington was acutely controversial, challenging joint Israeli-American rejection of any engagement with the PLO. Simcha Dinitz, Israel's ambassador to the United States at the time, reportedly discussed the matter with US secretary of state

Henry Kissinger. While there was apparently no legal means of forbidding the opening of a PLO office, as long as it was properly registered, it could only be staffed by those legally residing in the US. Jiryis had entered the US on a visitor's visa, which was set to expire at the end of November. His request for an extension was denied, ostensibly because he had falsely written that his place of birth was Sudan (rather than Palestine) on his initial visa application.[86]

By early February 1977, however, Benjamin Navon, an Israeli diplomat in DC, wrote in a secret memo to Moshe Raviv, director of the Foreign Ministry's North America department, that "it appears that the PLO is unable to open now an office in the US—more precisely it appears that they are prevented from manning it with Sabri Jiryis." Navon's unnamed source informed him that, according to American Jewish activist-scholar Norton Mezvinsky, "Sabri's stock was in decline."[87] One week later, the new US administration's secretary of state, Cyrus Vance, rejected Jiryis's application for a visa to return to the US to speak at an American Friends Service Committee conference.[88] A State Department official explained that Jiryis was not granted a new visa because "it was not American policy to have P.L.O. officials here on political business." Moreover, the official added, given Vance's upcoming trip to the Middle East, "it was thought better not to appear to be sending new political signals at a time when the Carter Administration was trying to work out a Middle East policy."[89]

The US government may have been somewhat more welcoming to Jiryis than was revealed at the time. On November 24, 1976, David Tourgeman, an advisor in the Israeli embassy in Washington, sent a "top secret" memo to Ephraim Evron, the assistant director of the Foreign Ministry reporting on information he had received from an unnamed informant who was in ongoing contact with Jiryis. (Tourgeman indicated that he fully trusted the informant but that he could not be certain about whether Jiryis was being completely honest with the informant.) In any case, Jiryis told the informant that he and the State Department officials had mutually agreed to keep their conversation secret and to deny its having taken place if ever asked. Jiryis also claimed that the Israeli government had advance knowledge of the PLO's intention to open a Washington office to promote its new political position and that the Israelis did not express any opposition. The State Department officials informed Jiryis that they would likely not be able to provide him with the sort of visa he had requested (presumably a diplomatic visa) but rather with one for a businessperson. On November 22, Jiryis's State Department contacts sent him a message asking him to keep a low profile for the time being. By November 24, Jiryis had been informed that his visa would not be extended, but that he would be granted a new visa from the consular department at the American Embassy in Damascus. His plan was to return to the US within a few weeks.[90]

Shortly after Jiryis left the US in mid-December 1976, Yasser Arafat sat for an interview with *Time* magazine. Arafat was asked about his perspective on "improving relations between the P.L.O. and the U.S." He replied: "We had hoped to establish a P.L.O. office in Washington, but our representative, Sabri Jiryis, was kicked out of your country on a technicality. This pained us. We tried but your reply was to kick out our representative."[91]

Jiryis ultimately returned to Beirut and resumed his work at the PLO Research Center, over which Arafat made him director general. Jiryis held this position until he and the PLO Research Center were expelled from Beirut in 1983.

PART II

Studying the Enemy

IN PUBLICATION after publication, the PLO Research Center's director, Anis Sayegh, emphasized that its goal was to help the Arab reader learn about the enemy. For example, in his foreword to a rather dry book on the founding and subsequent ideological and political history of the Israeli political party Mapai, Sayegh noted the following:

> After the PLO Research Center produced studies on the kibbutz and the Herut party (the fourth and fifth volumes of the Palestinian Studies series), it presents in the seventh volume in the series this study on the Mapai party. Following them in the course of 1967 will be another study on the Histadrut. It [the Center] hopes that these studies give the Arab reader—who constantly yearns to increase his knowledge about his enemy who usurped the heart of the Arab homeland—a clear, precise, and complete idea of the four main political institutions in occupied Palestine.[1]

This book on Mapai, explained Sayegh, "is intended to paint a full picture for the reader of the party that has ruled in 'Israel' since its birth in 1948." The worry marks surrounding Israel, which in the next sentence Sayegh calls "the usurper state,"[2] are indicative of Sayegh's derisive attitude toward Israel. But Sayegh's derision of Israel and his identification of the state as the "enemy" did not keep him, or the Center he led for a decade, from engaging in a serious effort to research all aspects of that enemy.

In the chapters that follow in this section of the book, I analyze several books and articles that the PLO Research Center published during its years in Beirut. I seek to understand what it meant, from the perspective of the Research Center's leaders and researchers, to learn about the enemy.

4

Zionist Colonialism in Palestine

ZIONISM AND EUROPEAN IMPERIALISM

IN NOVEMBER 1963, just months before becoming the founding chairman of the PLO, Ahmad Shukairy dubbed the Balfour Declaration "the first report on the Palestine refugees."[1] Shukairy conceded to his audience, the Special Political Committee of the United Nations General Assembly, that in the UN's official archives, the first report on the Palestinian refugee problem was that written by Folke Bernadotte, the Swedish UN mediator in Palestine. "But," insisted Shukairy, then chairman of the Palestine Arab Delegation, "it would be more equitable and comprehensive" if "we extend a request to the British Government, to the authorities of the British Museum wherein is deposited the original text of the Balfour Declaration, that this shameful document be transferred to the United Nations as the first instrument that led to this human drama, this human tragedy."[2] For Shukairy, the Balfour Declaration set in motion the policies and events that culminated in the exodus of some 700,000 Palestinian Arabs in the 1948 war. Half a year after he delivered this speech, Shukairy proclaimed in the Covenant of the newly established PLO that "the Balfour Declaration, the Palestine Mandate System, and all that has been based on them are considered null and void."[3] These initial denouncements by the PLO's founding leader were not the final statements made by the PLO concerning the Balfour Declaration. In the following decade, PLO intellectuals, especially those working at the PLO Research Center, engaged in substantial analysis and critique of the Balfour Declaration in numerous publications produced by the Center.

In the Balfour Declaration, the British government announced in November 1917 that it "view[ed] with favour the establishment in Palestine of a national home for the Jewish people."[4] It is thus unsurprising that PLO activists and intellectuals viewed the British government's declaration with extreme *dis*favor. But why, more than forty years after the Declaration was issued, and more than fifteen years after the establishment of the State of Israel, did the PLO deem the Declaration still relevant for discussion? And what do the arguments used by these PLO intellectuals to challenge the Balfour Declaration tell us about how they understood their predicament in the 1960s and early 1970s?

In this chapter, I first consider the prominent place of the Balfour Declaration in the PLO's founding covenant and propose an explanation for why the critique of the Declaration is linked to the denial of Jewish nationhood. Second, through an examination of several PLO Research Center publications, I offer a précis of the various arguments articulated by PLO intellectuals concerning the Balfour Declaration in the critical years surrounding the 1967 war. In presenting these challenges to the Declaration, I note the dissonance between two particular lines of argument: rejecting the Balfour Declaration because the British had already promised Palestine to the Hashemites (in the Hussein-McMahon correspondence of 1915–16), and rejecting the Declaration because the British had no right to promise Palestine to anyone. Third, I ponder whether those formulating these arguments were conscious of the logical inconsistency between these positions. In light of the complex, evolving, and tension-filled relationship between Palestinian nationalists and the Hashemite regime, and considering other contemporaneous writings about the Hashemites by the PLO Research Center director, I tentatively suggest that these intellectuals may have been aware of this dissonance. Indeed, the dissonance may have been deliberate, subtly unsettling the legitimacy of a regime that, not unlike Israel, was established in part as a consequence of a World War I–era promise. Finally, by exploring in closer detail one argument that distinguished the Balfour Declaration from the Hussein-McMahon correspondence, I consider the place of international law and pan-Arabist thought in the PLO intellectuals' arguments.

Fifty Years after Balfour

The Balfour Declaration reached its first jubilee on November 2, 1967, five months after Israel conquered those parts of British Mandate Palestine that it had not taken in the 1948 war—the West Bank, including the Old City of Jerusalem, and the Gaza Strip—along with the Sinai Peninsula and the Golan Heights. If the Balfour Declaration's drafters wrote of "the establishment *in* Palestine of a national home for the Jewish people"—intentionally not committing *all* of Palestine to this end—the Six-Day War had, it seemed, done away with that subtlety. Thus, the Palestine that the PLO set out to liberate from Israel when the organization was founded in May 1964 had suddenly become much larger—encompassing not merely large parts of Mandatory Palestine but all of it.

Though the June war of 1967 was surely the most dramatic event of that decade in the Palestinian-Israeli conflict, the entire period was transformative for the conflict and the history of the Palestinian national movement. The late 1950s and early 1960s had already witnessed the growth of the pan-Arabist Arab Nationalist Movement and the rise of the Palestinian nationalist organization Fateh. In January 1964, the first Arab summit was convened and established the Unified Arab Command to coordinate military preparations for war with Israel. In May of that year, as we have seen, in Jordanian-annexed East Jerusalem and with the support of Egyptian president Gamal Abdel Nasser and the Arab League, Shukairy spearheaded the founding session of the PLO. The delegates created the Palestine National Council and approved the organization's national covenant. In January 1965, Fateh officially launched its armed struggle, and later that year, the first units of the Palestine Liberation Army were formed.[5] Within months, scores of Palestinian guerrilla attacks were recorded by Israel and more still were claimed by the Palestinian militant groups themselves. Punishing Israeli reprisals followed.[6] All this was before those six fateful days in June 1967.

After the humiliating Arab defeat in 1967 and the resulting territorial losses, the transformations continued. In March 1968, at the Battle of Karameh in Jordan, Fateh was regarded as having proved itself militarily able to withstand an Israeli assault more adeptly than the Arab states had been the previous year. Palestinians' view of the Arab states' abysmal failure, combined with the perceived relative competence of the Palestinians' own guerrilla forces, paved the way for the younger militant activists, led by Fateh's Yasser Arafat, to seize the reins of the PLO. These years were capped in 1970–71 by Jordan's "Black September" assault on PLO forces and the expulsion of the PLO from Jordan to Lebanon.[7] In successfully asserting Hashemite sovereign power in Jordan, the offensive against the PLO, noted Hussein Sirriyeh, "undermined the credibility of Jordan in acting as 'defender' of Palestinian rights."[8] Thus, between Jordan's loss of the West Bank and its violent purge of the PLO, this period also marked a dramatic change in Palestinian-Jordanian relations.[9]

These years were also a period of prolific publication on the part of PLO Research Center scholars. It was in the analysis and polemics of these intellectuals that Palestinian nationalist views of the Balfour Declaration in the years leading up to and following its first jubilee were most extensively articulated.[10]

The Balfour Declaration and the PLO Covenants

The article of the PLO Covenant that concerns the Balfour Declaration (article 18 in the original 1964 version and article 20 in the amended 1968 version) is one of the most frequently quoted and, in certain circles, criticized, passages in the document. The particular sentence about the Balfour Declaration, however, often appears as a mere ellipsis or is otherwise ignored.[11] The article in full reads thus:

> The Balfour Declaration, the mandate for Palestine and everything that has been based upon them, are deemed null and void. Claims of historical or religious ties of Jews with Palestine are incompatible with the facts of history and the true conception of what constitutes statehood. Judaism, being a religion, is not an independent nationality. Nor do Jews constitute a single nation with an identity of its own; they are citizens [*muwatinun*] of the states to which they belong.[12]

Why did Shukairy, in composing the Covenant, choose to link the nullification of the Balfour Declaration with the denial of Jewish historic and religious ties to Palestine and with the assertion that Jews do not constitute a nation?[13] As we will see below, PLO thinkers in this period had many reasons to regard the Balfour Declaration as illegitimate, beyond denying the Jews' nationhood and their historic link to Palestine. In part, this linkage seems to be a response to the Balfour Declaration's use of the term "*national home.*"[14] Calling into question the nationhood of the Jews undermined a fundamental assumption of the Balfour Declaration; if the Jews were not a nation, they had no reasonable claim to a "national home." Hence, Shukairy linked his delegitimization of the Balfour Declaration (and the subsequent League of Nations' British Mandate for Palestine that incorporated the Balfour Declaration within it) directly to the claim that the Jews did not possess the necessary qualities of a nation.

When we consider Shukairy's statements about the Balfour Declaration in the months before the drafting of the PLO Covenant, however, we gain further insight into why he crafted this article as he did. In November 1963, just before declaring the Balfour Declaration to be "the first report on the Palestine refugees," Shukairy delivered the following remarks to the Special Political Committee of the UN General Assembly:

> The central factor for our refugee status is our non-existence as a people. I say our non-existence in the eyes of those who held world power in their hands. We do not exist in their eyes as a people. To them we do not exist as a people and our country is the ownership of none. When the Balfour Declaration was issued on 2 November 1917 by the British Government promising the establishment of a Jewish national home, our country was assumed to be a vacant land, and our people were assumed to be non-existent. This is the hotbed where the refugee problem was born and raised.[15]

For Shukairy, the Balfour Declaration was rooted in the assumption of the nonexistence of the Palestinian Arabs as a people. Shukairy reasoned that had they recognized Palestine's Arabs to be a people, the British would surely have consulted with them before endorsing a plan in which a different people would claim the land as its national home.

Thus, when Shukairy reached the topic of the Declaration as he composed the PLO Covenant, he dealt with the Jews as the British had done with the Palestinians in the Balfour Declaration—namely, he denied *their* peoplehood.[16] In the face of the claim of the Palestinians' nonexistence as a people, Shukairy not only countered that the Palestinians were indeed a people (the Covenant's preamble opens with and repeats the phrase "we, the Palestinian Arab people") but also redirected the alleged claim from the Palestinians to the Jews.[17] If there was a party to this conflict that did not truly exist as a people, it was, in Shukairy's mind, not the Palestinians but rather the Jews.

The line of argument against the Balfour Declaration outlined above was not the only, or even the most prominent, one developed in the PLO's early intellectual life—a life that during the 1960s and 1970s was concentrated in the PLO Research Center in Beirut. The other arguments that the PLO intellectuals articulated reveal much about how they viewed the Declaration, and equally important, how they regarded the major contemporary political challenges facing the Palestinian national movement.

"An Alliance of Convenience and Mutual Need"

The first book in the PLO Research Center's series Palestine Monographs was Fayez Sayegh's own *Zionist Colonialism in Palestine*.[18] In this short book, Sayegh narrated Britain's World War I–era calculations concerning the Middle

East. These evolving calculations explain the succession of British agreements, from the Hussein-McMahon correspondence to the Sykes-Picot agreement to the Balfour Declaration. "At first," wrote Sayegh, "Britain envisaged a new order for the Middle East, in which Arab autonomy would supplant Ottoman imperial rule in South-West Asia." This vision led to the "Anglo-Arab agreements" (the Hussein-McMahon correspondence) and consequently to the Arab Revolt against the Ottomans in 1916. "But," Sayegh explained, "the pressures of other European Powers—then wartime allies of Britain—precluded sole British overlordship." As a result, "secret agreements were . . . reached in the spring of 1916 between Britain, France, and Tsarist Russia, for division of the Ottoman spoils" (the Sykes-Picot agreement). Recounting Britain's evolving political logic, Sayegh continued that the agreements with France and Russia "soon proved irksome to the more empire-minded among Britain's policy-makers" because these agreements permitted France to come "perilously close to the eastern approaches to the Suez Canal." The war had demonstrated that the Sinai Peninsula was not the impenetrable barrier it had been imagined to be. Therefore, the "empire-minded British statesmen" viewed the internationalization of Palestine, as called for by the Sykes-Picot agreement, to constitute a serious threat to British security in Egypt. Moreover, asserted Sayegh, "the staking of French claims to the entirety of Palestine could hardly have served to allay the aroused apprehensions of British imperialists." This is the critical background for understanding why, in early 1917, a new British cabinet sought to extricate themselves from their Sykes-Picot commitments. "It was at that point," wrote Sayegh, "that formerly abortive Zionist attempts to secure British support for a Zionist-dominated Palestine were re-activated, at Britain's instigation."[19]

The crucial motivations behind British support for the Balfour Declaration, then, were intra-European power politics and concerns about French ascendancy in the region. "British Imperialism and Zionist Colonialism," as Sayegh labeled the movements that united in the form of the Balfour Declaration, thus entered into an "alliance of convenience and mutual need." The Zionists needed the British so as to undertake "large-scale colonization in the coveted territory under the auspices and protection of a Great Power." Meanwhile, the British needed the Zionists in order to justify British rule in Palestine as an extended buffer protecting British interests in Egypt and, above all, the Suez Canal.

Sayegh argued that this demanded a deliberately protracted process of Zionist colonialism in Palestine. After all, once Zionists attained statehood,

Britain would no longer have its justification for occupying Palestine. Thus, in looking back on the Mandate period, Sayegh did not see Britain's vacillating support for Zionism as a natural outgrowth of the balancing act inherent in the dual commitments (to Zionism and to "the existing non-Jewish communities in Palestine") the British government had articulated in the Balfour Declaration. Nor was it a response to Palestinian Arab revolts and violence in opposition to the Mandate, on the one hand, or to Zionist lobbying, on the other. Rather, Sayegh contended, "whenever Zionism sought to accelerate the processes of state-building (which would eventually render Britain's continued presence in Palestine neither necessary nor desirable in Zionist eyes), Britain pulled in the opposite direction to slow them down."[20] British steps during the Mandate that Zionists saw as backtracking on the Balfour commitment were thus carefully calculated stalling tactics aimed at indefinitely maintaining British control over Palestine. For the British, Zionism was useful only insofar as its aims remained unfulfilled.

Sayegh's assessment of British motivations for the Balfour Declaration was more sophisticated, and more conspiratorial, than Shukairy's. But Sayegh shared the PLO founder's view of the Declaration as "the first report on the Palestine refugees." In periodizing Palestinian responses to Zionism, Sayegh identified five stages, ranging from the "hospitable welcome" accorded to late nineteenth-century Jewish immigrants whom the Arabs regarded as "pilgrims" and "refugees" (the first stage) through the founding of the PLO (the final stage). The turning point in this narrative, the pivotal third stage, was the Balfour Declaration, which "at last opened Arab eyes to the true significance of what was happening, and brought home the realization that nothing less than dislodgment was in store for the Arabs, if Zionism was to be permitted to have its way."[21] For Sayegh and Shukairy, there was a direct logical and causal link between the Declaration and the Palestinian refugee problem (or, as Sayegh put it, "dislodgment"). The Balfour Declaration was not an irrelevant document but a prime agent in their people's ongoing tragedy.

The Hussein-McMahon Correspondence
as an Argument against the Balfour Declaration

Under the leadership of Anis Sayegh, Fayez's younger brother, the PLO Research Center supplemented Fayez's early attack on the Balfour Declaration with other lines of argumentation. Like Fayez, Anis regarded the Declaration to be the result of "conspiracy and coordination between imperialist interests

and Zionist ambitions," but he went further.[22] One of the additional contentions concerned the Hussein-McMahon correspondence. Recall that Fayez
Sayegh mentioned this correspondence in passing, noting the imperial interests driving British policy during the Great War. Fayez did not, however, stipu-
late a logical connection between the Balfour Declaration's illegitimacy and
that earlier Anglo-Arab agreement. For Anis, the Hussein-McMahon correspondence did not merely expose British interests, as they did in Fayez's rendering; they also constituted a serious British commitment. In a book published
in 1966, he claimed that the aim of the Arab Revolt that erupted following the
Hussein-McMahon correspondence was "the realization of '. . . the independence of the Arab countries'" within frontiers that, Anis contended, included
Palestine. "The British pretended to agree" that this territory included Palestine,
asserted Sayegh, "in terms which they [the British] later tried to distort so as
to justify their failure to keep their promises."[23]

The argument that the Balfour Declaration was illegitimate because Britain
had already promised Palestine to Sharif Hussein had already been articulated
in 1938, by the Lebanon-born George Antonius in *The Arab Awakening*.[24] Publishing the text of the Hussein-McMahon correspondence for the first time in
English, Antonius, who had served in the 1920s in the British Mandatory bureaucracy in Palestine, stated that "no one who has had the text of the McMahon Correspondence before him can legitimately" claim that Palestine was
excluded from the region offered for Arab independence.[25] He wrote:

> The Balfour Declaration . . . was issued from the Foreign Office on the
> 2nd of November 1917, and made public a few days later, that is to say, two
> years after the issue of Sir Henry McMahon's note of the 24th of Octo-
> ber 1915, and eighteen months after the outbreak of the Arab Revolt, when
> the Sharif Husain, relying on England's pledges of Arab independence,
> which he had every reason to believe applied to Palestine, had thrown in
> his lot openly with the Allies.[26]

For Antonius, the Balfour Declaration was a betrayal of both a previous promise and of a bargain that had already been acted upon by one side. Because the
Arabs, under Sharif Hussein, had fulfilled their side of the agreement by attacking the Ottomans, the British had no right to unilaterally change the terms
of the arrangement.

Under Anis Sayegh, this argument was brought into PLO Research Center
discourse—and there it remained. In the Center's 1969 *Dalil al-Qadiyya al-
Filastiniyya* (*Handbook to the Palestine Question*), Ibrahim al-Abid, asked: "Can

the Balfour Declaration be considered a legal document [*wathiqa qanuniyya*] granting the Zionists a right [*haqq*] to Palestine?" In compiling answers to the question, al-Abid noted that "the Balfour Declaration is in conflict with the obligations arising from the Hussein-McMahon negotiations, at the close of which Great Britain undertook officially to recognize the independence of the Arab states."[27]

This claim—that the British had already promised Palestine to Hussein— was the seventh of nine arguments al-Abid adduced to prove that the Balfour Declaration is illegitimate. Other arguments, in al-Abid's numbering of them, included (1) that the British had no claim to Palestine on November 2, 1917, given that they only began to conquer Palestine two weeks later and were first granted a League of Nations mandate over Palestine in 1922;[28] (3) that "the law of war" does not permit conquering powers to "dispose of the occupied territory" and, in fact, the Ottomans retained sovereignty in Palestine; (4) that the Balfour Declaration is "prejudicial to the acquired rights of the Palestine population" who, by the covenant of the League of Nations, were assured national liberation; (5) that the Declaration is also inconsistent with article 20 of the League's covenant, which claims that "all obligations or understandings *inter se* which are inconsistent with the terms thereof" are abrogated; (6) the view of Jules Basdevant, a French professor of law and former president of the International Court of Justice, that "international law does not recognize the British State as having competence other than over its territories and over its own subjects and nationals"; and (8) that the Balfour Declaration contravenes "Article 5 [of the League of Nations Mandate for Palestine], which makes it incumbent on the Mandatory State to ensure its protection against the cession or lease of all or part of its territory, and against the establishment therein of any foreign power."[29] These challenges to the validity of the Balfour Declaration were all variations of the same argument—namely, that the British had no legitimate claim to Palestine and therefore no right to offer it to any party.

Yet these same challenges would seem to render the Hussein-McMahon correspondence just as invalid as they do the Balfour Declaration.[30] The PLO Research Center *Handbook*'s claims, as numbered above, could be redirected— and no less compellingly—against Hussein-McMahon thus: (1) In 1915 the British were *years*, not weeks, away from conquering Palestine. (3) The "law of war" would presumably "not have allowed Britain to dispose of the occupied territory" regardless of whether the recipients were Zionists from Europe or Hashemites from the Hijaz. (4) Hussein-McMahon could well be regarded as "prejudicial to the acquired rights of the Palestine population," who ought to have been "liberated and given [a] national government." (5) If article 20 of the League of Nations covenant could abrogate the Balfour Declaration, it could also have abrogated the Hussein-McMahon correspondence. (6) Basdevant's view of the limits of British competence would also undermine the legitimacy of Hussein-McMahon. (8) Article 5 of the Mandate forbids the British from ceding part or all of Palestine to "*any* foreign power," which would seem, again, to describe the Hashemites no less than the Zionists.

Hussein-McMahon and the Question of Hashemite Legitimacy

This final consideration leads us to the heart of the comparison between the Balfour Declaration and the Hussein-McMahon correspondence: were the Hashemites a "foreign power" in Palestine? This question, ever sensitive for the Hashemites and the Palestinians, was especially delicate for the PLO to confront during the Balfour Declaration jubilee. While in the context of de-bates over Zionism the Hussein-McMahon correspondence was used as an argument against the Balfour Declaration, the Anglo-Hashemite agreement had contemporary political implications not only for Israel but also for the monarchy to its east. After all, Sharif Hussein's son was Abdullah, the first emir and then king of Transjordan and the ruler who annexed Palestine's West Bank in 1950 after his forces seized the territory in the 1948 war. The Hussein-McMahon correspondence was a piece of the argument for the legitimacy of Hashemite rule in Jordan and the West Bank (and in Iraq until the end of the monarchy in 1958).[31] The PLO Research Center was engaging in these polem-ics during the reign of Sharif Hussein's great-grandson, another Hussein, who ruled Jordan from 1952 until his death in 1999. To question the legitimacy of the Hussein-McMahon correspondence was to question the legitimacy of the Jordanian king's rule—on both sides of the Jordan River.

From the start, the relationship between the Jordanian kingdom and the PLO was, at best, ambivalent.[32] Until 1967, however, the PLO, beholden finan-cially, politically, and militarily to the Arab League, felt compelled to refrain from challenging Jordanian rule of the West Bank. In its original Covenant (approved, as we have seen, in Jordanian-annexed Jerusalem, surrounded by Jordanian intelligence agents), the PLO declared that "This Organization does not exercise any territorial sovereignty [*siyada iqlimiyya*] over the West Bank in the Hashemite Kingdom of Jordan."[33] Though Jordan continued to claim the West Bank until 1988, after the 1967 war, the PLO was less constrained on this matter; the revised Covenant of 1968 did not include the clause renouncing Palestinian sovereignty over the West Bank. "Black September" in 1970–71, when Jordanian forces killed thousands of PLO forces and expelled many more from the country, represented the nadir in PLO-Jordanian relations and laid bare the animus between the Hashemites and the PLO.

Given this broader context, we might wonder if the PLO Research Center authors of the texts reviewed above, some written before and others after the 1967 war, were aware that their arguments against the Balfour Declaration served to undermine the legitimacy of the Hussein-McMahon correspondence. We now turn to this question.

"Because He Was Silent"

It is impossible to know with certainty whether the PLO Research Center scholars intentionally articulated these arguments in order to challenge the legitimacy of Hussein-McMahon and of the Hashemites. Nonetheless, we might be able to speculate about the matter, using a historical-contextual analysis of the arguments. One piece of evidence can be found in a book published by Anis Sayegh in 1966, the year he assumed the Center's directorship. This work, *al-Hashimiyyun wa-Qadiyyat Filastin* (The Hashemites and the Palestine Question), was a screed against the Hashemites.[34] In this book, issued by a publisher unaffiliated with the PLO, Sayegh excoriated the departed Hashemite rulers—Sharif Hussein, his sons Abdullah and Faisal, and his grandson Abd al-Ilah—even as he claimed no implications of the analysis for the still-living Hashemites of Transjordan.[35] According to Sayegh, Sharif Hussein kept the Arab nationalists who joined his anti-Ottoman revolt in the dark about his correspondence with McMahon. Indeed, wrote Sayegh, Hussein even "hid the truth of it from his sons as well—or so said his sons."[36] When the nationalists learned about the correspondence, they were outraged. Hussein "treated important, fateful issues, such as the life, dignity, and future of an entire people," lamented Sayegh, "as though they were a local matter" affecting only "a few people." Moreover, Hussein "arrogated the matters to himself, insisted on a monopoly on everything, and refused to be enlightened by guidance from those more acquainted than he with international politics." Sayegh contended that Hussein "looked at the matter as the sheikh of a tribe trying to solve the problems of two families of his followers" using naïve methods of "reconciliation without angering either one." Lured by the promise of a kingdom, a caliphate, money, and arms, Hussein "had complete confidence in the

English," Sayegh charged, "representing the simplicity of the desert that ignores the evils, lies and ambitions of the city and that treats the most complicated of issues with the most naïve of means."[37]

And Sayegh's critique of Hussein went further. After the war, when it became clear that the British did not intend to fulfill the commitments that Arab nationalists believed the British had made to him, Hussein refused to denounce their duplicity. "Hussein was responsible," wrote Sayegh, "because he was silent."[38] In Sayegh's view, the only conclusion one could reasonably draw from Hussein's willingness to renounce significant Arab territories—parts of Syria and Iraq—was that he prioritized personal power over Arab independence. For Hussein, it was more important "to protect his interests from the Arab emirs" in the Arabian Peninsula than "to keep Syria and Iraq from foreign ambitions."[39] Following Elie Kedourie, Sayegh further contended that Hussein knew of the Sykes-Picot negotiations and did not object to them, so as to maintain good relations with the European powers.[40]

"Erasing the Name of Palestine from the Political Map of the Arab Homeland"

If, for Anis Sayegh, Sharif Hussein was a self-serving, cowardly buffoon, his son Abdullah was even worse. Discussing Emir and then King Abdullah's relations with the Zionists, Sayegh wrote that "the story of Abdullah and the Zionists is a tragedy . . . of the nation's disappointed hope in a leader" who "abandoned the nation and sided with its enemy."[41] Abdullah demonstrated his desire to place his own interests over those of the Palestinians "from the very first moment," notwithstanding the initial embrace he received from all levels of society.[42] Emblematic of Abdullah's shameful priorities, according to Sayegh, was his acceptance of the 1937 Peel Commission's proposal to partition Palestine into a Jewish state and an Arab state linked to Transjordan. Abdullah "blessed the plan" in private meetings, "but he didn't dare issue an official announcement of this," as "he feared the response." Abdullah thus became "the only Arab ruler who backed the partition plan," and this led many to regard demonstrations of support for his monarchy as "national treason."[43]

For Sayegh, the British abandonment of the Peel partition plan turned Abdullah's treachery into a mere mark of shame. Far worse was the king's conduct during the 1948 war, with its enduring political consequences. Sayegh listed thirteen separate charges against Abdullah in this regard. For instance, he criticized Abdullah's disregard for the demand of the Arabs of Transjordan,

Palestine, and elsewhere that "the Arabness of Palestine" be preserved. Sayegh further denounced Abdullah for attempting to foster Jewish immigration to Transjordan in order to enrich himself. Moreover, Abdullah collaborated with those "who deviated from the national covenant" and fomented Arab disunity, "especially as the crisis of Palestine was coming to a head and Arabs needed moral unity more than ever before." The king's aspiration to gain control of Greater Syria despite both the population's opposition and the way this plan would "complicate the demand for the liberation of Palestine" exemplified, for Sayegh, his power-hungry approach. Sayegh censured Abdullah for his suppression of the Arab national movement in Transjordan—preventing the movement from assisting the Palestinians—and for the king's loyalty to Britain "at a time when Britain was the greatest supporter of Zionism and the most dangerous enemy to the Arabs generally and to the Arabs of Palestine in particular." Sayegh even alleged that Abdullah tried to recast the conflict over Palestine as a "sectarian war" against Russian socialism rather than a struggle against "an enemy of Arab nationalism," thereby weakening the case for Palestinian liberation.[44] The catalogue of perfidies goes on.

Though Sayegh did not hold Abdullah solely responsible for the 1948 Palestinian Nakba, his assessment of the king was damning: "We do not find one Arab official or non-official who was as consequential as Abdullah in erasing the name of Palestine from the political map of the Arab homeland."[45] While "the myth is that Abdullah agreed to the loss of half of Palestine because he knew that 'Israel' would have to be established in that half," Sayegh contended, "the truth is that 'Israel' was established because Abdullah agreed to the loss of half of Palestine."[46] Though there may have been more assignable blame in Sayegh's mind, the lion's share was attributed to Abdullah.[47]

When he took over the PLO Research Center, Anis Sayegh naturally brought with him his views about the Hashemites. In the PLO's think tank, though, such blatant criticism of Arab rulers—the direct forebears of a contemporary Arab monarch who was himself the ambivalent host to PLO activities and activists—did not pass muster. A challenge to Hashemite legitimacy would require considerable subtlety. The Center may have found that opportunity in the pages of the *Dalil*, the above-mentioned 1969 *Handbook*.

Some of the arguments cited in the *Dalil* were originally collected in a book titled *The Palestine Question*, which emerged from a "Seminar of Arab Jurists on Palestine" in Algiers that met in late July 1967.[48] After June 1967, the implications of delegitimizing the Hussein-McMahon correspondence had clearly changed. The UN Security Council's state-centric Resolution 242 of November 22, 1967, seemed to call for Israel to restore control of the West Bank to Jordan. The Hashemite Kingdom, however, had already proved itself incapable of liberating those parts of Mandatory Palestine that Israel took in 1949 (even if it had been interested), and could not even maintain control over the West Bank. Considering the circumstances, perhaps this was precisely the time to highlight the foreignness of the Hashemites and to press for native Palestinian rule. Indeed, the fallout from the Six-Day War included Palestinian efforts to seize the reins of the PLO from the Arab League and the Arab states. Thus, when the PLO Research Center issued its *Dalil*, it is certainly possible that it intentionally referenced the Hussein-McMahon correspondence in the context of arguments against the Balfour Declaration in order to challenge Hashemite legitimacy. The scholars at the PLO Research Center would not have missed the observation that the very charges leveled against the Balfour Declaration could be leveled against Hussein-McMahon.

International Law, Pan-Arabism, and the Question of Palestine's "Lawful Owners"

Among the many arguments offered in the *Dalil* against the validity of the Balfour Declaration, all but one would seem to apply to the Hussein-McMahon correspondence. The second argument, which we skipped in the previous enumeration of al-Abid's challenges to the Balfour Declaration above, reads as follows:

> The Balfour Declaration is not the result of an agreement between States. It is no more than a letter addressed by Lord Balfour to a private person with no title to enter into an official contractual obligation, since its recipient, Lord Rothschild, a Zionist British subject, did not even represent the Jewish Community, which, in any case, was not a subject of international law [*al-qanun al-dawli*].[49]

In contrast to Lionel Walter Rothschild, the Anglo-Jewish financier and former parliamentarian to whom the Balfour Declaration was addressed, Sharif Hussein was essentially a head of state, and his correspondence with McMahon, Britain's high commissioner in Egypt, might thus be viewed as "an agreement between states."

The *Dalil*'s claim that the Jewish community was not "a subject of international law" was part of the PLO Research Center's broader interest in questions of international law in these early years. Indeed, in 1970, the Center published a book by Faris Yahia titled *The Palestine Question and International Law*. Yahia, born Godfrey Glubb in 1939 in Jerusalem, was the son of Sir John Bagot Glubb, the evangelical British commander of the Transjordanian Arab Legion who came to be known as Glubb Pasha.[50] A convert to Islam, Yahia was educated in England and studied for a time at the School of Oriental and Asian Studies. He then returned to the Arab world, living in Tunisia before moving to Amman, Jordan, in 1967. There, he taught at a school for Palestinian refugees and worked in journalism for the Hashemite Broadcasting Service and CBS News. In 1970, he moved to Beirut, where he served as a journalist and befriended Ghassan Kanafani, an author and activist for the Popular Front for the Liberation of Palestine (PFLP).[51]

In his discussion of the Balfour Declaration, Yahia remarked that many mistakenly assume that "the Balfour Declaration was given in a moment of carelessness by the British Government without an awareness of its full implications, in a desperate effort to win Jewish support in the First World War." However, Yahia clarified, "the British Government was fully aware of the broad long-term results likely from such an act," which was "not aimed at short-term benefits for British policy." In fact, he argued, immediate wartime British interests would have militated against supporting Zionism, given that "Zionism at that time was supported only by a small minority of Jews who were not in a position to influence the war decisively" and that declaring support for Zionism "risked losing Britain her ally in the Middle East, the Arabs fighting Ottoman Turkey." Instead, Yahia highlighted Palestine's strategic geographic importance for imperial powers, noting that "empire builders who sought world domination, whether Alexander the Great or Napoleon, have always made a point of trying to control Palestine and the surrounding area." Yahia thus claimed that it was the "broad strategic implications of a Zionist state" that lay behind the Balfour Declaration: "it would secure imperial domination of the Middle East, slice the Arab World in half and drive a wedge between Asia and Africa, a geographical obstacle to the unity of liberation forces in those two continents."[52] The desire to undermine anticolonial liberation movements was the ultimate goal of the Balfour Declaration, not the desire to gain the Jews' support.

Yahia then asserted that the Declaration was "completely meaningless in international law," for three reasons related to the terminology of the text. First, he wrote, "the term 'National Home' is unknown in international legal practice." International law deals with states, Yahia argued, "not with fantasy concepts like national homes that have never been properly defined." Second, Yahia asserted that the term "Jewish people" was "incorrect," because "a people," by definition, reside in "an internationally-recognized state area like Great Britain, China, France or Iran" and "share a heritage that is ethnic, geographical, linguistic, cultural or historical." The Jews do not qualify. "The only tie" that unites, say, "a Yemeni Jew with an Abyssinian or German of Jewish faith," is "religious," and "international law does not recognize" shared religion "as a basis for a nation-state's existence."[53] Yahia's third argument against the international legal significance of the Balfour Declaration began with a criticism of the Declaration's reference to the Arab population of Palestine. "To describe some 92 per cent of Palestine's inhabitants as 'existing non-Jewish communities,'" as the Balfour Declaration did, he said, "shows a disregard for the majority, whose rights anyway were bound to be affected adversely by a total transformation of their country to their disadvantage."

But the heart of the argument focused on "the circumstances in which the Balfour Declaration was issued," circumstances that, according to Yahia, "rendered it a totally illegal document." Yahia then made a claim we have already encountered: "In 1917, the British Government had no jurisdiction over Palestine, which was an Arab-inhabited territory governed by Turkey. The British Government, through a letter from their Foreign Secretary, were very generously disposing someone else's property without consulting the lawful owners." Moreover, even if the British had already conquered Palestine when they issued the Balfour Declaration, it "would still have been invalid, as it violated a previous solemn undertaking to the Arab people, the lawful owners of Palestine." Here, Yahia was referring to the Hussein-McMahon correspondence. He mentioned the historian George Antonius, who insisted that "there was no mention in this agreement that Palestine was to be excluded from the area of the Arab State."[54] Yahia wrote:

> It is axiomatic in international law that no state may undertake any action which is a violation of a previous solemn commitment. This is the whole basis of treaty international law. The prior commitment remains binding until terminated by the parties to it, and any contrary undertaking is automatically null and void. Thus both the Sykes-Picot Agreement and the Balfour Declaration were illegal and invalid, in that they were British violations of prior pledges in the Husain-Macmahon [sic] correspondence.[55]

Although his father, Glubb Pasha, had been dismissed from Jordan's Arab Legion in 1958 by Sharif Hussein's great-grandson King Hussein, Yahia maintained the value of the Hussein-McMahon correspondence. It was this agree-ment that brought Sharif Hussein's son Abdullah to Transjordan, and it was under Abdullah's rule that Yahia's father led the Arab Legion. The speculation raised earlier—that some PLO intellectuals may have paid lip service to the Hussein-McMahon correspondence in the context of other arguments against the Balfour Declaration precisely to challenge Hashemite legitimacy—does not seem to apply to Yahia. For Yahia, the Anglo-Hashemite agreement (and its chronological precedence vis-à-vis the Balfour Declaration) was the apex of the international legal case against the Declaration.

Why might some PLO researchers have upheld the legal validity and en-during relevance of the Hussein-McMahon correspondence while others simply used it as a rhetorical weapon against Zionism? Certainly, differing perspectives on the descendants of Sharif Hussein were at play. The Glubb family's associations with the Hashemites in Transjordan were thus a part of the picture, as was Anis Sayegh's perspective on the perfidy of those same Hashemite heirs.

More fundamentally, however, the debate may reflect the internal tension within the early Palestine liberation movement between pan-Arabist and ex-clusivist Palestinian nationalist tendencies. The core question was whether Palestine rightfully belonged to Arabs broadly or to Palestinians only. If the latter, it could be argued that there was little difference between offering the land to Jews from Europe or to Arabs from the Hijaz. If, however, Pales-tine belonged to the Arabs (and for Yahia, the lawful owners were "the Arab people"—not the Palestinians who populated the land or the Ottomans who ruled it), then the British agreement that the territory be included in an an-ticipated Arab kingdom was simply the application of the right of self-determination to another parcel of the Arab homeland. If one assumes that Palestine belonged to the Arabs as a whole and that the Hashemites were legitimate representatives of the Arabs, it is easy to see why the Hussein-McMahon correspondence would be privileged over the Balfour Declaration. It was patently superior to the Declaration in international legitimacy. If the Balfour Declaration involved "disposing someone else's property without consulting the lawful owners," under the theory of pan-Arabism, the Hussein-McMahon correspondence disposed that property *to* its lawful owners. In this sense, the way in which PLO intellectuals related to the Balfour Declara-tion and the Hussein-McMahon correspondence opened a critical window into the pivotal debate over pan-Arabism in the period between the 1967 and 1973 wars.[56]

"A Pluralistic, Humanistic, Secular, and Democratic State"

In 1970, Fayez Sayegh published *Palestine, Israel, and Peace,* in which he argued that "in proclaiming the creation of Israel, the Zionist community invoked the authority of three international instruments: the British (Balfour) Declaration of 1917, the League of Nations Mandate of 1922, and the General Assembly partition recommendation of 1947." Taking a different tack than Faris Yahia, Sayegh did not question the "intrinsic juridical worth" of these documents but rather argued that even if one accepts their legal value, "none of these documents granted Zionism a license to inflict upon the Palestinian Arabs what it has actually inflicted." Rather, Sayegh continued, "each contained built-in safeguards and guarantees of Arab rights—which were as much an integral part of the instrument concerned as was the limited and conditional support of Zionist political goals." For Sayegh, the Balfour Declaration's announcement of British support for a "national home for the Jewish people" was "predicated upon the condition stipulated in the clause that immediately followed: 'it being clearly understood that nothing shall be done which may prejudice the civil and religious rights of existing non-Jewish communities in Palestine.'" To understand what this "safeguard clause" meant, Sayegh cited what he called the "authoritative" explanation of the 1922 White Paper, which insisted that the British, in enacting the Declaration, did not intend "the disappearance or the subordination of the Arabic population, language or culture in Palestine." In Sayegh's view, disappearance and subordination were precisely what transpired, which demonstrated that the Zionists violated the Balfour Declaration.[57] Ultimately, Sayegh called in this piece for "a *pluralistic, humanistic, secular* and *democratic* state, of which all [Jews, Christians, and Muslims] will be equal citizens and all devoted builders."[58]

During the first half-decade of the PLO Research Center's activity in Beirut, the Palestinian condition changed dramatically. Among other developments, this period witnessed Israel's conquest of the entirety of Mandatory Palestine and Jordan's expulsion of the PLO. After 1967, the Balfour Declaration—as opposed to the later, more restrictive British White Papers or commission proposals, or UN General Assembly Resolution 181 that called for partition—had renewed relevance, as the Declaration made reference to only *one* "national home" in Palestine, that of the Jews. But the arguments assembled here also point to the centrality in PLO intellectual circles (and in PLO perceptions of what might convince others) of the discourses about anti-imperialism, anticolonialism, and international law. The PLO Research Center's arguments also hint at the internal struggle over the relationship between Palestinian liberation and the Arab states, especially the Hashemite Kingdom of Jordan. By studying the place of the Balfour Declaration in PLO Research Center writings of this period, we learn much about the organization and how it imagined it might convince fellow Palestinians, other Arabs, and the world beyond of the justice of the Palestinian national cause. This cause, as seen in Fayez Sayegh's call for "a *pluralistic, humanistic, secular* and *democratic* state, of which all will be equal citizens and all devoted builders," was itself developing.

5

The Zionist Idea

JUDAISM, CHRISTIANITY, AND THE
ARABIC TRANSLATION OF ZIONISM

THIS CHAPTER EXAMINES the PLO Research Center's turn to the Zionist canon through its Arabic translation of the writings of the founders of the Zionist movement, from Rabbi Yehuda Alkalai to Theodor Herzl to David Ben-Gurion.[1] I consider here the ways in which the Christian identity and education of the leadership and important members of the staff of the PLO Research Center may help us understand the PLO's particular focus on what they believed to be the fundamentally religious nature of Zionism. I show how these writers engaged with biblical arguments that were used to promote Zionism and then investigate how they dealt with a phenomenon they found especially objectionable: Christian Zionism.

As discussed in the preface to this work, in 1970, the Research Center issued a book called *al-Fikra al-Sahyuniyya: al-Nusus al-Asasiyya* (The Zionist Idea: The Basic Texts).[2] This was an Arabic version of *The Zionist Idea*, the classic English-language sourcebook of Zionist texts originally published in 1959 by the American rabbi and historian Arthur Hertzberg (1921–2006).[3] As noted, Hertzberg's name does not appear in the book.[4] Rather, the title page lists six other individuals involved in the project—all PLO researchers.

Comparing the Arabic and English editions allows us to assess how the PLO Research Center writers interpreted Zionism in the wake of the 1967 war and how they presented the Zionist movement's theoretical writings to their Arabic-reading audience. What we will find is that the PLO editorial team tended to present Zionism, especially at its roots, as a Jewish *religious* movement (in contrast to Hertzberg's conception of the movement). The researchers' emphasis on Zionism's religious aspects was no doubt driven by their close reading of the movement's primary sources. Additionally, however, I propose that the Christian upbringing and education of the PLO Research Center's leadership and of others involved in the translation project also informed the researchers' conception of Zionism. More specifically, I argue that the researchers' concern about the status of Christians as a religious minority among Palestinians (and other Arabs) and certain traditional, deeply rooted Christian ideas about the nature of Judaism together help to explain the particular view of Zionism that the Research Center developed in its foundational years. From this investigation, we learn not only about the PLO's view of Zionism but also about its view of Palestinian nationalism, as understanding how people conceive of others, not least their enemies, sheds important light on how they conceive of themselves.

This chapter engages with two distinct but related discussions concerning Palestinian nationalism. The first involves the nature of the PLO and its relationship to religion. Especially since the advent and rise to prominence of explicitly religiously inflected forms of Palestinian nationalism (e.g., Hamas, Islamic Jihad), the "secularity" or "secularism" of the PLO has been assumed.[5] Though scholars tend to use these terms reflexively, underlying them are two implications: that the PLO's leaders and members have been motivated by a will for national liberation disconnected from religious impulses, and that their vision of the fulfillment of national liberation is a state defined by nationality (understood ethnically, historically, or culturally) rather than religion. It is frequently pointed out that the words "Islam" and "Muslim" do not appear in the 1964 and 1968 PLO national covenants,[6] and that the PLO came to be associated, at least in the West, with the call for a "secular, democratic state" in Palestine (as seen in Fayez Sayegh's plea above). Recently, some scholars have complicated this view, arguing that, in their Arabic writings, the PLO and Fateh (the PLO's dominant constituent party since 1969) never actually described the democratic state they sought as ʿilmaniyya (the Arabic word that is generally used to mean "secular" or "secularist"). Moreover, some stress the Islamic connotations of the reverse acronym, Fateh (Harakat al-Tahrir al-Watani al-Filastini, or Palestinian National Liberation Movement), which include the sense of conquering for the sake of Islam.[7] Scholars have also noted the earlier involvement of Fateh's founders and leaders (e.g., Yasser Arafat, Khalil al-Wazir, Walid Ahmad Nimr al-Nasir, Hani al-Hasan, Rafiq al-Natsha) in the Muslim Brotherhood, as discussed earlier, and to the later use of Islamic imagery and iconography in Fateh and PLO publications and official speeches.[8]

Yet these valuable correctives all assume that, in the context of the PLO, the relevant religion is Islam. By exploring the work of an arm of the PLO in which Christians predominated, and by considering the impact of these intellectuals' Christian religious background and communal interests, this chapter suggests that there was a parallel Christian conception of the Palestinian condition and of Jewish nationalism. Like its Islamic counterpart, this Christian conception must be reckoned with for a full understanding of the history of Palestinian nationalism and, especially, of prevalent Palestinian theories about Zionism.

This chapter also engages with scholarship concerning Palestinian Christians.[9] Scholars commonly note that the PLO leadership insisted that Christians were legitimate members of the Palestinian nation.[10] Linking the argument about the PLO's secular nature to discussion of the place of Palestinian Christians within the nation, John M. Owen IV, for instance, argued that "the PLO, itself dominated by the al-Fatah movement, is explicitly secularist, owing in part to its determination to include Christian Arabs."[11] Christian Arabs were not, however, just "included" in the PLO; some played prominent, active roles, especially in the organization's intellectual and ideological development. By exploring the contribution of Christians to the PLO Research Center in the 1960s and 1970s, this chapter challenges the assumption that the multiplicity of religions within a single national movement necessarily removes theological concerns or religious-communal interests from the national agenda.

Translating the Zionist Canon

In his preface to *al-Fikra al-Sahyuniyya*, Anis Sayegh, who supervised the translation project, explained that one of the Center's aims was to increase Arabs' "knowledge of the enemy, its thoughts, and its work." Two years earlier, the Center had published a book of essays in Arabic translation by contemporary Israeli figures—including Zwi Werblowski, Shmuel Ettinger, Yehoshafat Harkabi, Shimon Peres, Simha Flapan, Moshe Sneh, and Nissim Rejwan. By 1970, Sayegh had published a translation of the classic Zionist texts, which his researchers found in Hertzberg's volume (without acknowledging as much), because "the Zionists regularly look toward them as they best express their basic idea."[12] Knowing the enemy required knowing the enemy's canon. And in order to know the canon, they had to translate it.

Notably, *al-Fikra al-Sahyuniyya* is only in a certain sense a translation of Hertzberg's *The Zionist Idea*. The original English version opens with an expansive introductory essay by Hertzberg about the intellectual history of Zionism, followed by thirty-seven chapters, each devoted to a different prominent Zionist from the 1840s through the 1940s. Each chapter begins with a brief biography of a Zionist figure, followed by the essays, speeches, or articles regarded by Hertzberg as representative or otherwise important.[13] *Al-Fikra al-Sahyuniyya* also has thirty-seven chapters devoted to the same thirty-seven Zionist thinkers. The primary source excerpts in *al-Fikra al-Sahyuniyya* precisely match those in Hertzberg's original and their translation is generally (though not always, as discussed below) faithful to the original—or, more precisely, faithful to Hertzberg's English versions, most of which were themselves translated from other languages.[14] *Al-Fikra al-Sahyuniyya* excludes Hertzberg's introductory essay[15] and, though its biographical sketches are generally based on Hertzberg's, some diverge from his substantially.

Aside from Anis Sayegh, the *al-Fikra al-Sahyuniyya* team included Lutfi al-Abed and Musa ʿAnaz, who translated the primary sources; Assʿad Razzouk, who authored the introductory biographies; and Hilda Shaʿban Sayegh and Ibrahim al-Abid, who proofread the text. Lutfi al-Abed was a Palestinian from the village of Safuriyya near Nazareth who, in 1948, at the age of eight, fled with his family to Lebanon.[16] His cotranslator, Musa ʿAnaz, wrote his master's thesis at AUB about the Israeli kibbutz, which he published as a book in 1970 under the title *al-Kibutz min al-Dakhil: Dirasa Siyasiyya wa-Idariyya* (The Kibbutz from the Inside: A Political and Administrative Study) in the PLO Research Center's Palestine Studies series. Hilda Shaʿban Sayegh was a Jordanian-born scholar who, several years earlier, had translated selections from Theodor Herzl's diaries into Arabic. She was married to Anis Sayegh.[17] Her coproofreader, Ibrahim al-Abid, also prepared the Research Center's *Handbook to the Palestine Question*, which we encountered above.[18] More relevant to the current discussion is the contribution of Assʿad Razzouk, author of the biographical introduction to each chapter. Razzouk, a Christian from Marjayoun in Lebanon (a mere five miles from the Israeli city of Metulla), was a seemingly indefatigable member of the Center, having written five books of his own between 1967 and 1970.[19] He had earned a PhD in philosophy in Tübingen, Germany, in 1963. These contemporaneous writings will prove useful as we try to understand the conception of Zionism in *al-Fikra al-Sahyuniyya*.

Emphasizing the Religious Motivations of Zionism

A comparison of the biographical introductions presented by Hertzberg and Razzouk reveals that the latter conceived of the factors that drove the rise of Zionism differently from Hertzberg in significant ways. To illustrate their distinct approaches, let us begin with the first source in the anthology, the writing of Yehuda Alkalai (1798–1878), a Sephardic rabbi from Sarajevo, whom Hertzberg named one of the "precursors" of Zionism. Razzouk's introduction to Alkalai closely follows that of Hertzberg. Like Hertzberg, Razzouk began with Alkalai's childhood as the son of a rabbi, noted the kabbalistic influences on Alkalai's thought, and explained the two-staged messianic redemption that Alkalai envisioned (the Josephite Messiah followed by the Davidic Messiah). But here the accounts begin to diverge. For example, Hertzberg argued that "the real turning point in Alkalai's life was the year 1840," when the Damascus affair saw a modern Middle Eastern Jewish community stand accused of ritually murdering a Capuchin friar and his Muslim servant. The resulting torture of a group of Damascene Jews "convinced Alkalai . . . that for security and freedom the Jewish people must look to a life of its own, within its ancestral home. After 1840, a succession of books and pamphlets poured from Alkalai's pen in explanation of his program of self-redemption."[20] In his rendering, Razzouk makes no reference to the Damascus affair. He may have omitted the event because it reflected unfavorably on Christians (and Muslims) in Damascus, but it is also possible that his perception of Zionism as a religious phenomenon led him to discount the impact of antisemitism and other external factors.

We find a similar omission in Razzouk's presentation of another of Zionism's "precursors," Rabbi Zvi Hirsch Kalischer (1795–1874). Hertzberg opened his biographical sketch by highlighting the political context in which Kalischer was raised. Like Alkalai, Hertzberg wrote, Kalischer "was born in a buffer area—not in the Balkans but in Posen," a province that was "the western part of Poland, which Prussia had acquired in the second partition of that country in 1793." Hertzberg then elaborated:

> Nationalism was the major force of European history during the whole of Kalischer's adult life, but he was particularly aware of it because of his geographic position. In 1830–1831 and again in 1863 unsuccessful revolts occurred across the border in the Russian part of Poland in attempts to re-establish the independence of the Poles. [The] Jewish population in this region was numerically significant, and in some places, including Warsaw during the

two Polish revolutions, it was of political, and even military, importance whether the Jews would regard themselves as Poles, Russians, or as a separate nationality.

A few paragraphs later, Hertzberg noted that "after completing his education in the conventional modes of the ghetto," Kalischer "settled in Thorn, where he served as the rabbi of the community for forty years."[21] In *al-Fikra al-Sahyuniyya*, this information is collapsed into three sentences: "He was born in Posen. At that time, the western region of Poland was under Prussian rule since 1793. He completed his traditional studies in the schools of the Jewish population and then settled in the town of Thorn, where he remained rabbi for forty years." There is no reference to European nationalisms, the acute problems of border regions, the Polish rebellions against Russia, or the identity challenges these nationalisms posed to Jews in particular. As he does with Alkalai, Razzouk portrays Kalischer as a thinker motivated almost exclusively by Jewish religious factors.[22]

If Razzouk had limited his emphasis on religious concerns to Alkalai and Kalischer, we might suspect he imagined that, as rabbis, they must have been mainly animated by religion—notwithstanding Hertzberg's contextualizing contentions. Yet Theodor Herzl (1860–1904), the paradigmatic "secular" political Zionist and founder of the Zionist Organization, received similar treatment under Razzouk's pen. While Razzouk acknowledged that in the Austro-Hungarian Empire, "German culture was dominant" and Herzl's "Hebrew culture was remarkably weak," he also asserted that "Jewish traditions influenced him [Herzl] on a subconscious level." Citing other scholars, Razzouk claimed that until his eighteenth birthday, Herzl's mind was heavily "influenced by the [biblical] book of Exodus and the idea of the awaited messiah." In contrast, Hertzberg wrote that Herzl's pre-Zionist writings "contained scarcely a dozen lines of passing references to Jews" and that his "early Jewish education had indeed been skimpy," despite Herzl's grandfather's friendship with Alkalai. It is worth mentioning that in his introductory essay, Hertzberg wrote provocatively that "messianism is the essence of his [Herzl's] stance, because he claimed the *historical inevitability* of a Jewish state in a world of peaceful nations."[23] But Herzl was not specifically motivated by the idea of a human messiah.[24] Razzouk perceived him as a believer in "extreme religious mysticism."[25]

And Razzouk did not stop at Herzl. Whereas Hertzberg's David Ben-Gurion "was born as David Green in Plonsk, Poland, in 1886," Razzouk's Ben-Gurion "was born in Plonsk, Poland, on 16 October 1886, and studied there in a religious school [*madrasa diniyya*]." Hertzberg did not see Ben-Gurion's Jewish religious education as critical for an understanding of this towering Zionist politician and ideologue who served as Israel's first prime minister. For Razzouk, however, Ben-Gurion's religious background was formative, and his Zionism could only be understood in its context.

In emphasizing the religious context and motivations of figures such as Herzl and Ben-Gurion, Razzouk seems to have been making a conscious selection. Among the many facts available to Razzouk about the lives of Zionism's two most influential leaders, Razzouk chose to stress certain religious elements. At times, however, he did acknowledge non-Jewish influences on Zionism. Following Hertzberg, Razzouk's biographical note on Eliezer Ben-Yehuda, for instance, mentions this Hebraist's embrace of "revolutionary ideas that were dominant among the Russian intellectuals and among the Nihilists in particular" and his "attraction to socialism" influenced by "the Russian movement known as Narodniki (i.e., Back to the People)."[26] Thus, Razzouk did not leave aside all such discussions in his rendering of Hertzberg's biographical sketches but he highlighted the "internal" Jewish, especially religious, sources of Zionism. The impulses that may have led Razzouk to do so will be addressed shortly.

That the PLO research team changed certain aspects of *The Zionist Idea* is hardly surprising. After all, unlike Hertzberg, these researchers harbored little sympathy for the Zionist idea. What is interesting is the particular form this modification took. Anti-Zionist inclinations could have spurred the PLO researchers to claim that Jewish nationalism, even in its earliest, ostensibly native, religious form, was a reaction to politics in Europe, characterizing it as another form of European colonialism. These researchers would have found ample evidence of modern Europe's critical role in the rise of Zionism in *The Zionist Idea*. Yet Razzouk chose to depict Zionism as a principally religious movement, mostly independent of historically contingent political considerations.

Magnes's Covenant of Peace vs. Jabotinsky's Terror

Before attempting to trace what may have led the PLO researchers to this view of Zionism, we should note the subtlety of the PLO team's changes to Hertzberg's depiction of the canonical Zionists. *Al-Fikra al-Sahyuniyya* generally strikes a dispassionate tone—a remarkable fact, considering the political context in which the text was produced. Polemics do, however, occasionally rise to the surface. Such is the case, for instance, in Razzouk's presentation of Judah Magnes, the American Reform rabbi who became the first chancellor of the Hebrew University in Jerusalem and a founding member of the organization Brit Shalom, which championed a binational solution to the tensions in Palestine. While he did not mention Brit Shalom by name in his sketch of Magnes, Hertzberg noted that "the only hope that he [Magnes] saw for the implementation of the Jewish aims essential to him was in a binational state."[27] Razzouk offered far greater detail:

> He created with a group of his supporters "The Covenant of Peace" ['ahd al-salam], Brit Shalom, in 1926, to strengthen mutual understanding and cooperation between the Arabs and the Jews. And he called for restricting immigration so that the Jews would not become a majority in Palestine. He announced its plan to found an independent, binational state on the basis of equality in law and public services. He presented this goal to [Palestinian leaders] Jamal al-Husayni, 'Awni 'Abd al-Hadi, and Musa al-'Alami, and established friendships with them.

Until this point, Razzouk provides a rather neutral account. In the following paragraph, however, we discern Razzouk's subjective voice:

> He [Magnes] continued his opposition to official Zionist policy . . . He was far-sighted [ba'id al-nazar] when he said, in 1931: "I am not prepared to grant justice to the Jew by means of inflicting injustice on the Arab. It is unfair to the Arabs to subject them to Jewish rule without their agreement. If I do not support the creation of a Jewish state, it is because of the one reason I mentioned: I do not want a war with the Arab world."

Razzouk's editorializing does not end with his assessment of Magnes's prescience in fearing "war with the Arab world." Despite Magnes's efforts, Razzouk wrote, "the majority of Zionists believed in violence and terror [bi-l-'unf wa-l-irhab]." Even as Magnes's "health began to deteriorate . . . he continued his opposition to partition and his criticism of the terroristic activity that spread around him by the Zionist groups and gangs." Binationalism, however, "collapsed before the events of 1948." Magnes's Brit Shalom signaled a Zionist road not traveled; the "majority of Zionists" disregarded his calls for peace and cooperation with Arabs and, as Razzouk put it, elected instead a path of "violence and terror."[28]

The "terrorism" designation reappears in Razzouk's biographical account of Vladimir Jabotinsky, founder of the right-wing Union of Zionists-Revisionists.

"When the Arabs began revolting against Zionism and its efforts to prepare a secret army under the leadership of Jabotinsky," Razzouk wrote, Jabotinsky "organized Zionist terrorist activities [al-'amaliyyat al-irhabiyya al-sahyuniyya] in Jerusalem (1920)." Later, Razzouk noted that

> Jabotinsky is like the spiritual father and the nominal leader of the terrorist group called the "Irgun Tsevai Leumi" that Menachem Begin inherited and that became the Herut party after the establishment of Israel. Throughout his life he demanded the establishment of an independent Zionist army, and he repeated the demand when World War II broke out. He is the rightful father of illegal immigration and all the secret movements and military organizations among the Jews of Palestine.[29]

For Razzouk, Jabotinsky's form of Zionism, not that of Magnes, was the version that ultimately dominated the movement and the state it created.

Considering the importance of Jabotinsky in Razzouk's reading of Zionism, it is instructive to note that the excerpt included in the section on Jabotinsky is one of the few instances where the PLO translators (Razzouk's colleagues Lutfi al-Abed and Musa 'Anaz) made a substantive—and critical—change. As noted above, the Research Center's Arabic translations of the primary source excerpts in *The Zionist Idea* are generally faithful to Hertzberg's English. This is not so, however, for the passage from Jabotinsky's testimony to the Peel Commission, the British commission of inquiry tasked with investigating the origins of the violence that erupted in Palestine in 1936. In this speech, Jabotinsky contended that "there is no question of ousting the Arabs." Rather, he insisted "Palestine on both sides of the Jordan" should "hold the Arabs, their progeny, *and* many millions of Jews." In the process, "the Arabs of Palestine will necessarily become a minority in the country of Palestine," but, he asserted, this would not be a hardship:

> It is not a hardship on any race, any nation, possessing so many National States now and so many more National States in the future. One fraction, one branch of that race, and not a big one, will have to live in someone else's State.[30]

The PLO rendering of this passage is a literal translation of the above until the final line. In his testimony, Jabotinsky contended that the Arabs of Palestine, remaining in Palestine, "will have to live in someone else's State," that is, in the Jews' state. In the Arabic translation, Jabotinsky instead says: "one fraction, one branch of that race will have to live in another Arab country [*fi balad* '*arabiyya ukhra*]."[31] The PLO translators changed Jabotinsky's testimony from a defense of making Palestine's Arabs a minority in a new Jewish state into a defense of expelling them from Palestine to Arab countries. This mistranslation was, I suspect, accidental; earlier in the same paragraph, the translators accurately rendered Jabotinsky's stated desire that "Palestine on both sides of the Jordan should hold the Arabs, their progeny, and many millions of Jews."[32] Reflexive as it may have been, this mistranslation reveals the deeply ingrained sense among those in the PLO Research Center, led by refugees from the 1948 war, that their expulsion was, from the beginning, fundamental to the Zionist plan.[33]

Why Stress Zionism's Religious Origins

Let us return to the question of the place of religion in Razzouk's conception of the rise of Zionism. Hertzberg, in his volume's introduction, argued that the Jewish view of Zionism as messianism was "really a kind of synthetic Zionist ideology presented as history."[34] If Hertzberg was not the source of this reading of Zionism, what could have led Razzouk to highlight religion in his biographical sketches? A look at Razzouk's larger oeuvre may be instructive. In addition to his contributions to *al-Fikra al-Sahyuniyya*, Razzouk, during the late 1960s and early 1970s, published numerous books, including *al-Dawla wa-l-Din fi Isra'il* (State and Religion in Israel), *Isra'il al-Kubra* (Greater Israel), *al-Majlis al-Amriki li-l-Yahudiyya* (The American Council for Judaism), *al-Talmud wa-l-Sahyuniyya* (The Talmud and Zionism), and *Qadaya al-Din wa-l-Mujtama' fi Isra'il* (The Problems of Religion and Society in Israel). Razzouk was clearly interested in the relationship between Judaism and Jewish nationalism, and he was regularly tapped by the Research Center's director to write on this subject. Thus, his portrayal of Zionism through a religious lens in *al-Fikra al-Sahyuniyya*'s biographical sketches intersected with research he was conducting contemporaneously in the PLO Research Center.

In the 1968 volume *al-Dawla wa-l-Din fi Isra'il*, Razzouk was tasked with elucidating the relationship between Judaism and Zionism. In the preface to Razzouk's volume, Anis Sayegh wrote that Israel is "one of the very few 'states' in our modern world that links its political existence to religion and makes religion a basis for its existence." Writing just one year after Israel's extensive territorial conquest in the 1967 war, which many Jews understood as a miraculous restoration of Jewish sovereignty over ancient sacred sites, Sayegh noted that "religion did not play a role in the lead up to the establishment, and then

in the establishment, of any modern 'state' as much as it did in the establishment of 'Israel,' then in its expansion, and in all of its past and present schemes
to increase its expansion."[35] Sayegh explained Razzouk's book as the investigation of this supposed historical peculiarity.

In preparing his 145-page analysis, Razzouk read not only Hertzberg's *The
Zionist Idea*, but also a wide range of Arabic, English, and German essays,
monographs, encyclopedia entries, and newspapers. On the basis of these
sources, Razzouk produced a nuanced portrayal of the relationship between
Judaism and Zionism. Let us begin with his presentation of Theodor Herzl's
views. Translating from Herzl's landmark 1896 pamphlet *Der Judenstaat* ("The
Jewish State" or "The Jews' State"), Razzouk quoted Herzl's expectation that
"our Rabbis, on whom we especially call, will devote their energies to the
service of our idea, and will inspire their congregations by preaching it from
the pulpit."[36] Razzouk argued that Herzl recognized "the importance of the
Jewish religion as an active agent in unifying Jews and preparing them psychologically to embrace the Zionist call."[37] Herzl perceived Zionism's potential to satisfy Jewish religious needs, explained Razzouk.[38] But Herzl was not
calling for a theocracy, Razzouk was careful to note. "One finds in Theodor
Herzl—who was German in culture, language, birth, and upbringing," wrote
Razzouk, "both a personal tendency toward humanism and an avoidance as
much as possible of the theocratic idea." Indeed, Herzl proved himself
throughout his writing to have been "a passionate advocate for the separation
of religion and state."[39]

Razzouk noted that Herzl's views on the religion/state divide did "not prevent him from daring to call upon religious fervor and to awaken zeal for the
faith of the ancestors, for the sake of gaining the great masses of religious Jews
and redirecting their love of Zion from its sense of spiritual longing and its
traditional supplicatory character."[40] Thus, he suggested, Herzl instrumentalized the religious faith of his fellow Jews to garner their support, even as he
himself lacked this faith. The father of Zionism, according to Razzouk, made
a "conscious use" (*al-istifada al-wa'iyya*) and "exploitation" (*taskhir*) of religion
for the benefit of Zionism.[41]

In Razzouk's reckoning, Herzl and the movement he founded had a complex relationship with religion. On the one hand, the author of *al-Dawla wa-l-
Din fi Isra'il* accepted Israeli scholar Jacob Talmon's claim that "the Orthodox
wing of Zionism had little effect on the general movement, for it feared secular
nationalism and had deep qualms about forcing the hand of the Almighty" by
engaging in actions to precipitate redemption. On the other, he insisted that

the limited influence of the observant Orthodox did not mean that religion's impact on Zionism was equally limited.[42] "Religious feelings of belonging," Razzouk contended, played a role "on an unconscious level in the course of the modern Zionist movement." In this way, Razzouk rejected Talmon's assertion that "most of the Zionist prophets and theoreticians, brought up in the liberal atmosphere of the nineteenth century, gave very little heed to the place of religion in their future state, apart from conventional insistence on religious freedom and inattentive assurance of respect for ancient traditions."[43] Believing that even secularist Zionists had a "religious motive," Razzouk insisted that they were secularist "on a conscious level only."[44] Zionists as apparently secularist as Theodor Herzl were motivated by wellsprings of which they themselves may not have been aware including, claimed Razzouk, Jewish religious and messianic ideas.[45]

Razzouk recognized that not all modern Jews believed that Judaism and Zionism were compatible or that Zionism emerged naturally and legitimately from Jewish religious sources. As we have seen, however, the PLO Covenant famously declares Judaism to be a "religion" (*din samawi*) and not a "nationalism" (*qawmiyya*), and the Jews to be "citizens of the states to which they belong" and not "a single people (*sha'b*) with a separate identity." These definitions have played an important role in the rhetorical battle against Zionism. I return to the PLO Research Center's interests in these matters below.

Christians and Christianity in the PLO Research Center

The PLO's conception of Judaism as religious-not-national was widely employed to earn political capital in the challenge against Jewish nationalism. The religious characterization of Judaism may have had particular meaning for the scholars at the PLO Research Center, many of whom, including Razzouk and the Sayegh brothers, were raised and educated in Christian communities. Anis Sayegh, as noted in part 1, was the son of a Presbyterian minister. In his autobiography, he described the central place of religion in his childhood home in Tiberias, where prayer and church attendance were obligatory and Bible recitation was a regular activity.[46] "Our main pastime," recalled his older brother Yusif, "was listening to the Bible and trying to read it . . . every day, every morning and every evening."[47] Their parents, according to Anis Sayegh, were "the most faithful believers."[48] As the Sayegh brothers related it, Christianity was fundamental to their rearing.[49] While Sayegh claimed to have ultimately embraced a humanistic, non-ritualistic religiosity and theology, he maintained a lifelong interest in Christianity,[50] and authored two hundred pages of entries for the Arabic *Dictionary of the Bible* (Qamus al-Kitab al-Muqaddas).[51] While less is known about Razzouk's upbringing, we know that he was educated at the Presbyterian mission's Gerard Institute in Sidon.[52]

The Christian background of the Sayeghs and many of their Research Center associates has a twofold importance to our discussion. Christians represented approximately 10 percent of Palestinians within and beyond mid-twentieth-century Palestine. As a religious minority, Palestinian Christians—and other Arab Christians in a Muslim-majority modern Middle East—were sensitive to the notion of religiously based political identities and nationalisms. The dangers of a one-to-one link between religion and nationalism were especially potent during this period in Lebanon, where the PLO Research Center was.[53] Portraying Zionism, reviled as the ideology was among Palestinians and other Arabs, as a *religious* nationalism, and emphasizing its religious qualities, could serve to tarnish the idea of religious nationalism generally.

The leadership of the PLO Research Center was deeply concerned about the place of Christians in the Palestinian nation. In his *Palestine and Arab Nationalism*, Anis Sayegh argued that Palestine's small size accounted for the exceptionally undifferentiated nature and high level of "accord and harmony" of the land's inhabitants:

> The smallness of Palestine throughout the various phases of its history since the Arab conquest in the seventh century, facilitated for its people, the process of accepting and absorbing most of the immigrant peoples and communities (and even the semi-conquering ones). This smallness facilitated also the process of fusion so that no great differences existed between one group and another; when there were differences, whether religious, ethnic, or cultural differences, they did not appear conspicuous. Even when such differences continued to exist, they did not divide the people among themselves.[54]

Sayegh highlighted the fact that "Arab minorities (e.g., the Christians) and the non-Arab minorities (e.g., the Armenians and the Kurds) upheld the Arab national aspirations in the area, and participated, as individuals, in political activities." Palestine's minorities engaged in "armed struggle" and even "martyrdom, side by side with the majority"—in contrast to minorities elsewhere in the Arab world, some of whom "oppos[ed] the national struggle."[55]

Though Sayegh wrote here of various Palestinian minorities, Christians were of particular concern to him. The smallness of Palestine, he said, was only one factor that contributed to its communities' cohesion. Another, equally important, consideration was this:

> The largest minority in Palestine, i.e., the Christians (forming 1/10 of the total population for the last seven or eight centuries), are Arabs who came from the Arab Peninsula or the adjacent areas, that is to say from the cradle from which originated the Arabs most of whom migrated to Palestine. The roots of both the majority and minority, therefore, go back to the same geographic and sociocultural background. This has played an important role in bringing together the Muslims and Christians in their daily living, and in their opposition to the political danger that suddenly threatened them in an unprecedented manner. Until a late period in the history of Palestine prior to the disaster [of 1948], scores of the important Palestinian families felt strongly tied to each other irrespective of sect or creed.[56]

Sayegh asserted that the common Arab ethnic origin of Palestine's Christians and Muslims accounted for their shared political interests. Palestine's Christians and Muslims were different in religion only and, it was implied, religion need not, ought not, and—until 1948—did not divide the communities politically.

Sayegh went further still in his argument for the integral place of Christians in the Palestinian Arab nation. It was not merely that Christians participated equally, "side by side," with Muslims in the national struggle. The Christian minority had been at the forefront of the struggle, especially in the development of national ideology. "The fact that the Christians in Palestine were pioneers in transmitting the concept of nationalism from Europe to the Arab world and into Arabic, just as the Lebanese did," contended Sayegh (in a book written and published in Lebanon), "gave strength to Christian participation in the Muslim national action." Proudly, Sayegh proclaimed that Christian Palestinians were "the first to come in contact with Western civilization, through the European and American religious missions to the East, the student missions to the West and through emigration to America."[57] And it was through these encounters that Palestinian Christians learned of and embraced the European concept of nationalism.[58] They translated the concept into an Arabic idiom and transmitted it into the Palestinian context where it was, only then, imbibed by Muslims. In *Palestine and Arab Nationalism* (a book ostensibly about Arab nationalism in Palestine and the place of Palestine in Arab nationalism broadly), Sayegh's tenacious emphasis on the critical historical role of Christians is indicative of his apparent desire to underscore the vital

place of his fellow Christians in the contemporary Palestinian Arab nationalist movement. The PLO Research Center's stress on the religious nature of
Zionism might therefore also be understood in this context. Palestinian nationalism, presented as transcending religion by encompassing both Muslims
and Christians, could thus be contrasted with a more parochial Zionism, religious to its core.

There is another way in which awareness of the Christian identities and education of important PLO Research Center leaders and contributors may help
us understand Razzouk's—and the PLO Research Center's—accentuation of
Jewish religious elements in Zionism. Christian Arabs could, on the one hand,
feel more threatened by the biblical legitimization of Zionism than their Muslim
counterparts; after all, faithful Christians also regarded the Hebrew Bible as
their own sacred text. On the other hand, the many Christians who, like Jews,
were biblically literate and could readily engage with the textual and theological arguments on their own terms could more directly challenge Bible-based
arguments for Zionism.

A "Divine Right" to Palestine?

The leadership of the Research Center engaged in precisely these arguments.
In September 1967, a mere three months after Israel conquered the West Bank,
the Gaza Strip, the Sinai Peninsula, and the Golan Heights, the Center's founding director, Fayez Sayegh, published a pamphlet entitled "Do Jews Have a
'Divine Right' to Palestine?" Sayegh argued against "the Zionist contentions"
about Jewish claims to Palestine that were based "on certain promises made
by God to Abraham, Isaac, and Jacob, and on certain predictions uttered by
the Prophets during the Babylonian Exile."[59] As a lifelong reader of the Bible,
Sayegh considered such Zionist claims seriously, and thus addressed them in
detail.[60]

Concerning the biblical predictions of a return to Zion, for example, Sayegh
insisted that these were "predictions of a return from a *specific* exile," and "*not*—
nor did they purport to be—predictions of a *recurrent act of return*." The biblical
prophets foretold the Jewish return from exile in Babylonia and these predictions "were in fact fulfilled," wrote Sayegh, with the reconstruction of the Jerusalem Temple and the institution of a "period of political independence, under
the Maccabees." Because they have already been fulfilled, "the prophecies of
the return cannot be viewed as still awaiting fulfillment."[61] Sayegh, informed at
least in part by his Christian religious education, did not question the authentic,

divine nature of the Hebrew Bible's prophets as he challenged Zionism's appeal
to these prophecies. Rather, he insisted that these prophecies, properly understood, were already actualized two millennia earlier and thus had no implications for contemporary Jews or for modern Palestine.

What of God's biblical promises to grant Palestine to the figures regarded
as the forefathers of the Jews? Drawing on Alfred Guillaume's 1956 essay "Zionists and the Bible," Sayegh cited the passages in Genesis where God promised the Land of Israel to Abraham, Isaac, and Jacob, and their descendants.[62]
These promises, wrote Sayegh, "were made to Abraham and his 'seed' in the
first instance. When they were subsequently made to Isaac and Jacob and their
'seed,' no exclusion of other descendants was indicated." In other words, *all* of
Abraham's descendants were included in God's promise, not just those who
descended from Isaac and Jacob. "The inclusiveness of the earlier promises,"
noted Sayegh, "was not cancelled by the relative narrowness of the later
ones."[63] The implication of this assertion is that those other, non-Jewish descendants of Abraham—including Arabs, Sayegh reminded the reader—have
equal claim to the biblical God's promise of Palestine. "Apart from Muslim
tradition," wrote Sayegh, "there is ample evidence in the Old Testament itself
that the term, 'the seed of Abraham,' includes Arabs." Citing Genesis 25 and
I Chronicles 1, Sayegh noted that "through Abraham's first-born son, Ishmael,
who was born to Abraham by Hagar the Egyptian, many an Arab tribe came
to be among the offspring of Abraham," and, through Abraham's second wife,
Keturah, "Abraham became the father of other Arab tribes also."[64] Moreover,
even if the promise to the "seed of Abraham" is intended for the descendants
of Jews, many Middle Eastern Christians would also be included in it. "A large
proportion" of the Jews who had been exiled by the Babylonians in the sixth
century BCE "preferred to remain where they were," explained Sayegh, rather
than return to the Holy Land when they were permitted. "Those Jews who
chose not to return formed the Diaspora," and, Sayegh contended, they subsequently became "the backbone of the Christian Church and an ethnically
indistinguishable component of the population of the Near East."[65] Abraham's
progeny to whom the Promised Land was promised included Arabs and especially *Christian* Arabs.

The second prong of Sayegh's challenge to the Zionist claim that all Jews
and only Jews constitute the "seed of Abraham," and are thus the rightful in-
heritors of Palestine, was the contention that many contemporary Jews are not
actual descendants of the biblical paterfamilias. "Throughout the centuries,"
asserted Sayegh, "conversion and proselytization have introduced into the

ranks of Jews many who were not the offspring of Abraham." He cited the *Universal Jewish Encyclopedia*, noting that "wholesale conversion of the Khazars of Russia to Judaism occurred in the Eighth Century A.D."[66] Sayegh retorted to the Zionist reliance on biblical promises to Abraham's offspring to legitimize modern Jews' claim to Palestine that "the over-simplified Zionist contention . . . is inaccurate from the standpoint of both its exclusiveness," that is, excluding Abraham's non-Jewish descendants, and "its inclusiveness," that is, including Jews who are not themselves the biological progeny of Abraham.[67] Finally, citing the American Presbyterian theologian Oswald T. Allis, Sayegh emphasized the conditional nature of the biblical promise, explaining that "possession of the land was conditioned on obedience" to God.[68] Even if contemporary Jews were all the progeny of Abraham and were his only surviving progeny, there would still be reason to conclude that God's promise had been revoked due to the Jews' defiance of God's commandments.

If the preceding arguments are remarkable for the degree to which they accept, and engage in, the logic of biblical reading in arguing against the "Zionist contention," the final section of Sayegh's short pamphlet on whether Jews have a "divine right" to Palestine rests on a different plane—or different Testament—entirely. "It is in the light of the Christian Gospel," wrote Sayegh, "that a Christian must understand the abiding truth and relevance of the promises recorded in the Old Testament." For Sayegh, articulating a form of supersessionism, the Gospel represents the ascendance of a "world-embracing universalism" over "the parochialism, provincialism, or 'nationalism' of the Jewish traditions."[69] Judaism was based on a "tribalistic belief in a 'chosen people,'" while Christianity involved "a revolutionary universalism which emphasized the fatherhood of God and the brotherhood of man."[70] As Sayegh saw it, Christianity's great innovation was its rebellion against the narrow particularism of Judaism in favor of a broad universalism.

There was nothing novel in Sayegh's contrast between Judaism's particularism and Christianity's universalism; it represented standard Christian critique of Judaism (a discursive tradition that remains relevant even though the PLO Research Center publications were not generally anti-Jewish).[71] Notable here, rather, are the ends toward which Sayegh employs this trope: to argue against Jewish nationalism. While Christianity taught the world universalism, the Jews, he said, still clung to their religion's particularism and hence to their antiquated nationalism. Jews failed to recognize that "Israel of the flesh" had given way to "Israel of the spirit" and that "within the revolutionary reinterpretation of old concepts which the Christian Gospel introduces, the spiritual importance of *places as such* vanishes, giving way to emphasis on the *spirit*; it is the spirit alone that possesses importance."[72] Jews, following an anachronistic Judaism, stubbornly persisted in seeing spiritual value in physical spaces, whereas Christians, enlightened by the Gospel, understood that earthly locations were of no spiritual import. For Christians, as Christians, wrote Sayegh quoting Allis, "the land of Palestine has a sentimental interest. But that is all."[73]

Recognizing that part of Sayegh's critique of Zionism was a well-worn—if creatively deployed—Christian argument against Judaism helps to explain why the Sayegh brothers, as successive directors of the PLO Research Center, and contributors to the Center's research agenda like Razzouk, honed in on the religious elements of Zionism. Demonstrating that Zionism was motivated by Jewish religious impulses allowed Christian Arabs to link the faults of Zionism to those they already recognized in Judaism. Some Jews—especially the nineteenth-century Reformers and their twentieth-century intellectual successors whom we will meet in chapter 7—effectively embraced the Gospel's universal message and understood that Judaism, as a religion, is a spiritual matter with no political implications or geographic boundaries.[74] Zionists, however, rejected this truth and, instead, held fast to traditional Judaism's particularist obsession with the physical land and the nation.

Challenging Christian Zionism

Given their proud insistence on Christianity's universalism, the PLO Research Center staff was especially disturbed by Christians who, qua Christians, embraced Zionism. For Razzouk, these Christians were epitomized by James Parkes (1896–1981), a well-known minister in the Church of England, who, by the late 1960s, had published numerous works on Jewish history, antisemitism, Israel, and the Arab-Israeli conflict. Not unlike the PLO researchers studied here, Parkes saw in Zionism an essentially religiously motivated movement, despite Zionist claims to the contrary. In "Judaism and Zionism: A Christian View," an essay Parkes contributed to a 1947 symposium on "Some Religious Aspects of Zionism," he wrote:

Neither anti-Semitism nor the need for a haven for the homeless nor political nationalism lie at the foundation of the Zionist movement, or form the inspiration even of those leaders and settlers who are not openly or even consciously moved by affection for the religious inheritance of Judaism and the Messianic dream of a return to Zion. At bottom lie the historic reality of the Jews as a people, and the nature of Judaism as a religion expressing itself in the life of an autonomous community.[75]

While the advent of increasingly virulent antisemitism and the rise of nationalism were important for understanding Zionism, religious forces, argued Parkes, were at the heart of Jewish nationalism. If Parkes, on the one hand, and the PLO Research Center team, on the other, shared the view of Zionism as religious (even if "not openly or even consciously"), the correspondence between their perspectives ends there. Whereas Parkes celebrated this religiously motivated drive for Jewish political independence, the PLO Research Center challenged it, both from an internal Jewish religious perspective and from a Christian religious perspective.

The PLO Research Center therefore found it necessary to attack Parkes and his views directly. In 1970 (the same year as the release of *al-Fikra al-Sahyuniyya*), it published Razzouk's *Partisan Views of Reverend James Parkes*. In this fifty-page essay, Razzouk argued that "prejudice seems to get the upper hand in the emotional approach pursued by the gentile Zionism of Rev. Parkes." Razzouk was insistent that Parkes had abdicated true Christian values in his embrace of Zionism, and consistently labeled his position "gentile Zionism" rather than "Christian Zionism." In fact, Razzouk contended that, "in posing the question of 'How to seek a proper Christian understanding of the State of Israel,' Rev. Parkes remained true only to his gentile Zionism, and thereby failed to give the proper Christian element its due credit."[76] Razzouk acknowledged Parkes's engagement with and contribution to "authentic" Christian theology, but asserted that where Zionism was concerned, "Rev. Parkes, the theologian" gave way to "Dr. Parkes, the historian and gentile Zionist."[77] Indeed, argued Razzouk, Parkes himself conceded this bifurcation in his writings by publishing his theological works under the pseudonym "John Hadham" and his Zionist compositions under his given name.

But why would a religious Christian—a respected Christian theologian—embrace Zionism so "overzealous[ly]," as Razzouk put it?[78] It was all about money, Razzouk claimed, highlighting throughout the essay Parkes's financial dependence on Jewish patrons. Parkes's "Zionist discoveries," said Razzouk, are in fact "the passionate and emotional voice of his Zionist masters and mentors," those "who are always eager and ready to 'pay the bills' with great pleasure."[79] Parkes had considered—but then backtracked—writing a book on the causes of the Palestinian refugee crisis, Razzouk alleged, so as "not to embarrass his Zionist benefactors."[80] Razzouk noted that in Parkes's autobiography, he made specific reference to funds he raised and gifts he received from Zionists.[81] There is no other way to explain Parkes's Zionism, Razzouk implied, than to understand who was bankrolling him.[82] Moreover, to Parkes's claim that "pro-Arab" Christians are not merely "anti-Israel" but also "both ignorant and mildly or virulently anti-Semitic," Razzouk retorted: "Apparently Dr. Parkes has met the wrong kind of Christians."[83] The right kind of Christians, it would seem, were those, like Razzouk and his colleagues, whose opposition to Zionism was informed by a proper understanding of Christianity, and of Judaism.[84]

I have argued here that, in the assortment of publications discussed above, the PLO Research Center presented Zionism as a movement that was mainly motivated by religious, messianic interests, values, and myths. Regardless of the precise historical relationship between Judaism as a religion and Zionism as a nationalism—a topic that remains a matter of scholarly debate[85]—the PLO Research Center's view of the question reveals an important insight: religious backgrounds and traditions shape how people see the world and engage in politics, even when they are unaware of these influences. Considering the PLO researchers' own religious traditions—ones that, as we have seen, animated their research program and the work they published—helps us to better understand their own relationship to and critique of Zionism.

By exploring the story of the PLO Research Center in Beirut, we bring into focus a part of Palestinian intellectual history that has been blurred by contemporary politics. The current prominence of Islam in Palestinian politics and in the discourse concerning the Palestinian-Israeli conflict, on the one hand, and the significant financial and political support that powerful American Christian evangelical groups bestow upon Israel, on the other, obscure the place of Christians and Christianity in Palestinian nationalism and in the development of Palestinian conceptions of, and polemics against, Zionism and Israel. Tackling the assumptions and interests of the Christian minorities engaged in the intellectual battles of Palestinian nationalism reminds us that when nationalist institutions such as the PLO Research Center imagined and presented their enemy, they were also constructing a vision of their own nation-in-waiting.

6

The Talmud and Zionism

REJECTING ANTISEMITISM IN THE NAME
OF PALESTINIAN LIBERATION

IN NOVEMBER 1970, *al-Talmud wa-l-Sahyuniyya* (The Talmud and Zionism), a book that accused Palestinians and other Arabs of swallowing wholesale European antisemitic myths and conspiracy theories about the Talmud, was published.[1] Arabs, this book claimed, engaged in "parrot-like repetition of traditional views" on the topic, without even bothering to open the Talmud. Remarkably, this fierce, Arabic-language indictment was published by the PLO Research Center in Beirut.

Here I contextualize and analyze this fascinating book, written by the same Ass'ad Razzouk[2] under the editorial guidance of the PLO Research Center's longtime director general Anis Sayegh. Three sets of questions drive this chapter. First is the issue of motivation. What led the PLO's think tank to task a researcher with writing about the Talmud? Even if the staff suspected that the dominant Arab view of the Talmud was drawn from polemical, antisemitic sources, why did the Center decide to correct these myths? Second is the question of sources. How did the researcher who undertook this myth-busting endeavor find his information in Lebanon? What books was he reading? And what does the presence of these sources on the Research Center bookshelf tell us about the world of PLO intellectuals in late 1960s Beirut? Finally, what can be learned from the conclusions the researcher drew about the relationship between the Talmud and Zionism and, more broadly, between Judaism and Jewish nationalism? What insights about this relationship were detected by the PLO's researcher given the unique vantage point from which he and his fellow intellectual-activists were reading the sources?

Motivations and the Protocols

Why the PLO, within the first half-decade of the organization's existence, would dedicate precious resources to learning about and reading the Talmud and then publishing the findings is a conundrum. To solve it, we must start with the views about the Talmud that were circulating in Arabic at the time. PLO researchers were not the first to express frustration about Arab ignorance of this foundational Jewish corpus. In 1967, at about the same time that the Research Center tapped Razzouk for this project, a different book was published in Beirut that bemoaned the problem. Its author, ʿAjaj Nuwayhid, though born in what is today's Lebanon, was educated in Jerusalem and lived there until the 1948 war.[3] In his book Nuwayhid lamented, "Until today, all that is possible to know about the Talmud, among the Arabs, after the passage of about fourteen centuries since its completion in Iraq, consists of hearsay and a few written fragments. And I do not imagine that any Arab—whether Muslim or Christian—in the entire Arab world has read one volume of the Talmud except if that person is a specialist student in a college or university."[4]

Nuwayhid offered three explanations for what he viewed as broad Arab ignorance about the Talmud. "Perhaps the first reason is the language"— namely, that Arabs cannot read Hebrew and Aramaic, the original languages of the Talmudic texts. "The second," he suggested, "is the Jews' perpetual attempt to keep it [the Talmud] far from the minds of non-Jews, and the third is the belief among a large number of Arab thinkers that the Talmud is old [and] obsolete," an irrelevant relic from the past. If Arabs mention any Jewish religious texts, Nuwayhid added, "they mention the Torah, and even the Torah interests few Arabs and [few] study it to know what images of Jewish morality are in it." Nuwayhid declared that finally "the time has come in 1966," when he was writing these lines, "for the Arab to know that the Talmud is the abode of 'the elders of Zion,' to which they return and from which they proceed, and from the spirit of which 'the protocols' derived and formulated decisions."[5]

This assertion of a clear and direct spiritual link between the Talmud and the *Protocols of the Elders of Zion* appeared in Nuwayhid's 1967 two-volume Arabic edition of the *Protocols of the Elders of Zion*. This edition, *Brutukulat Hukamaʾ Sahyun*, published in Beirut, quickly reached the PLO Research Center based in the same city. Indeed, the passage cited above from Nuwayhid was quoted by PLO researcher Razzouk in *al-Talmud wa-l-Sahyuniyya*.

Razzouk, whom we met as the author of the introductory biographies in *al-Fikra al-Sahyuniyya*, agreed with Nuwayhid about the problem of Arabs' Talmudic illiteracy.[6] However, unlike Nuwayhid, who complained about Arab ignorance of the Talmud but seems not to have studied it himself, Razzouk thought that the appropriate response to the charge of illiteracy was to become literate in the Talmud. And, as it happened, there was a new English edition of the Babylonian Talmud that had recently been published by the Soncino Press, the last volumes of which were completed in 1961.[7] Razzouk had the Soncino edition before him as he undertook his research.

Nuwayhid was no doubt correct that Arabs were, in the main, broadly ignorant of the actual contents of the Talmud (though surely the same was true of all other large ethnic groups, including for that matter Jews).[8] He was wrong, however, in his assertion that Arabs ignored the existence of the Talmud and its significance for Jews. In fact, in the modern Arab world, as Razzouk demonstrated in the first part of *al-Talmud wa-l-Sahyuniyya*, the Talmud was a major focus of speculation and denunciation. This preoccupation was especially evident during and in the wake of the Damascus affair, the blood-libel incident that took place in Egyptian-occupied Syria in 1840.[9] It was then, in the mid-nineteenth century, that the charge began to circulate in the Arab world, through Arabic translations not of the Talmud itself but rather of European-language antisemitic texts, alleging that the Talmud commanded Jews to murder Christian boys and extract their blood, which would then be used in the baking of Passover matzah. Indeed, the Arabic term that came to be used for Jewish ritual murder, especially since the late nineteenth century, was *al-dhaba'ih al-talmudiyya*—Talmudic sacrifices.[10] The Talmud, as an idea, was far from ignored by modern Arabs. On the contrary, the Talmud was the subject of fascination and fear.[11]

The *Protocols of the Elders of Zion* were of interest to the PLO not only because the title recalled the name of the competing nationalist movement, Zionism, that created the State of Israel, but also because the idea of a global Jewish conspiracy to wrest control of the world from non-Jews struck a particular chord with Palestinians—then, after the 1948 and 1967 wars, and later, as evidenced in the 1988 Hamas charter.[12]

In fact, Razzouk was not the only intellectual affiliated with the PLO Research Center who was concerned about the extent to which the Protocols had been employed as an explanatory device for understanding the Arab-Israeli conflict in the wake of the 1967 war. In 1968, the Syrian philosopher Sadik al-Azm (who attended high school with Razzouk, and who also eventually worked for the PLO Research Center in Beirut) penned an essay that came to be a landmark—and controversial—work in modern Arab intellectual history, *Self-Criticism after the Defeat*.[13] In the piece, al-Azm assessed the underlying causes for the Arab defeat in the Six-Day War. Criticizing those Arabs who failed to take responsibility for their societies' deficiencies and failures, al-Azm remarked on those Arab "writers who seek refuge in the *Protocols of the Elders of Zion* to prove that the Jews practice total control, through infernal international conspiracies, over the course of modern history (and perhaps ancient history, too). According to this superstitious logic, the Elders of Zion gather together at least once every century where they carry out discussions and studies in order to compose their frightening secret plan to enslave the world."[14] Al-Azm contended that "the diffusion of this kind of thinking among the Arabs to explain their defeat by Zionism and its colonialist allies indicates that the Arab mind (or better, the Arab imagination) still leans strongly towards the adopting of the simplest and most naïve explanations for the course of historical events."[15] Al-Azm was a staunch secularist and so, perhaps unsurprisingly, he attributed the appeal of the Protocols among the Arabs to "the influence of mythological or traditionally religious thinking that explains events, in the end, by recourse to divine will and the desires of supernatural beings, and that sees in the course of history a premeditated plan for the path of events and an intentional design for everything that happens."[16] Though in this discussion he cited a book by Shawqi 'Abd al-Nasir titled *Brutukulat Hukama' Sahyun wa-Ta'alim al-Talmud* (The Protocols of the Elders of Zion and the Teachings of the Talmud), al-Azm did not engage with the content of the Talmud. He was satisfied with demonstrating the absurdity of the Protocols by other means. For Razzouk, however, working on behalf of the PLO Research Center, the enduring link made between the Protocols and the Talmud merited substantive investigation.

The PLO Research Center's Jewish Studies Library

How did Razzouk undertake this investigation? What sources, aside from the Soncino translation of the Babylonian Talmud, did he turn to? Razzouk's bibliography begins with four pages listing and annotating Arabic books[17] that he saw as following the tradition of—and even simply republishing passages from—two different anti-Jewish Arabic works from the 1890s. The first was *al-Kanz al-Marsud fi Qawa'id al-Talmud* (The Guarded Treasure in the Laws of the Talmud),[18] originally published in 1899 in Egypt and reissued in 1968 and again in 1970 in Beirut. This was an Arabic translation of August Rohling's antitalmudic, antisemitic polemic *Der Talmudjude* (The Talmud-Jew) of 1871. The second book on which the others were based was *Surakh al-Bariʾ fi Buq al-Hurriyya wa-l-Dhabaʾih al-Talmudiyya* (The Cry of the Innocent with the Trumpet of Freedom, and Talmudic Sacrifices), written by Habib Faris and published in Egypt in 1891.

The next section of the bibliography lists other Arabic texts, including modern editions of medieval Islamic anti-Jewish polemics, such as Ibn Hazm's *al-Radd ʿala Ibn al-Naghrila al-Yahudi* (Refutation of Ibn Naghrila the Jew) and Ibn ʿAbbas's *Ifham al-Yahud* (Silencing the Jews),[19] and modern anti-Jewish works such as Amil al-Khuri Harb's 1947 *Muʾamarat al-Yahud ʿala al-Masihiyya* (The Jews' Conspiracy against Christianity)[20] and Muhammad Khalifa al-Tunisi's 1951 *al-Khatar al-Yahudi: Brutukulat Hukamaʾ Sahyun* (The Jewish Peril: The Protocols of the Elders of Zion).[21] Such works are the main subjects of the first part of Razzouk's book (part 1 is called "The Arabs and the Interest in Studying the Talmud"), which provides an eviscerating critique of the prevailing contemporary Arab discourse on the Talmud, judging the more recent works as even more problematic than the medieval polemical literature and tracing the modern texts to European Christian antisemitic tracts.

After listing these Arabic texts (highlighted mainly to repudiate them), Razzouk then listed a page of "Jewish Sources in Arabic,"[22] followed by eight pages of foreign-language texts and encyclopedias. This bibliography reveals that the PLO Research Center's library held much of what any basic, largely English-language Jewish studies library circa 1970 would have displayed on its shelves, a selection of which follows. These sources begin with Morris Adler's *The World of the Talmud* (1963) and end with Lucien Wolf's *The Myth of the Jewish Menace in World Affairs, or, The Truth about the Forged Protocols of the Elders of Zion* (1921). In between appear Leo Baeck's *The Essence of Judaism* (trans. from the German, 1936); Salo Baron's *A Social and Religious History of the Jews*, vols. 1–2 (1966); Eliezer Berkovits's *Toward Historic Judaism* (1943); Joseph Bloch's *Israel and the Nations* (trans. from the German, 1927); Norman Cohn's *Warrant for Genocide: The Myth of the Jewish World-Conspiracy and the Protocols of the Elders of Zion* (1967); Lucy Dawidowicz's *The Golden Tradition* (1967); Isidore Epstein's *Judaism: A Historical Interpretation* (1959); Eliezer Goldman's *Religious Issues in Israel's Political Life* (1964); Heinrich Graetz's *History of the Jews* (1893/1956); Solomon Grayzel's *A History of the Jews* (1947/1964); Jacob Katz's *Tradition and Crisis* (1958/1961); Bernard Lazarre's *Antisemitism: Its History and Causes* (1894/1967); Jacob Marcus's *The Jew in the Medieval World*

(1960); Michael Meyer's *The Origins of the Modern Jews* (1967); Howard Sachar's *The Course of Modern Jewish History* (1963); Alexander Altmann's selections from Sa'adiah's *Book of Doctrines and Beliefs* (1946); Solomon Schechter's *Studies in Judaism* (1945); and Max Weber's *Ancient Judaism* (1952/1967), among many others. In contrast to the Arabic sources listed in the bibliography's opening section, Razzouk treated these foreign-language texts mostly as reliable, legitimate scholarship. This Jewish studies library—with the Soncino edition of the Talmud at its core—was the basis on which Razzouk constructed his withering critique of Arabic writing on the Talmud.

After revealing previous Arabic writings to be poor translations and adaptations of libelous, fictitious drivel, Razzouk then aimed to provide his readers with an introduction to the actual Talmud. This section of the book consists of four chapters that focus on defining the Talmud, the composition of the Talmudic text, the areas of focus in the six "orders" (or main sections) of the Talmud, and the place of the Talmud in Judaism. In defining the Talmud, Razzouk turned to Solomon Schechter's *Studies in Judaism*, the *Jewish Encyclopedia*, Israel Wolfenssohn's Arabic work on Maimonides, and Isidore Epstein's *Judaism: A Historical Interpretation*.[23]

In his discussion, which includes an exposition on Talmudic hermeneutics, Razzouk regularly cited the Soncino Talmud to explain to his readers the broader context of the Talmudic passages to which his secondary sources refer. In his chapter on the orders of the Talmud, Razzouk followed and expanded on the introductions of the orders offered by the Soncino edition. In addition, Razzouk provided a synopsis not only of each of the six orders but of each of the sixty-three tractates of the Talmud.[24] All of the chapters, including the one on the place of the Talmud in the life of the Jews,[25] are strikingly dispassionate in tone. Razzouk relied on informed, sympathetic, and even, at times, apologetic Jewish secondary scholarship, and avoided tendentious descriptions.

Rejecting Antisemitism to Defend the Palestinians

If the PLO researcher ultimately concluded, after studying the Talmud, that the ancient text failed to prove Jewish moral iniquity, why did the PLO Research Center publicize these findings? Why bother to disabuse Arabic-language readers of their misapprehensions regarding the work? The answer, in part, may lie with the scholarly gravitas of the researcher, Razzouk, and of the director general of the Center, Anis Sayegh.[26]

The matter, however, may be more complicated, and connected to the broader interests of the PLO and its Research Center. Others in the Arab world, as we have seen, believed that the Talmud demonstrated Jewish moral depravity and the Jews' global conspiracy, both key features, as these critics saw it, of Zionism. That the readings of the Talmud on which these earlier and contemporary Arab writers relied were produced by European antisemites seemed of little import.

Upon completing his study of the Talmud, Razzouk was of a different mind. In his introduction to *al-Talmud wa-l-Sahyuniyya*, Razzouk wrote:

> The European tradition of antisemitism and hostility toward the Jews and oppressing them for religious or other reasons is a legacy with a weighty burden on the contemporary Western world. There are still European countries and peoples that sink to the ground under it [i.e., this burden] and suffer because of it in a variety of ways, despite all the attempts to get rid of it and overcome it or to transcend it by means of a "guilt complex." Why should we burden ourselves with such matters that harm our cause and disfigure its reputation and undermine its liberational and nationalist character? Disdain for facts will not serve our purposes at all.[27]

Razzouk asserted that, far from helping Arabs in their battle against Zionism, accepting antisemitism actually harmed them.[28]

Having earned his PhD in philosophy in post-Holocaust Germany, Razzouk was well aware of the costs of antisemitism, and not just for its victims.[29] Sayegh agreed. In the view of the PLO Research Center, the Palestinian cause was just, no doubt. As Sayegh put it in his foreword to *al-Talmud wa-l-Sahyuniyya*, the Palestinian conflict with Israel "is fundamentally and essentially a battle of right versus wrong."[30] Precisely because this was the case, there was no reason to associate the Palestinians' fundamentally just movement with a fundamentally unjust ideology such as antisemitism, thereby tainting the Palestinians' cause with this ugly product of Europe. Doing so was, in Sayegh's view, both unnecessary and ultimately self-defeating.

As this assertion was contained in a book written in Arabic, the intended readers here were, in the main, Arabs. The goal was to convince fellow Arabs of the fallaciousness of antisemitic theories (whether the blood libel or the *Protocols of the Elders of Zion*, both of which were allegedly linked to the Talmud) so that they would cease to employ them in their otherwise just battle against Zionism and Israel. In fact, before Razzouk published this book, even the Center had published works that casually defamed the Talmud. In *On*

Zionist Literature, for instance, which the Center issued in 1967, the influential Palestinian activist-author Ghassan Kanafani described the Talmud as "a book of bloody violence, hatred and extremism."[31] For this reason, moreover, it was critical that the publisher of this book be the PLO Research Center, rather than some other Arab institution. These PLO intellectuals, based in the Research Center, were arguing that for the sake of (and not despite the need for) the liberation of Palestine, antisemitism must be repudiated.

On the Relationship between the Talmud and Zionism

There was another separate, though related, motivation for investigating the Talmud and publishing the book about it. The two sections of the book thus far considered—the first on Arab misconceptions about the Talmud and the second an introduction to the text of the Talmud—build up to the third and final section of the book, which concerns the relationship between the Talmud and Zionism. If the Talmud was not the spiritual guide or blueprint for the *Protocols of the Elders of Zion;* if it was not some nefarious source of Jewish immorality and vice; if it was rather, as Razzouk demonstrated, a multivocal collection of all kinds of Jewish discourse from antiquity and late antiquity— what connection did it have to Zionism? Was the Talmud relevant for a proper understanding of Zionism? Underlying this question was a more basic one that, as we have seen, preoccupied the PLO Research Center in these years, especially after the 1967 war: What was the relationship between Zionism and Judaism?[32]

The opening epigraph of the first chapter of Razzouk's section on Zionism and the Talmud is a quote, translated into Arabic, from a 1959 article by Rabbi Richard Singer.[33] Singer wrote:

> Talmudic Judaism has an interesting attitude toward Palestine. The Talmud has little use for the mystique of land and soil and people so attractive to so many of our coreligionists. The religious emphasis of the Talmud was placed on the Torah—on the unique moral and ethical insights of Judaism. The religious leadership and emphasis of the Talmud was Torah-centered, Judaism-centered, rather than land-centered. This has been an embarrassment for contemporary Jewish nationalists.[34]

According to Singer, the Talmud is focused on the Torah, morality, and ethics, not on physicality or geography. The Talmud, Singer argued, was a religious source that Zionists had to explain away or ignore as they made their case for a Jewish nation-state in Palestine. Razzouk disagreed. Having reviewed the Talmud, he did not accept Singer's generalization about the Talmud's overall lack of interest in the Land of Israel.

In contrast to Singer, Razzouk offered a more nuanced assessment of Zionist engagement with the Talmud. As we have seen, at the same time that he was writing *al-Talmud wa-l-Sahyuniyya*, Razzouk served as part of the PLO Research Center team charged with translating Arthur Hertzberg's compendium *The Zionist Idea: A Historical Analysis and Reader*. Razzouk had thus read the classics of Zionist thought. From his reading of these texts, Razzouk concluded that Singer might have been right that the Talmud was insignificant in the thought of some later secular Zionists who, as Razzouk put it, "grew up in a non-talmudic environment." However, Razzouk asserted, based on his reading of the Zionist classics, the claim of the Talmud's irrelevance to Zionism "does not at all apply to those early Zionists who paved the way for the Herzlian call. We have in their writings . . . many of its [the Talmud's] statements and teachings." Razzouk contended that "the talmudic influence appears absolutely clearly among this first flock of Zionists who wrote in the middle of last century and since the beginning of the second half of it."[35] For the earliest Zionists, if not for all the later ones, the Talmud was crucial for the formation of their nationalist thought.

Next, Razzouk proceeded to introduce and analyze the writings of key early Zionists. Following the Zionist pantheon Hertzberg had constructed in *The Zionist Idea*, Razzouk started with Rabbi Yehuda Alkalai. "This Zionist advocate was influenced to a great extent," began Razzouk, "by the teaching of Jewish Kaballah, just as the talmudic influence is clearly reflected in his writings." Razzouk explained that "at the beginning of his article on 'The Third Redemption,'" which was excerpted in Hertzberg's compendium, "we find Alkalai citing the talmudic interpretation of a saying in the Torah: 'Return, O Lord, unto the many thousands of the families of Israel' (Numbers 10:36)." The Hebrew words used for "many thousands," *rivvot alfe*, can literally be rendered "tens of thousands, thousands." Addressing the double use of the plural form, "tens of thousands" and "thousands," Razzouk noted, the Tannaim in tractate Yevamot 64a explain that the verse demonstrates that "the Divine Presence can be felt only if there are at least two thousands and two tens of thousands [i.e., 22,000] of Israelites together."[36]

Though Razzouk generally followed Hertzberg's translation of Alkalai here, he substituted the word *Tannaim* (the term used for the rabbis of the mishnaic period), for Hertzberg's "rabbis." Razzouk knew that the rabbis referred to in this Talmudic passage were *Tannaim* because he followed the citation for Yevamot 64a in Hertzberg's endnotes and looked it up in his Soncino edition.[37] Having studied the terminology of the Talmud, with an interest in the different stages of rabbinic development, Razzouk apparently recognized the phrase "Our rabbis taught" (*tanu rabbanan*) as referring to a tannaic tradition.

Alkalai had argued that there must be large numbers of Jews living in the Holy Land before the redemption could occur and, by implication, that Jews could not wait until the messianic redemption before immigrating to Palestine. With the Soncino edition of Yevamot in hand, Razzouk investigated the literary context of Alkalai's Talmudic proof text: "If we look back to the conversations of the rabbis in the previous pages of this commentary, we find that they revolve around the question of procreation.[38] Rabbi Eliezer declares (Yevamot 63b, p. 426) that one who refrains from participating in increasing the Jewish race [*al-ʿirq*] is like someone who spills blood."[39] Razzouk noted that to support this claim, Rabbi Eliezer cited Genesis 9:6–7, biblical verses that forbid murder and command procreation, which, according to this interpretation, suggest that the failure to have children is tantamount to murder. When the Talmudic discussion reaches "the teaching of the *Tannaim*" that Alkalai addressed in his essay, Razzouk noted, the rabbis "link the necessary number of Israelites to the establishment of the divine presence among them." Razzouk explained that "If one man were missing from this magical number," 22,000, "and the duties of procreation were not fulfilled, the divine presence would depart Israel!"[40] None of this appeared in Hertzberg. Rather, it was Razzouk's attempt to understand Alkalai's view and explain it to Arabic readers by turning to the text of the Talmud in its modern English translation.

Similarly, even when Alkalai, in Hertzberg's edition, offered an interpretation of a biblical passage without providing a Talmudic basis, Razzouk looked to the Talmud to show the tradition in which Alkalai was operating. For instance, Alkalai highlighted that the biblical patriarch Jacob purchased land in Shechem "to teach his descendants that the soil of the Holy Land must be purchased from its non-Jewish owners." Razzouk noted that the concern for purchasing and owning territory in the Land of Israel "appears frequently in the Talmud in different and various ways. In the tractate 'Avodah Zarah' or idolatry (20b–21a, pages 108–109), we read, for example . . . one law of the Mishnah that says: 'One should not lease houses to them in the Land of Israel; and it is needless to mention fields.' But outside [the Land of Israel], this is permitted. By 'them' is meant all people who are not Jewish." Razzouk concluded that "As long as 'outside' was a far distance from Palestine, the Talmud expresses unrivaled tolerance." According to the Talmud, wrote Razzouk, "in Syria it is permitted to lease houses, but not fields, to non-Jews." Razzouk noted that "the talmudic justification for forbidding the sale of Jewish homes in Syria to non-Israelites" is the fear that this "would lead to selling houses also in 'the Land of Israel.'"[41] If Razzouk felt affronted by the Talmudic discussion of whether Jews are permitted to sell or lease land and homes to non-Jews in Syria or Palestine, he did not say so here. His contention was straightforward: to understand the value Alkalai placed on Jewish land ownership in Palestine, one needed to explore the Talmudic traditions in which Alkalai was immersed.

Razzouk had a similar view of the other religious proto-Zionist in Hertzberg's pantheon, the Posen-born Ashkenazic rabbi Zvi Hirsch Kalischer (1795–1874). To analyze his writings, Razzouk looked not only to Hertzberg's compendium but also to Moses Hess's *Rome and Jerusalem*, which cites and engages with Kalischer's ideas. "There is no doubt," asserted Razzouk, that Kalischer "was thoroughly familiar with the Talmud along with his mystical leanings." In fact, explained Razzouk, Jewish sources about Kalischer indicate that

> his extensive study of the Talmud is what persuaded him that the redemption requires the preparation of the masses, and this is not simply the Jews' observance of their religious duties and commandments in their Diaspora. Rather, its fulfilment requires the Jews' taking refuge in settlement activities and practical colonization in Palestine.[42]

Razzouk discussed Kalischer's plans for purchasing land in Palestine, resettling Jews there, establishing self-defense organizations, and training Jewish youth in agriculture along with sciences and traditional religious subjects. While the initial progress would necessarily be slow, the efforts would continue, wrote Kalischer, until "the country gradually comes into our possession, and we own the Holy Land in accordance with what the prophets prophesied." Razzouk cited Kalischer's assertion, quoted in *Rome and Jerusalem*, that the Jews' responsibility to "take the initiative and inaugurate the beginning" of the redemption by resettling Palestine was grounded in "numerous citations from Talmud and Midrash." In other words, "the talmudic roots" underlying Kalischer's ideas "are abundant here by the testimony of Rabbi Kalischer himself," concluded Razzouk.[43] Rabbi Singer's claim that there was no significant connection between the Talmud and Zionism was, in Razzouk's view, refuted by figures such as Alkalai and Kalischer.

Though he vigorously challenged the claim that the Talmud was wholly unrelated to Zionism, Razzouk did not argue the opposite—that Zionism emerged entirely from the Talmud or that all Zionists were driven by Talmudic mandate. Rather, Razzouk perceived a spectrum of Talmudic influence on various Zionists. Razzouk portrayed the Bonn-born socialist Moses Hess (1812–1875), for instance, as a liminal figure. On the one hand, contended Razzouk, the title of Hess's Jewish nationalist tract, *Rome and Jerusalem*, highlighted "the parallel that Hess sees between the movement for liberation and unity in Italy and its goal of Rome and the Jewish nationalist movement that looks toward Jerusalem." Hess, according to Razzouk, manifestly "borrows his nationalist ideas" from contemporaneous European nationalists.[44] On the other hand, notwithstanding the influence contemporary European nationalisms had on his philosophy, Hess's work was "filled with references and allusions that go back to Talmudic sources." Among the clearest examples of Hess's turn to the Talmud, for Razzouk, was the appearance in Hess's work of "the doctrine of the messiah in its Talmudic form." Razzouk pointed to Hess's reference to Rabbi Yohanan in tractate Sanhedrin who said "it is only with the coming of the messiah and the establishing of the messianic kingdom that the purpose of creation will be accomplished."[45] In Hess's "Sabbath of History," a notion he developed in *Rome and Jerusalem*, Razzouk heard "Talmudic echoes that repeat in these ideas, perhaps coming indirectly." Razzouk concluded his discussion of Hess as follows: "It might be that these chains of tradition [*al-asanid*] do not rest on the Talmud alone, but Hess's citing them . . . has significance concerning the Talmudic elements in the man's Zionism and concerning his concept of Jewish nationalism."[46] In other words, while the "chains of tradition" in Hess's proto-Zionism could be traced as much to European nationalism as to Talmudic texts and precepts, the considerable attention Hess paid to the Talmud suggests the enduring power of its ideas in the formation of his nationalism.

Perhaps the most incisive Talmudic reading that Razzouk provided was in his discussion of the Lithuanian-born Eliezer Ben-Yehuda (1858–1922). Still using *The Zionist Idea* as his guide to Zionist ideology, Razzouk analyzed Ben-Yehuda's 1880 letter to the publisher of the Hebrew journal *ha-Shahar*, which Hertzberg had translated. In that letter, Ben-Yehuda quoted the Talmudic adage that "Whoever lives outside the Land of Israel is like a man without a God." As in the previous cases, when he came across a reference to the Talmud in Hertzberg's reader, Razzouk turned to his Soncino translation to understand and then to explain the literary context.[47] Razzouk discovered that this

statement from tractate Ketubbot was contradicted by a statement of a different Talmudic rabbi, Rabbi Judah, on the same page: "Whoever goes up from
Babylonia to the Land of Israel transgresses a positive commandment." Show-
ing other related rabbinic disagreements in tractate Ketubbot, Razzouk concluded: "It appears through all this that the Talmudic position is not settled
on one opinion, except for the agreement on the distinction between the holy
lands" on the one hand, "and the unclean or impure lands," on the other. For
Razzouk, the Talmud's conflicting views on the question of whether it is obligatory for Jews to immigrate to and settle in Palestine were central. "The bottom
line," wrote Razzouk, "is that Eliezer Ben-Yehuda of course cites the expressions of the Talmud that meet his Zionist goal and support his argument."[48]
For him, Razzouk recognized, Talmudic knowledge was not a prime motivator
determining Zionist goals but rather a medium to be employed toward a priori
Zionist ends.

If, in Razzouk's view, Ben-Yehuda's appeal to Talmudic texts and precepts
was more instrumental than fundamental, this was even more pronounced for
Leo Pinsker (1821–1891).[49] The Russian-born author of the 1882 pamphlet
Auto-Emancipation cited the Talmudic aphorism of Hillel: "If I am not for
myself, who will be for me? And if not now, when?"[50] Notwithstanding the
pride of place Pinsker gave to this Talmudic quotation, Razzouk asserted that
"the author of *Auto-Emancipation* reflects in his writings and ideas the influence of Western ideas and culture more than he reflects anything clearly linked
to the Talmud."[51] Even beyond his extra-Talmudic ideas and his disrespect
for particular Talmudic concepts, Pinsker actually blamed certain Talmudic
beliefs for the deplorable condition of contemporary Jews. Razzouk wrote
that, for Pinsker, the Jews exhibited insufficient "national dignity and self-
respect" and Pinsker "attributes this deficiency on the part of the Jews . . . to
their doctrine of waiting for the 'messiah.'"[52] Razzouk concluded that "one
might say that Talmudism [*al-Talmudiyya*] has no influence in Pinsker's pamphlet on *Auto-Emancipation*." The true source of and motivation for Pinsker's
ideas were, rather, "nationalist ideas that were then prevalent."[53]

Whether because of the deep and explicit influence of Talmudic teachings
on Zionists, or because of the time they spent studying in Talmudic academies, or because of their instrumentalization of Talmudic precepts, or even
because of their active negation of those precepts, the Talmud was part of the early
proto-Zionist story. That changed, according to Razzouk's assessment of the
Zionist pantheon, with the Austro-Hungarian-born Theodor Herzl (1860–1904),
whose biography in *The Zionist Idea* we discussed above. Razzouk opened his

section on Herzl with the following appraisal of the relationship between Herzl and the Talmud: "When we come to Theodor Herzl himself it becomes entirely impossible to observe the Talmudic influences because the founder of political Zionism was raised far from the traditional Jewish environment. It is futile to search in the man's writings and diaries for clear reference to the Talmud."[54] The "foundation" on which Herzlian Zionism rests, wrote Razzouk, is not the Talmud but rather Herzl's "analysis of the Jewish condition," with the "prevailing conditions for eastern European Jews" seen "as the model and example of this condition." Razzouk knew that "surrounding Herzl at the start of his Zionist period was a circle of a number of Talmudists and Hasidim" and yet, argued Razzouk, there does not appear in Herzl's thought "any influence from their ideas."[55]

Razzouk, to be clear, did not deny the possibility of *religious* influences in Herzl's upbringing and even, perhaps, in his Zionism. Having read Alex Bein's biography of Herzl, Razzouk noted the interest Herzl's grandfather had in the writings of the religious proto-Zionist rabbi Yehuda Alkalai. Pointing to Herzl's annual holidays with his grandfather until the latter's death when Herzl was twenty years old, Razzouk cited Bein's suggestion that perhaps it was during his grandfather's visits "that the seed was sown which after long and invisible subterranean growth broke out in seed and flower in the sight of all men."[56] Notably, Razzouk mentioned this idea without expressing any particular skepticism about it. Similarly, following Bein's biography, Razzouk recounted Herzl's Reform synagogue attendance during his childhood and even his retrospective claims, later in life, of messianic pretensions.[57]

What mattered most for Razzouk in this study, though, were not religious but explicitly *Talmudic* influences on Zionism. On this question, Razzouk concluded concerning Herzl that his biography is devoid of such reference. While it is possible, conceded Razzouk, that "the founder of Zionism might have been exposed to Talmudic influences indirectly or through his reading and contacts with people close to him," Herzl's focus was, rather, "on scientific discovery literature along with his deep fascination with modern technology." The Talmud was not a text of concern for him. In contrast to pre-Herzlian proto-Zionism, then, beginning with Herzl, Razzouk discerned much less, if any, interest in Talmudic references and proof texts. This does not mean that Judaism disappeared entirely from Herzlian and post-Herzlian Zionist discourse, but rather that that Judaism was no longer centered on the Talmud.

In summarizing his conclusions about the relationship between Zionism and the Talmud, Razzouk wrote, "That religious longing for Zion found explicit expression in religious Zionism is not sufficient reason to grant the Talmud responsibility for the development of Zionism." Jewish religious longing for Zion can be found throughout the Jews' sacred texts, whether in the pre-Talmudic Hebrew Bible or in post-Talmudic medieval poetry; it is not exclusively, or even especially, Talmudic, acknowledged Razzouk. "Therefore," he explained, "it is difficult to discover and specify the direct influence of the Talmud." Indeed, Razzouk suggested, it is possible that "the mystical and kabbalistic tendencies among some circles in eastern Europe are closer to Zionism in certain ways than is the Talmud," even as "most of its teachings and beliefs derive from aggadic sources in the Talmud." Taken as a whole, "the religious influence in Zionism is difficult to deny, and the Talmud constitutes a primary element in the religious education for the Jews."[58]

The PLO, the Talmud, and the Claim of Anti-Antisemitism

This tripartite, PLO-sponsored study of the Talmud and Zionism ultimately yielded a rather sophisticated, and not especially provocative, assessment of the complex relationship between the Talmud and Zionism that not only denies but itself defies conspiracy theories. And that was exactly the PLO's point here: the case for their liberation movement stood on its own merits. There was no need to fear an engagement with a sacred Jewish text and its relationship to modern Jewish nationalism. The Palestinian cause required no manipulation or fabrication of the facts about the enemy. Jews, Judaism, Zionism, and Israel could be confronted with intellectual openness and even some degree of empathy, both because of the righteousness of the Palestinian cause, in the minds of the PLO researchers, and because, as we saw Razzouk explain above, the cause is only harmed when its advocates turn a blind eye to or, worse yet, themselves employ anti-Jewish prejudice. In his critique of Palestinian and Arab uses of antisemitism, Razzouk asked his readers rhetorically, "Until when will we remain our own worst enemy, continuing to prejudice the justice of our cause?"[59]

This argument calls for a reconsideration of the relationship between the PLO and antisemitism, a subject of continued interest and polemic, within academe and beyond. At least in official statements, the PLO generally maintained a practice (with precedents or roots going back to the Late Ottoman period)[60] of distinguishing between its enmity toward Zionism and Israel, on the one hand, and its amity toward Jews and Judaism, on the other. Recall PLO chairman Yasser Arafat's assertion in his landmark speech before the United

Nations General Assembly in 1974 that "since its inception, our revolution has not been motivated by racial or religious factors. Its target has never been the Jew, as a person, but racist Zionism and aggression. In this sense, ours is a revolution for the Jew, as a human being. We are struggling so that Jews, Christians, and Muslims may live in equality, enjoying the same rights and assuming the same duties, free from racial or religious discrimination."[61] In light of this expressed goal, Arafat was careful to "distinguish between Judaism and Zionism," explaining that "while we maintain our opposition to the colonialist Zionist movement, we respect the Jewish faith."[62]

Notwithstanding such assertions, charges of antisemitism are regularly leveled at the PLO.[63] In *A Genealogy of Evil: Anti-Semitism from Nazism to Islamic Jihad*, antisemitism and Holocaust scholar David Patterson portrays the PLO, represented by the organization's Covenant, as fundamentally and essentially antisemitic.[64] "In keeping with the anti-Semitism that characterizes Islamic Jihadism," argues Patterson, "the PLO Charter buys into the 'world Jewish conspiracy' libel." The PLO, Patterson contends, "with Arafat at its helm, is the champion and defender of humanity in the eternal struggle against the eternal Jew."[65] Accepting the view that the PLO's "mindset" was one of "absolute antisemitism," historian Joel Fishman similarly maintains that "even before the founding of the PLO in 1964, this mindset was current and has not changed to the present." Perceiving Palestinian perspectives on Israel as "intransigent hatred," Fishman argues that "the position of the Palestinians and their supporters has remained frozen in time and has not evolved. They have become entrapped by religion and ideology."[66] For Fishman, the PLO's religious and ideological fanaticism have made the organization not only obstinately opposed to Israel but also rigidly (and timelessly) antisemitic.

Those who see deep-seated antisemitism in the PLO tend to focus less on the words of the organization and more on its violent actions. Little dispositive value is thus assigned to statements by Arafat or any other PLO leader that the PLO was not antisemitic. Indeed, the PLO's denial of its own antisemitism is, for many critics, just another piece of the group's duplicity, a rhetorical tool in its battle against the Jews.[67] Insofar as this debate concerns underlying, even unconscious, motivations, my analysis of the PLO Research Center's writings about the Talmud cannot contribute much. Moreover, the PLO was an umbrella organization consisting of various constituencies with radically different ideological orientations.[68] Given this diversity, there is no reason to think that there existed a single "true motivation" for "the PLO" or PLO actors, let alone that that motivation might be ascertainable.

What is significant here is the window that Razzouk's text opens to us onto the explicit, intra-PLO—and, importantly, Arabic-language—consideration of and reflection on the impact of antisemitism on the PLO and Palestinian nationalism. Here was not simply an assertion of friendliness toward Jews and Judaism but an argument that the alternative—namely, hostility toward Jews and Judaism—was harmful to the Palestinian cause.[69] Partisans on either side of the PLO-antisemitism debate could seize this fact and employ it to support their respective positions: either, here is proof of the degree to which anti-semitism (or, in this case, its denial) was used, *functionally*, to serve the interests of the Palestinians, without meaningful concern for the moral implications of this form of hatred, or, here is proof of the degree to which PLO intellectuals were eager to root out antisemitism, using any argument available (even that of Palestinian self-interest) to convince supporters to desist from partaking in the morally loathsome ideology. Thus, while the analysis presented in this chapter does not resolve the question of whether the PLO was driven by anti-semitism, it does offer critical insight into the internal conversation among the PLO Research Center scholars and consideration of what was at stake in this question in the years following the 1967 war. Whether to embrace antisemitic tropes and assumptions, or to reject them, was a topic of substantive debate about how best to achieve the goals of the Palestinian national movement.[70] The PLO Research Center, through this publication, argued strongly to eliminate antisemitism and to base the movement's liberational goals and strategies on sounder historical and ideological ground.

For key intellectuals and leaders at the PLO Research Center, that ground was to be discovered, as we have seen, through study, including serious engagement with Judaism and core Jewish texts. These were texts that the PLO researchers found on the shelves of the Research Center library.[71] That the Research Center rested its argument against the embrace of antisemitism on such engagement is a critical legacy of the Center.[72]

7

The American Council for Judaism

AMERICAN JEWISH ANTI-ZIONISM

EVEN AS THEY emphasized the religious background and motivations of some of the early Zionist leaders, the PLO researchers were aware that there were Jews who considered Zionism problematic, objectionable, or even abhorrent from the perspective of Judaism.[1] To understand the PLO's engagement with this internal Jewish critique of Jewish nationalism and Zionism, we need to step back in time and cross an ocean, to Pittsburgh, Pennsylvania, in 1885.

There, a group of Reform rabbis declared, "We consider ourselves no longer a nation, but a religious community, and therefore expect neither a return to Palestine, nor a sacrificial worship under the sons of Aaron, nor the restoration of any of the laws concerning the Jewish state." The rabbis' message was meant to reach a variety of audiences: their fellow Jews in America and those back in Europe, along with their Christian neighbors, some of whom continued to question Jews' loyalty to the countries in which they resided.[2] One audience these nineteenth-century Reform Jews did not imagine as they penned these words was the PLO, an organization that would be founded nearly eighty years later. But the PLO's intellectual elite—including its founding chairman and those at the heart of the organization's think tank, the PLO Research Center— was indeed fascinated by the rabbinic declaration that became known as the Pittsburgh Platform, and by the classical Reform ideology that the Pittsburgh Platform embodied.

In this chapter, I consider the Research Center's engagement with Reform Jewish principles and its appropriation of classical Reform ideas for the PLO's ideological battle against Zionism. I then turn to the question of origin or influence, investigating the means through which the PLO researchers learned of the by-then long-overturned Pittsburgh Platform.[3] I identify a direct source, namely, the controversial twentieth-century American anti-Zionist Reform rabbi Elmer Berger. While the rabbis in Pittsburgh had no crystal ball, Berger made ample use of their Platform in his collaboration with Palestinian nationalists. I conclude the chapter with reflections on the broader question of how mutually hostile nationalisms relate to each other's religious traditions and on the unexpected alliances fostered by debates over the nature of Jewishness.

The Pittsburgh Platform and the PLO Covenant

The PLO's Covenant (Arabic: *mithaq*), drafted in 1964, offers the most famous Palestinian nationalist definition of the Jews and Judaism. The Covenant, as we have seen, was a carefully crafted document each word of which, Shukairy claimed, was contemplated fastidiously.[4] In the Covenant, the PLO insisted that Judaism is "a heavenly religion" (*din samawi*) and, as such, it is not "an independent nationality" (*qawmiyya dhat wujud mustaqill*)." Moreover, "the Jews do not constitute a single nation (*sha'b wahad*) with an identity of its own," but rather "they are citizens (*muwatinun*) of the states to which they belong."[5] Though the Covenant underwent revision in 1968, when it was again ratified, this conception of Jewishness (found in article 18 in the 1964 version and in article 20 of the 1968 version) was left intact.

Similar to the Pittsburgh Platform, the PLO Covenant denies contemporary Jewish nationhood. Unlike the Reform rabbis, however, who perceived—even *enacted*—a shift in Jewish self-definition, the Covenant's crafters presented an essentialist evaluation of the Jews and Judaism. There, Judaism is a revealed religion, and nothing more. Despite this difference, we are left with a striking sense of similarity between the two approaches to Jewishness.[6] How might we account for this?

I propose that the correspondence between the Pittsburgh Platform's and the PLO's positions was far from happenstance. In fact, the year before he drafted the PLO Covenant and undertook the role of chairman of the PLO, Shukairy was already citing the Pittsburgh Platform. As chairman of the Palestine Arab Delegation, he addressed the Special Political Committee of the UN General Assembly during its November 1963 discussion of the "Report of the Commission-General of the United Nations Relief and Works Agency for Palestine Refugees in the Near East." Challenging the claims of Golda Meir, Israel's then-minister of foreign affairs, who had pointed to the Bible as a source of Israel's legitimacy, Shukairy asserted: "If we are to go to the Bible, we must seek the authority of people who know the Bible. Mrs. Meir does not know the Bible. She is not Rabbi Mrs. Meir. She is Mrs. Meir, and that is all. Let us go to the Rabbis and see what they say about the Bible."[7] Shukairy first cited Rabbi Hermann Adler's 1878 essay in the journal *The Nineteenth Century* in which he asserted that "ever since the conquest of Palestine by the Romans we have ceased to be a body politic."[8]

Next, Shukairy wrote, "we have also the pronouncement of the Rabbis in 1885, a group of the most distinguished Rabbis of the day, meeting in Pittsburgh, Pennsylvania," who proclaimed that "we consider ourselves no longer a nation but a religious community and therefore expect no return to Palestine."[9] For Shukairy, "this is the verdict of the Rabbis meeting in congregation and saying that they have ceased to be a nation, and expect no return to Palestine. If the Bible has better information [about the rightful owners of the Holy Land], you must abide by the pronouncement of those who know the Bible, and those who know the Bible are the Rabbis."[10] When Shukairy penned the PLO Covenant, he clearly had the Pittsburgh Platform in mind.

Shukairy cast a long shadow on the PLO, but his leadership and direct influence was short-lived. As we have seen, the PLO was created by the Arab League in the age of Egyptian president Gamal Abdel Nasser, and was originally seen as a tool of Nasserism. When Israel routed the Arab armies in 1967, Nasser and all associated with him lost legitimacy in the eyes of many in the Arab world, not least the Palestinians, who witnessed Israel's conquest of the remainder of historic Palestine from Egypt and Jordan. Under these circumstances, it was not long before Shukairy, linked as he was to the Arab League and to Nasser, was pushed out of his chairmanship, soon to be replaced, not by another legalist with an academic bent but rather by Yasser Arafat, a young (two decades Shukairy's junior) militant leader of the Palestinian National Liberation Movement (Fateh), founded in 1959.[11] Notwithstanding the change in leadership and focus, PLO interest in the Pittsburgh Platform did not abate. In fact, it remained a central pillar of the PLO's conception of Judaism and its polemics against Zionism, especially in the work of the PLO Research Center.

The Pittsburgh Platform in the PLO *Handbook*

One of the Research Center's many published volumes was the 1969 work *Dalil al-Qadiyya al-Filastiniyya* (an abridged version of which was issued in English the same year as *A Handbook to the Palestine Question*).[12] The *Dalil*, which we encountered above, is a 261-page myths-versus-facts style, questions-and-answers guide for defenders of the Palestinian cause.[13] Anis Sayegh, the second director general of the Research Center, explained in his foreword to the handbook that it is intended for "the thousands of Arab citizens, especially students, who travel beyond the Arab homeland," who feel uncomfortable when "the Zionist enemy poses questions to which they are unable to give satisfactory answers based on facts."[14] To compose the book, Ibrahim al-Abid, along with a number of PLO Research Center researchers, reviewed "hundreds of the enemy's books and articles and extracted the questions that appear in Zionist books." In addition to its review of Zionist texts, the Center also surveyed "the tens of Arab students who are studying in European and American universities and collected the questions that they said had been posed to them."[15] Combining analysis of Zionist texts with personal surveys of Arab students at Western universities, the questions found in the *Dalil*, Sayegh contended, represented the questions about the "the Palestinian problem" that an Arab abroad might expect to encounter. The answers the *Dalil* offered to these frequently asked questions, Sayegh asserted, were presented in a manner "far from the sentimentality that oftentimes is the cause of Arabs' failure in debates with foreigners."[16] Moreover, the answers offered were not those of "a particular point of view" but rather expressed "the view of the Palestinian national movement in general."[17]

In the book's second chapter, on "the Jewish question," al-Abid twice cited the Reform movement's Pittsburgh Platform. The first time, it was to answer the question "Have the Jews been continually conscious of being a nation and a people [*ka-shaʿb*] throughout the ages?"[18] Among his proposed responses, al-Abid wrote that "in 1883 [*sic*] the Jewish Congress at Pittsburgh, Pennsylvania declared: 'We consider ourselves no longer [*baʿd al-yawm*; literally: after today, or from this day forward] a nation [*umma*] but a religious community [*jamaʿa diniyya*].'"[19] The second time, al-Abid offered a response to the Zionist claim that "Jews consider every country except Palestine a land of exile and Palestine the only guarantee for their continued existence." Al-Abid repeated the Pittsburgh assembly's insistence that they were no longer a nation, adding that they "therefore expect neither a return to Palestine, nor a sacrificial worship under the sons of Aaron, nor a restoration of the laws concerning the Jewish state."[20] To refute the claims that Jews had always retained their national consciousness and that they regarded anywhere outside of Palestine as "exile," there was no better proof, from the perspective of "the Palestinian national movement in general," than the Jews' own Pittsburgh Platform.

By the 1960s, however, when Shukairy cited the Pittsburgh Platform at the UN and when al-Abid sat in Beirut to compile the *Dalil*, the Pittsburgh Platform was a distant memory for most Reform Jews, not only because eight decades had passed since it was proclaimed in 1885, but also because the Reform movement had long since officially disavowed its implied anti-Zionist stance.[21] In 1937, forty years after the First Zionist Congress and four years since Hitler's rise to power in Germany, American Reform rabbis re-reformed their Judaism. "In view of the changes that have taken place in the modern world and the consequent need of stating anew the teachings of Reform Judaism," the Central Conference of American Rabbis (CCAR) declared in Columbus, Ohio (in what became known as the Columbus Platform), "in the rehabilitation of Palestine, the land hallowed by memories and hopes, we behold the promise of renewed life for many of our brethren." Moreover, the rabbis asserted that "all Jewry" had an "obligation" to assist in Palestine's "upbuilding as a Jewish homeland by endeavoring to make it not only a haven of refuge for the oppressed but also a center of Jewish culture and spiritual life."[22] While these Reform rabbis in 1937 still maintained that Jews everywhere "assume and seek to share loyally the full duties and responsibilities of citizenship and to create seats of Jewish knowledge and religion," their embrace of the upbuilding of a Jewish homeland in Palestine was a dramatic reversal of classical Reform ideology.

The PLO was founded nearly three decades after the Columbus Platform overturned the Pittsburgh Platform. How then, did Shukairy or al-Abid come to rely on that of Pittsburgh? There were Palestinian Arab intellectuals interested in arguments against the Jews' claim to nationhood ever since there were Jews who sought to establish themselves as a nation in Palestine.[23] But the PLO's appeal to the Pittsburgh Platform and principled Reform anti-Zionism had a more direct source: Rabbi Elmer Berger and his American Council for Judaism (ACJ).[24]

Rabbi Elmer Berger

Berger, born in Cleveland, Ohio in 1908, studied at the University of Cincinnati before undertaking rabbinical studies at Hebrew Union College, the American Reform seminary.[25] After his ordination in 1932, he served as rabbi of various Reform congregations in Michigan for a decade.[26] In 1942, a half-decade after the Columbus Platform redefined the classical Reform Judaism Berger had imbibed at HUC,[27] and three years into World War II, Berger wrote an essay titled "Why I Am a Non-Zionist."[28] Shortly thereafter, he was appointed head of the American Council for Judaism, a newly founded organization that promoted the Reform movement's earlier anti-Zionism.[29] Berger propagated his anti-Zionist views, first at the helm of the ACJ, which he led from 1942 until 1955; then as its executive vice president until 1968; and, finally, in his remaining three decades leading a still newer one-man organization called the American Jewish Alternatives to Zionism (AJAZ). For Berger, the idea of a "Jewish people" was a fallacy.[30] "I cannot write about a Jewish people because there is none," he asserted in 1945 in his first full monograph, *The Jewish Dilemma*.[31] "To designate them [Jews] as a national group is a vestige of the past," Berger wrote. "Enlightened states always refer to Jews as citizens of Jewish faith," he continued, and thus "as nations emerge from absolutism and oligarchy and join the march of freedom into representative government, Jews slowly get out from under the concept of a restrictive, separate nationality group."[32] In these lines, Berger affirmed the historical process whereby Jews became "no longer" (in the language of the Pittsburgh Platform) a separate nation but rather an emancipated, integrated religious community among other religious communities of fellow citizens. In a 1957 book, *Judaism or Jewish Nationalism: The Alternative to Zionism*, Berger wrote that "the Council's approach to Judaism is essentially the same as that of the Pittsburgh Platform."[33]

Berger's stance provoked a fierce response from fellow Jews. As one contemporary reviewer of *The Jewish Dilemma* put it in the *American Sociological Review*, classical Reform's anti-Zionism "was understandable in the light of achievements of emancipation in the first half of the [twentieth] century . . . but the retention of these effete shibboleths in the era of genocide is scarcely realistic." In Berger's "acidulous tract," this reviewer continued, "there is scant recognition of the bitter realities of the plight of Jewry in the age of crematoria," but rather "only homilies on the promise of democracy as providing automatic insurance of the safety of the Jews."[34] For many American Jewish readers, like this reviewer, Berger's position—written in the midst of the Holocaust—was outrageously, even dangerously, detached from reality.

American Jews were not the only ones to take note of Berger's work. The American Council for Judaism, and Berger as its chief spokesman, also caught the eye of Palestinian critics of Zionism and Israel. One such Palestinian critic was Fayez Sayegh. At some point in the early 1950s, as Berger recalled in his *Memoirs of an Anti-Zionist Jew*, he "received a letter on the stationery of the Lebanese Embassy in Washington." This letter, wrote Berger, "was from Fayez A. Sayegh," who "suggested that the next time I might come to Washington he would welcome an opportunity to meet and talk."[35] Berger accepted this invitation, which sparked an extended intellectual friendship. Of Sayegh, Berger wrote, "I enjoyed his intellectual coolness, which was not without passionate conviction and commitment to the cause of justice and political rights for the Palestinians." Remarking on the development of their relationship, Berger wrote that "we each had some things to learn from the Other. And without ever saying so, we explored each other's thinking. The process made us life-time friends."[36] Berger described his friendship with Sayegh as his "first genuine, free-wheeling and sustained relationship with any Arab."[37]

But Fayez Sayegh was decidedly not just "*any* Arab." More than a decade before he established the Research Center, Sayegh had invited Berger to address the convention of the Organization of Arab Students, meeting in Colorado, where Berger's topic was "How Should Arabs Present Their Case to the American Public?"[38] This was a question Berger was to confront again in the wake of the 1967 war, when he spoke at a banquet in Beirut on the topic "How Can the Arabs Explain Palestine to the West?"[39] at the invitation of sponsors Americans for Justice in the Middle East (founded by Americans at AUB after the Six-Day War); the Fifth of June Society (led initially by the Jaffa-born refugee Shafiq Kombargi);[40] and Friends of Jerusalem (a Christian Lebanese organization that advocated for the welfare of Christians in the Israeli-occupied West Bank).[41]

And when Berger spoke, Palestinian nationalists and their Arab supporters listened. Indeed, in the aforementioned speeches delivered before the Special Political Committee of the UN General Assembly in November 1963, Shukairy cited Berger's *Who Knows Better Must Say So*.[42] Though Shukairy stepped down from PLO leadership at the end of 1967, Berger's writings, and those of his associates in the American Council for Judaism (including William Thomas Mallison and Moshe Menuhin[43]) were cited frequently in PLO Research Center publications in the years immediately following the 1967 war. In fact, one of these publications was a 271-page book published in 1970 titled *The American Council for Judaism* (*al-Majlis al-Amriki li-l-Yahudiyya*). In introducing this book, the younger Sayegh brother, Anis, then director of the Center, wrote that "one of the oft-repeated claims among Arabs . . . is that every Jew is a Zionist, and that Judaism and Zionism are two names for the same thing." The Research Center aimed instead "to offer an honest picture of . . . Jewish tendencies, organizations, and movements that oppose or publicly challenge Zionism."[44] The book's author, Assʿad Razzouk, whom we met above, explained that drawing a distinction between Jew and Zionist was essential for the Palestinian nationalist effort.[45] Conflating "Jew" and "Zionist," he wrote, "is a mistake that leads to confusion in the strategy of the opposition and yields negative results for the struggle."[46] Emphasizing this distinction, Berger advised his Palestinian and Arab colleagues, held the key to their success.

In Razzouk's section on the "religious background" of Jewish opposition to Zionism, the Pittsburgh Platform takes pride of place. Razzouk noted the central role of the Bohemian-born American Reform rabbi Isaac Mayer Wise in articulating the Reform ideas, which "found their classical expression in the platform known as the Pittsburgh Platform," which Razzouk proceeded to translate into Arabic.[47] (The very next source Razzouk cited is Elmer Berger's *A Partisan History of Judaism* of 1951.[48]) The Pittsburgh Platform was central to the PLO Research Center's conception of Jewish opposition to Zionism and thus the critical element of historical, "religious background" that explained the outlook of the American Council for Judaism.

In 1968, two years before the publication of the PLO Research Center's book on the ACJ, Berger was forced out of the organization due to his response to the Six-Day War.[49] A *New York Times* article published on July 16, 1967, just over a month after the conclusion of the war, began by noting that while "most of the 5.5 million Jews in the United States reacted with pride and rejoicing" to Israel's swift military victory, "a small but prominent minority of American Jews looked upon the Arab-Israeli war as a 'tragedy,' and their leaders charged that their fellow Jews in Israel had embarked on 'aggression.'"[50] Notwithstanding their opposition to Zionism, the members of the ACJ were unwilling to tolerate this public attack on Israel after its sensational military victory and Berger was pushed out of the organization. As a former president of the ACJ explained in a note to the new executive director, "I know that our members, by and large, want to be assured that their continued support for the Council does not mean their undying hatred of the State of Israel or, of even greater importance, their endorsement of the position and tactics of the Arabs."[51]

Berger went on to found American Jewish Alternatives to Zionism. Although AJAZ had been in existence for less than two years when he published the aforementioned book, *The American Council for Judaism*, Razzouk subtitled the volume *Dirasa fi al-Badil al-Yahudi li-l-Sahyuniyya* (A Study in the Jewish Alternative to Zionism). Following Berger, Razzouk saw the ACJ as having betrayed its anti-Zionist values in its reaction to the 1967 war. Insofar as the ACJ "compromised its principles and shirked responsibility for the implications and applications" of those principles, wrote Razzouk, "it failed to embody the Jewish alternative to Zionism." Berger's AJAZ is thus the subject of the final pages of Razzouk's *al-Majlis*.[52] Noting that AJAZ's principles "do not differ much" from the stated values of the ACJ, Razzouk asked, "Will the successor succeed where the predecessor failed?" Only time will tell, answered Razzouk, but the success or failure of "the new alternative" will depend on whether it maintains "the line separating Judaism and Zionism." The narrower that line, the less viable a Jewish alternative to Zionism becomes. Even more relevant for the readers of *al-Majlis*, effacing the line between Judaism and Zionism "is not in the interests of the Arab perspective on Zionism." Rather, Razzouk concluded, "the single beneficiary of the deliberate confusion of universal religion and narrow racial [or racist, *al-'unsuriyya*] nationalism is undoubtedly the Zionist movement."[53]

Israel's Ambiguous Relationship to World Jewry

As Anis Sayegh wrote in his foreword to the April 1969 book *Isra'il wa-Yahud al-'Alam* (Israel and World Jewry), its assumed links to Jewish citizens of other countries made Israel an exception in the world of modern states. Indeed, according to the author, the asserted links between Israel and world Jewry were "illegal in terms of international political principles and international law." A study of this relationship would help explain, Sayegh asserted, why "the Arab countries do not consider Israel to be a regular state with sovereignty among the states of the region of the Middle East." The State of Israel has chosen to define itself and to act as something other than "a regular state";[54] its declared affiliation with Jews beyond its borders is a prime example of the state's anomaly.

In this book, PLO researcher Mustafa 'Abd al-'Aziz articulated three separate, albeit related, arguments concerning Israel's relationship with Jews abroad. The first was that by claiming a special relationship with and a certain responsibility for Jewish citizens of other countries, Israel violated a basic principle of international law—namely, that states exercise sovereignty only over their own territories and their own citizens.

The second argument 'Abd al-'Aziz set forth was that by claiming a connection to world Jewry, Israel undercut the proclaimed loyalty of Jews to the countries of which they were citizens. Moreover, Israel's claims complicated life for Jews abroad. Whereas a "policy of tolerance toward the Jews" currently "prevails in the world," 'Abd al-'Aziz argued, Israel was effectively working in opposition to this trend. Israel "slows the extent of Jews' integration in their societies and works to . . . isolate them from their nations [*shu'ubihim*]." Israel, through claiming this link to world Jewry, "actively helps to bring about waves of antisemitism that break out from doubt surrounding the loyalty and allegiance of the Jews of the world." For the welfare and security of world Jewry, ʿAbd al-ʿAziz contended, all "states of the world that desire peace for their citizens" must resist Israel's presumptions of responsibility for Jews beyond the state's borders.[55]

Third, ʿAbd al-ʿAziz claimed that Israel's asserted connection to citizens of other states violated basic principles of international law. Citizenship, wrote ʿAbd al-ʿAziz, was properly based on "a political bond, that is, belonging legally to a particular state," and not on "religious ties."

Yet ʿAbd al-ʿAziz identified what for him was a "glimmer of hope": that many Jews opposed Israel's claims of responsibility for "the Jewish people."[56] The publications of Elmer Berger and others associated with the ACJ filled a significant portion of ʿAbd al-ʿAziz's bibliography: twenty of the eighty-five English-language sources listed were either written by Berger or published by the ACJ.[57] Such Jews, wrote ʿAbd al-ʿAziz, "insist that they are an inseparable part of the national majority among whom they live" and that "they do not believe in Israel's proclamation that it is the natural place for all of the world's Jews." Moreover, ʿAbd al-ʿAziz noted in conclusion, these Jewish anti-Zionist heroes "oppose mixing the spiritual and the worldly."[58] For ʿAbd al-ʿAziz, in line with the views of the ACJ and of the PLO Covenant, Jewishness belonged in the realm of *al-ruhaniyat*, the spiritual, and had no proper place in the realm of temporal or secular law. The mixing of the two realms was a fundamental flaw in the logic and, consequently, the legitimacy of Zionism and Israel.

"The Heart and Soul of the Revival and Renaissance of the Palestinian Nation"

As we have seen, the PLO Research Center scholars saw Berger as a kindred spirit with respect to his perception of Jewishness. What did Berger, for his part, think of the PLO? While he was regularly accused of being more interested in the welfare of Arabs than of Jews, Berger denied this accusation. In his memoirs, published in 1978 by the Institute for Palestine Studies,[59] Berger wrote that his ACJ was

> *not* a pro-Arab organization nor were our primary concerns, in the first instance, with "Arab rights." All of my new Arab friends understood this. In fact, I have been told by more than one of them and more than once that it

was precisely my point-of-departure from American interests and my concern for the integrity of Judaism against the pollutions of Zionism's politics which gave me credibility in the Arab world. This Arab perception of my motivations never prevented the Zionist propagandists from charging me with "pro-Arabism," even of being paid by the Arab League.[60]

Berger's motivations remain open to debate. What is clear, however, is that he was right on the money in thinking that the more his views were perceived as part of internal American Jewish discourse and motivated by "authentically" American Jewish values and interests, the better these views served the Arab critics of Israel.

Notably, Berger's critique of Zionism went well beyond his insistence on the rejection of Jewish nationhood, and exposed what he saw as Israel's racist laws and acts.[61] Moreover, he ultimately expressed profound sympathy for Palestinian nationalism and specifically for the PLO. In 1983, a few years after the publication of his *Memoirs* and in the wake of the 1982 Israeli war against the PLO in Lebanon, Berger reviewed a book about the PLO published that same year. This book, Cheryl Rubenberg's *The Palestine Liberation Organization*, Berger wrote, "breathes a living soul into the recognized leaders of the Palestinian nation" and "eliminates any excuse for caricaturing the PLO as one-dimensional 'terrorists,' single-mindedly devoted to the 'destruction' of the State of Israel." Adopting a laudatory tone, Berger opined that the PLO's "dedication to the total welfare of its forcibly dispersed people approximates a religious commitment." In fact, the PLO's "network of institutions serving Palestinian education, arts, health services, labor organizations, and many other needs," Berger declared, is comparable "to only enlightened, humanistic, socially conscious States."[62]

Berger's encomium did not stop at the PLO as a whole. He singled out the Research Center as its crown jewel. "Perhaps the best reflection of the breadth and depth of the PLO's commitment to a long struggle," he wrote, "is the Palestine Research Center." The Center "was the heart and soul of the revival and renaissance of the Palestinian nation." Moreover, as the Research Center's work was intellectual and cultural rather than material or territorial, Berger wrote, it is "an element of Palestinianism which defies F-16's or cluster bombs," for "the intellectual and spiritual products of the Center would surmount the blitzkriegs of the Zionist State."[63] It is worth mentioning that Berger made no reference to the Center's dissemination of his own ideas and the potential conflict of interest that that might have entailed.

Berger, the ACJ, and the CIA

Another layer of complexity in this nexus between the PLO Research Center and the American Council for Judaism is the fact that Elmer Berger apparently had, as late as the 1950s, professional ties to the Central Intelligence Agency (CIA). Historian Hugh Wilford has recently argued that the network of the ACJ and the American Friends of the Middle East (AFME), on the board of which Berger served, was "both a government front and a lobby group with an agenda of its own."[64] Of AFME, Berger, who acted as its "chief pamphleteer," wrote in his 1978 memoirs that "by now . . . everyone knows it [AFME] was conceived and financed by the CIA."[65] In private correspondence, also from 1978, Berger wrote to an associate that "at one point in my life, when [Kermit] Kim Roosevelt was running the Middle East section of CIA, I served as a consultant—part time."[66] Wilford contended that Berger was not doing the CIA's work so much as engaging in coordinated efforts to advance interests he shared with the CIA Arabists (and with the anti-Zionist Arabist Protestants at the helm of AFME). "Berger and his friends did not see Kim Roosevelt as their boss," according to Wilford, but rather as "a partner working in a common cause."[67] Nonetheless, the CIA's support of Berger and its role in connecting him to figures in the Middle East lead us to ponder how the conception of Judaism espoused by the PLO and its Research Center may have been, however indirectly, informed and influenced by an American intelligence agency.

Strange Bedfellows

In this chapter, I have aimed to expand the context in which we understand the early years of the PLO, its intellectual roots and ideological development, and particularly its perspective on Jews, Judaism, and Jewishness. We have found that to more fully understand the PLO delegitimization of Zionism, one must consider Jewish religious developments, even, and especially, those outside Palestine or Israel—indeed, across the Atlantic. American Reform Judaism's late-nineteenth-century mainstream (unwittingly) and its mid-to-late-twentieth-century renegade-stalwarts (purposely) played a crucial role for Palestinian nationalists as they made their case against Zionism. This chapter thus might be seen as part of a broader project of cross-regional intellectual historiography that takes careful note of the often-counterintuitive points of intersection and appropriation between the Middle East and the West, in this case the United States.[68]

This argument might also be seen as part of the growing interest in not only the elements of conflict between Jews and Arabs over the Holy Land but also in shared Jewish-Arab interests and mutual influences concerning the problem of Palestine and Israel that persisted, sometimes across vast territorial distances, deep into the twentieth century.[69] To the extent that these contacts have been explored in the context of the Arab-Israeli conflict, the focus tends to be on those developed in Palestine and Israel or between Zionists/Israelis and Palestinians. However, insofar as Zionism was understood to make claims on Jews beyond Palestine and Israel, exploring the connections between Western Jews, especially American anti-Zionist Jews, and the Palestinian national movement is particularly important. The story of the PLO's embrace of the American Jewish Reform Pittsburgh Platform and of the organization's intellectual and personal relationship with Rabbi Elmer Berger represents a vivid case of unexpected and generally forgotten points of encounter between Jews and Arabs concerned about modern Palestine and Israel.[70]

Furthermore, study of religio-nationalist conflicts—or nationalist conflicts with religious undercurrents—reveals how, on the one hand, each side employs its own religion (or religions) as motivator and legitimizer and how, on the other hand, each challenges and attacks its opponent's religion(s) as a way of contesting the legitimacy of the opposing nationalism. The case of the PLO's use of classical Reform Judaism reminds us that as we research the relationship between religion and nationalism, we must also be sensitive to the ways in which one nationalism might combat another, not by delegitimizing the latter's associated religion, but by privileging one stream—however idiosyncratic—of the enemy nationalism's religion.

Finally, the question of the nature of Jewishness in the modern period has from the start fostered curious commonalities and unexpected alliances. The presumption or demand at the heart of eighteenth- and nineteenth-century Emancipation was that Jews were, or must become, connected to one another by religion only, and that they were conationals only of the other residents of their respective states.[71] This claim was opposed both by antisemites hostile to Jewish integration into European society and, no less, by traditional Jewish religious authorities anxious about losing control over their communities. Later, from the end of the nineteenth century, Zionists rejected the presumption of the Jews' nonnationhood and insisted that—whether essentially or circumstantially—the Jews constituted a nation in the modern sense. Just as Emancipation's claim of Jewish nonnationhood was opposed by strange bedfellows, so too was Zionism's assertion of Jewish nationhood. These latter opponents included Orthodox Jews committed to a messianic narrative that would keep the Jews in the Diaspora until the divinely appointed time, Reform Jews wedded to the integrationist ideology of Emancipation, and Palestinians and other Arabs who perceived in the affirmation of Jewish nationhood a severe, even existential, threat.[72] In all these cases, political interests intersected with religious principles and, as we have seen here, the views of one group could inform and be employed by very different others. As the debate over the nature of Jewishness persists into the twenty-first century, and as the implications of the definition of Jewishness appear no less weighty, new and perhaps similarly peculiar convergences and coalitions may be on the horizon.

8

The Jewish Woman in Occupied Palestine

THE PROMISE OF GENDER EQUALITY

IN HIS ASSESSMENT of the 1967 war, in *Self-Criticism after the Defeat*, the Syrian philosopher Sadik al-Azm wrote, "The greatest example of entirely wasted human resources is the completely and utterly excluded half of the Arab people, and I mean by this Arab women." He continued,

> We see that the Arab people do not comprise one hundred million people, as the broadcasts tell us, but only fifty million. Arab women form today, undoubtedly, the greatest reserves of latent human power in our society, still unused and untouched. It is the greatest bloc of raw intellectual and human material that the nation possesses that does not benefit the Arab revolutionary movement in any aspect.[1]

Moreover, al-Azm contended, it was not merely the conservative forces in Arab society that were responsible for squandering women's potential. Rather, he wrote, "Arab socialists themselves still view women through romantic ideas of motherhood and the raising of future generations, and through tribal values that revolve around dignity, sexual honor, and obedience to the husband, and that 'men are the protectors and maintainers of women,' and 'have been preferred [by God] over them [women] by one notch.'"[2] In his attempt to explain the Arab states' humiliating defeat in 1967, al-Azm included in his list of Arab societal flaws what he viewed as antiquated ideas about women and the resulting forfeiture of women's full participation in and contribution toward the advancement of their society.

Wasting half of a society's human potential was not inevitable, according to al-Azm. Some societies took full advantage of both their men and their women. One such example, he wrote, was Vietnam, "which mobilizes all its available human resources without exception." Al-Azm quoted a Vietnamese writer, who reported that "the women's army, 'the army of long hair,' is feared for its perseverance and fearlessness by officers, functionaries, and workers. . . . This direct participation of the masses, especially the women among them, has played a decisive role in the war."[3] If women were able to participate fully in Vietnamese liberation efforts, as al-Azm believed, there was no reason why they could not also participate fully in the battle for Arab liberation.[4]

Sadik al-Azm and the Model of Zionist Women

Vietnam, though, was the second example al-Azm offered, a mere aside within an extended discussion of a different case-in-point much closer to home: Israel and the Zionist cause. "Zionism," wrote al-Azm, "knew from its beginning how to benefit from all the human powers available to it without exception" while "the Arab revolutionary movement has not yet managed to learn this."[5]

Al-Azm's main source on the subject of Jewish women in the Zionist movement was *The Jewish Woman in Occupied Palestine*, an Arabic book written by the Nazareth-born Adib Qaʿwar and published by the PLO Research Center in April 1968.[6] This chapter is dedicated to analyzing Qaʿwar's book. I am especially interested here in understanding how the PLO Research Center's perspective on women among the Zionist enemy reflected and informed the Center's approach to the place of women in Arab society in general and within the Palestinian nationalist movement in particular.

Qaʿwar's book is presented as a neutral assessment of Jewish women first in Mandate Palestine and then in Israel. For al-Azm, however, the implications of Qaʿwar's review were far from neutral. Al-Azm cited Qaʿwar's reference to the French feminist Simone de Beauvoir's visit to Israel just before the 1967 war.[7] When de Beauvoir "wanted to get to know the Jewish women who left their imprint on the creation of Israel and contributed to the colonizing of Palestine, she went to interview working women in the kibbutz and women in cities and in free professions."[8] Qaʿwar had quoted from an article that de Beauvoir had written in May 1967, following her visit to the country.[9]

To whom would de Beauvoir have gone, al-Azm tartly asked, had she "wanted to get to know the Arab women who left their imprint on the creation of the Arab liberation movement and participated in the building of modern progressive societies in the Arab states possessing revolutionary regimes"? In case there was any doubt, he answered his own question: "In truth, there is nothing called the Arab working woman who left her fingerprints on the formation of modern Arab society."[10] The contrast between Zionist and Arab societies that al-Azm sensed as he read Qaʿwar's book demonstrated to him that the Zionists' interests were better served than the Arabs' interests because the former took advantage of the strengths of the women among them.

The Arabs' antiquated mode of thinking concerning women not only prevented Arab societies from taking advantage of women's physical labor and intellectual talents but also had hindered the Arabs' ability to fight effectively against the Israelis in the most recent war. "We found ourselves in a war in which ʿAbd al-Rahman ʿArif," then Iraq's president, "told his troops marching to the front to be harsh with the enemy but not to kill a woman or child." Perhaps, "the rightly-guided caliphs" in the earliest generations of Islamic history "could give this sort of advice to their troops and fighters," al-Azm commented acerbically. How, though, he asked, "can our leaders offer the same advice in almost the same words to our troops after the passing of fourteen centuries, while knowing that a large part of the enemy army is composed of women?"[11] Arab backwardness vis-à-vis women not only prevented Arab *women* from fighting against Israel, al-Azm contended, but even kept Arab *men* from fighting effectively.

Yet Qaʿwar did not explicitly present Zionist women as a model for Palestinian women. Within the framework of the PLO Research Center, it would have been taboo to offer Zionism or Israel as a standard to be emulated in any sense. The Center did publish research about Palestinian women, but such studies appeared in separate volumes distinct from those that concerned Zionist women. In 1975, the Center published, in Arabic, an anonymously written *The Victory of the Palestinian Woman* and, two years later, also in Arabic, *The Palestinian Woman and the Revolution* by the young PFLP activist Ghazi al-Khalili.[12]

Introducing Arab Women to Their "Female Zionist Opponent"

If the purpose of researching and publishing a book on Jewish women in Mandate Palestine and Israel was not (at least not explicitly) to offer a model for Palestinian women, why did the PLO Research Center undertake this project? The answer, it seems, stems from the basic role the Research Center played in helping Palestinians to "know the enemy." On the most fundamental level, "knowing the enemy" meant identifying who or what it was that constituted "the enemy," and for this it was essential to determine the relationship between Jewish women and the enemy. Were Jewish women a component of the enemy, bystanders who benefited from Zionism, victims of Zionism, or something else?

In his preface to the Center's book *The Jewish Woman in Occupied Palestine*, Anis Sayegh expressed his exasperation about previous Arabic writing on Jewish women in Zionism. "Most of what has been published in Arabic about the Jewish woman and her role in the Zionist aggression against Palestine over the last fifty years," wrote Sayegh, "is limited almost to one aspect of women's Zionist activity, and this is the aspect whose roots reach back to the ancient period of the Torah." In Sayegh's estimation, Arabic-language books about Jewish women failed to shed light on the modern woman. Moreover, asserted Sayegh, most of what had been written in Arabic about Zionist women was "based on the role that the *Protocols of the Elders of Zion* assign to Jewish women in building 'the Kingdom of Zion.'"[13] Once again, we hear Sayegh's complaint that the Arabs misunderstood the Zionist enemy because they drew their information from a worthless source.

By conceiving of Jewish women only in the context of the Bible or the conspiratorial *Protocols*, Arab critics had overlooked Jewish women's real, crucial role in Zionism, argued Sayegh. The actual Jewish women who should be studied are "the Zionist woman who works in the factories, the farmer, the writer, the teacher, the soldier, the terrorist, the politician, the social researcher, the free professional, the government employee, the ambassador, and other Zionist women who take part in Zionist activity." These women "came to Palestine, expelled its Arab people, and founded a foreign entity that aggressively expands into neighboring territories"—words that resonated loudly with Sayegh's Arab readers in the months following the 1967 war and Israel's trebling of its territory.

Sayegh thus called on his readers to dismiss their idea that women's activities contributed only marginally toward Zionism's goals. It is a mistake, he warned, to believe that the Zionist woman "did not play an almost equal role to the Zionist man."[14] Qaʿwar argued much the same, noting that his book "aims only to give the Jewish woman her due and to acknowledge her active participation in the effort that succeeded in inflicting the defeat upon us in more than one battle and achieved for the Zionists a staged victory."[15] Without acknowledging Jewish women's role in Zionism, wrote Qaʿwar, "we prevent ourselves from the complete understanding of the Zionist victory," an understanding "that is necessary [for us] to stand in the face of Zionist colonialism, to fight and eliminate it."[16] Jewish women were, in the view of Sayegh and Qa'war, crucial to the Zionist enterprise. Only armed with this knowledge, they maintained, would Palestinians have a chance to defeat the enemy.

It is worth mentioning that, notwithstanding the loaded language Sayegh and Qa'war used to describe Israel (the "usurper entity" or "Israel" in quotation marks), Sayegh assured readers that *The Jewish Woman in Occupied Palestine* was "a completely objective study." He made this claim regularly about the Research Center's publications. The general goal, as Sayegh articulated it, was "to inform the Arab reader about half of Jewish society in Palestine," the female half, about which the Arab reader knew even less than the male half. He offered a more specific goal as well: "to inform the Arab woman reader in particular about the activity of her female Zionist opponent [*gharima*],"[17] including the methods of Zionist women's activities and their results.

Why was it important for Arab women, in particular, to know about Zionist women's activity? Sayegh did not elaborate. Perhaps, though, we can glean something from the term that he used to describe the relationship between Arab women and Zionist women. The Zionist woman, said Sayegh, constituted the Arab woman's *gharima*, her opponent, adversary, or rival. Sayegh posited a direct—and perforce oppositional—relationship between Arab and Zionist women. For Arab women, "knowing the enemy" meant learning not merely about Zionists generally but about Zionist women in particular. Though Sayegh did not expressly present Zionist women as a *model* for Arab women (as al-Azm would), this relationship may have been implied in his call for Arab women to learn about Zionist women, so that Arab women would know what they were up against but also what they, too, would need to do to compete successfully.

Qa'war's book consists of eleven chapters. The first deals with the Jewish woman before the advent of the modern Zionist idea. The second focuses on the Jewish woman in Palestine in the years before 1948. The subsequent chapters consider Jewish women as a "human element," and discuss their position in the labor force, their role in the military, their legal status, their function in political and official life, and their position in the field of education. The final chapters analyze Jewish women in culture, literature, and in the free professions, and survey Jewish women's unions and organizations in Israel and abroad.

Biblical Gender Equality?

A major focus of Qaʿwar's book, beginning with the preface, was the issue of gender equality in Israel. The book, Sayegh explained from the start, "is especially interested in tracing the steps that the Jewish woman took until she reached the situation in which she finds herself presently inside the Zionist movement and inside 'the State of Israel,' where she has become equal with the Jewish man in almost all areas in which it is possible for men and women to be equal."[18] As the book progressed, however, Qaʿwar critically assessed the claim of gender equality in Israel, arguing that the reality was not quite as rosy for Israeli women as Israel's advocates portrayed it to be.

First, though, Qaʿwar engaged with the question of the extent to which gender equality was rooted in Judaism and ancient Jewish religious sources. For Qaʿwar, following English-language Jewish apologetic literature of the day, this meant turning initially to the Bible. Qaʿwar relied in these opening pages on Benno Jacob's essay "The Jewish Woman in the Bible," from a 1934 essay collection on Jewish women. However, Qaʿwar's assessment was more critical than that of the liberal German rabbi and Bible scholar.[19] According to Jacob, through "the strict laws that regulate the life of the Jew down to the smallest details," the Bible "has assigned to the Jewess her particular niche: she has her own sphere of duties." While the Jewish woman "is excluded from a variety of other obligations," insisted Jacob, "this exclusion defines her individuality." Moreover, "with every one of its words," wrote Jacob in a literary flourish, "the Bible has captivated her [the Jewish woman's] heart; the Holy Scriptures have entered into the soul of the daughter of Israel."[20] While biblical and rabbinic laws treat women differently from men, these distinctions are advantageous for Jewish women and productive for their "individuality," argued Jacob, demonstrated by Jewish women's affection for the Bible.

Qaʿwar accepted the facts presented in Jacob's essay but did not reproduce the value judgments that the rabbi drew from them. Opening his first chapter, on Jewish women in the era before Zionism, for instance, Qaʿwar wrote: "If we turn back to the status of women in the Torah, which is the Jews' holy scripture, we find a clear contradiction between the rights it grants to women," on the one hand, "and women's equality with men in punishments that are imposed on both [men and women] for the same crime," on the other.[21] As Qaʿwar saw it, the Bible offers women equality in the realm of punishments but inferiority in the realm of rights—a rather different assessment from the romantic view Jacob had presented to his readers.

Again, following Benno Jacob, Qaʿwar referenced a number of biblical women who were active in politics. Qaʿwar cited the biblical figures Miriam, who "held political leadership alongside her brothers" Aaron and Moses; Deborah, who "served as a leader, and declared war against the Canaanites;" and Athalia, who "ruled as queen of Judah for six years after she reached the throne through a series of terrible crimes."[22] Unlike Jacob, who enumerated these instances of "the woman in politics" and then moved on to his next subject, Qaʿwar concluded with this assessment: "On the whole, however, the place of the Jewish woman in antiquity was the home and her work was limited to the traditional spheres of women's work except in extremely exceptional cases."[23] Not constrained by his source's apologetic mission, Qaʿwar presented what he viewed to be exceptions as such rather than as representative of women's general experience in ancient Israel.

Even as he challenged the notion that pre-modern Jewish women were treated equally with men or were especially powerful and emancipated, Qaʿwar noted that the treatment and condition of Jewish women was generally on par with that of the non-Jewish women in the population among or alongside whom they dwelled. "Though in most cases," wrote Qaʿwar, the Jewish woman "lived in 'the ghetto' (i.e., the closed Jewish neighborhood) that the Jews imposed upon themselves, she adapted and lived the life of the women of the people [al-shaʿb] among whom she lived except for basic differences that were imposed by the nature of religious difference."[24] That Qaʿwar attributed Jewish residential segregation to Jews' own preferences is noteworthy.[25] For present purposes, however, the key point is that Qaʿwar perceived the status of Jewish women to be, in general, similar to that of their non-Jewish women neighbors.

The Role of Women in Herzl's Zionism

If apologetics, such as those of Rabbi Benno Jacob, concerning pre-modern Jewish women were less than entirely accurate, what might be said of the view of Zionism as an emancipatory movement for women? Was Zionism, popularly identified with the collectivist kibbutz, fundamentally feminist, as was often asserted?[26] To tackle this question, Qaʿwar looked first to the writings of Theodor Herzl.

Based on his analysis of Herzl's published diaries, Qaʿwar found the father of modern Zionism to hold distinctly sexist views. In fact, he claimed, Herzl utterly instrumentalized women.[27] Qaʿwar cited Herzl's entry from June 1895 as a prime example: "As stipends for my brave warriors, ambitious artists, and loyal, gifted officials I shall use the dowries of our wealthy girls," noting that he would need to "carry on marriage politics." Imagining how he might take advantage of the awe that he expected personally to generate among wealthy Jews, Herzl anticipated calling upon the Jewish elite to "give your daughters to up-and-coming vigorous young men." Using Jewish women to attract talented and ambitious Jewish men to the Jewish nationalist movement was necessary, Herzl contended, for the sake of the mission. "I need this for the state," he wrote. "It is the self-fertilization of the nation."[28]

Herzl, according to Qaʿwar, "did not give women any active role in the Zionist movement or in realizing his dream of building a Jewish state."[29] The diaries, he emphasized, made no mention of women working or fighting but rather envisioned women's roles as limited to "narrow, traditional fields, aiming to apply aristocratic customs on the national scale."[30] In support of this assertion, Qaʿwar offered another diary entry from June 1895:

> No women or children shall work in our factories. We need a sturdy race. Needy women and children shall be taken care of by the State. "Old maids" will be employed in kindergartens and as nurses for the orphans of the working class, etc. I shall organize these girls who have been passed over by suitors into a corps of governesses for the poor. They will be given housing by the State, enjoy due honors (just as every gentleman treats a governess courteously), and eventually will be pensioned. But they can rise in the ranks in the same way that men can.[31]

For Qaʿwar, Herzl's view of the proper place of women in the model society he imagined was far from the ideals of gender equality that some would later claim for the Zionist movement. Women, Qaʿwar contended, came to play a crucial role in Zionism not because of Herzl but rather despite him.[32]

Women's Independence in the Service of the Nation

However, Qaʿwar argued, once the Zionist idea progressed from theory to practice, it required the active participation of Jewish women. Thus, Jewish women joined the current of "western women," who, wrote Qaʿwar, "had already set out on the path of liberation, independence, and equality in most aspects of working life." Given the Zionist movement's need for women, Qaʿwar's narrative continued, "when the World Zionist Organization was founded, it gave the Jewish woman the opportunity to participate in official, national work," allowing women "to be active in realizing Zionist goals."

Yet, wrote Qaʿwar, women did not spontaneously enter the ranks of Zionist activists. Rather, "this required exhausting educational work" to encourage them to participate actively in the movement. But, transforming Jewish women into Zionist activists required more than words. In fact, according to Qaʿwar, even "the educational work among Zionist women themselves failed to push them to apply this theory" of gender equality. Such difficulties led to the founding of separate Zionist women's organizations.

Eventually, many Zionists came to believe that "increasing the power of the Zionist Organization required great effort by Jewish women." Once Jews began immigrating to Palestine, this effort was divided into two spheres of Zionist activity: first, "the Jewish women pioneers" who had settled in Palestine and second, "the women in what the Zionist movement calls the Diaspora (the outside world)." Those women who had immigrated to Palestine strove "to apply these principles in Palestine by means of female manual labor," while the focus abroad was on indoctrinating Jewish women in the principles of Zionism and on training Jewish girls and young women to work. There was presumed to be a direct relationship, elaborated Qaʿwar, between women's labor and constructing the nation.[33] Zionism demanded progress toward women's "social and economic independence," not for the sake of women's fulfillment but rather for the sake of Zionism.

At the end of his chapter on Jewish women in pre-1948 Palestine, Qaʿwar offered several justifications for his having focused particularly on Jewish women workers. The final explanation in his list returned to the ultimate purpose of this PLO Research Center book: to explore "an aspect of Zionism that has led to the conquest of Palestine." Accordingly, Qaʿwar deemed it necessary "to turn the bulk of our attention to the Jewish woman who participated in the process of colonization, namely the Jewish working woman in Palestine and, to some extent, beyond [Palestine]."[34]

As he aimed to comprehend who Zionist women were, Qaʿwar turned to population statistics prepared and published by the Israeli government. He cited and translated for his readers numerous charts that he found in the latest issue of *The Statistical Abstract of Israel* from 1966. For instance, Qaʿwar presented and analyzed a chart entitled "Immigrants and Jewish tourists who settled in occupied Palestine above the age of 15 sorted according to sex and family status." The chart divided Jewish men and women immigrants who had arrived in Israel since 1948 into categories: single, married, divorced, or widowed. Analyzing this two-page spread of statistics, Qaʿwar noted that, whereas before 1948 and especially in the years before World War I, women represented only a fraction of the total number of Jewish immigrants to Palestine, since 1948 women had immigrated in nearly equal numbers to men. The vast majority of the Jewish adults who had immigrated in this period (1948–65) were married and, in this demographic group, men and women came in about equal numbers.

This overall gender balance among the Jewish immigrants, Qaʿwar cautioned his readers, should not obscure the many differences between the Jewish men and women who had come to Israel. There were, for example, 49 percent more single men than single women among the immigrants who had arrived in the country's first eighteen years. In contrast, 237 percent more divorced women than divorced men immigrated during this period. The most gaping percentage divide was in the category of widows and widowers, as widows exceeded widowers by 411 percent. Qaʿwar offered an explanation for these demographic differences: divorced women and widows found that immigrating to Israel offered "a change that relieved the tragedy that had occurred in their lives."[35] In clarifying that Jews moved to Israel for a variety of reasons, Qaʿwar—whether intentionally or not—humanized the immigrants, indicating that each was impelled by his or her own life story. Moreover, his analysis implicitly acknowledges that many who relocated to Israel did not seek to displace or dominate Palestinians. Indeed, in many cases, they were not motivated by Zionism at all.

Zionist Women and Zionist Violence

A central topic of interest for Qaʿwar in this study was women in pre-1948 Zionist militias and later in the Israeli national military. From the very start of Zionist settlement, women participated in the armed activities of the movement. "With the founding of the first Jewish colony on the land of Arab Palestine," Qaʿwar wrote, "the organization Ha-Shomer was created to defend it" and to assist in establishing new Jewish settlements. Already then, "the Jewish woman participated in this movement."[36] In the midst of World War I, shortly after the Balfour Declaration of 1917, Jewish women in Palestine, under the leadership of Rachel Yanait, joined the Jewish Legion of the British army to battle the Ottomans. "Some went so far as to demand to participate in direct military work, exactly like men, while the rest participated in the war effort" in the roles of cooks, nurses, laundresses, and other such noncombatant positions.[37]

After the fall of the Ottoman Empire and the advent of the British Mandate in Palestine, the objectives of Jewish women's armed activities necessarily changed. Qaʻwar noted that many women joined the British Mandate-era Jewish militia known as the Haganah, though Herzl had not foreseen nor particularly wanted women in the army of the Jewish State. "When the number of members of the Haganah ('the Jewish Self-Defense Movement in Palestine') was 50,000," wrote Qaʻwar, "the number of women who had joined it exceeded 10,000, including working women and mothers."[38] "During the successive Arab uprisings"[39] of the British Mandate period, wrote Qaʻwar, "the Jewish woman participated in the defense of the Jewish settlements. This repeated in the revolutions of 1929 and 1936–1939, as Jewish women were drafted and armed women protected Jewish transport routes." In the 1940s, Qaʻwar noted, women were trained alongside men within the Palmach, the Haganah's "striking force," to assist illegal Jewish immigrants in reaching the shores of Palestine. Women also participated in destroying railroad lines in Palestine and in attacking the illegal immigrant detention camp at Atlit in order to help Jewish detainees escape internment and enter Palestine. Beyond the fighting roles that women played in the Mandate era, women also managed the secret radio stations for the various Zionist militias.[40]

Though women played active and at times armed roles in the Mandate-era Zionist militias, women did not achieve full equality with men even in this context, argued Qaʻwar. In highlighting the disparities, Qaʻwar challenged what he regarded as the mythology of gender equality in Zionism. Through painstaking analysis of the evidence, Qaʻwar concluded that the extent to which women could rise in power in these organizations was limited. "The role of women" in the militias, or "gangs" as Qaʻwar labeled them, "rarely ascended to the sensitive and leadership centers." Instead, women played humbler roles such as militia youth recruiters and trainers, message deliverers, arms thieves, internment camp attackers, immigrant smugglers, publication distributors, secret radio operators, and so on.[41]

The IDF's Use, and Exploitation, of Israeli Women

After the establishment of the State of Israel, women continued to serve in military roles, in the new official state army, the Israel Defense Forces. Qaʻwar emphasized that "'Israel' is the only country in the world that demands conscription of women during peacetime." Again, Qaʻwar did not see the conscription of women in Israel as an expression of the state's principled gender egalitarianism but rather as a consequence of the new state's "need to exploit [*istighlal*] all manpower to the greatest extent possible."[42]

And exploit it did, claimed Qaʿwar, by including women not only in regular military forces but also in its clandestine intelligence units. Qaʿwar appeared to have been especially interested in salacious reports he read about Israel's sexual exploitation of young women within its spy network. In these "secret realms," Israel is "willing to use any means to reach the desired 'Israeli' objectives," Qaʿwar wrote, "even the means of sex."[43] Qaʿwar was relying here on the recently published *Soldiering for Peace*, a 1966 memoir by the Swedish major general Carl von Horn. Von Horn had served as commander of the United Nations Truce Supervision Organization from 1958 through 1960 and worked for the UN on Arab-Israeli matters in the region through 1963.

In his memoir, von Horn complained about corruption within the ranks of his own UN staff and the ways in which both the Arabs and Israelis (the latter much more effectively than the former) fostered and instrumentalized that corruption. Von Horn wrote of Israeli intelligence's often successful efforts to extract sensitive and classified information from the UN mission in Jerusalem and the Mixed Armistice Commissions. A primary tool that the Israelis used, von Horn contended, was sexual temptation of the UN's male staff by young Israeli women. For instance, von Horn recalled an Israeli official who "kept open house for United Nations personnel in a lavish style quite inconsistent with his salary." In particular, von Horn noted "the attractive Israeli girls who embellished" this Israeli official's home and who "assisted in entertaining UN visitors." Upon investigation, von Horn's team "discovered that some of these alluring creatures had been released from their National Service for 'special duties.' So special that we nicknamed them 'the Commandos' (with no slur intended on that fine body of men), as we unearthed other members of this sisterhood in Tel Aviv and Tiberias."[44] Qaʿwar translated this lengthy passage in full (rendering "the Commandos" as *al-fadaʾiyyat*, that is, the female fedayeen) as it revealed, in his view, the peculiar roles assigned to women in serving Israel's interests.[45]

Qaʿwar also quoted other prurient anecdotes from von Horn's memoir that further revealed the state's use of Israeli women. Von Horn related the story, for instance, of "a luscious, raven-haired Sabra girl," who allegedly seduced more than one "sex-starved" UN employee stationed in the country. In one case, after a rendezvous in her home, a different Israeli agent blackmailed the UN official, threatening to disclose to the man's wife what had happened unless he would serve as a spy for Israel within the UN.[46]

Self-conscious, perhaps, about his keen interest, Qaʿwar explained why he felt compelled to include these titillating stories in his study. "We tried," Qaʿwar wrote, "not to touch this aspect of the duties of women's units in the 'Israeli' intelligence and army in this scientific study of all aspects of Jewish female life." However, "we saw that disregarding" this facet of women's roles in Israeli society "would leave a gap in this chapter on the different activities of the Jewish woman in military life in occupied Palestine." Qaʿwar thus only reluctantly included the piquant details, he explained, for the sake of scientific accuracy.

Women in Israeli Law

After exploring the roles Jewish women played in the Zionist militias and the Israel Defense Forces, Qaʿwar turned to the question of women's status under Israeli law. Qaʿwar was especially interested in analyzing the areas of dissonance between ancient Jewish legal approaches to women and those of modern Israeli law. With more than four hundred pages of Israeli legal code before him (in Joseph Badi's 1961 compilation *Fundamental Laws of the State of Israel*), Qaʿwar argued that the Israeli legislature's decision to enact Torah-contravening laws concerning women was not a surprising or revolutionary act of a new, radically progressive state, but rather the natural outgrowth of developments in Palestine over the preceding decades. Indeed, because they participated actively in the efforts that ultimately led to the establishment of the state, while struggling for equality in work opportunities, women demanded that the state grant rights which they "already believed legitimately to be theirs and took for granted." Qaʿwar acknowledged that some leaders of the Jewish women's movement argued that Israeli law did not go far enough in upending traditional patriarchy. Yet, in his view, and notwithstanding the de facto inequalities, "the laws of 'Israel' created political, social, and economic equality between men and women."[47]

To demonstrate the de jure gender equality in Israel, Qaʿwar offered his readers a brief overview of the most important Israeli laws that established equality between men and women. He began with the Women's Equal Rights Law of 1951 and cited what he took to be the law's four principal aspects. It affirmed the full equality of men and women before the law and annulled any law that discriminated against women on the basis of gender. Next, the law declared that married women had the same rights to their money as unmarried women. Third, this act acknowledged the "natural right" of both parents as guardians of their children. Finally, Qaʿwar explained, the law incorporated an article of the 1936 British Palestine Mandate penal code, with the addition of a clause that imposed up to five years imprisonment on a man who, without a court judgment, annulled his marriage against the will of his wife.[48]

In Qaʿwar's view, Israel legislated complete equality between women and men and instituted multiple safeguards to protect women from discrimination and abuse. And yet, as he noted, traditional Jewish religious law is not egalitarian in this sense. When Jewish religious law is simply ignored by Israeli law, the contradictions are of no practical relevance. But Israeli law, in particular instances, invokes or appeals to Jewish religious law and, in these cases, the incongruities concerning gender equality are brought into relief.

Such is the case in the law concerning marriage and divorce. Qaʿwar cited the 1953 Rabbinical Courts Jurisdiction (Marriage and Divorce) Law, which declared that "marriages and divorces of Jews shall be performed in Israel in accordance with Jewish religious law."[49] "Jewish religious law" is the English translation that Badi's compilation provides for the Hebrew *din Torah*.[50] Along with Badi's anthology, Qaʿwar had before him Shulamith Schwarz-Nardi's English translation of Ada Maimon's *Women Build a Land*. Maimon, an Israeli feminist politician elected to the first Knesset, also cited this law and Schwarz-Nardi used the literal translation of the phrase *din Torah*: "the law of the Torah."[51] Qaʿwar rendered the phrase as *taʿalim al-tawrat* (literally: the teachings of the Torah). Apparently understanding "Torah" narrowly to mean "Bible" (rather than broadly to mean Jewish scripture and subsequent religious law), Qaʿwar noted the differences between biblical marriage practices and Israeli law and thus warned his reader against assuming that the 1953 law made Israeli marriage law identical to biblical law. In fact, Qaʿwar contended, "the law looks at the teachings of the Torah in this regard as obsolete [*baliyya*] and not in keeping with the requirements and customs of modern life." In particular, Qaʿwar wrote, while "the Torah allows polygamy, the law observed among the Jews of occupied Palestine forbids it," in accordance with "its prohibition among the Jews of Europe since the Middle Ages." In Qaʿwar's view, the practical relevance of the Israeli law was that it established that "the authority of the religious courts is the only authority in occupied Palestine that is authorized to annul divorces between Jews and to set the support of a divorced woman."[52]

In recounting the Israeli discussion surrounding this law, Ada Maimon wrote that "the legislation introduced by the Government occasioned much debate in the Knesset, and Israel's women still look upon it as a betrayal of the principle of equality and personal freedom, and a perpetuation of a system that relegates women to a position of inferiority."[53] In Qaʿwar's version, which closely followed Maimon in this section of the book, this same idea appeared: "Some non-religious women in occupied Palestine see this law as having established a lower status for women in relation to men despite the law on equality of women and men."[54] Whereas Maimon declared "Israel's women," without distinction, to have opposed this law, Qaʿwar, who of course had a very different agenda from Maimon's, explained more subtly that only some Israeli women, especially those who did not identify as "religious," opposed the law.

Maimon herself came from a religious Jewish home. She did not think that a person's identity as "religious" necessarily dictated one's position on questions of feminism.[55] Following Maimon, Qaʿwar explained that those who supported this law reasoned that instituting civil marriage in Israel could lead to a fundamental split within Israel's Jewish community between those married by rabbinic law and those married in civil proceedings. The fear, as Maimon elucidated and Qaʿwar relayed, was that rabbis would rule intermarriage between these two Jewish communities to be religiously impermissible. Even apologists for the law granting sole authority to the rabbis conceded that more ought to be done "to adapt Jewish tradition to present-day reality and make Judaism attractive to the modern Jew."[56]

Maimon wrote that "women members of the Knesset, who took an active part in the debate, stressed the need to include women in the rabbinical tribunals dealing with marriage and divorce. It was also necessary, they insisted, to have female secretaries so that Jewish women from the Middle East, or others unused to dealing with men, would be able to present their cases without undue restraint." Qaʿwar rendered this passage as follows: "The women members of the 'Knesset' have raised the issue of including women in the Jewish religious courts that render decisions on matters of marriage and divorce, but until now they [the women] have not been able to penetrate the fortifications of this fortress forbidden to them."[57] In his adaptation of Maimon's account, Qaʿwar omitted the specific concern about the cultural sensibilities of Middle Eastern women. To understand this excision, it is important to consider the context in which Qaʿwar was writing.

In 1960s Beirut (and long after as well), marriage and all other matters of "personal status" were in the hands of the various religious authorities.[58] Thus Qaʿwar was not citing the absence of legalized civil marriage in Israel in order to allege the backwardness of Israeli law compared to that of neighboring Arab countries. On the contrary, he may well have highlighted the debate in the Israeli legislature concerning these matters to offer an implicit model for debates in Lebanon and elsewhere.

At the same time, Qaʿwar removed Maimon's reference to the particular challenges faced by Israeli women who had immigrated from the Middle East. He also chose not to translate Maimon's concluding paragraph of this section in which she wrote that "we must bear in mind that tens of thousands of women in Israel, especially those who come from Islamic lands, still fail to realize the humiliating nature of their position."[59] Qaʿwar similarly elected not to include material from Maimon's chapter "The Arab Women in Israel," which opens by declaring proudly that "Israel was the first country in the Middle East to extend suffrage to Arab women and give them the right to hold elective office."[60] Maimon's chapter is markedly condescending in its depiction of the attitude toward and treatment of women by Muslim and Arab culture and society; Qaʿwar did not address these topics.[61] Considering the context, one reasonably wonders whether, in making these editorial decisions, Qaʿwar was determined to keep the contrast between women in Israel and women in Arab countries implicit only.

Qaʿwar noted that the Bible and the rabbis privileged men in matters of inheritance as well, citing Benno Jacob's article "The Jewish Woman in the Bible" along with the entry "Inheritance" in the 1966 printing of *The Standard Jewish Encyclopedia*. Sons and their descendants inherited before daughters and their descendants, brothers and their children before sisters and their children, and fathers and grandfathers rather than mothers and grandmothers. He discovered in this area, too, a fundamental distinction between biblical and rabbinic law and contemporary Israeli law. Qaʿwar pointed out that Israeli law overruled Jewish religious law in this sense. "Today," because of Israel's Women's Equal Rights Law and particularly its affirmation that "a man and a woman shall have equal status with regard to any legal proceedings, and any provision of law which discriminates, with regard to any legal proceeding, against women as women, shall be of no effect," wrote Qaʿwar, "women are equal to men." Qaʿwar also highlighted this Israeli law's declaration that "a married woman shall be fully competent to own and deal with property as if she were unmarried; her rights in property acquired before her marriage shall not be affected by her marriage." Qaʿwar concluded that notwithstanding biblical and rabbinic laws, "from the perspective of inheritance, the woman, in the laws of 'Israel,' is equal to the man and she has all of the rights to share with her brothers on an equal footing, and she maintains her ownership of this inheritance after her marriage."[62] In these particular matters, according to Qaʿwar, Israel had in fact overturned traditional law in favor of legal gender equality.

Women Teaching Hatred

Qaʿwar did not accept Israel's reputation for gender equality uncritically. In fact, he carefully studied a variety of demographic, government, and employment statistics, with an eye to the exceptions and contradictions. For instance, in his section on "the Jewish woman in official and public positions," Qaʿwar posited that it is "necessary not to look at it [this topic] in general" and thereby to draw broad conclusions about "the proportion of women in official and public positions." Rather, insisted Qaʿwar, "this sort of study must seek the proportion of women in the different levels and ranks in the government and public positions." Considering the granular detail of these statistics is essential, Qaʿwar contended, to assess the true degree of gender equality in public life. He insisted on investigating questions like "How many women directors general and how many secretaries make up the government staff in occupied Palestine,"[63] to achieve a fuller, more honest view of the actual situation for women in Israel.

So, Qaʿwar warned his readers "not to be deceived" by, for instance, the apparent increase in women's employment in government positions, which rose from 17.7 percent to 23.4 percent between 1960 and 1965.[64] After all, Qaʿwar noted,

> if we compare the number of senior women government employees, that is, on the level of director general of a ministry and heads of departments and sections in the "Knesset" and the office of the president of the state and the office of the heads of the government and the ministries and the independent governmental agencies and Zionist institutions, we find that the percentage is much lower than this. Rather, it is also lower than the percentage of representation of women in the Knesset, which reaches an average of 10%. From a total of 2,141 senior employees in the government, the number of women in these centers reaches approximately 90 women, that is less than 4% of the group of senior employees.[65]

In other words, Qaʿwar demonstrated that the true degree of gender equality in Israeli government positions is far lower than a glance at the broad statistics might suggest. Women were disproportionately concentrated in the lower ranks and largely absent from true positions of power. The same was true when one carefully examined the number of women in senior roles in government ministries.[66]

If women were grossly underrepresented in senior level Israeli government and public positions, they were well represented, and in certain spheres even overrepresented, Qaʿwar argued, in the field of education in Israel. For Qaʿwar, this was a field of enormous significance because of education's pervasive impact on a society. "The Jewish woman in Palestine, before and after the Zionist occupation," wrote Qaʿwar, "had an active role in the realms of culture, education, instruction, propaganda, and services." In fact, he continued, "we see that the Jewish woman in occupied Palestine has a monopoly on teaching in kindergartens, and 70% in primary schools, and 40% in secondary education." As a result, women played "a foundational role in creating political Zionist Hebrew culture and in steering the youth to follow Zionist principles (as education and culture in occupied Palestine are joined in one ministry)." Jewish women were thereby essential for Zionism in "teaching the new immigrants the Hebrew language and 'educating' them according to the goals of the expanding 'Israel.'"

No less importantly, Qaʿwar contended, women were indispensable in "planting hatred in their [Jewish youths'] hearts toward the Arabs and preparing them to fight them."[67] Notwithstanding the discrimination they faced in government employment and in gaining promotions, Jewish women were absolutely crucial in the Zionist enterprise, especially in education and in fostering faith in Zionism and hostility toward Arabs. If one purpose of Qaʿwar's book was to determine whether Jewish women were part of "the enemy" or just more victims of Zionism, the conclusion was resoundingly that Jewish women were indeed "the enemy" for Palestinians even if they were also victims of Zionist patriarchy.

In the course of his analysis of women's role in Zionist education, Qaʿwar took the opportunity to reflect more broadly on the role of education in Zionism. "There is no doubt," wrote Qaʿwar, "that some of the topics that are taught to the youth and the new immigrants—among them, the Hebrew language and its literature, the Jewish religion, the history and geography of Palestine and the region surrounding it, 'Greater Israel,' in particular, and the Arab homeland in general—rely on falsification of facts and fabrication and distortion of history."[68] For Qaʿwar, Zionist education demanded deceit; an honest study of Judaism, Jewish history, Jewish culture, and of Palestine would, Qaʿwar implied, militate against Zionism. Facts about these topics needed to be manipulated, contorted, ignored, or altered in order to produce Jewish nationalist ideology and expansionist politics.

Israel's Effort to Know the Enemy

But Zionist education, Qaʿwar noted, was not limited to studying Jews and Judaism. As part of their education, Zionists also studied and taught about Arab society and culture and the Arabic language. "Faculties for Arabic studies," explained Qaʿwar, "were founded in the universities of occupied Palestine." These departments "teach the Arabic language and its literature, the different dialects, the organization of Arab regimes, the ways of life and traditions in each part of the Arab homeland, and so on."

Why did Zionists invest in researching and teaching about Arab society, politics, language, and culture? The Zionist goal in this enterprise was, as Qaʿwar put it, to "know your enemy" (*aʿrif ʿaduka*). As we have seen, Anis Sayegh regularly used that same phrase, "knowing the enemy," to describe the Research Center's work. One can only wonder whether Qaʿwar viewed his work at the PLO Research Center and his book about Zionist and Israeli women as a mirror image of Zionist efforts to "know the enemy." It is difficult to believe that the parallelism of the projects was lost on Qaʿwar and his colleagues.

Either way, for Qaʿwar, the Zionist research and teaching was all part of "the malevolent plot aiming toward 'educating' [Qaʿwar's worry marks] the youth and the new immigrants and all the Jews of occupied Palestine and the rest of the world according to the Zionist political plot."[69] Curiously, whereas Qaʿwar accused Zionists of distorting the facts of Jewish history, religion, and culture, and the history of the region, for the purposes of instilling their nationalist ideology into the Jewish masses, he did not make the same allegations concerning the Zionists' and Israelis' research on Arabic and Arab culture. The Zionists' goal was "malevolent," because they aimed to "know the enemy" (so as to dominate it), but Qaʿwar did not challenge the substance of the knowledge about Arab society that the Zionists produced toward this effort.

9

Jews of the Arab Countries

THE QUESTION OF RACISM

Did Middle Eastern Jews Need Saving?

In his monograph on the history of Jewish women in Zionism discussed in the previous chapter, Adib Qaʿwar translated into Arabic a lengthy section of Ada Maimon's *Women Build a Land*. In the English version on which Qaʿwar relied, this section is called "Immigrant Youth from the Neighboring Lands"; in Qaʿwar's Arabic translation, it is called "The Immigration of Young Jewish Girls from the Arab Homeland [*al-watan al-ʿarabi*]." This passage concerns Jewish girls and young women who immigrated to Palestine from Lebanon and Syria in the years before and especially during World War II. It begins with Maimon's narrative, followed by a lengthy quotation from "one of the Syrian girls" who had immigrated to Palestine in 1943. Qaʿwar translated this section in a straightforward way, with little commentary—that is, until he came to the following line in the account: "During the Second World War the Jewish Agency and the Histadrut took active steps to rescue as many young people as possible from the poverty and hardships of their lives in the Middle Eastern countries." Here, Qaʿwar placed his rendering of the word "rescue" (*li-najdat*) in quotation marks.[1]

In the footnote he appended to the four-page quotation, Qaʿwar focused on Maimon's presentation of Jews in the Arab world as necessitating rescue. Explaining that he "decided to quote these two texts verbatim to give an idea of the style of Zionist propagandistic thinking and the fallacies that are found in the two of them," Qaʿwar went on to assert that "the Jews of Syria, Lebanon, Iraq, Egypt, and most other parts of the Arab homeland lived—and those who still live there continue to live—in prosperity and comfort that were not known by Jews from other parts of the civilized world." Moreover, Jews in these Arab regions achieved their exceptional level of wealth and security even though they "never tried to assimilate into Arab society."[2]

The Nazareth-born Qaʿwar chose his adopted city as a case in point to refute Maimon's portrayal of the status of Jews in the Arab world. Turning to the entry on Beirut in Cecil Roth's English-language *Standard Jewish Encyclopedia*, Qaʿwar noted that the city's Jewish community, which had reached six thousand members in 1940, was described in the work as "excellently organized." He was especially impressed by the fact that, as the encyclopedia pointed out, "the community was renewed on a small scale with the arrival of exiles from Spain." In fleeing from Spain to Beirut after their expulsion at the end of the fifteenth century, Jews "took refuge from oppression in a safe place," wrote Qaʿwar. Thus, according to reliable Jewish historiographical sources, Jews were rescued *by* the Middle East.[3] Middle Eastern Jews—whether girls or boys, women or men—were in no need of "rescue," contended Qaʿwar. That they ultimately left the countries they had called home for more than four centuries begged other explanations.

Those explanations were offered by PLO Research Center authors in numerous other publications they wrote during their years in Beirut. This chapter begins with a close reading of the Center's 1971 book *Jews of the Arab Countries*—issued in Arabic and in condensed versions in English and French. Cowritten by Ali Ibrahim Abdo and Khairieh Kasmieh,[4] this is a study of the modern history of the Jews in nine different Arab regions: Iraq, Syria, Lebanon, the Arabian Peninsula, Egypt, Libya, Tunisia, Algeria, and Morocco. Using Abdo and Kasmieh's book as a starting point, the chapter expands into a broader analysis of the PLO Research Center's writing about the place of race and racism within Zionism. The Center focused on what it perceived as Zionist discrimination against Middle Eastern Jews as part of, and in the service of, its larger contention that Zionists related to Palestinian Arabs in a racist manner.

Palestine was conspicuously absent from the list of Middle Eastern countries that Abdo and Kasmieh chose to study in their book. "This study does not deal with the Jews in Palestine," Abdo and Kasmieh explained, for "to do so would require lengthy discussions of the complex problems which their advent to that country has created." In the Arabic, the authors explain in greater detail why they excluded the Jewish community of Palestine in their analysis. "Before the rise of the Zionist movement," they wrote, "Palestine had only a few thousand Jews who were not distinct from the Jews of Syria and Lebanon." The Jews of

Palestine, rather, "came suddenly from Europe after the start of the twentieth century and particularly after the British Mandate." The story of these Jews— the "vast and complex" set of "problems that their presence created in the region"—did not fit within the bounds of Abdo and Kasmieh's book.[5]

"Indigenous Jews"

With the Jews in Palestine out of the picture, the argument that Abdo and Kasmieh advanced was clear: the Jews of Arab countries were to be regarded as "indigenous Jews"[6] who "have formed an integral segment of the whole indigenous Arab population." These Jews, "though numerically few," have "participated in the general life of the greater community, speaking the same language, adhering to the same mores and living under the same economic, social and political circumstances."[7] Abdo and Kasmieh insisted that such deep integration into the surrounding community had "never been available to Jews throughout their long history" anywhere else. This idyllic treatment of Jews was unique, rather, to this region. While Jews "have been repeatedly exposed to pogroms in Europe, they have always been able to seek refuge in the Arab world."[8] Abdo and Kasmieh presented their study as a revisionist work. "All past studies," they boldly declared, "represent a slanted viewpoint."[9] Zionist studies portrayed these communities as though "they were living in 'exile' and awaiting their return to the Holy Land."[10] Meanwhile, the authors asserted that no previous Arabic study of these Jewish communities had investigated their "economic, social, and cultural conditions" because the Jews were not viewed separately from the rest of the population.[11]

Who were the "Jews of the Arab countries" in the view of the PLO Research Center? The history of the Jews in the Arab world dates back to the sixth century BCE, these researchers explained, when waves of Jewish migrants arrived during the Babylonian Exile. Another such wave followed the destruction of Jerusalem in the first century CE. These communities "migrated eastward toward Iraq or southward toward the Arabian Peninsula or southwestward toward Egypt and some of them flowed into North Africa." These migrants "mixed with the native peoples and spoke their language. Some of the natives referred to the migrants as 'the settlers.' These were the oldest Jewish communities in the region."[12] The descendants of these early settlers were later joined by "immigrants from various parts of the world." The largest "wave of immigration came in the wake of the mass exodus of Jews from Spain after the fall of the Arab rule there."[13] Another sizable immigration came in the seventeenth century from Italy. These two groups "differed from indigenous Jews mainly in that they [the newcomers] enjoyed a higher standard of education and greater wealth."[14] As time passed, however, the distinction between the Spanish and Italian Jews and the original "Eastern Jews" became less clear, though it did not entirely disappear.[15] Despite the fact that the Iberian Jews spoke Ladino until the late nineteenth century, "when they replaced it with French, like the rest of the Levantines who engaged in trade," Arabic, "the mother tongue of indigenous Jews [in the Arabic edition: *al-mutawatinin al-qudama*, "the ancient indigenous residents"], became a *lingua franca* among all Jews in the area."[16] For Abdo and Kasmieh, the term "indigenous Jews" seemed to refer to Arabic-speaking Jews who lived in the Middle East before the influx of Iberian Jews at the end of the fifteenth century.

At the same time, the authors contended that "Arab[s] and Jews have the same origin."[17] After the advent of Islam, Jews, like other non-Muslim communities, "were granted the freedom to organize their internal affairs in accordance with their particular religious laws and social customs." Under this system, "non-Muslim communities enjoyed not only freedom of worship, but also freedom of movement, thought, and education."[18] As the PLO Research Center presented them, these were "optimum conditions" under which "the Jewish communities in the Arab world flourished."[19] There were "no complaints of persecution or mistreatment."[20] The authors stressed that it was in this context that Jews achieved major "intellectual accomplishments," including the Sura, Nehardea, and Pumbedita academies; the Babylonian Talmud; the centers of the Geonim; the Exilarch; responsa literature; and religious missions to Egypt, North Africa, South Asia, and the Far East.[21] Later, important Jewish figures such as Solomon Ibn Gabirol, Abraham Ibn Ezra, Judah ha-Levi, and Moses Maimonides wrote key works of Jewish literature in Arabic.[22] In the Ottoman period, the Jews were able to find refuge from Spanish persecution in Arab lands and were permitted to thrive in ways completely unparalleled in the European sphere.[23] "Antisemitism is a European invention that did not have an influence in the Arab countries," the authors asserted.[24]

"A Reverse Side to Arab-Jewish Relations"

Abdo and Kasmieh acknowledged that there was "a reverse side to Arab-Jewish relations," namely, certain problematic aspects of the Jews' position in the Middle Eastern societies in which they lived.[25] The Jews in the Ottoman Empire came to play an important role in the economy as agents of European trade by acquiring European passports "in ever increasing numbers." In addition, the authors explained, "missionaries and Jewish philanthropists" constituted "another means of foreign penetration in the Arab world," such as through the Alliance Israelite Universelle school system and Jewish colonization in Palestine.[26] The argument that the authors subtly constructed here is that the problems that Jews came to face in the Arab world originated not in the Arab world but rather in Europe, whether through local Jews' political and economic associations with Europeans or by rich European Jews' establishing schools in Arabic-speaking lands.

Relying on the Soviet historian Vladimir Lutsky's work on the Middle East, the PLO authors wrote denigratingly of the "kind of Europeans" who immigrated to the Arab world. "The overwhelming bulk of them were parasitic elements of the worst kind," they explained, "such as dealers, speculators, stock-jobbers, money-lenders, smugglers, brothel owners, swindlers, thieves, corrupt journalists, prostitutes and other." Benefiting from the Capitulations (treaties between the Ottoman Empire and various European states) and the protection of their consuls, "these scum of Europe, who regarded themselves as representatives of 'high culture,'" Abdo and Kasmieh related, "exploited the working people of Egypt and poisoned the atmosphere."[27] Though Lutsky was not alluding exclusively to Jews, Abdo and Kasmieh wrote that "whenever he refers to European immigrants . . . he is referring mostly to Jews."[28] One wonders whether the authors considered how this remark perpetuated classic antisemitic canards about the unethical foreign Jew.[29]

During the period of European encroachment on the Ottoman Arab world—an era that the authors refer to as a "dark period in Arab history"— "members of indigenous Jewish communities and descendants of early settlers moved increasingly away from their Arab neighbors and acquired Western culture, sometimes to the point of total alienation, as in the case of the Jews of Algeria who threw in their lot with the French colonialists." Ever since this distancing between the Jews and their neighbors in the Arab world, "friction between the majority of the population and the Jewish minorities should be viewed as a symptom of Arab dissatisfaction with the general situation in the Arab world." The authors highlighted "the fact that Arab nationalist leaders have sought to foster an Arab national sentiment among all members of the Jewish communities in the area and to induce them to bear their share of the general responsibility of citizenship."[30] In other words, according to these Research Center authors, "indigenous" Jews in the Arab world were consistently invited into the fold of Arab nationalism. That they declined the invitation was their own choice.

Zionism among the Jews of the Arab Countries

Though *Jews of the Arabs Countries* generally avoided the topic of Jews in Palestine, the authors addressed the question of the relationship between the Jews of the Arab world and Palestine.[31] "The Jews in the Arab countries were connected to Palestine through their religious heritage," they wrote.[32] But this sense of connection was distinct from political Zionism, which the authors presented as decidedly European (indeed, driven by the rivalry between European powers). Thus, "when the Zionist movement began its organized efforts to direct Jewish emigrants to Palestine, the Zionist leaders neither paid much attention to Oriental Jews [the term used here in the English edition], nor did the latter respond to the call of the Zionist movement."[33]

Abdo and Kasmieh explained that until World War II, "Zionist activities in the Arab countries were intermittent and scant. In fact, the Jews in the Arab countries played no great part in the Zionist emigration program to Palestine."[34] It was only after the establishment of Israel and "the new factor which its creation introduced in the area" that "Jewish communities in the Arab countries became the principal source of immigrants to Israel. They were to be instrumental in fulfilling Israel's need for manpower and military strength." Abdo and Kasmieh blamed Zionists for the dissolution of the Jewish communities in the Arab lands. "By harping on 'imminent' persecution and other means of propaganda, Zionist agents succeeded in destroying the peaceful existence which Jews had enjoyed among their Arab brethren for centuries."[35]

Once the Eastern Jews arrived in Israel, Abdo and Kasmieh noted, they were not viewed favorably by the Ashkenazic Jewish elite in the new country. "The European Israelis (the Ashkenazim)," the PLO authors wrote, "looked upon the Eastern Jews as primitive and lacking culture."[36] Ashkenazi Jewish discrimination against Mizrahi Jewish immigrants (from the Middle East and North Africa) after their arrival in Israel would become a crucial element in the PLO Research Center's assessment of Zionism, we shall see, in some of the Center's more polemical publications.

"The Best Evidence of the Tolerance of the Arabs"

The PLO Research Center's studies about the Jews in and from Arab and Muslim countries were useful in bolstering the PLO's rhetorical arsenal in its battle against Israel and for the liberation of Palestine. As we saw above, in 1969, the PLO Research Center published its *Dalil al-Qadiyya al-Filastiniyya*, and then abridged and adapted it into English as *A Handbook to the Palestine Question*. This book, as we learned, was meant to familiarize Arabs and their supporters with Zionist claims and to furnish them with compelling rejoinders. The *Dalil* addresses the issue of Jews from the Arab and Islamic world in several places. For instance, in answering the question "Do the Arabs propagate [*sic*] the elimination of the Jewish race," Ibrahim al-Abid offered, "The Arabs' treatment of the Jewish communities in different Arab countries and over history . . . is the best evidence of the tolerance of the Arabs and their humanitarian approach to minorities." Moreover, al-Abid contended, even now, "despite the bitterness of the violent conflict between the Arabs and Israel and despite all the massacres and tragedies and oppression that Israel has committed," the Jews in Arab countries are still well treated. The continued protection of Jews in Arab countries, al-Abid claimed, "is the best evidence of the lack of Arabs' hostility toward Jews as a religious and human community."[37]

Addressing the questions of what is meant by the liberation of Palestine and what will happen to the Jews of Israel after the PLO succeeds in its liberation effort, al-Abid asserted that the PLO's target is Israel as a state and as a set of institutions that represent Israeli sovereignty. "The Palestinian resistance movement," wrote al-Abid, "does not look with an eye of hate or animosity toward individual Jews regardless of whether they reside in the occupied land [that is, Israel] or in their original native countries throughout the world." In fact, al-Abid elaborated, "the Palestinian resistance movement aims to build a democratic Palestinian state in which all its citizens without exception or discrimination based on religion or race enjoy all rights and duties under Arab sovereignty. The Arab people has demonstrated over the passage of time its tolerance and its sheltering of the Jews." Moreover, "this reality continued after the establishment of Israel. And the Palestinian resistance movement did not aim any act on its behalf to influence the Arab citizens of the Jewish religion [*al-muwatinin al-'arab min al-diyana al-yahudiyya*] or citizens of the Jewish religion in any country as long as they do not support the Zionist movement and its expansionist and aggressive goals."

So long as Jews did not support the Zionist movement, al-Abid asserted, the Palestinian resistance movement was not hostile to them, regardless of where they lived. The supposedly continued safety of "the Arab citizens of the Jewish religion" (in the English version al-Abid used the term "Arab Jews") even after the rise of Zionism and even after the establishment of the State of Israel was, according to al-Abid, proof of this fact.[38]

A "Population Exchange"?

The PLO Research Center was aware, of course, that most Jews who had once lived in Arab countries had in recent years left those countries—primarily for Israel. Al-Abid thus asked, "Is it possible to compare the emigration [*hijra*] of the Jews who had inhabited [*kanu yaqtanun*] the Arab countries to the exodus [*khuruj*] [of Palestinians] as a result of the establishment of Israel?" Al-Abid noted the political ends this comparison sometimes serves for advocates of Israel who perceive "a process of 'population exchange' between the Arab states and Israel."[39]

For al-Abid, the two events had no equivalence. In contrast to the emigration of Palestinian Arabs, who "were forced to leave Palestine under the shadow of Zionist terror," "the Jews of the Arab countries emigrated to Palestine after the establishment of Israel," al-Abid asserted, "willingly and voluntarily without being subjected to any pressure or push to emigrate." In fact, again in contrast to the emigration of Palestinian Arabs from Israel, "it was in the interest of the Arab states and of Palestine that the Jews of the Arab countries remain [where they were] and not to permit them to emigrate because the arrival of more Jews to Israel strengthened it and enabled it to usurp the Arab land and made it easy for it [Israel] to carry out its expansionist plans." Because Jewish emigration was voluntary while Palestinian emigration was coerced and because Jewish emigration was against the interests of the Arab states that Jews left behind while Palestinian emigration was in the interests of the new Israeli state, the notion that the two phenomena constituted a simple "population exchange" was, al-Abid concluded, a false—and dangerous—equivalence.[40]

It is worth mentioning, in this context, that al-Abid's perspective on Jewish emigration from Arab lands differed markedly from that later offered by another important Palestinian observer of Zionism, based not at the PLO Research Center but rather, at the time, in Damascus: Mahmoud Abbas. In 1977, Abbas wrote, "The way in which the Arab regimes dealt with their Jewish subjects, whether intentionally or not, is regrettable and painful to recall. It cannot be described as anything but a shameful disgrace. Did these regimes not give Zionism the key to its existence and success? Did they not defend and preserve it? The number of Jewish Arabs in Israel is now more than 1.5 million, out of some 2.75 million [Israeli Jews]. Two-thirds of Israelis are our people, our brethren. We made them enemies and forced them to oppose us by leaving them no choice. We forced them to choose between immigrating to Israel and death and annihilation, with no other alternative."[41]

Discrimination against the Eastern Jews in Israel

The writings of the PLO Research Center focused less on why Jews left the Arab countries than on what happened to those Jews once they arrived in Israel. On the latter subject, PLO intellectuals wrote a great deal, including a monograph, published in July 1971, titled *al-Tamyiz didda al-Yahud al-Sharqiyyin fi Isra'il* (Discrimination against the Eastern Jews in Israel). *Al-Tamyiz* was written by Hilda Sha'ban Sayegh, wife of the Center's director general, Anis Sayegh, and a long-time researcher at the PLO Research Center.[42] In his preface to *al-Tamyiz*, Anis Sayegh lamented that, until then, though the Arabic press often commented on the "divisions that exist in the society of the usurper entity in occupied Palestine, and especially on its division between Eastern Jews and Western Jews, or between Sephardic Jew and Ashkenazi Jews," the Arabic library, "even one that specializes in the affairs of the enemy, does not include one scientific study of this important aspect of the reality of Israeli society."[43] The PLO Research Center sought to fill this lacuna.

In *al-Tamyiz*, Sha'ban Sayegh explored the tensions between European and Middle Eastern Jews in Israel. In one section of her book, she translated and expanded upon parts of Michael Selzer's 1967 polemical work *The Aryanization of the Jewish State*. Sha'ban Sayegh explained European Jewish discrimination against Middle Eastern Jews in three ways—all connected to the similarities between (Christian and Muslim) Arabs and Eastern Jews.[44] First, Ashkenazi Jews discriminate against Middle Eastern Jews because the latter remind the European Jew of the Arab "enemy who threatens to destroy the Jewish State." Second, because the Middle Eastern Jews are culturally so similar to the Arabs, their presence undermines the Zionist claim that the arrival of the Jews brought civilization to the Arabs. Finally, there is a basic fear among European Jews, Sha'ban Sayegh claimed, that one day the Middle Eastern Jews might ally with the Arabs against the European Jews.[45]

Sha'ban Sayegh argued that the European Jews quickly became wary of large-scale Eastern Jewish immigration to Israel. She cited an official 1951 Israeli report on the need to reduce the flow of Jewish immigration to Israel, a report that, she suggested, was delivered only to Middle Eastern countries— not, for instance, to the United States. The more Eastern Jews immigrated to Israel, Sha'ban Sayegh contended, the more alienated the country would be from European culture, which for Zionist leaders represented the ideal.[46] Though Sha'ban Sayegh suggested that Ashkenazi Jews worried that Eastern Jews might support the Palestinian cause, she and her fellow PLO intellectuals understood that most Jews from the Arab world did not support the Palestinian revolution (even if a small number did).[47] In any case, it is clear that Jews from the Arab world played a key role in the way Palestinian intellectuals thought about and argued against Zionism and Israel.

"A Form of Racism and Racial Discrimination"

In September 1975, not coincidentally just two months before the vote on UN General Assembly Resolution 3379 declaring Zionism "a form of racism and racial discrimination," the PLO Research Center issued an anonymously authored pamphlet called *Israeli Racism*. In this text, the Center proclaimed that while "the main victims of Israeli racism are, naturally, Israeli Arabs . . . racism also extends to the large Oriental Jewish community in Israel." The author explained that "the basis of this racial discrimination lies in the history of the Zionist movement. Zionism was and is not simply a movement of Jewish nationalism." Rather, "more specifically, it was a movement of *European* Jewish nationalism, born in Europe in the minds of European Jews, led throughout its history by European Jews, and primarily serving the interests of a small group of European Jews."[48]

Later in the pamphlet, the author argued that it is the discrimination against Eastern or "Oriental" Jews that demonstrates Israel's inherent racism: "While the racism against Arabs is in some sense the inevitable yet peculiar product of their status as a non-Jewish minority in a Jewish State, the racism against Oriental Jews is of a more classical, albeit no less oppressive, nature." These Jewish immigrants from Arab and Muslim countries "are the objects of racial hatred because they are dark-skinned, speak Arabic or Persian rather than German or Yiddish or Russian as a first language, as do European immigrants, and share none of the cultural traits of their European co-religionists," the pamphlet asserted. "It is precisely because Judaism is a *religion, not a common culture or race*," wrote the author, echoing the PLO Covenant, "that discrimination between the two Jewish communities is so marked in Israel, even today, 25 years after the last significant wave of Oriental Jewish immigrants."[49]

Jews Are Members of a Religion (Not a Race) but Zionism Is Racism (Not Religious Discrimination)

For the PLO Research Center, as for many ideological opponents of Zionism from the very beginning of the Jewish nationalist movement, it was vital to insist that religion alone was the unifying thread among Jews. They did not comprise a race nor did they constitute a unique ethnicity. They did not even have a shared culture or language. As such, Jews lacked the fundamental elements of nationhood. Curiously, however, the Center characterized Zionism's, and later Israel's, discrimination against non-Jews as racism. There were many other ways to categorize (and critique) Israel's alleged discrimination against non-Jews—the terms "confessionalism" or "anti-non-Judaism" or "religiously defined bigotry" or "religious xenophobia" spring to mind. Why choose one that militates against a central plank of your ideology?[50]

Though the PLO asserted that the Jews do not constitute a race, it argued that Zionists *believed*, mistakenly, that they do. Thus, discrimination against non-Jews was, from the perspective of the perpetrators of the discrimination, racism. Consider a contemporary parallel. Many people today maintain that race is socially and historically constructed; at the same time, they recognize the existence of "racism," namely, discrimination enacted by those who believe, however mistakenly, that there is an objective category called "race."[51] This perspective helps to explain the PLO's claim that while the Jews do not constitute a race, Israel's discrimination against non-Jews is a case of racism.

Fayez Sayegh made precisely this argument in the UN debates preceding the vote on Resolution 3379. "By its very essence," said Sayegh in a speech before the Social, Humanitarian, and Cultural Committee of the General Assembly in mid-October 1975, "Zionism implies a system of 'distinctions,' 'exclusions,' 'restrictions' and 'preferences'—to use the four key-words employed in article 1 of the International Convention on the Elimination of All Forms of Racial Discrimination to define 'discrimination.'" If, as Sayegh contended, Zionism constituted a form of discrimination, was that form of discrimination properly deemed "racial"? Put differently, "is *Jewishness* a 'racial' attribute?" Sayegh asked. For Sayegh, the answer to this question was clear. "My Delegation," Sayegh argued, "maintains that Jewishness is primarily a religious attribute. But it is not what *we* maintain that is relevant: in the present context, it is what Zionism itself believes that counts!"[52]

Moreover, wrote Sayegh, the UN General Assembly's definition of racism was more expansive than a narrow sense of discrimination based on race. For the UN, race also encompassed discrimination based on color, descent, national origin, and ethnic origin.[53] Not included among these categories, crucially, was religion. If Zionism discriminated based solely on religion, this discrimination would not qualify as racial. But, Sayegh stressed, "from the very beginning, Zionism opted to discard the *purely religious* interpretation of Jewishness. Jews, it proclaimed, are a people; and Jewishness, therefore, is a national/ethnic bond."[54]

But perhaps the more important reason to describe Israeli discrimination as racist was that this usage linked the struggle against alleged apartheid in Israel to the struggle against apartheid in South Africa. Toward the end of his presentation in the UN committee, Sayegh mentioned the "growing intimacy and collaboration between Israel and South Africa." Just as "the international community was acting to isolate the South African regime, Israel was stepping up its activities to de-isolate that regime," Sayegh asserted. This "unholy alliance," as the UN General Assembly termed the bond between Israel and South Africa, was not merely one of convenience, argued Sayegh, but was based on the regimes' shared principles. "The expanding relations" between the countries "is a manifestation," Sayegh contended, "of an underlying ideological affinity that attracts the bastion of racism in western Asia and the stronghold of racism in southern Africa to each other."[55] The term "racism" thus constructed a rhetorical link between South African apartheid and Israeli discrimination against non-Jews.[56]

The Link between Zionism's Two Racisms

The PLO and its Research Center argued, as we have seen, that racism in Israel existed on two levels. The first and most severe was the racism that targeted non-Jews. The second, less severe but nonetheless significant, was the racism that targeted Jews who were not of European or Ashkenazi heritage (that is, racism against "Oriental" or "Sephardic" Jews who had immigrated to Israel from Africa or Asia). The latter was, in the PLO's view, a more "classical" form of racism, namely, discrimination against a group based on the color of its members' skin. A potential problem with this argument, however, is that it assumes that Zionists do not in fact consider the Jews to be a single race, while the claim that Zionists do (mistakenly) regard the Jews to be a single race was, as just discussed, critical to the PLO argument that Zionist discrimination against non-Jews constituted a form of racism.

"Race-thinking," in Hannah Arendt's apt characterization, has infinite potential.[57] Simply because certain Zionists considered Jews to be racially distinct from non-Jews did not mean, necessarily, that these Zionists considered Jews to be a homogenous racial unit. So perhaps the PLO argument was that Zionists regarded Jews as a race separate from non-Jews *and* that within the Jewish race there were internal racial differences. This argument appears to be what Fayez Sayegh had in mind when he said, at the United Nations in 1975, that "like a cancer, racism has a propensity for expansion: it defies containment. Having adopted a racist approach to non-Jews, Zionism soon came to draw a color-line or a racial line among the Jews themselves." Here, Sayegh was arguing that intra-Jewish racism was a side effect of Zionism's fundamental racism against non-Jews. "The Zionist myth of 'one Jewish people' was exploded," asserted Sayegh, "as soon as Jews from different cultural, ethnic and racial backgrounds were assembled together." The racial hierarchy in Israel thus emerged: "If the 'white' Jews from Europe and America, who constitute the backbone of the 'Establishment,' are Israel's first-class citizens, the Oriental Jews and the Black Jews constitute the second-class and third-class citizens of the *Judenstaat* respectively. This makes the Arab citizens, the remnants of the Palestinian Arab people in Israel, the fourth-class citizens in their own land."[58]

In his writings and speeches arguing that Zionism constituted a form of racism, Sayegh regularly referred to Israel as "the *Judenstaat*." This German term for a Jewish state or a state of the Jews was borrowed from Theodor Herzl, who titled his foundational German-language Zionist pamphlet *Der Judenstaat*. But Sayegh may also have been using this term in order to emphasize Zionism's German roots and to associate Zionism with another German ideology, namely, Nazism.[59] Indeed, in various ways, more or less explicitly, Sayegh linked Zionism with Nazism. For instance, arguing to the UN in November 1975 that criticism of Zionism ought not be regarded as antisemitism or anti-Judaism, Sayegh asked rhetorically, "Is criticism of Nazism a criticism of the German people and of Christianity? Why should criticism of Zionism automatically be considered criticism of Judaism and of the 'Jewish people?'"[60] When writing of the debates within Israel over the question of "Who is a Jew?," Sayegh cited Israeli Supreme Court Justice Haim Cohen's 1963 opinion that "it is one of the bitterest ironies of fate that the same biological and racist approach which was propagated by the Nazis and characterized the infamous Nuremberg laws," which defined Jewishness in genealogical terms, "should . . . become the basis for the official determination or rejection of Jewishness in the state of Israel."[61]

In concluding his earlier October 1975 UN committee speech, Sayegh cited Arnold Toynbee, who wrote in his book *Experiences* that "the age through which I have lived has . . . seen the moral implications of mankind's common humanity repudiated in outrageous doctrines that have served as excuses for atrocious acts."[62] Toynbee listed three varieties in what Sayegh described as "descending order of outrageousness": first, "genocide" (with the Nazi genocide of the Jews as the paradigmatic case); second, "eviction of entire populations" (such as the "the Palestinian Arab evicted persons and refugees"); and, third, "the penalization of a weaker section of a population" (e.g., South African apartheid).[63] Through Toynbee, Sayegh sandwiched Israel's refusal to permit Palestinian refugees to return to their homes between Nazism and apartheid, thereby rhetorically linking the three.

Given that characterizing Ashkenazi discrimination against Mizrahim in Israel as "racism" complicates the argument that Israeli Jewish discrimination against Palestinians is "racism," why use the same term to describe both?[64] Again, one explanation may be simply that PLO Research Center intellectuals were eager to explore any and all ways in which Israel could be denounced as "racist."

But there may have been another motivation in addition to the analytical, theoretical claim these researchers were making (i.e., that Israeli society and politics were marked by both internal and external Jewish racism). At the time, some Israelis and Palestinians were considering a political alliance between non-Jewish Palestinian Arabs and Middle Eastern Jews in challenging Israel's legitimacy. This same period, the early 1970s, saw the rise of the Israeli Black Panther movement in which Middle Eastern Jews protested the state's discrimination against them. As Black Panther leader Kokhavi Shemesh noted in 1971, in Israel, "in poor [Mizrahi] neighborhoods . . . one can hear expressions like 'the Ashkenazim are worse than the Arabs.' Everybody says that today," Shemesh asserted. The political implications of Mizrahi and Palestinian shared antipathy toward Israel's Ashkenazi elite were clear. "Any identification between [Mizrahi] Jewish and Arab workers will help ease the tension between the two peoples and push them towards a common struggle against Israel's rulers," argued Shemesh. "The Sephardim realize that the Arabs are worse off than they are in this country," he explained, "and that could lead to a joint struggle."[65] Very much aware of the Israeli Panther movement, some PLO Research Center intellectuals may have been interested in the potential for such a collaborative effort.

Historian Hillel Cohen has recently argued that the advantages gained by Mizrahim in linking themselves to the Palestinians were miniscule compared to the advantages of emphasizing their links to Ashkenazim and, by implication, their differences from Arabs. Mizrahim were aware of this disparity and, according to Cohen, acted accordingly. It is no wonder, given the benefits of aligning with the dominant party (namely, the Jews) rather than those viewed as the enemy, Cohen wrote, that "most Mizrahim emphasized their differences from the Arabs—socially and politically—and not their bonds with them." And yet, according to Cohen, "on the Mizrahi margins," occasionally there were some Mizrahim who desired to ally with Palestinians, whether "politically, culturally, or as an expression of anger." It was apparently these few Mizrahi exceptions who fueled what Cohen described as a "Palestinian fantasy" of a potential alliance with a significant portion of Israel's Jewish population.[66]

A decade later, according to Joseph Massad, there was a "growing trend" among Mizrahi Israelis, "toward solidarity with the Palestinians." In his estimation, non-Ashkenazi Jews "spanning the entire social spectrum linked discrimination practiced against them with that used against the Palestinians." They were, wrote Massad, "prominent in the Committee for Israeli-Palestinian Dialogue formed in 1984, whose meetings with Palestinians prompted the government to issue, in August 1986, its 'Counter-Terrorism Act' banning contact with the Palestine Liberation Organization (PLO)." Massad noted that former Black Panthers Kokhavi Shemesh and Saʿadya Marciano, "who had launched their Eastern (Mizrahi) Front in support of the Palestinians in 1986, were in the forefront of Israeli groups protesting Israeli repression during the intifada."[67] Notwithstanding the law aimed at preventing engagement with the PLO, "the Dialogue Committee, which also included Ashkenazim, met with PLO officials in Romania in November 1986 and in Budapest in June 1987," wrote Massad, and "a specifically Mizrahi-Palestinian dialogue was soon established, which, with the support of the Paris-based *Perspectives Judeo-Arabes*, held a historic meeting in Toledo, Spain, in July 1989 attended by thirty-eight Mizrahi intellectuals and a large Palestinian delegation including Mahmud Abbas (Abu Mazin) and the poet Mahmud Darwish."[68] The PLO Research Center's 1970s-era writing on what its researchers regarded as Zionist racism helped lay the theoretical and political foundations for this remarkable, if ephemeral, alliance.[69]

10

The Role of the Zionist Terror in the Creation of Israel

ON THE NECESSITY OF VIOLENCE

THE SCHOLARS at the PLO Research Center did not pretend that the Palestinians' conflict with Israel was merely academic in nature. They knew that violence played a central role in this conflict, and so they also engaged with the topic of militance—with a greater focus on violence targeting Palestinians than on the violence perpetrated by Palestinians.

During its years in Beirut, the Center published *The Terrorist Roots of the Israeli Herut Party* (1966); *The Balance of Military Power between the Arab States and Israel* (1967); *Violence and Peace: A Study in Zionist Strategy* (1967); *The Role of the Zionist Terror in the Creation of Israel* (1969); *Crime and No Punishment: Zionist-Israeli Terrorism* (1972); *The Israeli Air Force* (1973); *The Israeli Armored Forces through Four Wars* (1975); and *Haganah, Etzel, Lehi: Relations between the Zionist Armed Organizations* (1981), among other works focused on Zionist and Israeli armed forces and violence.[1] In this chapter, I examine several Center publications on the topic of Zionist and Israeli violence, especially Bassam Bishuti's *The Role of the Zionist Terror in the Creation of Israel*, with the aim of understanding how the Center authors understood and depicted the violence of the enemy. I also consider the ways in which Zionist violence was seen as a model for Palestinian violence.

The Necessity of "Terror"

In *The Role of the Zionist Terror*, published in English (evidently aiming for an international audience) in April 1969, Bishuti used a rather broad definition of "terror."[2] He explained in his preface that by "terror" he meant "a number of different actions by which pressure was used in order for the Zionists to achieve their aims." While he wrote that terror's "more obvious forms are the physical acts of violence, murder, destruction and military aggression," Bishuti also included within the rubric of terror "diluted violence," such as "propaganda, spying, and threats."[3]

Bishuti opened the book by exploring "the causes of the terror" that the Zionists inflicted on the Palestinians. He clearly felt uneasy with this task, apparently concerned that noting the reasons for the "terror" might be perceived as justifying it. "The only excuse I give for writing this introductory chapter," Bishuti noted, "is my wish to be as complete, balanced and coherent as possible." In order to comprehensively "discuss the terror and deal with its effects and influence," he wrote, "I must discuss the reasons for it, the factors which made it so instrumental and so important to Zionism in the first place."[4]

For Bishuti, the cause of Zionist terror was simple: necessity. If Zionism was to achieve its aim of a "purely Jewish state on the soil of Palestine," the Zionists had no choice but to engage in terrorism.[5] Given that "the odds against this goal being realized proved to be so many," Zionists recognized "that swift and dedicated action had to be undertaken" in order to overcome these odds.[6] Bishuti explained why the Zionists engaged in this terror:

> How could the Zionists control a land when the Jews in the land were such a small minority and when they owned only a small fraction of its territory? Clearly, something had to be done. The Zionists' answer was of two branches. First, swell the Jewish population in Palestine by immigration into the land, and second, obtain control over more areas of the land. This was the Zionist program and it constituted, in fact, the causes of the terror I am discussing.[7]

The British, who stood in the way of Zionist goals by limiting Jewish immigration to Palestine, thus became the first targets of Zionist terror.[8] After the British announced that they would withdraw from Palestine and the UN approved the 1947 partition plan, Bishuti explained, the Zionists no longer had reason to engage in terror against the Mandate forces. "Having accumulated enough arms and experience in terrorism," the Zionists thus "turned to the Arabs."[9] They "had seven months in which to terrorize the Arabs into leaving the Jewish State, and also to expand into, control and de-Arabize as much as they could of the projected Arab State." The Zionists were aware that, upon the British departure, they "would have to face the Arab armies," continued Bishuti, so "a quick and concentrated campaign of terror" was necessary for the Zionists "to achieve their aims and also to put themselves in a position of strength when the Arab armies came." As a result, he concluded, "the Arabs of Palestine faced the Zionist bands of cut-throats for seven months of most horrible terror."[10] The Zionists succeeded in their goal of "driving the Arabs out of Palestine" primarily "as a result of what happened at Deir Yassin," wherein Zionist militia forces massacred Palestinian civilians in their village outside Jerusalem.[11]

As Bishuti framed matters, terror was not a Zionist choice but rather a necessity if the Zionists were to achieve their aims. "We see that terror was inevitable from the Zionist point of view," Bishuti contended. For the Zionists to succeed in securing a Jewish state in Palestine, they had to overcome several major challenges: "they had to create a Jewish majority in Palestine, they had to get rid of the British presence and they had to acquire control over a large area of Palestine to be able to achieve a respectable and secure status of nationhood." In Bishuti's view, "these problems could not be solved except by terrorizing the people who stood as obstacles. These, in fact, were the causes of the Zionist terror, directed against the British and then against the Arabs."[12] For various reasons, the British, Americans, and Soviets all chose not to interfere with the Zionist terror against the Arabs of Palestine and, as a result, "Zionist terror . . . was able to achieve all its aims. The results were: the State of Israel was created, and the Arabs of Palestine became the bitter refugees of today, sworn to revenge and the liberation of their Palestine."[13]

"Sworn to Revenge"

The idea that along with establishing Israel, Zionist terrorism also transformed the Palestinian Arabs into refugees who were now "sworn to revenge and the liberation of Palestine" is a crucial subtext of Bishuti's book. While Bishuti's focus was on Zionist violence, he was clearly thinking about its relationship to Palestinian violence. If the Palestinians engaged in terror, they were simply using the same means as the Zionists did—albeit in the Palestinians' case, to right a historic wrong. Bishuti complained that "People would heartily condemn the Arab resistance to Israeli occupation of their lands on the grounds that it was a type of terrorism and violence. Hardly anyone realizes that the Arabs are merely repaying the Israelis with acts they have already committed against them."[14] Bishuti's assertion here is critical for understanding a prominent PLO Research Center perspective on violence during this period. For Bishuti, the violence directed at Israel was "Arab resistance to Israeli occupation of their lands." This, in his view, was justified and legitimate violence. At the same time, he acknowledged that these acts constituted "a type of terror-ism and violence" comparable to those committed previously by the Zionists against the Palestinians.

The implicit argument is that Arab "terrorism" against Israel is distinct from Zionist "terrorism" against the Arabs not in the nature of the acts but in their contexts.[15] The Zionists engaged in terrorism in order to occupy Arab lands; the Arabs engaged in terrorism in order to resist and undermine that occupation. The Zionists engaged in terrorism against a population that had not provoked it;[16] the Arabs engaged in terrorism against a population that had previously engaged in terrorism against them. For Arabs, terrorism against Zionists was simply repayment in kind.

Practical Lessons from Zionist Terror

Given the contentions that terrorism was necessary for the achievement of the Zionists' goals, and that contemporary Palestinian terrorism was justified ret-ribution for what the Zionists had inflicted upon the Palestinians and neces-sary for achieving Palestinian liberation, Bishuti's narration of the history of Zionist terrorism might be read as a guide for Palestinian terrorism. Bishuti thus appears to be offering not only a portrayal of Zionist history but also a prescription for the Palestinian present and future.

Bishuti's assessment of Zionist duplicity concerning terrorism is a case in point. Zionist leaders, according to Bishuti, publicly condemned terrorism enacted by fellow Zionists even as they privately supported it, understanding that violence was key to the success of their cause. It was for this reason, Bi-shuti argued, that the distinction between "the Irgun terrorists"—who "were responsible to no authority except their own"—and the Haganah—which "was run and supervised by the Jewish Agency and therefore owed this Agency its allegiance"—was so useful to the Zionist leaders. "Since it was clear that those who stood to gain most from the terror were the Zionist leaders, who became Israel's leaders later, because the terror made the aim of statehood possible," he wrote, "it was best for these beneficiaries to pretend that the ter-ror and its aims did not coincide with their programmes." This pretense of disapproval "was the official public attitude."[17] Thus, notwithstanding how crucial terrorism was for Zionists, "some Zionist commentators—understandably—have alleged that both goals" of removing the British and expelling the Arabs "were achieved by diplomatic, or at best military means, and not by terror."[18] If for Zionism's past political leaders it was essential to engage in terrorism in order to achieve their aims even as it was crucial to deny publicly that this was so, the same might be said of contemporary Palestinian leaders.

Bishuti further explored the potential use of terrorism for the purposes of gaining international attention and sympathy. This, he asserted, was the Zionists' approach as they strove to bring Jewish refugees into Palestine far beyond the numbers that British Mandate policy permitted. Because the British Mandate forces sought to prevent the entry of these refugees, the Zionists would "inevitably engage in bloody battles with the British authorities and security forces trying to stop the ships at the ports." At times, the Zionists succeeded in smuggling in the "unfortunate people and would hide them in Jewish settlements." In other instances, the Zionists would fail and "out of frustration and in an attempt to win international sympathy . . . would blow up the ships, killing or drowning the Jews in them together with the British soldiers." Bishuti alleged that violence and terrorism—inflicted upon fellow Jews—were exploited to attract the attention of the press and sympathy in the broader world. "The propaganda connected with these incidents," wrote Bishuti, "would, undoubtedly, have great effects all over the world, especially in the USA. There the propaganda was directed at the American public in an effort to win sympathy for the terror (portrayed as a war of liberation) by spicing the behaviour of the British authorities in Palestine with an anti-Semitic flavour."[19] If, as Bishuti suggested, earlier Zionist terror served as not only a justification but also a model for contemporary Palestinian terror, he showed that terror can be used to engender sympathy rather than antipathy for the perpetrators' cause in global public opinion.

Bishuti also discussed how Zionists used negotiations to gain crucial time to prepare and arm their forces for future violence. On the truce of June–July 1948, for instance, Bishuti wrote, "the truce gave victory to Israel and defeat to the Arabs." He explained that "the Arabs accepted it from a position of strength while the Israelis accepted it in a position of weakness." During the period of the truce, "while the Arabs sat and waited, the Israelis ignored their promises under the truce. They armed themselves, made their terrorists into an army, eased the blockade over Jerusalem and when the war came again, the balance had been changed."[20] For Bishuti, the Israeli forces' clandestine violations of the terms of the agreement allowed them to win the war.

In the years since the establishment of the State of Israel, Bishuti argued, those who engaged in terrorism in the Mandate period were fully embraced by the state. "Israel has shown its gratitude and admiration for the terrorists,"

Bishuti wrote, "by opening its arms to them and making respectable citizens out of them." In Israel, Bishuti contended, "the terrorists of yesterday are not murderers, cut-throats or professional thugs; they are the heroes of the state." Contemporary Israeli society and culture willfully ignore the history of terrorism in the pre-state years, and the relationship between the political leadership and the terrorists, Bishuti alleged. In support of this assertion, Bishuti cited British Zionist Harry Sacher, who noted that "much is still obscure as to the relation between the Haganah or the Government and the Irgun" and that this is no accident. "For comprehensible reasons," wrote Sacher, the Israeli government "does not think the time has come to tell its story fully and frankly."[21]

Moreover, Zionism's reliance on terrorism did not end with the establishment of the state, argued Bishuti. The sort of violence that Zionist forces used against Arabs during the British Mandate continued, "although now 'terrorist' is hardly the right word to describe these activities because those who engaged in them were now the officials of a state." Nonetheless, alleged Bishuti, "they preserved the same pattern of murder and destruction. Now we must call them examples of Israel's policy of violence."[22] Bishuti's primary example of Israel's continued "policy of violence" in the years following 1948 was the 1956 massacre of nearly fifty Arab civilians in Kafr Qasim by IDF forces.[23] This mass killing constituted, in Bishuti's view, "one of the most savage examples of post 1948 Zionist terror," resembling "the [1948] massacre of Deir Yassin in many ways, except that this new one was the work of the Israeli 'Defense' Army, while the other was the work of pre-army terrorists."[24]

With the 1967 war having recently passed, Bishuti concluded that "Israel owes its existence to the effectiveness of terror." The state expanded beyond the borders offered it by the UN as a result of the Zionists' use of terror during the 1948 war. "Now," he wrote, "after the 1967 war, Israel controls the rest of Palestine plus further Arab territory." Bishuti opined that "it seems that Israel's frontiers are and will always be, as they have always been, decided upon by the latest victory in battle—in other words as a result of the right of force."[25] This message was received loud and clear by the Palestinian guerrilla groups, which assumed leadership of the PLO after the 1967 war.

After the Munich Olympics

The PLO Research Center published Bishuti's book about Zionist terror in 1969. As the years progressed, and as Palestinian militants engaged in increasingly spectacular acts of public violence, "terrorism" came to be closely associated with, and even seen as synonymous with, Palestinian nationalism. The Black September group's widely televised capture of the Israeli Olympic team in Munich in September 1972, leading to the deaths of eleven Israeli athletes, did much to solidify the link in Western consciousness between the Palestinians and terrorism.

Two months after the Munich attack, the PLO Research Center published another book about Zionist and Israeli terrorism. This new book was called *Crime and No Punishment: Zionist-Israeli Terrorism, 1939–1972*. The book was written by Sami Hadawi (1904–2004), a Palestinian Christian refugee from Jerusalem who, between 1965 and 1968, had directed the nearby Institute for Palestine Studies. Hadawi argued that "it is necessary to distinguish between acts of violence intended to remove a grievance or an injustice, and acts of violence committed in order to impose and perpetuate an injustice." This distinction was crucial for Hadawi because it permitted him to categorically differentiate between the two sides of the Palestinian-Israeli conflict. "The acts of Palestinian Arabs are those of the dispossessed and, therefore, fall within the first category" (namely, "acts of violence intended to remove a grievance or an injustice"). On the other hand, "the acts of Israel and its predecessor structure—the Zionist organizations in Palestine—are those of the colonialist possessive and, consequently, conform in nature to the second," namely, "acts of violence committed in order to impose and perpetuate an injustice, i.e., terrorism."[26] Put differently, the Palestinian cause is just and violence for a just cause is not terrorism. In the Palestinians' case, violence is simply "the only avenue left open to them to achieve their liberation."

Addressing his English-reading audience in terms to which he presumed they would relate, Hadawi cited a paragraph from the conclusion of the Continental Congress's July 1775 "Declaration on Taking Arms":

> In our native land, in defence of the freedom which is our birthright, and which we enjoyed till the late violation of it, for the protection of our property, acquired solely by the honest industry of our forefathers and ourselves, against violence offered, we have taken up arms. We shall lay them down when hostilities shall cease on the part of the aggressors and all danger of their being renewed shall be removed, and not before.

Hadawi argued that "if the American people, whose homes and country were not taken away from them by aliens, and whose very existence was not threatened with extinction, were within their human and legal rights to adopt such a stand," then "surely the Palestinian Arabs, after twenty-five years of solicitude, argument, appeal and protest at the doors of the United Nations and the Big Powers, have a greater right to adhere to the principles of the American Declaration [of Independence] and take up arms in defense of their property and homeland."[27]

While Hadawi defended the Palestinians' recourse to violence, he was evidently uncomfortable offering a full-throated justification of the massacre at the Munich Olympics. Instead, he blamed the course of events on others. "Responsibility for the actual shape of the Munich tragedy rests squarely with the West German Government," Hadawi alleged, "for having deceived the Arab commandos into believing that they would be allowed to leave German soil with their hostages unmolested, but who then opened fire on them." If only the Germans had permitted the hostage takers to escape with the captive Israeli athletes, Hadawi asserted, the hostages as well as the Arabs whom the hostage takers sought to free from Israeli prisons would have been safe and free. Citing "some students of the Palestine problem and Zionist methods and tactics during the period of the Mandate," Hadawi further added the possibility that "the death of the Israeli athletes may have been allowed to happen on the advice of the Israeli 'advisers,' who arrived in Munich to assist the West German authorities in handling the situation."[28] Hadawi thus deflected responsibility for the murders first onto the West Germans and then onto the Israelis themselves. At the same time, he held fast to the principle that the violence in which Palestinian militants engaged against Israeli targets was legitimate because its goal was just.

"A Perfect Symbiosis of Antipathy, Fear, and Envy"

This phenomenon of enemies projecting assumptions on each other has been observed by scholars of antagonistic encounters in other historical contexts. For instance, describing France-Germany mutual perceptions in the years preceding the World War I, historian Michael Nolan observed "an inverted mirror—a perfect symbiosis of antipathy, fear, and envy." Each of these two nations, Nolan explained, "projected certain assumptions about national character onto the other by way of creating its primary enemy. Most notably, the qualities each country ascribed to its chief adversary were exaggerated or negative versions of precisely those qualities it felt to be lacking or inadequate in itself." Nolan's insight concerning early twentieth-century Europe seems to apply rather aptly to our case. In this period of rising Palestinian militancy, the PLO Research Center argued that the Zionists were the model. As Nolan put it, "paradoxically, though we fear the enemy, we embrace him as well, because he is a clear focus of the unspeakable hatreds that dwell within us." And yet it is difficult for parties to a conflict to acknowledge the obvious similarities of the opposing sides' acts of violence, and of their corresponding rhetorical and ethical justifications. "The necessity of presenting a stark contrast between 'us' and 'them,'" wrote Nolan, "overrides the evidence of reality and militates against a balanced evaluation of facts."[29] In its studies of Zionist and Israeli terrorism, the PLO Research Center presented the Israeli enemy as a model to be at once emulated and abhorred.

Arms vs. "the Decisive Factors Leading to Victory"

In May 1974, just seven months after another Arab-Israeli war, the PLO Research Center published an Arabic book on the topic of Israeli military force. This time it was a study of contemporary Israeli weapons, *The Arms of the Israeli Forces*, compiled by Hisham Abdallah for the Center's Facts and Figures series. The book is divided into three broad sections. The first outlines the tools and weapons of Israeli ground forces, including tanks, armored cars, artillery, antitank missiles, and guns. The second covers the air force, detailing Israel's fighter jets, reconnaissance planes, transport aircraft, and the various weapons attached to the planes. Finally, the third section concerns the navy and its submarines, light units, and landing ships. Abdallah opened the book by explaining that "the armed forces in Israel are considered one of the primary elements of this aggressive state, and an urgent necessity for it to live and remain as 'a garrison state' [*ka-dawlat mu'askar*] in the midst of the Arab homeland."

Because Israel existentially depends on its military, wrote Abdallah, "these forces in Israel enjoy an importance that exceeds their importance in most other countries." Given the "numerical gap between them [the Israelis] and the Arab forces that surround them," with the Israeli population so much smaller than the populations of the Arab states in the region, "the Israeli armed forces pay special attention to the issue of armaments, and they attempt to acquire the newest and strongest arms to ensure superiority" over the neighboring militaries. Abdallah explained that initially Israel procured arms from a variety of both Eastern and Western countries. In the 1950s, however, "France became the main source of Israeli arms, especially in the area of airplanes and artillery," while Britain and the United States provided weapons for Israel's tank corps. Abdallah recounted that "the good relations between France and

Israel lasted until the aggression of 1967." By means of this close relationship with France, "Israel acquired equipment, arms, and military factories, and nuclear generators. And there is no doubt," added Abdallah, "that French arms participated to a great extent in Israel's victory in the 1967 War."[30]

After the Six-Day War, the French imposed an arms embargo on Israel. In place of France, Abdallah explained, "the United States became the main source of arms for Israel in all areas." The US supplied the Israeli "air force with all the necessary fighter planes, transport planes, helicopters, and special munitions that it needed and air-to-air, air-to-surface, and surface-to-air missiles." The Americans also outfitted Israel with "devices for [radar] jamming and electronic warfare, and unmanned aircraft." At the same time, "the Israeli army acquired the best American machine guns and the strongest and newest American tanks and armored personnel carrier tanks, along with the new anti-tank missiles." In addition, the US offered the Israelis "technical assistance and factories necessary for developing Israeli weapons" produced locally.[31]

With these American-aided weapons factories in Israel, Abdallah explained, Israel had also developed a weapons industry of its own. Israel has over time "established workshops to make alterations to the arms that it has acquired, and it has developed a military industry that manufactures transport planes, airplane engines, gunboats, air-to-air missiles, and different types of ammunition." Israel's difficulties during the 1973 war that had just passed, however, "revealed the weaknesses of this industry and Israel's inability to depend upon it."[32] Hence, concluded Abdallah, Israel remains deeply reliant on foreign-produced weapons.

What did the PLO Research Center wish to achieve by publishing this volume? According to Abdallah, the book's aim was "to contribute to disseminating the facts" about the enemy's "military knowledge" and "the arms that the enemy uses" as these "have a direct impact on the strategy that it follows and on its tactics and military concepts." In order to comprehend how Israel behaves, Abdallah contended on behalf of the PLO Research Center, one must understand the military tools at Israel's disposal. At the same time, Abdallah asserted, weapons are not the sole, or even the most important, factor in determining the results of a military conflict. "No matter how much the power of weapons is increased, or how much their gunfire and thrust and effectiveness are intensified," wrote Abdallah, weapons "remain in modern war mere combat tools that do not constitute the decisive factor in any war (whether traditional or revolutionary)." What matters most, he insisted, are the human aspects of the military. "The trained soldier, a good military system, a strong political system, and balanced economic and social conditions"—rather than the sophistication of the weaponry—"represent the decisive factors leading to victory."[33] In a conflict as militarily imbalanced as that between Israel and the Palestinians, for any hope of success through "armed struggle," one had to believe that there was more to determining the fate of a war than the weapons each side possessed.

Planning Terror in the PLO Research Center?

Was this research on Israel's armed forces and Zionist and Israeli violence and terrorism the extent of the PLO Research Center's relationship to the PLO's armed struggle? Or was the PLO Research Center more directly involved in PLO armed activity against Israeli targets? In January 1976, two years after the PLO Research Center published Abdallah's book on Israeli arms, journalist Walter W. Howard wrote an article in the *Boston Globe* called "Terrorists: How They Operate a Worldwide Network." Howard opened the piece with a scene of "a lavish headquarters" in Beirut in which a man, in a single day, plots a terrorist attack in France with Latin American agents, communicates with a Japanese secret organization, plans a raid into Israel, requests payments from the Libyan government, and follows up with the Irish Republican Army about a scheduled delivery of Czech-made submachine guns with silencers and folding butts—all before heading out to golf with a Basque Nationalist agent. The headquarters in which all this scheming was said to have taken place was the PLO Research Center.[34]

If PLO violence was in fact being organized at—if not *by*—the PLO Research Center, this might explain Israel's apparent targeting of the PLO Research Center and its staff beginning in the mid-1970s. It would also explain why, as we shall see, in 1982, the Israeli military attacked the building and confiscated its contents. While the official work of the PLO Research Center may have been unobjectionable, if its offices were used for militant purposes, Israeli decision-makers may have expected to find documents related to these militant activities in the library. These documents could then be used for intelligence and counterterrorism ends.

But ought we to trust reports like Howard's? The level of detail in the account suggests that the journalist himself witnessed the scene. Yet the sensational, all-in-a-day's work nature of those details arouses skepticism. When one looks more closely at the story, one notices that only two people are quoted: Major-General Eliyahu Zeira, a former Israeli intelligence director (one of four officials blamed by the Agranat Commission for Israel's unpreparedness for the Yom Kippur War), and a Captain Paul Herst of the West German police. The "squat, bespectacled little man named Habib Bakary" allegedly organizing all the activity is, as far as I am aware, otherwise unknown. Though the author did not mention the date on which all this took place, given that the article was published in a daily newspaper in January 1976, one imagines that it had occurred recently. However, the PLO, under the leadership of Fateh, had at least officially suspended attacks outside of Israel several years earlier, after the 1973 war.

Even if PLO officials were continuing to plan attacks outside Israel and were doing so from the offices of the PLO Research Center, it stretches credulity that they would have permitted an American journalist to look on. Howard may have fabricated elements of this story to make it more titillating. Or perhaps some details were rooted in allegations of Israeli officials such as Zeira, or other enemies of the PLO, whether Israeli or Lebanese or even Palestinian. Parties to the conflict may have deliberately misinformed journalists in an attempt to weaken the PLO by disparaging the organization or by provoking Israeli or Lebanese parties to act against the Center as an arm of the PLO and thus a symbol of the PLO's legitimized presence in Lebanon.[35] Ultimately, however, a report such as this need not have been accurate for it to have been impactful. The real question is whether Israeli officials directing the activities against the PLO gave the report credence.

Is there more reliable evidence linking the PLO Research Center to PLO militancy? Can one find the Center's fingerprints on materials more directly linked to PLO-initiated violence? I address these questions, which were at the heart of a fiery international debate following Israel's invasion of West Beirut in September 1982, in part 3.

PART III

Invasion, Confiscation, and Return

11

The PLO Research Center
in Tel Aviv

War in Lebanon

THE LATTER HALF of the 1970s was a period of great upheaval in the Middle East. A complex, multisided civil war (that also involved foreign powers) erupted in Lebanon in 1975, dooming the country to a decade and a half of bloodshed. In May 1977, for the first time in Israel's history, a right-wing government won a majority in the Knesset, Israel's parliament, under the leadership of former Irgun militia head and long-time opposition chief Menachem Begin, an outspoken opponent of an independent Palestinian state. Aiming to exploit Egypt's relative success in the 1973 war, President Anwar Sadat initially pursued a comprehensive, regional peace agreement with Israel that would include the Palestinians—bringing his case directly to the Knesset in a dramatic visit in November 1977—but acceded to what was effectively a separate peace with Israel.[1] By the end of the decade, Israel and Egypt had signed a peace treaty while the Pahlavi ruler of Iran who had long maintained relations with Israel had been overthrown by a profoundly anti-Israeli Islamic Revolution.

Meanwhile, thousands of Palestinian guerillas who had been driven from Jordan between September 1970 and July 1971 established bases in southern Lebanon and strongholds in Beirut and surrounding refugee camps. Palestinian fighters now in Lebanon sought, and sometimes succeeded, to enter Israel and attack Israeli targets. The Israeli military regularly retaliated with deadly raids. The civil war in Lebanon only exacerbated the tension between Israel and the PLO as the latter managed to entrench and expand its power in significant portions of the country, establishing what many viewed as a "state-within-a-state." From this relatively secure position, PLO militants increasingly undertook raids south of the nearby border with Israel, continuing to spark punishing Israeli military reprisals. PLO fears during these years that the cause of Palestine was being forgotten or sacrificed on the altar of Egypt's peace with Israel further enraged Palestinian nationalists and militants in Lebanon.[2]

In March 1978, the violence came to a head when Palestinians infiltrated Israel's coast from Lebanon, commandeering two buses and ultimately killing over thirty civilians, including thirteen children. Three days later, Prime Minister Menachem Begin ordered the Israel Defense Forces to undertake Operation Litani. The aim was to clear PLO forces from Lebanese territory south of the Litani River, to create a buffer zone between Palestinian militant bases and Israel's northern communities. The harsh military assault left more than a thousand dead, including both militants and civilians, and approximately 250,000 displaced people. The United Nations demanded Israel's withdrawal and established the UN Interim Force for Southern Lebanon (UNIFIL) to administer the border. Israel did indeed withdraw, but not before handing control over a ten-kilometer-wide buffer region to its Lebanese Christian Melkite ally from Marjayoun, Major Saad Haddad.[3]

Neither UNIFIL nor Haddad's Christian forces were successful in preventing either Palestinian attacks on Israel from southern Lebanon or Israeli assaults on PLO militants and positions there. In fact, Israel's attacks extended north of the UNIFIL-controlled buffer zone. The cycle of attack and counterattack peaked again in July 1981 when Israel's air force launched an offensive on Palestinian artillery and rocket positions near the coastal city of Sidon and the inland city of Nabatiyeh, both north of the Litani River. In response, the Palestinian militants shelled northern Israeli communities and the region under Major Haddad's forces. The Israelis then took their assault further (foreshadowing the approach they would take the following year) by extending their attack far north of the Israel-Lebanon border region all the way to the country's capital. From the air, Israeli forces bombed Palestinian organizational offices in Beirut, leaving hundreds of casualties, mostly civilian. This stage of the conflict came to a close with an Israeli-PLO ceasefire brokered by American and Saudi diplomats.[4]

The fragile ceasefire did not hold long, especially as Israel viewed Palestinian attacks against Israeli or Jewish targets anywhere in the world (not just from Lebanon) as violations of the agreement. While Israel's right-wing Likud government was eager to push the PLO farther and more fully from Lebanon's border with Israel, a group of Israeli government and military officials led by Defense Minister Ariel Sharon had a more ambitious goal: to remove the PLO entirely from Lebanon.[5] After the completion of Israel's April 1982 withdrawal from the Sinai Peninsula (signaling the firm establishment of its peace treaty with Egypt and ensuring a quiet southern border), Israel prepared for the next Palestinian provocation. At the beginning of June 1982, members of the Abu Nidal group—hardliners who violently opposed any softening of the Palestinian determination to recapture all of historic Palestine—provided it by attempting to assassinate Israel's ambassador to the United Kingdom, Shlomo Argov.[6] Three days later, on June 6, 1982, Israel launched Operation Peace for Galilee.[7]

Since then, Israel's ultimate plan in its summertime invasion of Lebanon has been hotly debated. On the day the operation began, the Israeli cabinet announced that it had instructed the Israel Defense Forces "to remove all of the residents of the Galilee from the range of the terrorists, their headquarters, and their bases in Lebanon."[8] This directive may be interpreted in ways that run the gamut from limited to expansive—from the more modest aim to create a wider and less permeable buffer zone within Lebanon to the more ambitious goal of expelling the PLO from all of Lebanon.[9]

The more expansive interpretation won out. The Israeli military assault did not halt in southern Lebanon. Rather, it pushed deeper northward into Lebanon, taking on Syrian forces stationed there, and finally, within a week of the start of the invasion, the Israeli military laid siege to the country's capital, Beirut. By the end of August, the PLO leadership, which had been based in Lebanon for a dozen years, was expelled, and Israel's Maronite Christian Lebanese ally Bashir Gemayel was elected president.

The turmoil did not end there. On September 14, 1982, days before his inauguration as the president of Lebanon, Gemayel was assassinated by a bomb planted at the headquarters of his party, known as the Kataeb or Phalanges, in East Beirut.[10] Israeli troops then invaded West Beirut.[11]

Israel's invasion of West Beirut provoked speedy international condemnation (and a sizable backlash among the Israeli population).[12] Already on September 15, the spokesman for West German chancellor Helmut Schmidt warned that "this one-sided and unjustified step can lead to a serious threat to the peace process."[13] Similarly, Egypt, which had signed a peace treaty with Israel only three years earlier, decried Israel's invasion as an "obstacle in the way of the peace process."[14] The next day, the White House and the State Department asserted that "there is no justification in our view for Israel's continued military presence in west Beirut and we call for an immediate pullback."[15] The

UN Security Council held an emergency meeting on September 16 to address the Israeli invasion and Lebanon's request for a resolution condemning Israeli actions.[16] By the following day, the Council had unanimously condemned Israel's incursion and called for its withdrawal from West Beirut.[17] Once reports began to circulate concerning Phalangist militia massacres of Palestinians in the Sabra and Shatila refugee camps, at the time surrounded by Israeli forces,[18] the condemnation of Israeli actions became all the more severe, not only from Arab, Soviet, and Western governments, but also from within the Jewish Israeli political mainstream.[19]

Seizing the PLO Research Center

On the very first day of the invasion of West Beirut, a battalion from the IDF's Golani Brigade, under the command of Baruch Spiegel, entered the Hamra neighborhood of Ras Beirut. Knowing that the area was a PLO stronghold, the Golani soldiers went door to door, and came upon the library and archive of the PLO Research Center. Spiegel radioed his intelligence colleagues to inform them of this discovery.[20]

Israeli intelligence had prepared for this call. After the 1973 war, which Israelis widely regarded as a major intelligence debacle, the Israeli intelligence regime was overhauled. One result was the formation of a unit known as AMShaT (a Hebrew acronym for *Isuf Mismahim ve-Shalal Tekhni*, namely, "Gathering documents and technical spoils"). The AMShaT unit was trained to undertake on-the-spot Arabic document analysis to discern whether data discovered in the midst of battle was of operational value.[21] AMShaT members soon arrived at the PLO Research Center and began combing through the files they found. Though they apparently unearthed nothing immediately usable, over the next few days, Israeli forces loaded truck after truck with the materials found in the building and shipped them south toward Tel Aviv.[22]

With international newspaper headlines such as "All Hell Breaks Loose," "Survivors of Massacre Tell of Reign of Terror," and "Evidence Suggests Israelis Were Aware of Killings"[23]—all focused on the massacres at Sabra and Shatila in the days immediately following Israel's invasion of West Beirut—it is no wonder that the confiscation of an archive and library was not regarded as a major news item. Nonetheless, on September 19, just four days after the start of the West Beirut invasion, wire services were reporting Israel's assault on the PLO Research Center. According to these early reports, "the PLO's political headquarters in West Beirut and the Palestine Research Center that served as the PLO's headquarters in the Hamra shopping district were raided by Israeli troops on Friday," September 17, 1982. "Lebanese police said that troops wielding axes seized 'files and documents' from these buildings," the reports continued.[24]

Matti Steinberg amid the "Heaps"

The confiscation of the PLO Research Center's library and archive and their removal to Israel in mid-September 1982 were thus amply reported upon from the first days of the West Beirut invasion. Speculation about the whereabouts of these materials has abounded ever since. During my years studying the intellectual production of the PLO Research Center, I have also tried to reconstruct the story of its fate in Israel's hands. At one point Israel Gershoni, a renowned scholar of modern Middle Eastern and Egyptian history, advised me to speak with Matti Steinberg about the matter. This advice proved pivotal for my project.

Like that of his mentor Yehoshafat Harkabi (who had served as chief of Israel's military intelligence in the late 1950s and then as a professor of international relations at the Hebrew University), Matti Steinberg's career crisscrossed the line between academia and intelligence.[25] In 1974, Steinberg (b. 1946) began his doctoral research on modern Palestinian nationalist thought; at the same time, he was recruited as a reservist to Israeli intelligence.

From the mid-1970s until the 1982 war, Steinberg wrote reports for Israel's intelligence agencies about what he regarded as transformations in PLO political positions vis-à-vis Israel. He wrote about those same developments in his doctoral dissertation. Given that his academic research and his intelligence work were essentially focused on the same questions and used the same sources, the two "cannot be disentangled," Steinberg told me.[26]

In both his research and his reports, Steinberg's primary source for his conclusions about ideological and pragmatic transformations within the PLO was, he told me, PLO Research Center publications, especially articles the Center published in its journal *Shu'un Filastiniyya*. When I met with him in his Jerusalem home, Steinberg explained his approach from that period: "If you want to detect big changes, mega-trends, in PLO thinking, you need to follow the publications of the PLO Research Center." One needs nothing more than "open sources," Steinberg elaborated, to understand PLO thought.

Steinberg's claim, which he first shared with me in 2017, was consistent with what he had been arguing for decades. In July 1975, after delivering an analysis of the differences between the various member parties of the PLO, Steinberg was asked by an audience member about his sources. He responded that his presentation was based "on their own testimonies, how they view themselves and what they see." Much like the PLO researchers we encountered earlier, Steinberg argued that "in order to fight an adversary, you must know how he sees himself."[27]

After spending more than half a decade studying the literary output of the PLO Research Center, Steinberg had the opportunity to examine the Center's library and archive, the sources that the PLO intellectuals had been using as they wrote the books and articles he had been reading for his academic and intelligence research. Steinberg hadn't been invited to the Center, to be sure. Rather, the Center was brought to him.[28]

When the Research Center's contents arrived in Israel, Steinberg recalled, he was summoned for "reserve service in [his] capacity as an analyst."[29] At the warehouse where the materials had been delivered, he found thousands of books "dumped in a garage . . . like garbage." His mission was to singlehandedly review the material and produce a report within one week. The timeframe for this task was laughable, by his own account. Ultimately, Steinberg did write a report based in large measure on the Research Center's card catalogue that he "found in the heap" in the garage.[30]

After more than two years of effort, I located and succeeded in securing declassification of what appears to be a revised summary of Steinberg's report, in the Israel Defense Forces and Defense Establishment Archives (IDF Archives).[31] The secret document, "Captured Material from the Archives of the PLO in Beirut: Preliminary Inventory and Characterization," was issued on October 13, 1982, less than a month after the invasion of West Beirut. According to the report, from Sunday, October 3, through Friday, October 8 (*hol ha-mo'ed*, the intermediate days of the Jewish Sukkot festival that year), Steinberg analyzed the materials that had been seized from the PLO Research Center in a hangar in the Hatsav base of the IDF.[32]

The PLO Research Center materials were not alone in this hangar. According to the intelligence report, the space housed, along with the Research Center's library and archive, three other Palestinian collections that had been seized in Beirut: those belonging to the PLO's "Western Sector," the PLO's Planning Center, and the newspaper of George Habash's Popular Front for the Liberation of Palestine (*al-Hadaf*). The materials taken from the Research Center, however, constituted most of what Steinberg found in the Hatsav hangar. Indeed, the report noted, the library of the Research Center, "nearly all of which is in our hands," represented "the glory" of that institution. The report reflects Steinberg's frustration with the condition of the materials, which he recalled in our conversation before I found this written report. The document noted that the captured material (*ha-homer ha-shalal*) had been "concentrated (more precisely: heaped) in a car garage."[33]

After describing the scene in which Steinberg undertook his analysis, the report turns to the central question of the intelligence value of the seized archives. The document asserts that "the material that has come into our hands was gathered from *open sources* only, such as Arabic, Israeli, and world newspapers and radio broadcasts" from the mid-1960s and following.[34] This assessment applied even to the archive from the PLO's Western Sector (the unit that planned sabotage and other attacks west of the Jordan River), "which meticulously followed events in Israel and the territories of Judea and Samaria and the Gaza Strip, and that served clear operational needs." This does not mean that these archives had never contained more sensitive information. Rather, concerning the Western Sector, the report claimed that Israel had received intelligence indicating that, "during the siege of Beirut," the Sector's staff worked "to destroy the classified documents and they brought some of them with when they were evacuated."[35] What arrived in Israel, then, may have been a sanitized version of the original content of these archives.

Sabri Jiryis's Suitcases

The Israeli intelligence report's assessment that files had been removed from these offices before Israel's conquest was later confirmed by the PLO Research Center's director himself. In February 1985, less than three years after the war, Sabri Jiryis was interviewed about the fate of the PLO Research Center by the journalist Salah Qallab. In response to a question about whether the Research Center held any "irreplaceable rare documents," Jiryis answered: "I would like to state for the first time ever, that rare and very valuable documents were shipped out of Lebanon prior to the Israeli invasion. We also transferred all files including sensitive information such as personnel files."[36] At least as the interview was recorded in the *Journal of Palestine Studies* a few months later, Qallab did not ask Jiryis any further questions on this matter.

I did, though—many years later. In an interview with Jiryis in August 2015, three decades after he sat with Qallab, I asked him about those "rare and very valuable documents" and those "sensitive" materials. What were they? "It's not for disclosure," Jiryis told me curtly. But he shared with me a bit more than he had with Qallab about how he had removed those materials:

> I went there at midnight. I took two suitcases. Big ones. And alone. Just one hundred percent alone. Nobody was there. And I picked what should be picked from there because I was afraid that the Israelis would come there. And they did later in any case. And I packed these two suitcases with whatever I did there. Put them in my diplomatic car. . . . And took it somewhere. And from there it was sent somewhere else.

The materials eventually made their way back to Jiryis, he said, and then "they went to where they are supposed to be. And that's it."[37]

Of "Operational" Value?

We will return to the issue of the materials Jiryis removed before the Israeli forces raided the building in mid-September 1982. For now, let us consider the materials that the Israeli forces did find there. If all that reached Israel in these collections was material based on open sources, were they of any value from an intelligence perspective? On this question, the report offered a subtle conclusion. "The value of the archives from an intelligence perspective does not flow," the report asserted, "from the type of sources, which are accessible to anyone who wishes, but rather perhaps from the method of collection of the open material and its variety (especially the Arabic press). They are fit for use mainly as raw material for basic research, not to be confused with basic operational needs." If there was any intelligence value in what had been seized (and the "perhaps" here suggests that the author of the report was not entirely convinced), it was simply in revealing what sorts of open sources the Palestinians were gathering.[38]

With tens of thousands of books and archival files scattered in a warehouse and just six days to assess them, how did Steinberg proceed? "A comprehensive and relatively reliable picture of the inventory in our possession," explained the report, "may be attained by analyzing the wonderfully organized catalogues of 'the Research Center' and the indexes of the different archives." Here, the report strikes a note of reverence. "Seventeen years of labor was invested in this library," the report asserted. "Not only is the scope of the library impressive, but so too is the methodicalness [*shitatiyut*] upon which it was organized and administered," the report continued. "The catalogue of the library in English, Hebrew, and Arabic is made up of several sections: names of authors, titles of books, and, separately, there is even a catalogue by topic." Moreover, the catalogue categorized not only books but also articles in the collection. In terms of the range of topics covered by the library, the report explained that it consisted of "books, periodicals, and articles that were published since February 1965 (when the 'Center' was founded) that deal with the topics of Palestine, the Arab world, Zionism, Judaism, and Israel." (Note the worry marks surrounding 'Center.') However, because the topic of Palestine had wide ramifications, "the library includes a notable portion of the literature from the Arab world that has been published since the mid-60s," including "all of the prominent cultural and political periodicals of the Arab world."[39]

The PLO Research Center's library also contained, according to this report, a special section dedicated to the publications of the PLO and the various Palestinian organizations. There was a separate catalogue for these Palestinian publications and "there is no doubt that this is the most complete catalogue of its kind." While the author of the report saw no clear operational intelligence value in the Research Center's library, this did not lead him to express regret that Israel had taken it. "One hopes," the report read, "that all of the material" listed in the catalogue of Palestinian publications "is in our possession." Thus far, "we have found part." The library contained multiple copies of the PLO Research Center's own publications as well as those of the nearby Institute for Palestine Studies.[40]

Beyond the publications that the Research Center collected as they were produced following the Center's establishment, the Center also gathered "historical documentation and microfilms." These are the subject of the next section of the report. The Center, according to the report, "invested special effort in collecting documents and reports of importance for historical research. A list of documents and personal archives that were deposited in the 'Center' is found in our possession." Among these historical documents were the personal papers of Fawzi al-Qawuqji, the commander of the Arab Liberation Army in the 1948 war, and documents from Palestinian figures associated with the Arab Higher Committee in the 1950s. There were also more recent documents, such as those concerning the events of September 1970 in Jordan.[41]

Along with these archival documents, the Center "had in its possession a rather large library of microfilms," the index of which had also made its way to the Israeli hangar. The Research Center's microfilms included copies of

Mandate-era documents, such as files from the British Foreign Office found in the Public Records Office. There were also microfilms of the protocols of the Zionist congresses, the full yearbooks of foreign newspapers, and material on such topics as the position of Arab states on the Palestine issue from 1965–67, Arab oil from 1966–74, Egypt and the Middle East crisis, speeches of Arab leaders from 1969–71, and Arab Summit conferences. The report noted that "a special branch of the microfilm archive was dedicated to basic facts— economic, social, demographic, and historical—about Arab sites in the past and present in Palestine," such as Acre and Beisan/Bet She'an. The Research Center also maintained a Rolodex of Palestinian students who were employed by the Center. In addition, the captured files contained "archives of pictures that included the 'Who's Who' of the Arab world, Israel, and beyond."[42]

"Incriminating Material"

The final section of the intelligence report is called "'The Palestinian Research Center'—Incriminating Material." Here, the report asserted that the Center was not a run-of-the-mill academic institution. Because of the Center's "subordination to the PLO," wrote the author, the Center "did not merely provide cultural and ideological services but deviated into clearly operational areas, that is: giving assistance to terror activities." To support this allegation, the report cited a book called *Dalil al-Muqatil al-Filastini* (Handbook for the Palestinian Fighter), published by the Research Center in 1972. This book offered, in the report's assessment, "operational intelligence [*modi'in likrat mivtsa'*]— literally—about Israeli military bases in the regions of the Galilee and the Golan, paths to reach them, and primary traffic routes." The report highlighted the fact that this book did not include the name of its author but listed only the Research Center, "thus emphasizing sevenfold the responsibility" of the Center. Further incriminating details about the book include that it was marked as of "limited and special" circulation and that "it was duplicated in stencil and not published as a regular publication." These facts "only strengthen the suspicion that the heads of the 'Center' sensed that their hands were not clean," the report asserted.[43]

What did the intelligence report conclude about this "incriminating material"? The existence of this material raised the question, according to the report, as to "whether the public academic facade [*hazut*] that the 'Center' wore was merely camouflage [*masveh*] designed to hide direct assistance to acts of

THE PLO RESEARCH CENTER IN TEL AVIV 195

terror." The report added here that the Center's press archive collected material about the "Black September" underground organization and that "secret documents about the September 1970 crisis in Jordan were deposited in it [the archive] by the PLO," some of which Israel had seized. The closing lines of the report read: "A basic contradiction exists, therefore, between the pretense [*yumrah*] of the 'Center' being an academic institute and its formal and essential subordination to the PLO. The identification with the goals of the PLO leads the 'Center' out of necessity and knowingly to be a tool in the hands of the PLO also in the field of operations."[44]

In this report, the author made two separate assessments: one concerning the seized materials and another concerning the Research Center more generally. The first assessment was that the material from the PLO Research Center held no value for operational intelligence purposes. Sitting in the Hatsav hangar were, in the main, recently published books, journals, and newspapers along with historical documents and microfilm collections. Even the secret documents that had been seized were not, in the report's view, of operational value. However, that the collection was innocuous did not mean that all the activities of the Research Center had been harmless. On the contrary, the report's second, more tentative assessment was that considering the PLO Research Center's status as a branch of the PLO, it perforce supported the PLO's aims—including its militant objectives. The primary piece of evidence for this support was that the Center had published, a decade earlier, a book explicitly intended for use in violent attacks against Israeli targets. Though this intelligence report, based on Matti Steinberg's analysis, remained classified until 2018 when the IDF Archives declassified it for me, the book to which it points, *Dalil al-Muqatil al-Filastini*, would play a key role in Israel's public presentation of the PLO Research Center.

Handbook for the Palestinian Fighter

Given the degree of attention the *Handbook for the Palestinian Fighter* received in the following months, as we shall see, it is worth pausing here to look at it closely.[45] The title of the book makes patently clear its goal of assisting Palestinian militants. This *Handbook*, sixty-four pages in length, presents itself as the first in a series of four books. This one, prepared in April 1972 and printed in July of the same year, focuses on "the Galilee and the Syrian Heights," the latter another name for the Golan Heights. The subsequent three volumes in the series were to cover the Jordan Valley and the West Bank, Gaza, and the "lands occupied before 1967."[46] The handbook offers a geographical and topographical description of the region, information about its transportation systems (paved roads, unpaved roads, railroads, military roads, bridges), facts and statistics about the region's communities (population, national and religious identity, electricity stations, water facilities, gas stations, factories, and military bases). Additionally, the book provides precise geographical coordinates of Israeli military bases, power lines, nuclear facilities, water pipes, and the like. Though the information assembled in the book may have been based on open sources, as the revised summary of Steinberg's report concluded, rather than espionage, it nonetheless belongs to a realm distinct from that of the other PLO Research Center publications we have studied here.

At the same time, even this work seems aimed to preserve cultural knowledge in addition to preparing fighters for violent missions. Consider, for instance, the handbook's section on the population of the Galilee, which it defines as "a rural Arab region":

> In 1967 its [the Galilee's] population was 220,000, only a quarter of whom live in the two main regions: in Nazareth (42,000 including its suburb known as Nazareth Heights—Nazareth Illit) and Safed (13,000). Non-Jews constitute three-quarters of the population in all of the Galilee, and the majority in every part of the Galilee with the exception of the northeast around the city of Safed and behind it. The Galilee has a relatively fast population growth, as its population grew by a third between 1961 and 1967. Despite the settlement of Jewish immigrants, they played a modest part in the growth of the numbers of the population in the Galilee; the main reason for the growth is the high birth rate among the Arabs.[47]

This section on the Galilee then proceeds to describe the topography of the region:

> From a geographical perspective, the Galilee can be described as a hill region of the Mediterranean Sea. It is very different from the plains in the west, the south, and the east. The southern or lower Galilee consists of low hills or of a steppe region mixed with water basins. The northern or upper Galilee consists of hills that reach 1200 meters. There are scattered basins among the hills. Though these regions get the greatest percentage of rains in the winter in the country, the sources of water in the dry summer are not abundant, thus limiting their development.[48]

Next, the *Handbook* discusses the cultivation techniques of the Arabs in the Galilee:

> The Arabs live like the rest of the fellahin [peasant farmers] in the Mediterranean, most in the villages cultivating their lands in Mediterranean farms, and using the agricultural techniques of Mediterranean fellahin. The Arabs grow olives and grains and so on in the valley basins that are blessed with fertile silt soil and abundant irrigation water. The high and flat regions are cultivated with wheat and barley that are irrigated by rainwater. Most of the harvest is not good because the soil in most of the region is not fertile and the sloping ground is left for grazing. But they plant it with olives and seasonal fruits in some instances.[49]

Perhaps this level of detail about a region of the homeland was regarded as important information for a fighter. It seems more likely, however, that the goal was to spread cultural knowledge about Palestine.

Yet there is no denying that the bulk of the 1972 *Handbook for the Palestinian Fighter*—such as the locations of IDF military bases—was meant to help the Palestinian fighter *fight*. How does this fact impact our broader assessment of the Center? Does this unabashedly militant volume, published by the Research Center, render more plausible Howard's *Boston Globe* article from 1976?

Such questions were asked—and answered in radically different, though equally emphatic, ways—by supporters of Israel and of the Palestinians following the Israeli seizure and transfer of the PLO Research Center. We turn now to that debate.

12

A Global Debate about the PLO Research Center

THE STORY of the seizure of the PLO Research Center was quickly fitted into one of two broader narratives. Some presented the confiscation as part of systematic Israeli efforts to seize everything connected to the PLO. Journalist Trudy Rubin of the *Christian Science Monitor* wrote on September 24, 1982, that "Israel is also collecting arms from caches left by PLO and Lebanese leftists." Throughout Beirut, Rubin wrote, "Israeli soldiers with trucks and flatbeds can be seen collecting boxes of ammunition and heavy weapons from schools, apartments, and mosque basements where they were stored." According to Rubin, "scores of trucks deliver loads of these arms to Israel daily." As part of this same process, "Israeli soldiers can also be seen searching for documents, carting out books, archives, and manuscripts from the PLO's Palestinian Research Center, according to reliable Lebanese sources."[1]

Other observers saw the Israeli action as part of a different pattern: widespread looting by Israeli soldiers during their invasion of West Beirut. Jewelry, radios, television sets, clocks, cigarette lighters, surgical equipment, antique Syrian pots, and more were missing from homes and offices that had been searched by Israelis. Cars and trucks were allegedly placed on flatbed trucks and seen heading south toward Israel.[2] So, too, the archive and library of the PLO Research Center. In this latter narrative, the seizure of the PLO Research Center was an act of spite, a theft for the sake of theft, on par with other acts of vandalism and wanton destruction.[3]

Edward Said and the "Assault on Palestinian Culture"

Among the first to ascribe deeper symbolic meaning to the seizure of the PLO Research Center was Columbia University English professor and Palestinian advocate Edward Said (1935–2003). In a September 29 *New York Times* op-ed titled "'Purifying,' Israelis Called It," Said argued that the Sabra and Shatila massacres were part of a "larger pattern of hostility," which included "not only the killings . . . but an assault on Palestinian culture." Underlying Israel's attack on the PLO in Lebanon, Said contended, was Israel's intention "to destroy the fabric of a displaced nation." Said noted that while physical violence against Palestinians was widely known of, "what is not sufficiently reported is the cultural extension of this: Israeli Army units have been entering Palestinian research institutions, libraries and homes in West Beirut, either to remove or destroy the cultural artifacts of Palestinian society." Prime evidence of this attempt at cultural erasure, as Said saw it, was Israel's decision to invade and commandeer the PLO Research Center, which Said described as "an official repository of Palestinian history, contemporary and past." The Research Center was "emptied of [its] contents and destroyed."[4] Along with its seizure of other private Palestinian libraries, the destruction of the PLO Research Center "can only have been designed to leave the Palestinian people destitute of its history."[5]

Two days after Said decried the confiscation in his op-ed, the *New York Times* published a full article on the seizure of the Center. The *Times* presented the affair as a case of "looting"—the piece was titled "Israelis Looted Archives of P.L.O, Officials Say"—but Said's symbolic interpretation of the incident was echoed, according to the article, by Sabri Jiryis, the director of the Center. "They have plundered our Palestinian cultural heritage," Jiryis said. Noting that the Israelis also occupied the main office of the PLO and, before leaving, removed the word "Palestine" from the sign outside, the *Times* correspondent Ihsan Hijazi cited a Palestinian source who asserted that "the Israeli invasion was intended to obliterate all memory of Palestine, the country we have left behind."[6]

UNESCO and the PLO Research Center

Once this symbolic view of the confiscation of the Research Center's library was articulated, the seizure in the midst of Israel's invasion became a matter of concern for those committed to preserving threatened cultural heritages. The affair was thus referred to the United Nations Educational, Scientific and Cultural Organization (UNESCO). The Executive Board of UNESCO was meeting in Paris during this same period (September 8 through October 7) and, in its report from this session, issued on October 22, 1982, the Executive Board noted that it had learned the following:

> the Israeli army has seized and taken away with it archives and documents of every kind concerning Palestinian history and culture, including cultural articles belonging to those institutions—in particular the Palestinian Research Centre—archives, documents and materials such as film documents, literary works by major authors, paintings, objets d'art and works of folklore, research works, etc., serving as a foundation for the history, culture, national awareness, unity and solidarity of the Palestinian people.[7]

These "acts of destruction and plunder," in the view of the UNESCO board, "constitute serious violations of the human rights defined by the Universal Declaration of Human Rights, Unesco's Constitution and all other relevant international instruments concerning in particular the right to education and the right to cultural identity in all its forms." The UNESCO officials regarded Israel's seizure of the PLO Research Center as a "deplorable act of violence . . . against the educational and cultural values of the Palestinian people." As such, UNESCO requested that the Israeli government "make full restitution of all the archives and documents removed from the Palestinian Research Centre as a result of the Israeli aggression."[8] Only after expressing this censure of Israel's confiscation of the PLO Research Center did the UNESCO report turn to the massacre of civilians at the Sabra and Shatila refugee camps.[9]

UNESCO's condemnation of Israel's seizure was reported in Israel even before the official statement was issued. On October 5, 1982, journalist Tamar Golan wrote in *Ma'ariv* not only that Israel was accused of violating the Declaration of Human Rights but also that this accusation was viewed as a first step toward expelling Israel from UNESCO altogether. Golan did note that this move was led by a group of Third World nations (i.e., not countries expected to be sympathetic to Israel). Nonetheless, from Israel's perspective, there were unsettling surprises in the vote tally as two African states that then maintained diplomatic relations with Israel—Zaire (now the Democratic Republic of the Congo) and the Kingdom of Lesotho—supported the measure as well.[10]

At a plenary meeting of UNESCO in early November 1982, Israel's representative to the international organization, Hadassah Ben-Itto, lambasted her colleagues for their discrimination against Israel, and argued that Israel was judged by a higher standard than were all other countries. "It is only of us," she stated indignantly, "that some delegates speak as a Member State not fit to be part of the international community." She continued: "Others may murder thousands of people, they may torture and flog people in the public square, they may execute people without even giving them a fair trial, without any-body suggesting taking away their credentials, but their delegates accuse us of the massacre in Sabra and Chatila, knowing perfectly well who were actually the perpetrators of this crime." She asserted that "it is a matter of public knowl-edge that no Israeli took part in these massacres" and despite this fact Israelis were conducting an "unprecedented" public inquiry. This inquiry, she claimed, was not intended "to satisfy the international community," but rather "to satisfy our own conscience, because to us life is sacred—any life." Of the ac-cusation that Israel attempted to destroy Palestinian cultural heritage, she asserted that "not only do we not destroy the cultural heritage of the Palestin-ians, but there are seven universities in the administered territories [the term then preferred by Israeli authorities for the West Bank and the Gaza Strip] for 1¼ million people, where there was but one college before 1967. The last of these universities was established only last year in Abu-dis." Israel, Ben-Itto contended, was responsible for expanding Palestinian cultural sites, not shut-ting them down.

Following this public harangue, Ben-Itto concluded with "a word about the Research Institute for Palestinian Studies, which we have been accused of hav-ing plundered. Some have referred to it here as an 'institute for humanistic studies.'" Ben-Itto insisted that this was a gross mischaracterization of the PLO Research Center. In fact, she contended, "There is no time to list all the mate-rial inciting to violence and preaching the destruction of Israel which was found in this institute." Despite the presence of this violent provocative mate-rial in the Research Center, she told her fellow delegates that she had been authorized by her government to inform them "that in due course, the research material will be placed at the disposal of the legitimate Government of Leba-non, in whose capital it was found."[11]

Israel's Foreign Ministry

The international press and UNESCO were just two of the theaters where pressure was placed on Israel to justify its seizure of the PLO Research Center. Israel's ambassadors abroad also felt this burden and turned to the Foreign Ministry for instructions on how to respond. On October 14, 1982, one day after the revised summary of Steinberg's report was issued, the Foreign Ministry's legal advisor Elyakim Rubinstein wrote a classified memo to the Ministry's director general, David Kimche.[12] In the memo, Rubinstein explained that "based on what I have heard, the IDF captured in Beirut, among other things, the library and archive of the Center for Palestine Studies of the PLO." This library "contains, according to what I understand," wrote Rubinstein, "many books and archival materials, mainly old." Rubinstein was aware that Military Intelligence had produced a report about the contents of the library and archive, but he apparently had not yet seen this report. "It appears that it would be worthwhile," he wrote in what reads as a rather strange understatement, "to obtain from Military Intelligence sources the report that describes the contents of the material." Despite not having seen Steinberg's report, Rubinstein offered Kimche the following advice about how to respond to "claims that we captured 'Palestinian cultural material,' etc.":

> It appears that the "Center" was a unit of the PLO and not only this but also that as far as is known 'PLO' diplomatic immunities were granted to its people. Moreover, it is possible that within the material, elements that are not merely 'research' literature will be found but rather also material about the Center's intelligence or subversion activity (though probably most of the material in these fields was removed or destroyed).[13]

The fact that this Research "Center" (note again the worry marks) was under the PLO umbrella was sufficiently incriminating. That the Center's staff received diplomatic immunity was, it seems, not a reason (from the Israeli legal advisor's perspective) for legal concern about what Israel had done there. On the contrary, this status represented further evidence of the Center's pernicious purposes. After all, these were not just *any* diplomatic immunities; they were "'PLO' diplomatic immunities" (*hasinuyot diplomatiyot 'asha"fiyot'*). If Rubinstein harbored any concerns about the international legal implications of the seizure, he did not reveal them to Kimche. Instead, he closed the memo by noting that "it would be worthwhile to check which other archives were captured and if there is material that could interest us."[14]

Outrage among Archivists

Before Israeli officials began mounting a full-fledged public relations defense of their military's capture of the PLO Research Center, American archivists began to raise concerns. On October 20, 1982, the Society of American Archivists (SAA) held its annual business meeting in Boston. The first items for discussion dealt with minor changes to the organization's own constitution. The final two items on the agenda were of a different sort entirely. Eva Moseley of Radcliffe College's Schlesinger Library proposed that the SAA issue a call to the American government to adopt an agreement between the US and the Soviet Union concerning nuclear weapons. This was a matter of SAA concern, according to the resolution, because "the use of nuclear weapons could cause immense indiscriminate destruction" not only of people but also of "the records of people." Moseley's resolution was adopted on the spot.

The final resolution, submitted by archivists Sybil Milton, a scholar of the Holocaust at the Leo Baeck Institute, and Claudia Hommel, was more directly linked to the SAA's mission. "The SAA," they wrote, "calls on the Israeli Government to preserve intact the records of the Palestine Liberation Organization's research center, Beirut, which were removed by Israeli troops in late September." In addition, the resolution "urge[d] the government of Israel to make the records accessible on an impartial basis and to repatriate the collection to the original creators or their legally designated successor organization as soon as possible." In contrast to the resolution on nuclear weapons, this one was not passed at the business meeting. Instead, the group passed a motion to refer the resolution to the International Archival Affairs Committee for further investigation.[15]

This committee lost no time in responding. Two days later, during the SAA's leadership council, Canada's dominion archivist Wilfred Smith submitted a statement on behalf of the committee, indicating that its members "wish to express concern regarding the reported seizure of the archives of the research center of the P.L.O." and requesting that the SAA Council "take action appropriate for a national professional association of archivists in the circumstances." The International Archival Affairs Committee was apparently divided over what action would be appropriate given that this was not a domestic matter but one of "intervening in a diplomatic sphere." There seems to have been a consensus in the committee, however, that it would be appropriate for the International Council on Archives (ICA) to become involved as it had previously done "in the question of repatriation or 'migrated' archives." Thus, the committee recommended raising the matter with this international archival association. Additionally, it delivered this more direct statement:

We believe that archivists everywhere have a legitimate concern in the conservation of the archival heritage of mankind and that if the facts are indeed

as reported in the *New York Times*, October 1, 1982, then the action is a violation of accepted archival principles and practice. While 'protest' may be an
inappropriate term, an expression of concern in an objective way does seem
legitimate for professional archivists, but it seems to us that the ICA as
representative of the entire international community is in a better position
to ascertain the facts and to communicate to the appropriate authorities the
concern of archivists than is the SAA.[16]

The SAA's leadership voted to adopt the committee's recommendation and to
request that the international organization of archivists investigate and
intervene.

A Challenge from Stockholm

On November 12, 1982, Israel's ambassador to Sweden wrote a memo to the
Foreign Ministry's legal advisor about a discussion in the Riksdag, the Swedish
parliament, concerning the PLO Research Center. The memo explained that
Sweden's foreign minister, Lennart Bodström, noted in the parliament that he
had been asked what he planned to do to facilitate the return of the PLO Research Center archive to the PLO. According to the Israeli ambassador's
memo, Bodström then reported to the parliamentarians on what had happened in Beirut. "Thousands of books, the entire microfilm and document
archive in the institute and other inventories of value," he explained, "were
brought away according to unanimous information by Israeli soldiers." On the
contents and importance of this material, Bodström noted that it "is said to
be the biggest collection about history of Palestine," and thus "an important
part of the cultural inheritance [*sic*] of the Palestinians and of great importance
to their national identity."[17]

   Following this account of the events, Bodström offered his opinion on what
had occurred. The Israeli action was "contrary to the international law principles" concerning "the responsibility of fighting and occupation powers" to
protect civilian property from "plundering and theft." Moreover, Bodström
contended, the Israeli seizure "further violates the international law principles
saying that [the] fighting party must try to prevent the confiscation or the destruction of objects of cultural, historical or scientific value." As a result, "the
Swedish Government urgently calls upon the Israeli Government to do everything" necessary to ensure "that the material brought away from the PLO Re-

search Center in Beirut may be returned and that compensation will be paid for material destroyed." Bodström expressed his support for UNESCO's intervention on this matter and concluded by suggesting that Israel's confiscation of the PLO Research Center was "a tragic expression" of "a vain belief" that the national ambitions "of the Palestinian people can be stopped by bringing away or destroying documents and archives about its history."[18] This was a severe indictment in a European hall of power.

In the classified memo accompanying the translation of this report, Israel's ambassador asked the legal advisor how to react. The ambassador thought it important to respond considering the foreign minister's "appeal to the government of Israel to return the material and even to pay compensation for damages." Of particular concern for the ambassador was that never before had Bodström made a statement that was "entirely negative" about Israel. What Israel had done with the PLO Research Center was sparking outrage even among those generally sympathetic toward the state.

Oded Granot and the Research Center's "Two Faces"

The conquest of the PLO Research Center's library and archive was turning out to be a public relations and diplomatic disaster for Israel at a time when the country was facing severe criticism for the massacres of Palestinians that took place during its invasion of West Beirut. It was not until December, however, that a rebuttal of Edward Said's conception of the PLO Research Center as a benign repository of Palestinian cultural heritage appeared in the Israeli press. On December 2, 1982, in the newspaper Ma'ariv, Israeli journalist Oded Granot published an article called "Two Faces of 'The Palestinian Research Center' in the Capital of Lebanon: Aiding the PLO in Attacks and Terrorism—Behind an Academic Cover in Beirut."[19] The article reported on the recent renewal of the PLO Research Center's activities in Beirut following the forced suspension that came with Israel's conquest of the Center during the war in September.

The essence of Granot's article was that though the Research Center was a *"seemingly* academic [*akademi likh'orah*] body of the 'Palestine Liberation Organization,'" in reality, in addition to its academic pursuits, the Center served a secret, malicious, decidedly violent agenda. Granot explained that "since its inception in 1965, the heads of the Palestinian Research Center[20] made sure it kept an academic image, dealing with the Palestinian problem and offering its services to foreign researchers."[21] Within the scope of these "public activities," Granot noted,

> a large staff of researchers gathered material about Israel and the Palestinian problem from many sources, mostly books, newspapers, periodicals and academic studies written in Israel, in Arab countries and in other countries. A special team listened regularly to the broadcasts of Israeli radio and television. The center library had many books in Hebrew, not only about the Palestinian problem but also the history of Zionism, Judaic subjects and works by Israeli and Jewish writers and thinkers.

With this extensive collection, Granot elaborated, the Center published two journals—*Shu'un Filastiniyya* in Arabic and the *Journal of Palestine Studies* in English (the latter was actually published by IPS, an error we address below)—as well as a daily report monitoring Israeli radio and television broadcasts.

If the public face of the PLO Research Center suggested that the institution was a legitimate research unit, the Center's other face revealed it to be something far more insidious. "Few people knew about its other side," asserted Granot, "that behind the academic façade was a PLO intelligence center gathering information on Israel and on Israeli and Jewish objectives for terrorist acts."[22] Since "the IDF captured center documents and publications" in September 1982, however, the Center's "covert activities" had been exposed. These captured documents, wrote Granot, included:

- *A Handbook for the Palestinian Fighter*, a guide published in 1972 with data on IDF camps in the Galilee and the Golan Heights.[23] This is the first of a series which apparently [*kanir'eh*] includes all parts of Israel. The first page specifies it has "limited and special circulation."
- *Maps of Transportation Roads in Occupied Palestine*, published in 1969. The pamphlet includes seventy-four maps of Israel's various areas with geographic and other data. The introduction states circulation is limited, since it is intended to help in terrorist acts. It was issued in two parts, one without a cover, to make it easier for terrorists going out on a mission against Israel to conceal it in their clothes.
- Detailed list of gas stations in Israel, apparently [*ke-khol ha-nir'eh*] for operational purposes.

In addition, Granot noted that the Center's archive maintained individual files on the members of the IDF leadership and tracked changes in personnel. Finally, according to Granot, also among the files seized from the PLO Research Center were "entire files of the PLO intelligence services, including requests from senior terrorist commanders for special investigations for the terrorist organizations."

Granot's list was clearly meant to justify Israel's seizure of the PLO Research Center library. What the Israelis found, he asserted, was indisputable evidence of the Center's involvement in providing intelligence to support violent attacks on Israeli targets. If the Israelis took everything on the shelves, even innocuous historical and cultural documents, this was only because they were in the midst of an offensive and had no time to sift the dangerous from the anodyne on the spot. Such sorting would need to be done on Israeli turf. And when Israeli officials were able to undertake this process, Granot's article alleged, the dangerous material was indeed found.

While the *Handbook* to which Granot referred was mentioned in the intelligence report based on Steinberg's analysis, the other problematic projects do not appear in that report. When I spoke with Granot in 2018, I asked him about the source of his information. Granot, who had previously served in Israeli intelligence, told me that he had been permitted to visit the garage where the PLO Research Center material was stored and he based his *Ma'ariv* article on his own assessment from this visit, though he left open the possibility that perhaps he had been shown an intelligence report about the Research Center while he was writing his article. Regardless of its source, Granot essentially turned a question raised in the October 13 intelligence report into an emphatic answer. The intelligence report suggested that the existence of "incriminating material" published or housed by the Research Center "raises the question" about whether the Center's academic activities were a cover for its efforts to aid terrorism. Granot answered in the affirmative.

Granot's article contained a number of inaccuracies. The English-language *Journal of Palestine Studies* was published not by the PLO Research Center, as Granot reported, but by the Institute for Palestine Studies. The October 13, 1982, intelligence report noted that the PLO Research Center collected the publications of IPS, so it is possible that Granot, or one of his sources, saw the *Journal of Palestine Studies* in the Hatsav garage and assumed that it too was published by the Research Center. The conflation of the two institutions appears as well in Granot's claim that Elias Shoufani was "one of the senior workers of the center." Shoufani was a leading member of IPS, not of the PLO Research Center.[24]

Granot was not mistaken, however, about the Center's having published a book of maps. In November 1969, the Center issued its *Khara'it Turuq al-Muwasalat fi Filastin al-Muhtalla* (Maps of Transportation Roads in Occupied Palestine), complete with seventy-four maps of Israel and the occupied territories, just as Granot had reported. Publishing a book of maps is, of course, not in itself a militant act. The goal might have been to help preserve Palestinian refugees' connection to the geography of the homeland for the sake of cultural memory, or in the hope of an eventual return.

Anis Sayegh's preface to the volume, however, explains otherwise. The Center had produced a wall map in 1966 that, according to Sayegh, "greatly served the purposes of awareness, media, and heritage preservation." Why produce a series of much more detailed maps? Sayegh did not make the reader guess: "The purpose of these maps is to benefit the *feda'i* work." Because these maps were meant to assist Palestinian fighters, the maps would not be sold to the public "so that what we know, and what we do not know, will not leak out to the enemy." As a result, only "a limited number of them have been printed to be distributed only to the fedayeen and soldiers." Moreover, Sayegh explained that while half of the copies were bound, the others remained unbound "so that the fedayeen can use the maps more easily."[25] *Khara'it*, this book of maps, was produced to assist in violent attacks against Israeli targets.

Granot's article had extensive reach, in part because it was translated from Hebrew into English by the US Central Intelligence Agency. The CIA's Foreign Broadcast Information Service (FBIS) issued translations of foreign press reports for public consumption; in its February 3, 1983, report, Granot's article from the previous December was translated in full.[26] Interested Americans, especially American Jews monitoring Israeli political affairs, as we shall see, appear to have relied on Granot's translated report in retrospectively defending Israel's seizure of the PLO Research Center.

"A Legitimate Defensive Action"

Despite Granot's article and the implicit justification it offered for Israel's confiscation of the Center's contents, international criticism continued unabated. Israel's state archivist, Paul Abraham Alsberg, was one of the primary targets as his counterparts in archives across the globe expressed outrage at the wholesale pilfering of another national group's archive. Alsberg turned to his colleague Haim Sarid, then director of the IDF Archives, who in turn asked Haim Israeli, the head of office of the IDF Chief of Staff, to explain what had occurred. Israeli passed the question on to the head of AMaN, namely, Israeli military intelligence.

On December 21, 1982, less than three weeks after Granot published his newspaper piece, Moshe Sinai, a lieutenant in the bureau of the head of military intelligence, sent a classified (*shamur*) report to Israeli.[27] Sinai's report offered advice about how to respond to those who criticized Israel's confiscation of the PLO Research Center's library. First, Sinai corrected a misunderstanding that had apparently been circulating about whose archive the Israelis had seized in Beirut: "A. There is no truth to the claims of any harm to the Lebanese National Archive," he insisted. "The claim is libel with no factual basis. IDF forces had no contact whatsoever with the Lebanese National Archive." Then Sinai continued, addressing the matter of the PLO Research Center:

B. We are relating here to what is called "The Center for Palestinian Studies" as an innocent academic institution, as the PLO agents are trying to present it. Behind its innocent appearance hides an institution that served the terrorists, for their different organizations, to collect intelligence information about Israel and about Israeli and Jewish targets for the purposes of attacks and terrorist acts. The institute itself defines this: "meticulous surveillance of Israeli sources and preparing documents related to the enemy."

C. In the material that is in our hands there is much evidence that:
  1. A significant portion of the institute's library was utilized as an archive for surveilling targets, installations, and individuals in the Israeli army, security, and political system as targets for attack.
  2. The institute publishes classified publications, in limited distribution, aimed for terrorist activists. Included among these is intelligence information on IDF bases, roads, and civilian-economic targets, such as gas stations.
  3. The institute's systems and collecting capabilities were used by attack and terror arms of the terrorist organizations to gather operational intelligence about Israel.

D. The members of the administration of the institute and a portion of its members are known to Israeli intelligence as active members of terror organizations and active in matters of intelligence and recruiting terrorists to serve in the organizations.

The head of the institute himself, Sabri Jiryis, participated in the early 70s in planning attacks inside Israel but he fled before he was arrested.

E. In summary, the claim of destruction or looting of what is called "The
   Center for Palestinian Studies" is an attempt to distort a legitimate act
   of locating information that sheds light on terrorist activity against
   Israel and on all the efforts of the terrorist organizations to attack it.

Sinai added a final note: "After it finishes reviewing the discoveries, AMaN
would not prevent giving to the government of Lebanon the material that is
defined as academic research material (subject to the approval of the political
echelon)."[28]

Alsberg relied on the information he received in Sinai's report to respond
to questions from his colleagues. In early February, Alsberg wrote to Eric Kete-
laar, Deputy General State Archivist in the Netherlands: "The Palestine Research Center is, on the face of it, a research institute of a recognized academic
level, though," Alsberg added, "not an archival institution." But the Research
Center played another role, as well, he noted. It served "as a front to hostile
intelligence operations of the P.L.O. as proved by the fact that it conducted
documentation of a purely military character and concern." Given the Center's
military activities, insisted Alsberg, "any confiscation of material must be considered a legitimate defensive action."[29] As we will see, this response did not
staunch the flow of condemnation that Alsberg faced from the international
community of archivists.

A few days earlier, on January 23, Anne-Marie Lambert-Finkler, an Israeli
official responsible for overseeing relations with international and human
rights organizations, wrote a secret missive to Shmuel Divon, the assistant
director of the Foreign Ministry's Middle East bureau. Lambert-Finkler recalled that in the wake of the "wave of protests and criticism" that followed
Israel's seizure of the PLO Research Center, "Israel claimed that the Center
included, among other things, intelligence material that was designed to assist
PLO terror activities." She noted, however, that Hadassah Ben-Itto, Israel's
representative to UNESCO, had informed her colleagues in the organization
that "in the right time Israel would transfer the contents of the Center to the
legitimate Lebanese government and that, indeed, the Minister of Defense
approved the delivery of the material to the government of Lebanon (referring
to the academic-research material, not the intelligence material)."[30]

Lambert-Finkler was evidently pleased by this development and sought to
stress its significance to Divon. "The propagandistic importance of transferring
the contents of the Center to the Lebanese government is non-negligible," she
wrote. "The capture of the Center ignited criticism," explained Lambert-

Finkler, as "the protesters waved the banners of freedom of expression, academic freedom, etc." Moreover, "the topic was raised in appeals to us by the director general of UNESCO and appeals of other sources known as our supporters." Lambert-Finkler thus asked Divon to inform her whether the restitution of the PLO Research Center was indeed being discussed in Israel's negotiations with the Lebanese government.[31]

The Revival, and Bombing, of the Research Center

On February 5, 1983, two days after the CIA published its translation of Granot's article, the PLO Research Center suffered a devastating car-mounted rocket attack that killed eight staff members, including Hanneh Shahin Jiryis, the wife of the director Sabri Jiryis. The explosion also took the lives of two Lebanese soldiers standing guard outside and at least six neighbors and bystanders.[32]

With the library and archive of the PLO Research Center relocated to Israel and the Center itself a mere shadow of its former self, who would have bothered to bomb this institution now?[33] The Front for the Liberation of Lebanon from Foreigners (FLLF) took responsibility for the attack—but what was the FLLF? According to author and journalist Ronen Bergman, it was the creation and tool of three renegade Israeli military officials: IDF chief of staff Rafael "Raful" Eitan, regional commander Avigdor Ben-Gal, and special operations expert Meir Dagan.

Though Bergman referred to the FLLF as "a terrorist organization that Israel ran in Lebanon in the years 1980–83,"[34] by Bergman's own account it is misleading to claim that the FLLF was operated by Israel. "The operation," Bergman wrote, "ran almost entirely without the authorization or knowledge of the rest of the military, the defense ministry, the intelligence agencies or the government."[35] Bergman cited David Agmon, head of the IDF's Northern Command staff, who apparently knew of this scheme: "The aim was to cause chaos among the Palestinians and Syrians in Lebanon, without leaving an Israeli fingerprint, to give them the feeling that they were constantly under attack and to instill them with a sense of insecurity." To achieve this goal, the group recruited local "Druze, Christians, and Shiite Muslims who resented the Palestinians and wanted them out of Lebanon."[36] Bergman highlighted Israeli agency in this and correspondingly minimized the agency of the Lebanese participants who undertook the violent acts. If Bergman's sources were correct that the FLLF was established by Israelis, it seems more reasonable to see here not an Israeli effort with Lebanese individuals lacking agency but rather a joint effort among Israelis and Lebanese opponents of the PLO in Lebanon.

In any case, the question arises: why *then*? Why target the Research Center in Beirut when, in February 1983, the Center's contents were languishing in a Hatsav hangar in Israel? Any answer would lie within the realm of speculation, but two theories come to mind. One concerns what the PLO Research Center represented in this period and the other focuses on the particular activities in which the Center was then engaged.

As we have seen, in 1982 the PLO leadership was expelled from Beirut. However, while the other PLO-affiliated offices were shuttered and their people sent packing, the Research Center, protected by diplomatic immunity in Lebanon and perhaps perceived as harmless, remained. Slowly but surely, research and publication resumed.

The Center proudly publicized its continued operations in Beirut after the war. Despite the devastation inflicted upon the PLO Research Center by Israeli forces in September 1982, "the Palestinian people's desire for life and its ability to revive and persist" prevail, proclaimed the editors of *Shu'un Filastiniyya* when the journal resumed publication in October 1982. The revival of the Research Center was a manifestation of the Palestinian ideal of steadfastness, *sumud*. This national quality lay behind the Center's "resolve to replace what the Israeli savages plundered and destroyed, and its resolute decision to renew its activities." *Shu'un*'s editors vowed to remain stalwart in their efforts to rebuild the Center, and pledged to resume full publication activities.[37] As the editors put it, "the first goal of publishing" this latest issue of *Shu'un* "is to announce with a great voice: the national Palestinian life is stronger than all attempts of destruction."[38]

This "great voice" was heard far beyond Lebanon. In October, the Israeli newspaper *ha-Aretz* reported that the Research Center was still active in Beirut. This was a "breach of agreement," the article's title asserted, as the PLO was supposed to have completely ceased operations in Beirut over the summer. Amos Elon reported that, according to Faysal Hourani, seventy-eight people were back at work in the Center.[39] In November, the Kuwait News Agency reported on the reappearance of *Shu'un*, citing an announcement about the Center's defiant return issued by WAFA, the Palestinian News Agency.[40] And the Center's operation made the pages of US newspapers, with David Ottaway reporting in the *Washington Post* in December 1982 that "the only PLO institution that seems to have survived—if not intact at least as a functioning body—is the Research Center in downtown West Beirut."[41]

For those Lebanese parties that sought the removal of the PLO from Lebanese soil—and this was precisely the goal of the Front for the Liberation of Lebanon from Foreigners—the Research Center embodied the PLO's refusal to abandon its foothold in Lebanon.[42] For the Center's enemies, as for its participants, its persistence in Lebanon represented Palestinian *sumud*. Bombing the Center, then, might have been an attempt to put the final nail in the coffin of PLO activity in Beirut.

But there may be more to the timing of the decision to bomb the PLO Research Center. In the months following the Israeli seizure of the Center's library and archive, the Center might not have been viewed by anti-PLO Lebanese nationalists as a mere ideological thorn. Rather, it was reportedly preparing to take an action that would potentially stir up internal trouble in Lebanon.

On January 30, 1983, just as Israel's Kahan Commission of inquiry into the Sabra and Shatila massacres was expected to issue its report, Thomas Friedman wrote in the *New York Times* that the PLO Research Center, "which is still operating in Beirut, has done its own investigation" of the mid-September massacres in the Palestinian refugee camps. The Research Center, wrote Friedman, "will be publishing its report in the next few weeks" and "officials at the center said their conclusion would reveal that some 3,000 people were either dead or missing as a result of the Shatila massacre."[43] By the end of the same week, the PLO Research Center was targeted by rockets launched from a car parked outside the building, timed to detonate just as the staff was assembling to leave for the day.

Was the PLO Research Center attacked in anticipation of the report it was preparing to issue on the Sabra and Shatila massacres? We don't know. What we do know is that the timing of the attack raises important questions.

Debating the Center in the Wake of the February Bombing

Regardless of the bombers' motivations, and despite (or perhaps because of) the ruin in which the PLO Research Center lay in Beirut, debate about the true nature of the Center persisted across the Atlantic in the United States. *Newsview: The Israeli Weekly News Magazine*, an English-language, self-declared independent publication focused on Israel-related events, reported on the bombing in an article entitled "Terrorist Academic," in its February 22, 1983, edition.

Newsview had published an earlier article, written before the bombing, titled "PLO Back in Beirut," on February 8. This first piece reported on the "renewed activities of the PLO Research Center for Palestinian Studies, which has been combining academic and intelligence operations for some years." Like Granot, *Newsview* confused or conflated the PLO Research Center and the Institute for Palestine Studies. "Best known for its *Journal of Palestinian* [*sic*] *Studies* (published in the US in cooperation with Georgetown University and Kuwaiti funding and grants)," the article continued, "the center has also maintained a staff of researchers who duly monitor the Israeli media for intelligence purposes." In addition, the Center has "prepared special booklets for direct use by PLO sabotage teams, outlining the gas station infrastructure in Israel, files on senior IDF officers—including those in supply tasks—and publications on army base locations as well as road maps in Israel."[44] While *Newsview*'s writer did not provide sources, the information broadly matches that found in Granot's article (and the FBIS translation), including the detail of the cooperation between Georgetown University and Kuwait in producing the *Journal of Palestine Studies*.[45] The notion that the PLO oversaw a "two-faced"— seemingly innocuous but actually deadly—Research Center, now entered American Jewish discourse.

The second article focused on the Center's director Sabri Jiryis and his slain wife, Hanneh. The Research Center, *Newsview* wrote, "was considered by Israeli intelligence to have been a PLO front for many years, and to have become the terrorist organization's main headquarters in Beirut since it was forced out of the city last summer." The article offered this brief biography of Sabri Jiryis's public face:

> In 1960, he published an article in the campus newspaper defining Israeli Arabs as second-class citizens, and comparing their plight to that of European Jewry during the rise of Nazism. After graduating, Sabri joined a prestigious Arab law firm in Haifa, spending much of his spare time engaged in political activity and writing a book on the Arabs in Israel.

But there was another side to Jiryis's activities (just as there was a clandestine side to the Research Center he ultimately led). "Eventually, he secretly joined the Fatah terrorist faction, and is believed to have cooperated with Abu Jihad, the head of the Fatah branch responsible for attacks against Israeli citizens." In this period, Jiryis "defended Arab youths accused of security crimes, but apparently became involved in some of his own and so was handed a restraining order from the authorities." In 1969, the article continued, Jiryis "set out to write his own version of Zionist history, but his research was interrupted by his arrest for alleged involvement in setting up an arms cache in northern Israel."[46] (Decades later, as we have seen, Jiryis's daughter would suggest something similar.) *Newsview* perceived a clear pattern in Jiryis's years in Israel: a double life of publicly licit and privately illicit attempts to undermine Israel's security.

Jiryis's double life, as *Newsview* portrayed it, continued after he and his wife left Israel in 1970 and moved to Beirut. In Lebanon, "he worked with the PLO top leadership as an intelligence advisor. They in turn availed themselves of his considerable knowledge of Hebrew and Israeli life." The author evidently struggled to make sense of Jiryis's actions when they did not appear to fit the pattern of public academic and secret terrorist. "At one point," the author wrote, "Sabri, apparently still remembering his Israeli period favorably, arranged the release of two Israeli youths who mistakenly crossed the Lebanese border in the Galilee and were captured by the PLO." Why Jiryis had "favorable" memories of Israel at this one point is left unexplained. In any case, "after becoming head of the Palestinian Studies Center, he mixed academic pursuits with the preparation of intelligence reports for terrorist squads operating in Israel."[47] *Newsview*'s perception of Jiryis and of the PLO Research Center matched Granot's: the Center and its leadership were facilitating acts of violence against Israel, even if they also engaged in academic research.

Sustained American interest in the PLO Research Center extended beyond small Israel-focused magazines like *Newsview*. On February 20, 1983, the Research Center once again landed on the pages of the *New York Times*. David Shipler, then the Jerusalem bureau chief for the *Times*, wrote an article on what he regarded to be Israel's "blind spot"—the Israeli "national consensus on the illegitimacy of Palestinian nationalism." Shipler placed Israel's war against the PLO in Lebanon in the context of the "rejection by most Israelis across most of the political spectrum of the notion that the Palestinians are also a people laden with a history and a dream." This was the "frame of mind," asserted Shipler, in which "Israel sent its army into Lebanon" the previous year.

Toward the end of this critical article, Shipler quoted Meron Benvenisti, former deputy mayor of Jerusalem, who, at the time, was based at the American Enterprise Institute conducting research on the West Bank and Gaza. Israel's seizure of "the extensive archives on Palestinian culture and history" from the PLO Research Center was, in Benvenisti's mind, "revealing."[48] Benvenisti told Shipler that Israel's purpose in seizing this material "was not only to destroy them [it is unclear whether 'them' referred to the PLO or to the Palestinians] as a political or a military power ... but also to take from them their history, to erase that because it is troublesome." Benvenisti accused his fellow Israelis of harboring "a profound need or urge not to allow the Palestinians to be a respectable or historic movement."[49] Confiscating the library and archive of the PLO Research Center was not in any way essential, or even relevant, for military or security purposes, Benvenisti argued. It was, rather, an act aimed exclusively at pilfering—in order to deny—Palestinian history.[50]

Cynthia Ozick, Don Peretz, and "Calling the Thugs Librarians"

At least one *New York Times* reader was disturbed by this article: the acclaimed American Jewish author Cynthia Ozick, who was no stranger to debate on matters of Jewish interest. In 1974, for instance, she penned an article for *Esquire* called "All the World Wants the Jews Dead."[51] When, in February 1983, she read Shipler's article in the *Times*, Ozick was enraged by what she regarded as the flagrant mischaracterization of the PLO Research Center as "archives on Palestinian culture and history." She seems to have read the *Newsview* article about the Center from earlier that month and perhaps other articles on the subject as well.

The very day that the *Times* piece was published, Ozick responded in a letter to the editor about this "so-called cultural archive."[52] Citing Israeli press reports, Ozick relayed that the PLO Research Center "compiled personal files on high-ranking Israeli military officials, monitored Israeli police, military and civilian radio and television broadcasts and served as a clearing house for communications exchanged by terrorist organizations all over the world." Moreover, asserted Ozick, among the Research Center's "faculty" (Ozick's quotation marks) was Sabri Jiryis, "an advisor to Arafat and to Abu Jihad, the PLO's chief terror strategist (whose code name 'Jihad' means holy war), as well as Elias Shoufani, a highly situated member of Fatah, Arafat's personal terrorist organization." Considering the work done there and its staff's close association with the most important PLO militant leaders, the PLO Research Center "was in actuality," charged Ozick, "a leading PLO intelligence center"—notwithstanding "any other purpose it may have served." Thus, "to represent the military capture of a camouflaged military arm as an 'erasure' of culture and history is," Ozick argued, "a stunning falsehood."[53]

The debate Ozick opened about the nature of the PLO Research Center continued on the pages of the *New York Times*. Responding to Ozick's accusations about the Center and her implied defense of Israel's confiscation of its contents, a group of Middle Eastern Studies scholars wrote a letter of their own to the *Times* (the letter was dated March 8 and published on March 16).

The letter's published signatories were Eqbal Ahmad, Richard Bulliet, Irene Gendzier, Don Peretz, George Saliba, and Stuart Schaar, all established scholars of the medieval and modern Middle East with PhDs from Princeton (Ahmad and Schaar), Harvard (Bulliet), Columbia (Gendzier and Peretz), and the University of California, Berkeley (Saliba).[54] In addition to the signatories listed in the *Times*, several others signed the letter but were excluded in the published version owing to the newspaper's editorial policies. Those not listed were Edmund Burke III (University of California, Santa Cruz), Masao Mioshi (University of California, Berkeley), Alan Richards (University of California, Santa Cruz), Miriam Rosen (Fordham University), Jeanette Wakin (Columbia University), and Donald Will (United Methodist Office for the United Nations). The signatories were a diverse and distinguished group of scholars (several of them Jewish) with significant academic gravitas.[55]

In their letter, these scholars asserted that "the Palestine Research Center had been a most valuable resource for the study of Palestinian history and culture" and that "access to it had been easy and open." Not disputing Ozick's claim that the Center collected information on Israeli leaders and Israeli television and radio broadcasts, the scholars noted that the Center also profiled "other world leaders, including Arabs," and reviewed Palestine-related broadcasts from countries other than Israel as well. "These," the writers asserted, "are standard holdings for a research library." That Jiryis, the Center's director, was affiliated with the PLO was well known, the letter granted, just as, they hastened to add, was "the fact that he is one of the first Palestinians to have spoken out for a negotiated Palestinian accommodation with Israel." (I address this fact at length below.) The scholars' letter went on to challenge Ozick's understanding of the Research Center. Her piece "betrays a certain ignorance," they wrote, highlighting her apparent confusion between East and West Beirut and between the PLO Research Center and the Institute for Palestine Studies (the latter, rather than the former, being the institutional home of Elias Shoufani).[56]

The scholars were "deeply saddened," they wrote, "by the destruction of an educational institution that housed the archives, family records and manuscripts of an ancient people" and that had been "useful to several of us." They concluded with an appeal to the US government to "ensure that the Israeli authorities restore the library and archival material to their rightful holders."[57]

Thus, in a matter of six weeks, the PLO Research Center had been variously described as the repository of "extensive archives on Palestinian culture and history," as a "camouflaged military arm," and as an "educational institution"—all on the pages of the *New York Times*.

The controversy did not end there. Having read the scholars' letter to the *Times*, David Partington, a Harvard librarian and member of the Middle East Librarians Association (MELA), wrote to Don Peretz to offer assistance in trying to secure the return of the Center's holdings.[58] Peretz forwarded the note to Stuart Schaar, who had helped marshal the letter's signatures; Schaar responded by asking Partington to compose an appeal on behalf of MELA to the US State Department and to the Israeli government requesting that the Israelis "return the materials to their rightful owners." Schaar also suggested that Partington and his fellow librarians send a letter to the *New York Review of Books* calling for the same.[59] It is unclear what if anything came of MELA's involvement in the matter, but there was at least one librarian at Harvard (who would soon become the librarian association's president)[60] who shared the view expressed by the *Times* letter signatories that the fate of the PLO Research Center's holdings was a matter of concern not for terrorists or counterterrorism efforts but for professional librarians.

Ozick would have the last word in the *Times*. As she did when she read Shipler's original piece, Ozick penned her letter to the editor the very day the *Times* published the scholars' statement (though her letter was printed a few weeks later). This time, she assailed "Don Peretz and other signers" of the letter for obfuscating the distinction "between 'profiles on Israeli leaders' as 'standard holdings for a research library' and a hit list of key Israeli military targets."[61] Jiryis's "highly visible PLO affiliation" seems to have been all the proof necessary to determine that the profiles produced by the Research Center about Israel's leaders clearly fit the latter category; they were "a hit list." Of Jiryis's academic credentials, Ozick wrote, "surely it is an abuse of every civilizing value to mix academic pursuits with the preparation of intelligence reports for terror squads."[62]

Though her second letter to the *Times*, published April 9, 1983, was the last of her public statements on the matter of the PLO Research Center, Ozick persisted in private. On April 15, she wrote a personal letter to Don Peretz, to whom she had been introduced some ten years earlier.[63] Ozick's letter began with a personal attack on Peretz's religious identity. Having heard (erroneously) that Peretz, who was born Jewish, had become a Quaker, Ozick asserted that the founder of the Society of Friends George Fox "was not free of antiSemitism" and that, considering their approach to the Palestinian-Israeli conflict, "the Quakers today add up to a moral nonenity [*sic*]." After all, she wrote, "only a moral nonentity refuses to distinguish between two competing parties when one is openly contending for the destruction of the other."

After her broadside on Quaker morality, Ozick returned to the subject of the PLO Research Center. Responding to the claim in the scholars' letter to the *Times*—namely, that researchers had made productive use of the archives and resources of the Research Center—Ozick posed the following questions to Peretz:

> What use might a scholar like yourself have made of a detailed list of gas stations in Israel? Of a 1969 pamphlet, called "Road Maps for Occupied Palestine," published in a format without a cover and marked "circulation limited," designed for "missions" into Israel? What use might a scholar have made of a 1972 handbook . . . called "A Guide for the Palestinian Fighter," containing data on Israeli military camps in the Galilee and the Golan Heights? The latter being the first of an ongoing series dealing with IDF camps throughout Israel? What use might you, as a serious scholar of the Middle East, make of entire files of PLO intelligence services, including details of the "investigations" of senior terrorist commanders?[64]

These publications of the PLO Research Center demonstrated, for Ozick, the true, violent purpose of the Center. This was no "Brooklyn yeshiva," no "Widener Library at Harvard." As the Center was patently an intelligence unit assisting Palestinian attacks on Israeli targets, Ozick wondered, rhetorically, what use scholars such as Peretz might have had for it and why they would assail Israel for confiscating it.

In response to the scholars' mention of the killing of Hanneh Jiryis in the February 5, 1983, bombing of the Center,[65] Ozick used the life stories of Hanneh and Sabri Jiryis to highlight not the faults but rather the virtues of Israeli society. "It is of further interest—especially to feminists concerned with the subjection of women in traditional Arab societies—that Hani Shaheen Jiryes, whose life was ended by fellow Arabs at age 34," wrote Ozick, "emerged from the Arab village of Fassuta, in the Galilee, to take advantage of Israeli freedom of opportunity." Ozick continued: "surely it is coals to Newcastle for me to tell you that she graduated as an economics and statistics major from Hebrew University in Jerusalem, where she met [Sabri] Jiryes." Noting as well that Sabri Jiryis had studied law at the Hebrew University and joined a prominent law firm in Haifa, Ozick highlighted "the right of both Arabs and Jews to higher education in the Israeli university." Ozick concluded disdainfully: would Peretz and his fellow cosigners of the *Times* letter—"scholars who appear to honor archives riddled with hit lists"—regard the educational and employment opportunities with which Israel provides Arab men and women "as still another abuse of

Palestinian rights?"[66] If for Peretz and his colleagues the biographies of the Shahin-Jiryis couple illustrated the problems in Israeli society, for Ozick they represented precisely the opposite.

When Peretz received this note, he tried to gather more information about the PLO Research Center. Though he had visited Lebanon at least twice in the 1960s and apparently spent time at the Center, when pressed regarding the substance of the Center's holdings he wished to have more information at his disposal.[67] Peretz's archive reveals that he wrote to colleagues in the Association of Arab-American University Graduates (AAUG) who sent him materials about the Center's collections.[68] This information served as the basis for Peretz's point-by-point rebuttal of Ozick's allegations.

In his letter, written on June 28, 1983, Peretz began with an impassioned defense of the Society of Friends. He explained that, though Ozick was mistaken in taking his appreciation for the Quakers as an indication that he had left Judaism, he was indeed "an admirer of, supporter of, and participant in the work of the American Friends Service Committee (AFSC)." Peretz then denied additional charges Ozick had leveled against him in her letter, including that he was a PLO supporter and a binationalist. He was neither, he asserted, though he noted that many Jews "who gave far more of themselves to the establishment of a Jewish homeland than either you or I" were in fact binationalists (e.g., Judah Magnes, Martin Buber, Hugo Bergmann, Ernst Simon).

After contesting Ozick's personal attacks against him, Peretz turned to the matter of the PLO Research Center. Peretz asserted that he never saw any of the materials Ozick mentioned in her letter "nor has anyone else I know who used the archives mentioned them." Such materials, he continued, were not of interest to him and his academic colleagues:

> Of far greater interest to us, among the 25,000 volumes that were there, are: collections of literature in Arabic, Hebrew, and English about the Palestinians; memoirs in diaries and on tape from Arab families that lived in the country; collections of family photographs; records of landholdings that date back to the nineteenth century; radio broadcasts from Israel, the US and the Arab world on the Palestinians; and thousands of newspaper articles from all over the world about the Palestinians. I assume it takes no extraordinary familiarity with historical, political and cultural scholarship to recognize that these items are invaluable and have little if anything to do with, as you state in your letter, "missions" into Israel, "hitlists" or "terrorism."[69]

Without denying the possibility of the existence of militant materials in the Research Center, Peretz insisted that he and his fellow scholars valued the Center for its collection of historical sources that had nothing to do with and served no use for militants.

The exchange between Ozick and Peretz continued through the summer of 1983. At the end of June, Ozick passed on to Peretz a news article from the *Washington Post* she had come across that she believed confirmed her view of the Research Center.[70] The article ended with a report about the closing of the PLO Research Center and the Lebanese authorities' detention of Sabri Jiryis and two others. "Lebanon accuses them," the article noted, "of participating in plots leading to a series of bombings here" and, therefore, the "military prosecutor Assad Germanos asked the Foreign Ministry . . . to declare them persona non grata so that they can be expelled."[71] Peretz replied by questioning the reliability of the news article's source. Germanos, after all, had led the Lebanese government's investigation into the September 1982 massacres at the Sabra and Shatila refugee camps and had recently decided to terminate the investigation without any prosecutions.[72]

If Ozick had ever had any patience for Peretz, at this point she lost it. In one diatribe, she wrote: "You know Goddam well that Jiryes is a practiced terrorist, and you won't speak of it. . . . Jiryes is a killer, Arafat is a killer, Arafat's enemies in the disintegrating PLO are killers; what in the name of human decency are you defending?"[73]

Shortly after she dispatched this challenge to Peretz, Ozick read a Foreign Broadcast Information Service bulletin that, in her view, removed any last shred of doubt about the nature of the Research Center. The report relayed a Lebanese official's claim that explosives, grenades, and a gun had been found in the Center. "The difference between us," wrote Ozick to Peretz, "is that I call a thug a thug. You, the political scientist, so much more sophisticated than I, see a 'library' run by thugs and persist and persist in calling the thugs librarians. When are you going to admit that Jiryes is a terrorist?"[74] Ozick concluded: "You committed a Lie of Omission in the *Times*. Do you want to go on living with that?"

For Ozick, there was only one way to explain Peretz's stubborn defense of the PLO Research Center. "There is an obscuring lens over your heart that denies you the clarity to see the claims I am making in this letter," she wrote him on July 11, 1983. "I am sorry; it is known as *Selbsthass*."[75] Only self-hatred could prevent a Jew from acknowledging the true, malevolent nature of the PLO Research Center, Ozick insisted.[76] This, as far as I am aware, was the last in the exchange of letters.[77]

American Archivists, and Israel's State Archivist, Seek More Information about the Center

As Ozick and Peretz engaged in this epistolary battle, American archivists were continuing to investigate the nature of the PLO Research Center. Some were clearly dissatisfied with the decision of the Society of American Archivists to punt the issue to the international association of archivists.

In late May 1983, three New York University–affiliated archivists met with Hatem Hussaini, then a member of the PLO delegation at the United Nations, and with Philip Mattar, a Palestinian American scholar who had conducted dissertation research at the PLO Research Center in 1978. In this meeting, the archivists sought to collect information about the Center and to pass it on to the leadership of the SAA. Mattar, according to the letter the archivists penned after the meeting, explained that "access to the Center was quite open (more so than, for example, the Hebrew University Archives)."[78] Nothing beyond a passport was required for entry and Mattar recalled being shown anything he requested. Mattar kept notes on the subject headings in the Center's collection and these, the archivists wrote, included "Studies of the Palestinian Problem, 1918–1964; Jerusalem; Palestine War—general matters; Palestine and the United Nations; Papers of the Arab Higher Committee;" and "The Anglo-American Committee." The Center, according to Mattar, did not focus on contemporary events. Its collection concentrated on historical matters.[79] With a staff of university students and alumni, the PLO Research Center, suggested Hussaini, was tantamount to "the Brookings Institute of the Palestinian government-in-exile." The archivists stressed that the Research Center was not "the PLO Archives" as "none of its records are institutional records of the PLO."

The meetings with Hussaini and Mattar had left the archivists convinced that the PLO Research Center was indeed an academic institution that housed valuable historical archives concerning Palestine and the Palestinians. In light of the reports they received, the three archivists asserted:

> It seems clear to us, as archivists, that the Palestinian Archives belong to the Palestinian people, that no other state should confiscate and prevent access to the records by their own creators. We stand in agreement with the Geneva Accords, that occupied peoples must not be plundered of their social, cultural, historical objects and institutions.

In the letter, the archivists declared their wish that the SAA publicly express its opposition to the seizure of the PLO Research Center archives and send letters to the UN secretary-general, UNESCO, the US secretary of state, the American president, the Israeli prime minister, and the Israeli minister of education calling "for the return of the PRC Archives to the Center, under the protection of the Lebanese government." Moreover, the archivists suggested offering the Research Center assistance in the way of books, journals, and microfilms on Palestine-related matters as well as supplies and even a travel award to Jiryis or a colleague to visit the US to meet with American archivists.

On June 10, 1983, the Israeli newspaper *Yedi 'ot Aharonot* ran a special interview with Paul Abraham Alsberg, the head of the Israel State Archives. The occasion was the publication of the third volume of a series called *Israeli Foreign Policy Documents*. In a three-page spread, Alsberg discussed the codenames used in Israeli documents to refer to Arab leaders during the 1948 war; the potential for political misuse of archives; the 1933 assassination of Haim Arlosoroff; the inaccessibility of Arab state archives; the effort to remove Franz Kafka's papers from Israel; Israeli policies concerning destruction of official documents; the Israel State Archives' budget and microfilming efforts; and more.

Toward the end of the interview, the journalist Raphael Bashan asked: "Are the PLO's archives, which were captured by the IDF in Beirut, found in the State's Archives?" In Bashan's record of the interview, Alsberg responded emphatically: "No! They are found in the hands of security apparatus and, as one recalls, the state announced at the time that it is prepared to return them" to the PLO Research Center, "as part of a broader agreement." Bashan then asked Alsberg whether, as a professional, he would have wanted the PLO documents transferred to the Israel State Archives. The archivist responded that such documents are outside the bounds of the mandate of the State Archives, which are meant to deal exclusively with state institutions. But Alsberg did not, in principle, oppose Israeli use of the Research Center's archives. On the contrary, he explained that "the Palestinian archive has operative value and I hope that the intelligence corps, the Shiloah Institute,[80] and the Truman Institute are deriving from them the maximal benefit."[81]

If Alsberg, Israel's state archivist, was publicly confident about the nature of the PLO Research Center materials and the justice of Israel's having confiscated them, he seems to have been less certain in private. In early August 1983, Alsberg wrote again to Haim Israeli at the Ministry of Defense. "It appears," wrote Alsberg, "that the topic [of Israel's seizure of the PLO Research Center] will again be raised for discussion in the international organization of archivists

[International Council on Archives] that will take place in October in Bratislava." Alsberg asked Israeli for "updated information in order to know what to respond and how to relate."

A New Intelligence Report

By the end of the month, the research division of Israel's military intelligence had produced an updated report that included more detailed information about the PLO Research Center. Haim Israeli forwarded this report to Alsberg. Curiously, this report largely matched not only the information but also the language of the article Oded Granot had published in *Ma'ariv* eight months earlier. The three-page report, marked "secret," was titled "The Center for Palestinian Studies" and dated August 28, 1983. The document began with a basic description of the Research Center: "The Center for Palestinian Research was founded in 1965 by Dr. Fayez Sayegh as an academic body whose primary occupation was gathering political and historical information and producing publications on the topic of the Israel-Arab conflict and the Palestinian problem." The report continued with information about the source of the Center's funding and its diplomatic immunity in Lebanon.

Next, the report listed three periodicals that the Center produced: the Arabic *Shu'un Filastiniyya*, the English-language *Journal of Palestine Studies* (once again confusing, as Granot did in *Ma'ariv*, the Institute for Palestine Studies, which published this journal, with the PLO Research Center), and daily listening reports. The surveillance reports, the document explained, included summaries of information from Israeli radio and television broadcasts along with introductions and commentary by the Center's researchers. Approximately 1,500 copies were published and distributed to, among others, the leaders of the PLO organizations for intelligence and attacks. In addition, the Center served as a publishing house for books and pamphlets that dealt broadly with the Palestinian problem and Israel.

This new military intelligence report further explained that the Center "did not serve only as an academic institution" and was not engaged merely in "offering cultural and ideological services." Rather, the report asserted, it also "veered into clearly operative areas, that is, assisting terror activity." Here, the report cited the same three documents that Granot had listed: *The Handbook for the Palestinian Fighter*, *Maps of Transportation Roads in Occupied Palestine*, and a detailed list of gas stations in Israel. In addition, the report noted that the topics covered in the Center's newspaper archive included activities of

Fateh's "underground organization, 'Black September'" and that the Center's document archive included secret documents on the 1970 crisis in Jordan. The archive also tracked changes in IDF leadership, organized folders of documents from PLO entities, and accepted requests from senior terrorists for special research on behalf of the terrorist organizations. The report added, parenthetically, that "according to our information, during the siege of Beirut, Center staff worked to destroy classified documents" and "brought others with them when they were evacuated."

The next section of the report noted that members of the Center's monitoring unit were active in the surveillance unit of Fateh's "Western Sector," which was charged with militant operations inside Israel and which monitored the IDF, Israeli police, and Israeli radio news reports. The intelligence report continued with a list of five Research Center staff members who were formerly Israeli residents but were expelled due to criminal terrorist activity or criminal political activity. "Most," the report asserted, "were active in terrorist organizations through recruiting volunteers and setting up close ties with heads of the Palestinian organizations." These formerly Israeli researchers included Sabri Jiryis, Elias Shoufani, Imad Shakur, Makram Yunes, and Nazih Murad. After the PLO was pushed out of Beirut, the report noted, Arafat ordered that the Research Center renew its activities under the directorship of Sabri Jiryis. By July 1983, "the Center was closed by the Lebanese authorities after terrorist materials were found in it." Jiryis was therefore arrested and expelled from Lebanon and, according to the report, the PLO was presently searching for a new location in which to reopen the Center.

The report concluded with a line that already appeared, in almost the same words, in the October 13, 1982, intelligence report: "In summary, there exists a basic contradiction between the Center's pretense of being a proper academic institution," on the one hand, "and its formal and essential subordination to the PLO. The identification with the aims of the PLO leads the Center, necessarily and knowingly, to be a tool in the hands of the PLO, including in the sphere of executing acts of terror."[82] In the Israeli intelligence's assertion of a "basic contradiction" in the identity of the PLO Research Center, we might recall the skepticism Fayez Sayegh attributed to Walid Khalidi and Constantine Zurayk nearly two decades earlier about how a think tank could adhere to the highest academic standards while existing under the auspices of a political organization such as the PLO. Of course, while upholding the misgivings of the IPS founders, Israeli intelligence had different purposes in stressing these contradictions.[83]

A remarkable feature of the debate about the PLO Research Center analyzed in the present chapter is that, like the Palestinian-Israeli conflict itself, it was a global controversy. Indeed, the debate involved a full cast of characters familiar to us from the broader conflict. We encountered a Palestinian Israeli scholar living in Lebanon (Jiryis); a Palestinian diasporic scholar and activist in the US defending fellow Palestinians (Said); an international cultural organization recruited to exert political pressure (UNESCO); an Israeli journalist disseminating—or composing?—Israeli intelligence reports (Granot); American foreign interest (the CIA); international media (the *New York Times*); a Zionist in the Diaspora committed publicly to defending Israeli actions (Ozick); an American Jew critical of Israeli policy (Peretz); and, finally, an Israeli intelligence analyst (Steinberg).

That so many people bothered to enter the arena on this issue speaks volumes about the PLO Research Center's importance both as an institution and as a symbol. For supporters of the PLO and others sympathetic to the Palestinian nationalist cause, the Center represented the hope of Palestinian cultural and intellectual progress and integration. For those who opposed the PLO, the Center represented yet another threat to the State of Israel. The Center's apparent innocence made it all the more threatening, precisely because its cultural and intellectual activities complicated the violent image that the PLO had gained in the West. On both sides, the Research Center became a key emblem.

The True Face of the PLO Research Center?

In the public debate over the nature of the PLO Research Center's collections and activities, the dueling narratives were diametrically opposed. Some portrayed the Center as a storehouse of Palestinian cultural and historical heritage. Others depicted it as a den of terrorists. Each of these narratives, especially as they emerged in the United States, drew on selective data. In point of fact, the bottom line was how one perceived the Palestinian national cause. Those who regarded the PLO as a legitimate national liberation movement relied on descriptions of the Center as a legitimate academic research institution. Those who regarded the PLO as an illegitimate terrorist organization relied on sources indicating that the Center's academic research was but one of its "two faces," meant to disguise sinister pursuits. In this battle of the politics of knowledge, Edward Said trusted Sabri Jiryis; Cynthia Ozick trusted Oded Granot.

Lost, however, in such binary portrayals is the extraordinary nature of the PLO Research Center. Its halls and its publications, especially the journal *Shuʾun Filastiniyya*, served as a space for internal Palestinian political debate, and for hashing out new directions in Palestinian nationalist politics. The Center housed an expansive Jewish and Israel studies library, filled with books written by Jews and Zionists about Judaism, Zionism, and Israel, right in the heart of the PLO in Lebanon. The Center employed Hebrew-reading and Hebrew-speaking researchers to follow and translate contemporary Israeli press and radio programming, offering an ampler and more accurate view of Israeli discourse and debate. All these features of the PLO Research Center were missed in the 1982–83 debate as each side sought to portray the Center as either purely academic or secretly terroristic.

Was the Research Center a two-faced organization, as Granot and the Military Intelligence reports alleged? The Research Center indeed investigated historical, political, ideological, religious, sociological, and economic questions that were not in any obvious way connected to violent attacks against Israel. *And* the Research Center investigated topics and published materials explicitly aimed at facilitating the PLO's armed struggle against Israel. For those committed Palestinian nationalists involved in the Center, these were not two faces, but two aspects of the same face, aiming to combat Israel. The Center's researchers were dedicated not merely to the pursuit of knowledge but also to the pursuit of the PLO's political aims. In this regard, however, the PLO Research Center was in no sense exceptional. It was a think tank that straddled the spheres of academics and politics, under the umbrella of an organization that was, among other things, engaged in a violent struggle against an enemy. Think tanks of all kinds regularly engage in politically driven knowledge creation and dissemination.

However, even if we regard these various pursuits as the reflection of two faces, it is not obvious which face was masking the other. In the Israeli intelligence reports and newspaper articles we have seen, the Center's academic pursuits covered for its true, violent purpose. At the same time, those scholars and archivists advocating for the library's return did not mention to UNESCO, and likely did not know, that the Center occasionally prepared operational intelligence for attacks on Israel.

Yet, there may be another way to look at this question. It is possible that publishing a set of maps for the fedayeen gave the Research Center the flexibility to publish, the following year, a book such as *al-Talmud wa-l-Sahyuniyya*, a book that, as we have seen, called upon Palestinian nationalists to renounce antisemitism. There is little reason to question whether the Research Center's leaders and staff supported Palestinian armed struggle against Israel when it published its book of Galilee and Golan Heights maps or its *Handbook for the Palestinian Fighter*. But in the Palestinian context of this period, support for the armed struggle was the norm. The Research Center, as we saw in Sayegh's preface to the *Handbook for the Palestinian Fighter*, felt no need to hide its advocacy of violent attacks on Israeli targets. The secret that Sayegh sought to conceal was not the desire to attack but the particular information that the Research Center had gathered ("so that the enemy does not know what we know—and what we do not know").

Recall that at this time, the PLO Covenant insisted on armed struggle as the sole means to liberate Palestine. This position was taken for granted within the PLO. What was not taken for granted was the reading of Zionist texts or the study of Jewish history. In this serious attempt to understand the enemy, the PLO Research Center was engaged in something radical. In other words, it may have been this academic face that demanded cover.

The debate that raged after the confiscation of the Center in 1982 echoed in certain ways the argument between Fayez Sayegh and the IPS leaders when Sayegh was founding the Center in 1965: how independent—intellectually and otherwise—could the PLO Research Center be, considering its status as an arm of the Palestine Liberation Organization? This question bookended the life of the PLO Research Center.

13

Exchanging Prisoners,
a Library, and an Archive

AFTER FOURTEEN MONTHS in Israeli custody, on November 24, 1983, the PLO Research Center's library and archive returned to the PLO. As we have seen, PLO intellectuals and their supporters had publicly decried the confiscation and demanded restitution of the Research Center's materials within days of the Israelis' seizing them. However, the materials were not returned in direct response to condemnation by Edward Said or Meron Benvenisti or in answer to UNESCO or international archivist pressure, nor were they shipped back as soon as Matti Steinberg determined that they held no intelligence value. Instead, they were returned as part of a human prisoner exchange.[1]

In the course of the 1982 war, the PLO had captured six Israeli soldiers.[2] At the same time, Israel took more than four thousand Arab prisoners, detaining them primarily in the Ansar prison camp in southern Lebanon. As part of its mission to protect prisoners of war, the International Committee of the Red Cross sought to help the parties negotiate a prisoner exchange when the war ended. According to the ICRC's account, the Red Cross spent months negotiating with the Israelis and with the PLO; the negotiations were conducted separately as the Israelis and the PLO refused to negotiate directly with one another. The two Israeli negotiators were Shmuel Tamir, chairman of the staff for prisoners of war and missing soldiers, and Amos Yaron, head of the human resources division in the General Staff.[3] Finally, in late November 1983, the parties came to an agreement. In exchange for the six Israeli soldiers held by the PLO in Tripoli, the Israelis would release some 4,400 (reports of the precise number vary) Arab prisoners, including several dozen who had been held in Israeli prisons before the war.[4] Some three thousand would be sent back to their families in southern Lebanon while another thousand would be expelled to Algeria. But the PLO demanded the return not only of the Arab prisoners but also of its Research Center.

The "Relief" of Return

The Israeli negotiators consulted their colleagues in intelligence, who informed them that from their perspective there was no need for Israel to keep the Center's materials. Contributing to this recommendation was Amos Gilead, an intelligence officer who was present during the 1982 assessment and then confiscation carried out in Beirut. When I interviewed Gilead in his office at the Interdisciplinary Center's Institute for Policy and Strategy, he remembered the library as impressive and well organized. He also said it did not take long to determine that the materials in the collection were worthless from an operational point of view.

If this was so, why did Israel bother to send the library and archive down to Israel, I asked. The act, said Gilead, had less to do with strategic decision-making and more to do with "emotions" and "symbolism." Because Israelis viewed the PLO as the enemy, they dealt with the PLO Research Center emotionally rather than rationally. No "real thought" had been given to the matter, according to Gilead. "Conquering 'the PLO's archive'" was considered a symbolic triumph in the war against the PLO.[5]

Gilead commented that "in retrospect, I would never have taken the archive." It was a wartime blunder, "a mistake" that, in his view, cost Israel dearly in terms of international legitimacy while providing the state with no benefits. "We needed more copies of *ha-Aretz*?" he asked rhetorically. "We didn't need to take their copies of *Shu'un Filastiniyya*. We already had them." If Gilead was guarded about his part in seizing the Center, he was unequivocal about his role in the decision to return it. "I was very happy," he stated several times in the course of our conversation, to have had the opportunity "to be part of the decision to return it" the following year. "Getting rid of it," Gilead said of the Research Center, was a major "relief."[6]

So, at Ben-Gurion Airport, as the thousand-plus Algeria-bound prisoners boarded the cabins of three Air France 747s provided by the French government, Israelis down below on the tarmac, under the supervision of Yigal Sheffy, loaded more than one hundred wooden crates filled with the PLO Research Center's archives and library into the cargo hold. In the passenger cabin, human prisoners; in the cargo hold, a library.[7]

On November 24, 1983, the *New York Times* correspondent David Shipler reported from Jerusalem on the prisoner exchange. "Six Israeli soldiers, held prisoner for more than 14 months by the Palestine Liberation Organization in Lebanon, returned home today," wrote Shipler, "to a tumultuous, passionate welcome." In exchange, Israel "completed the release of 4,500 Arab prisoners, including some who were serving life sentences for terrorist attacks on Israeli civilians," and closed the Ansar detention center it had created in southern Lebanon for the prisoners it took during the war. In addition, Shipler commented, "the P.L.O.'s archives, seized in West Beirut during the 1982 Israeli invasion, were also returned."[8] While the article focused on the human prisoners who were freed—and the jubilation and distress that this caused on either side of the conflict—it ended with the matter of "the P.L.O. archives," which were "turned over to the Red Cross." Shipler noted here the debate about the contents and mission of the Research Center. On the one hand, he paraphrased Jiryis, who claimed that "the files contained only historical information on Arab families and villages in pre-1948 Palestine" and "microfilms had been made of everything except some old and valuable books." On the other hand, he reported that "the Israelis have said that the research center was less an academic than an intelligence organization, and that much of the data could be used in planning terrorist attacks."[9] Even as the Research Center's contents were in the air on their way to Algeria, their true nature continued to be contested.

Was the PLO Research Center's Archive "the PLO Archive"?

In the above-mentioned article, Shipler referred to the materials returned in November 1983 as "the P.L.O. archives." While the PLO Research Center collected thousands of books in its library, by all accounts it also housed an archive. The question of whether this archive, assembled by the PLO Research Center, should be regarded as "the PLO archive" has been the subject of intense debate.

"The Center does not have secrets," Jiryis insisted in a 1985 interview—the same interview in which he claimed that there were some "rare and very valuable documents" and "sensitive information" that he hid from the Israeli conquering forces (and that he told me, more than thirty years later, were still "not for disclosure"). I am therefore not certain what he meant by "secrets." In any case, in 1985 Jiryis elaborated on the contents of the Center's library and archive:

> What have been described as documents are simply academic books available at many research institutes and centers, in addition to books found at any normal library throughout the world, including Israeli books. These number about 3,000 books dealing with the Zionist entity and society. The value of the books stems from the efforts spent collecting these sources and from the fact that they are specialized in the Palestine problem. Even the documents do not contain any secrets pertaining either to the activities of the PLO or to the activities of friendly or adversary forces. They simply include valuable collections of old British, Ottoman, Israeli and Arab documents pertaining to the Arab-Israeli conflict dating from the last several decades. These documents are purely for academic research aimed at writing the history of the Palestine problem and the Middle East. In addition, there are large collections of regular publications such as newspapers and magazines pertaining to the Palestine question in some form or another. These are, briefly, the possessions of the Research Center.[10]

When I spoke with him in 2015, Jiryis essentially repeated the above claim. The Research Center had "a classical academic library. There were no secrets, nothing of unique value that we lost." Later, he insisted that the Center's collection "would be very similar to the library of the faculty of history" in any university and that "if they give me some money now, I can create another one better than it. It's a matter of economics only."[11]

From the writings of Jiryis's predecessor, Anis Sayegh, however, it is not clear that replacing what was taken from the Center's archive was simply a question of sufficient funding. In the 1984 Arabic *Palestinian Encyclopedia* entry about the Research Center, presumably written by Anis Sayegh (who edited the encyclopedia), the Center's archive department was described as follows:

> It collects all published documents about the [Palestine] problem. It continuously strives to acquire unpublished documents and to sort them. This department follows what is published in 80 newspapers and periodicals in different languages, and sorts the materials by its particular field. It copies the acquisitions of its archive on microfilm, and works to acquire historical documents that have been out of print for several years, including English and Hebrew documents. The department publishes a monthly volume that contains summaries of current events each month, arranged by topic, in

order to make it easy to review it and to use it as a source for facts at any time. And this volume is distributed to concerned parties.[12]

According to this account, the Research Center's archive consisted of published documents and newspapers and assorted unpublished documents that the staff would compile and copy to microfilm. The staff also had a particular interest in collecting published but out-of-print documents. Complementing the library, the archive was meant to serve as a resource for researchers.

In his memoirs, published in 2006, Anis Sayegh offered additional details about the nature of the documents that the Research Center held in its library and archive. Assuming Sayegh's account is accurate, it would seem that the loss of these documents was more significant—and, if permanent, more devastating to the historical record—than Jiryis suggested. According to Sayegh, the library contained a special section for documents under the leadership of the researcher Khairieh Kasmieh. This section, Sayegh wrote, was "rich in private papers and unpublished memoirs." These included the private papers of Frances Emily Newton (1871–1955, a British missionary in Palestine who came to be an outspoken opponent of Zionism);[13] a "huge collection" of papers from the British Mandate–era Criminal Investigation Department (CID) of the Palestine Police Force;[14] documents from the All-Palestine Government (established by the Arab League in 1948); papers from the Arab Liberation Army (created by the Arab League to fight against the Zionists in 1948); and "a large part" of the papers of Hajj Muhammad Amin al-Husseini (1895–1974). In addition, Sayegh recounted, the library held memoirs and papers of leading Palestinian figures such as Husayn Fakhri al-Khalidi (mayor of Jerusalem in the mid-1930s and member of the Arab Higher Committee); Hanna ʿAsfur (an Executive Committee member of the Mandate-era Palestine Arab Workers Society);[15] ʿAwni ʿAbd al-Hadi (a member of the Arab Higher Committee and then of the All-Palestine Government); Fawzi al-Qawuqji (field commander of the Arab Liberation Army); Kamal Nasser (editor of PLO newspaper *Filastin al-Thawra* and member of the PLO Executive Committee); and, by Sayegh's estimation, files from "tens of other leading figures, political parties, and groups."[16]

Among the most important documents that the Research Center held, according to Sayegh, "from both a legal and practical perspective," was a complete collection of the statistics and statements of the British Mandate Lands Department. This collection was valuable because, through its "specific, detailed, reliable, and official" information about the ownership of Palestine's lands during the Mandate, it "demonstrates clearly the right of the members of the Palestinian nation to the ownership of their lands from which they were forcibly uprooted." These "rare, secret files" were removed from Palestine "covertly," revealed Sayegh in his memoirs, and given to the Center by Sami Hadawi, whom we met above as the author of *Crime and No Punishment*. Hadawi, who died in 2004 (two years before the publication of Sayegh's memoirs), had been a senior officer in the Lands Department of the mandatory government.[17]

Beyond these documents, Sayegh wrote, there were "thousands" of other files all pertaining to Palestinian-"Israeli" (Sayegh would rarely name Israel without quotation marks) matters, all properly indexed and catalogued. These files, under the supervision of the researcher Salma Haddad, came from "over one hundred press or official sources—Arab and foreign." According to Sayegh, "no researcher on any contemporary topic" could manage "without turning to these files."[18]

Yet another section of documents held in the Research Center, beginning in the 1970s, was a special collection of sources related to the Palestinian resistance and its factions, organizations, and departments. Sayegh wrote that this department, headed by Rashid Hamid, was able to collect "all of the official communiques (and they were in the thousands) that were issued by the Liberation Organization and its departments, offices, and divisions, along with those issued by factions and combat organizations." Not even the groups themselves had such complete collections of their own papers, Sayegh asserted, and, from time to time, groups would request a publication or leaflet that they had lost.[19]

Given this extensive collection of historical and organizational files, along with the Research Center's own publications, archivist and scholar Hana Sleiman argued that "the Center's archive did in fact serve as an official archive for the PNM [Palestinian National Movement] for the years from 1964 to 1982." While it was "not produced by a state bureaucracy," Sleiman wrote, the PLO Research Center "archive collected the documents produced by the factions of the contemporary liberation movement, and the documents of past administrations and figures relating to modern Palestinian history. It thus constitutes an integral part of the PNM's archive."[20] Sleiman emphasized that "the Center's archive is neither the only, nor the most complete, archive of the PNM. Several others exist: the archive of the PLO Chairman's Office, the PLA archives, and the archives of the individual factions and affiliated unions and social organizations."[21] However, in Sleiman's view, the PLO Research Center's library and archive clearly constituted an archive of the PNM.

Jiryis, however, denied that the PLO Research Center served as an archive for the PLO and the movement. When I spoke with him in 2015, before the publication of Sleiman's article, Jiryis stated that "the Israelis thought, and up to now some of their ignorant people say, that it was the PLO Archive. In fact, it has never been the PLO Archive." The idea of a "PLO Archive" was unimaginable, Jiryis argued. He elaborated: "The PLO never centralized its archives. It would never put it in one single place. Because of security, that would be in danger, of course." Rather, Jiryis insisted, "every department, every organization, every corner here and there had their own archive by themselves."[22] It appears that the PLO Research Center's archive, such as it was, was not a "PLO archive" in the sense of an archive of all internal PLO documents and correspondence from the organization's various divisions.

After reading Sleiman's article, Jiryis reiterated that the Research Center had "never been the archive medium of the PLO, never. We did not receive, or keep, any single document from any PLO department or institute, as each was keeping its own 'archives.' Besides, for security reasons, keeping all of your eggs in one basket was too dangerous for the PLO in general to be even contemplated." Rather, "what we had was simply a research library, similar to those found in any university department. No more and no less."[23]

Though Jiryis dismissed the idea of the PLO Research Center as the archive of the Palestinian National Movement as "fantasies," Sleiman's claims about the contents of the Research Center's archive are solidly grounded in Anis Sayegh's memoirs. Why would Sayegh, who headed the Center for a decade (1966–76), have such a different recollection of the library's holdings from that of Jiryis, who worked at the Center from the early 1970s and headed it during its final years in Beirut (1978–83) and afterward, as we shall see, in Cyprus?

It seems reasonable that sensitive materials would not be housed in one place. It was also reasonable to think that the materials held in the Research Center might one day be destroyed or captured. After all, as we have seen, the Center had, in the 1970s, been targeted on multiple occasions. Moreover, as noted, until Jiryis assumed stewardship of the Center in 1978, it was run by individuals who had a highly conflictual relationship with Arafat. It seems unlikely that the PLO chairman would entrust sensitive documents to such a staff.

Perhaps the issue comes down to the definition of "archive." If one defines an archive as a place to which internal, unpublished organizational documents ("secrets," as Jiryis might put it) are regularly sent to be stored, the PLO Research Center may not have been the PLO's or the PNM's archive. However, if the term is taken more loosely, as referring to a place that, of its own accord (rather than by the policies of those producing the documents), systematically gathers the official pamphlets, leaflets, and other publications of groups affiliated with a movement, then perhaps the PLO Research Center ought to be understood as at least a *kind* of archive of the PLO and the PNM.

The depiction of the Research Center as an academic library of books along with historical documents intended for research purposes is further supported by the fact that Israel ultimately returned the contents in 1983. Yet, that the Israelis returned these materials so soon after capturing them might reflect the sacrifices they were willing to make to bring home their prisoners of war.[24] Yitzhak Shamir, who became prime minister a month earlier, said at the time: "We paid a high price for the release of the six, but in the negotiations we were faced with the fact that their lives were in peril, and that any moment the worst could happen."[25] If the Israeli government was willing to release *people* it regarded as dangerous, it might have been even more open to returning dangerous *documents*.[26]

Where Are the Center's Library and Archive Now?

If we want to see what was held in the Research Center, why not just visit it now and see what is there? The Israelis, after all, returned the Research Center's materials in 1983. Here is where the story gets even more complicated. By all accounts, Israel returned much, if not all, of what it had seized. But by the time this exchange was negotiated, the PLO Research Center was no longer in Beirut. As we have seen, the PLO leadership had been forced out of Lebanon during the war, but the PLO Research Center, because of its diplomatic status, was permitted to remain in the country. Soon, though, as part of the preparations for an Israeli-Lebanese peace treaty, and in response to Palestinian attacks on Israeli forces in Lebanon, Jiryis and a few other remaining PLO officials in Beirut were arrested.[27] In June 1983, Jiryis was deported to Tunis and eventually settled in Cyprus. So, in November 1983, the Research Center was not sent back to Beirut. Instead, as we have seen, it was sent to Algeria.

According to Jiryis, the Israelis returned what they had captured "in the most convenient and nicest way." They loaded the materials into "boxes of good, strong wood—80 by 100 by 100 cm," costing Israel, by Jiryis's estimation, "some tens of thousands of shekels." These wooden crates, which Jiryis personally surveyed in Algeria in March 1986, evidently made quite an impression on

Jiryis: "if you were to dismantle them," he told me, "they would make furniture for a big building." Those boxes were sent on an Air France 747 jet from Tel Aviv to one of the Palestine Liberation Army (PLA) camps in Algeria, where Jiryis found them; as he recalls, "all of the materials were in them."[28] Jiryis told me that the Israelis returned absolutely everything, "even things that I thought that they should have destroyed," such as the original copies of newspaper clippings that had already been microfilmed.[29] Samih Shabeeb, who accompanied Jiryis, recalled their visit to Algeria differently. He wrote that the two did not have the opportunity to review each box so it is not clear whether they would have noticed if something had been missing.[30]

After Jiryis was deported from Lebanon, he and PLO chairman Arafat decided that it would be best to reestablish the Research Center in Cyprus. Cyprus, Jiryis liked to say, "turned out to be the best Arab state." As Jiryis told it, the PLO was anxious about the safety of shipping the Research Center's collection out of Algeria and the feasibility of storing it in Cyprus. "We were not sure, after what happened [in Beirut], that it would be safe to get it back to Cyprus," he explained, and, in any case, "we had no place to put it." Instead, in Cyprus, Jiryis recalled, "we started our new small library and continued our work on a small scale."[31]

Confused, I asked Jiryis if he was telling me that, after demanding that the Research Center's library be returned in the prisoner exchange with Israel, the PLO then just left it in Algeria. "That's what I'm saying," answered Jiryis, "we left it there in Algeria." According to Jiryis, there were numerous proposals of places and institutions to which the library could be sent:

> Some wanted to take it for themselves. For example, the University of Birzeit. My friend Dr. Hanna Nasser, who was the president of the university, came and talked to me about that. And other people wanted to send it to Egypt. And a third person talked to the Saudis that they would take it there. And I was against all of these . . . I told them that the most secure thing would be to stay in Algeria.

After the Oslo Accords were signed in 1993 and Arafat moved to Gaza, there was discussion of transporting the library to Gaza as well. "But again," Jiryis recalled, "we didn't think that it was a good idea." They thought it advisable first to allow the Palestinian Authority to develop and take control over further areas of the West Bank and Gaza before bringing the library to Palestine. "But then things started moving," as Jiryis put it, referring presumably to the breakdown and failure of the Oslo process, "and everybody just forgot about it."[32]

Since then, Jiryis said, the fate of the Research Center's library has been a matter of speculation. As far as he knows, it never left Algeria, but whether it is still extant is uncertain. "Some Algerians say that it vanished, that it was destroyed due to rain, to all kinds of things. Some say, no, that it still exists. But we really don't know exactly." Jiryis explained that those PLA officers responsible for the library when it was stored on their base in Algeria returned to Palestine after the Oslo Accords. The Palestinian officials "left it [the Research Center's library] behind them, entrusting the Algerian army with it. And from there we couldn't trace exactly what happened with it."[33]

Having learned from Jiryis that, as far as he was aware, the library never left Algeria, I contacted Robert (Bobby) Parks, founding director of the Centre d'Études Maghrébines en Algérie, the Overseas Research Center in Algeria of the American Institute for Maghrib Studies. I had heard from a colleague that if one wishes to locate something in Algeria, Parks is the first port of call. After inquiring into the situation, he reported back that he had "come up with nothing. A shocking degree of nothing, as a matter of fact—nobody knows what I'm talking about."[34] Intriguingly, archivist-historian Hana Sleiman found what appears to be an inventory, apparently prepared in 2003, of the contents of the Research Center. She used this document as well as other sources to try to piece together the fate of the archive. Sleiman, too, acknowledged, that "there are still significant gaps and contradictions in accounts of the whereabouts of the archive, the convoluted path it took, and the motives of the actors involved." Given the uncertainty, she presented a story not of locating or recovering an archive but rather of "archival silencing."[35] Thus, to return to the question posed above, we cannot examine the Research Center materials that Israel shipped to Algeria because we don't know where they are.

Did Israel Return the Entire Library and Archive in 1983?

According to the Red Cross, despite "very careful preparation and meticulous co-ordination," the prisoner exchange did not proceed exactly as agreed. In its annual report that year, the ICRC claimed that more than two hundred prisoners who ought to have been released remained in Israeli custody after the exchange. "Some," charged the ICRC, "had been secretly removed from Ansar camp in the weeks prior to the operations; others were not released on 24 November from the interrogation centres at Sidon and Nabatiyeh, while a few other prisoners were removed from Ansar and Tel Aviv airport at the time of the operation."[36]

One of those whom Israel had agreed to free but who, at the last minute, was allegedly kept prisoner was Ziad Abu Ayn. The United States had extradited Abu Ayn to Israel to face charges of planting a bomb that killed two Israeli teenagers in Tiberias in 1979. He was convicted and sentenced to life in prison. He was meant to be one of several scores of prisoners freed not from the Ansar prison in Lebanon but from prisons inside Israel as part of the deal with the PLO.[37] After it was revealed that he had not been sent to Algeria but rather remained in prison in Israel, Israeli officials claimed that Abu Ayn's name was missing from the final list of prisoners to be released, as a result of a Red Cross error. In a note sent to the representative of the International Red Cross in Tel Aviv on December 6, 1983, IDF lieutenant colonel Dov Shefer recounted that because Abu Ayn's name did not appear on the Red Cross list of the sixty-three non-Ansar prisoners to be released, an IDF officer agreed with the Red Cross to instead release Naif Awad Hassan Abu Asba, who had also been sentenced to life in prison. Likewise, when it was discovered that a female prisoner on the list had been released years earlier, Israel instead released someone else: Majhad Ahmad Jabar al-Hubani. "In this way," wrote Shefer, "the IDF fulfilled its commitments, namely, to release 63 prisoners."[38]

If some human prisoners had been kept in Israel—intentionally or not—was the same true of any of the documentary "captives," that is, the PLO Research Center library and archive?[39] According to Ilana Alon, director of the IDF and Defense Establishment Archives, Israel indeed returned everything. In 2015, Alon wrote me that "it's true that the IDF confiscated the PLO Research Center during the [19]82 War. The archive was returned in agreement to the PLO in November 1983. Israel [r]eleased the ANSAR PRISONS and returned the Archive."[40] Since I began studying the PLO Research Center, however, I have heard all sorts of rumors that contradict Alon's claim. For example, Gadi Zohar, who served as commander of the Human Intelligence unit of the Military Intelligence Directorate from 1981 to 1985, informed me that it was safe to assume that "we did not return everything."[41] I conclude this chapter by sharing what I know and acknowledging what I still do not about the presence in Israel of materials seized from the PLO Research Center.

At least one document from the Center was formally transferred to the National Library, according to Matti Steinberg: a seventeenth-century Hebrew manuscript from Yemen about the laws of kosher slaughtering. With permission from his Military Intelligence superiors, Steinberg recalled, he gave the document to his friend Professor Shaul Shaked of the Hebrew University, who deposited it in the National Library.[42] According to Steinberg, this text was the sole item he was permitted to take from the cache.[43]

The Shiloah Institute

But there were rumors of more wholesale Israeli appropriation of PLO Research Center materials. For instance, I heard that many of the Arabic periodicals now found in the Moshe Dayan Center for Middle Eastern and African Studies at Tel Aviv University were from the PLO Research Center's collection. These rumors were not entirely baseless.

Before 1983, the Dayan Center was called the Shiloah Institute, one of the institutions Israel's state archivist Alsberg had said, in his June 1983 interview with *Yedi'ot Aharonot,* he hoped was making productive use of the PLO Research Center materials. Shiloah had been founded in 1959 and was, as sociologist Gil Eyal has written, "a joint endeavor of the Foreign and Defense ministries, the military, the Hebrew University, and the Israeli Oriental Society." Shiloah was designed to produce research on "contemporary problems of Arab countries" and was "staffed by career officials from the Foreign Office and some doctoral students from the Hebrew University." In 1965 (the year the PLO Research Center was established), scholar Shimon Shamir recommended that the new Tel Aviv University absorb the Shiloah Institute. Shamir's proposal was soon accepted and implemented.[44]

Alsberg's hope that, among other institutions, the Shiloah Institute was reaping "maximal benefit" from the materials seized from the PLO Research Center appears to have been informed by more than a mere hunch. Already in the October 1982 preliminary intelligence report, produced after Matti Steinberg's week-long exploration of the PLO materials in the Hatsav base hangar, the Shiloah Institute's role was mentioned. The report had noted that in order for Steinberg to have a chance of assessing the contents of the seized materials, *reshit hokhma,* the first order of business, was to search "the catalogues and indexes" that the PLO Research Center had created to organize its library and archive. "Indeed," the report noted, "they all were found (these are now in the hands of the representatives of the 'Shiloah' Institute)."[45] Later in that same report, in the section on the historical documents that the Center had collected, the author noted:

Part of the historical documentation has already been deposited in the hands of the representatives of "Shiloah" (for example: the documents of

[Fawzi al-]Qawuqji) and the representative of "Hatsav" (the secret papers
of the crisis of September 1970). Another part of this primary material has
yet to be found and one assumes that it is still hidden under piles of books.[46]

In other words, less than a month after the invasion of West Beirut, some
primary historical documents that had been collected by the PLO Research
Center had, according to the intelligence unit analyzing the materials, been
handed over to the Shiloah Institute.

Before I saw the summary of Steinberg's intelligence document, I asked the
then-director of the Dayan Center, Professor Uzi Rabi, about rumors indicating that some periodicals and other sources found in the Dayan Center originated in the PLO Research Center. He replied unequivocally that "the Dayan
Center does not possess any of the [PLO] Research Center's documents."[47]

After viewing the 1982 intelligence report that mentioned the Shiloah Institute, I asked Professor Itamar Rabinovich, who served as director of Shiloah
in 1982, about his recollections of the affair. Rabinovich recalled that the Israeli
government offered the archive to Shiloah but that he had refused to accept it.
"My firm position at the time," Rabinovich told me, "was that on grounds of
principle an academic entity must not come to possess the archive of another
research institute taken under such circumstances."[48] The intelligence document did not mention Rabinovich; it referred, rather, to "the representatives
of 'Shiloah.'" One wonders whether some other Shiloah official accepted the
transfer of the materials without Rabinovich's knowledge. Moreover, the intelligence report was written in October 1982 and the subsequent reports do not
mention Shiloah. If PLO Research Center materials were held by Shiloah at
that time, they might have been returned along with the rest of the sources in
November 1983.

If, however, the Shiloah Institute had held on to materials from the Research
Center, those captured sources would not be unique among the institute's holdings, according to Gil Eyal. When the Shiloah Institute boasts of "a large collection of Middle Eastern newspapers and archival material from the archives of
several institutions within Israel and outside it," Eyal explained, this is "a euphe-
mistic way of referring to, among other items, Syrian, Egyptian, Jordanian, and
Palestinian documents captured by the army during Israel's wars and used by
the institute's researchers in preparing their monographs."[49]

This is a sensitive matter that scholars in Israel are often loath to discuss for
fear of the political and professional repercussions. One colleague, who requested anonymity, told me about a conversation he had had with the late

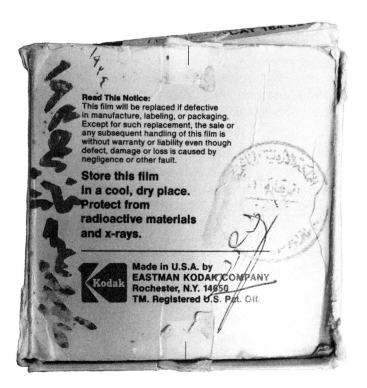

FIGURE 1. The Hashemite Kingdom of Jordan censor stamp found on the microfilm box of *al-ʿAlam al-Israʾili* in the Moshe Dayan Center for Middle Eastern and African Studies. Photograph by author.

Haim Gal, director of the Arabic Press Archive at the Dayan Center from 1979 through 2011. Gal once acknowledged to this colleague that a particular set of microfilms in the Center's collection had come from the PLO Research Center.[50] I went to the Dayan Center to see if I could confirm that this microfilm, an Arabic Jewish newspaper from Beirut in the early 1920s, *al-ʿAlam al-Israʾili*, had in fact been seized from the PLO Research Center. I scrolled through three fascinating microfilm rolls in search of evidence on the images themselves of a PLO connection. While I found no marking on the images, I did find something curious on the box encasing one of the three rolls: a smudged and faded stamp of the censor of the Hashemite Kingdom of Jordan. Was this microfilm acquired directly from Jordan at some other point or was it first given to (or taken by) the PLO Research Center? While it is impossible to be certain, notably, Jan Dayah published an article in the PLO Research Center's journal *Shu'un Filastiniyya* in 1978 regarding this same Beirut newspaper and the precise years covered in the microfilms at the Dayan Center.[51]

There is further evidence that the Israeli government was willing, perhaps even eager, to transfer the materials the IDF had seized from the PLO Research Center to an Israeli academic institution. In December 1983, not long after the prisoner exchange, *Yedi'ot Aharonot* reported on a recent article by Sabri Jiryis in *Shu'un Filastiniyya*, in which he alleged that it was Israel's "jealousy" of the success of the PLO Research Center that drove the IDF to try to conquer or destroy it. The *Yedi'ot* article ends with a revealing question. "How," the anonymous author wonders, "will Jiryis respond when he hears that all the institutions of higher learning in Israel refused to absorb the PLO's archive and overcame the temptation to benefit from its research as the booty of war that is now returning to its owners."[52] This seems to be an acknowledgment that the Center's holdings had, in the months that the Israeli military held them, been offered to Israeli university libraries, which, according to this article, roundly refused them. This is consistent with what Rabinovich told me years later.[53]

Mementos from the Center's Bookshelves

While it appears that no Israeli university was willing to accept the PLO Research Center's library and archive as a donation from the IDF, I discovered that some books that Israeli soldiers found in the Center's library never even made it to the Hatsav hangar. During my research for this book, I met a Jewish Israeli scholar of antiquity who, on hearing that I was writing a book about the PLO Research Center, said: "My brother was there. He has a book from the Research Center on his bookshelf at home!" Upon speaking to this brother, I learned that he had not been inside the Research Center, but he was in Beirut with his Golani Brigade unit at the time and indeed has two books that were taken from the Center's library.[54]

According to this veteran, a group from his unit decided to use a few hours of free time to tour Beirut in their military jeep. It was a Saturday, he recalled, and because he is a Sabbath observer, he did not join his comrades. Their excursion included a stop at the PLO Research Center, and they brought back as mementos several Hebrew books they pilfered from the library's shelves. When they returned to the base, the person I spoke with took two of these books:[55]

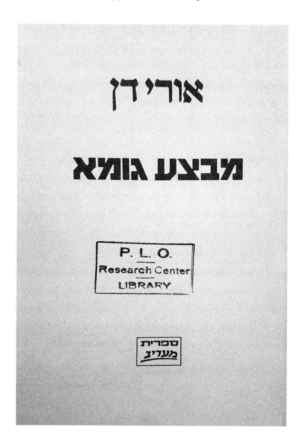

FIGURES 2 AND 3. Cover page and spine of Uri Dan's *Mivtsa ʿ Gome*, with the stamp of the PLO Research Center Library, held in a private Israeli home. Photograph shared with author.

The Revolt, a work by Menachem Begin about the Irgun, and *Mivtsaʿ Gome*, a book by Uri Dan about the secret negotiations leading to the Israeli-Egyptian peace agreement.[56] How many other PLO Research Center books sit as keepsakes on the shelves of Israeli veterans of the events Israel now calls the First Lebanon War is a question likely to remain unanswered.

Israel's National Library and Donor #2300

Thus, despite the claims of both Sabri Jiryis and Ilana Alon that Israel returned everything its forces had taken from the Research Center, the prisoner-book exchange of November 1983 was not entirely complete. The whispers about the Dayan Center holding significant portions of the PLO Research Center's collection remain uncorroborated, but they are bolstered by a confirmed fact: namely, that contemporaneous secret and public reports indicate that the Dayan Center's predecessor, the Shiloah Institute, held portions of the collection for a period between September 1982 and November 1983. And there are intimations that some of the collection may remain there today. Moreover, as we have seen, individual soldiers swiped books as mementos and these were not returned on the Air France planes to Algeria.

Along with the rumors about the Dayan Center, I also heard allegations that the National Library of Israel (NLI) possessed materials from the PLO Research Center's library. Such a theory was not unreasonable, as the NLI in Jerusalem has, in recent years, become known for having in the past accepted materials of problematic provenance into its collection. Over the last two decades, scholars, artists, and activists—spearheaded by author and educator Gish Amit—have been exploring the history of parts of the National Library's collection. Amit began writing, first in Hebrew and then in English, about the library's acquisition of books taken by Israelis from private Palestinian homes and libraries during the 1948 war. Many of these books were easily identified because they had been catalogued separately in the National Library under the label "AP" (Abandoned Property), a euphemism that exacerbated the scandal. In 2012, this story was the subject of a documentary film, *The Great Book Robbery*, directed and produced by Benny Brunner.[57] The same year, the AP collection was the focus of a book of photography by Palestinian artist Emily Jacir, who focused her cell phone's lens on the Arabic nameplates and inscriptions that revealed aspects of the lives of the books' Palestinian owners.[58] In 2014, Amit published a Hebrew monograph, *Ex Libris: Chronicles of Theft, Preservation, and Appropriating at the Jewish National Library*, exploring this collection in the context of two others that also made their way onto the National Library's bookshelves in the late 1940s and early 1950s: books seized by the Nazis from Jews during World War II and books and manuscripts taken from Yemenite Jews when they immigrated to Israel during the first years of statehood.[59]

I began my search for the PLO Research Center library shortly after Amit published his *Ex Libris*. Given the public consciousness of this affair at the time, it is no surprise that some suggested I look in the National Library for the Research Center's library. Aside from the one text that Matti Steinberg told me had been given to the National Library, though, I knew of no other item that had found its way from the Hatsav intelligence base hangar to the National Library.

One day, during a year I spent researching in Jerusalem, I was contacted by Hillel Cohen of the Hebrew University. Cohen sent me a photo of a library "Due Date" page marked in Arabic *Markaz al-Abhath* (Research Center) above the words *Munazzamat al-Tahrir al-Filastiniyya* (Palestine Liberation Organization) alongside *al-maktaba al-ʿamma* (Public Library). Cohen had found this page glued to the back of a book that he had requested from Israel's National Library, Frank George Jannaway's 1914 *Palestine and the Jews; or The Zionist Movement an Evidence that the Messiah Will Soon Appear in Jerusalem to Rule the Whole World Therefrom.*

I wondered whether, with Cohen's scoop, I might have found the first clue to a previously unknown collection of books added to the National Library of Israel's stacks from those captured in the PLO Research Center. With the help of a librarian at the reference desk, I learned that the copy of Jannaway's book that held the PLO marking in it was given to the library by Donor #2300. I further discovered that that same donor had also given seventy-two other books to the library. This list of seventy-three books was readily available through the library's online catalogue.

I began ordering the books donated by Donor #2300 to the reading room. Most of them were English-language books about Jews and Zionism, and none of the first few books I ordered had any marking from the PLO Research Center. I wondered if the book that Cohen had found had perhaps been borrowed from the Research Center and then, through some circuitous route of secondhand booksellers, made it to the National Library. I noticed, though, that several of the books had ex libris stamps of a certain Ibrahim Abaza.

For a couple of weeks, I set this mystery aside to work on other questions and to acquaint myself with the Center's latest activities in Ramallah. The Palestinian book fair was then taking place and I was eager to visit the PLO Research Center booth I heard would be there. When I returned to the mystery of the books at the National Library, I was advised by the reference librarian

FIGURE 4. Frank George Jannaway's *Palestine and the Jews*, with Due Date slip
from the PLO Research Center library, held in the National Library of Israel.
Photograph by author.

who had initially assisted me to speak to Yaniv Levi-Korem, then head of Technical Services in the National Library.

A friendly man in his forties, Levi-Korem informed me that, according to
the library's records, *he* (Levi-Korem) was Donor #2300. No, he was not the
one who brought those seventy-three books to the library. Rather, he found
them there, he explained, in three boxes labeled "PLO" in a storage area when
he began his job at the National Library in 2010. He had been hired by the library to help bring order to aspects of the institution that had long been neglected and so, he told me, he simply emptied those boxes and added them to
the library's catalogue with the next available donor number in the system:
2300. When word reached him that I was looking into these books, Levi-
Korem consulted veteran workers in the library who, he explained, told him
that at "some point in the 1980s" those boxes had been given to the National
Library and simply left aside.

Realizing that, with the help of colleagues and librarians, I had come upon
a modest trove of books from the PLO Research Center that had not been
returned in November 1983, I decided that I ought to request the rest of these
books through the online system to see what I might learn from examining
them. When I returned to my computer, though, I found that Donor #2300
was no longer listed. Three weeks earlier I had been able to view the full list of
books. Now: nothing.

FIGURE 5. National Library of Israel web page listing book donations by donor number, missing Donor #2300. Screenshot by author.

Why was Donor #2300 removed from the list? I might have suspected that I had come upon (or even caused) some sort of cover-up had Levi-Korem not just told me the whole story.[60] Moreover, he expressed no concern whatsoever when I informed him that I would be discussing the episode in my book. Upon discovering the removal of Donor #2300's list, I emailed Levi-Korem to ask whether he could help me regain access. He agreed and invited me to meet him in his office. There we were joined by Elchanan Reiner, the library's academic director, and Raquel Ukeles, curator of the Islam and Middle East collection at the library.

Sitting on Levi-Korem's table was a handful of books from the Donor #2300 list that he had requested from the stacks. As I examined them, I found that most had some marking from the PLO Research Center—an ink stamp or a sticker—and those that did not bore the residue of a sticker that had been removed or had fallen off. The missing sticker revealed the same ex libris stamp I had seen in the first book from this collection that Hillel Cohen had found: Ibrahim Abaza. (More on Abaza to come.) Ukeles thanked me for having pursued this issue, enabling the National Library to be better aware of its holdings. I asked for permission to photograph the books on the spot (worried that they might somehow disappear along with Donor #2300) and took several photos of each book. Then, Levi-Korem told me that he would return the books. "Return them to whom?" I asked, wondering whether the library had decided to send the books to the PLO in Ramallah.

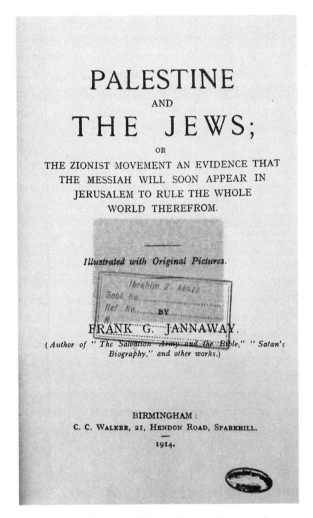

FIGURE 6. Title page of Frank George Jannaway's
Palestine and the Jews, with Ibrahim Z. Abaza's ex libris
stamp, in a volume held in the National Library of
Israel. Photograph by author.

"Back to the stacks," he responded. Ukeles asked Levi-Korem to mark the
books in some way so that the collection could be viewed as a unit and Levi-
Korem agreed. Shortly thereafter, Levi-Korem emailed me the full list of
seventy-three books. As of this writing, Donor #2300 is still missing from
the catalogue and there is no way for the public to see this collection. The
list can be found as an appendix to this book.

Why did Israel not return these books when Sheffy and his Israeli col-leagues loaded thousands of others onto those Air France planes sent to Alge-ria in November 1983? In the absence of the PLO Research Center library catalogue, it is impossible to know what, if anything, distinguishes these books as unique among the collection. However, examination of the list revealed a number of common features. First, the vast majority of the books—fifty-seven—are in English. Of the remaining volumes, five are in German, four are in Hebrew, three are in Yiddish, two are Hebrew-English dictionaries, and two are in Arabic (a periodical and a reproduction of comics).[61] The books were published between 1844 and 1971. Most fit into the following categories: Holy Land photo books and guidebooks, ancient and modern histories of Palestine, and works on Jewish history and Zionism.

I would speculate that someone with an interest in these subjects, who was given access sometime between September 1982 and November 1983 to the cache seized from the PLO, removed the books for personal or profes-sional reading—along with a couple of English-Hebrew dictionaries. Then, perhaps after learning of the international outrage about the confiscation of the library, either feeling embarrassed or just wishing to avoid trouble, de-livered the volumes to the National Library. Or perhaps that person initially took many more than seventy-three books but kept the rest in their private library.

Returning to the ex libris stamp, who was Ibrahim Abaza? I found the an-swer in Anis Sayegh's autobiography. Sayegh wrote of "two anonymous sol-diers" who served the Center's library:

> One of them was a Palestinian lawyer who immigrated to Britain in 1948 and settled there. His hobby was collecting rare books concerning Jewish/ Zionist thought, history, and society. He collected several hundred of such books. At the end of the 60s, he presented them to the Research Center as a long-term "loan." But the Center did not return them to their owner because the hands of the enemy army were faster and captured them in 1982. The name of this lawyer who had insisted upon not being revealed was Ibrahim Abaza.[62]

The Palestinian British lawyer Ibrahim Abaza had collected hundreds of books on Judaism, Zionism, and Israel and lent these books to the PLO Research Center. They were seized, along with the rest of the library, by the IDF. Thus, we might say that Ibrahim Abaza ought to be regarded as the National Library of Israel's inadvertent Donor #2300.

A Sidenote about PLO Research Center Publications
in the National Library of Israel

The seventy-three books that traveled from the PLO Research Center's shelves in Beirut to the National Library of Israel's stacks in Jerusalem were not my initial draw to the NLI. Rather, it was the fact that, as noted earlier, the NLI holds one of the world's most complete collections of PLO Research Center publications. How did the NLI come to acquire this collection?

By and large, as we have seen, the Research Center's publications were not meant to be kept under wraps. On the contrary, the idea was to disseminate them widely. While there may have been clandestine trading with book dealers in countries officially regarded as enemy states, agents of the NLI could have easily purchased these books in Cyprus or Europe or the US and shipped them to Jerusalem.

There were, however, other ways that at least some of the NLI's collection of the Center's publications found its way to Jerusalem. The stamp on one such publication in the National Library—a copy of Ibrahim al-Abid's book on the Mapai party—reveals that it was part of the collection in the officers' library in the Syrian army base at Quneitra. Israel conquered this base on the final day of the 1967 war and, apparently, some of the books found in the library were added to the collection of the National Library in Jerusalem.

Had the Reestablished PLO Research Center
in Ramallah Located the Library in Algeria?

After finding refuge in Cyprus and reestablishing a much-contracted PLO Research Center in Nicosia over the course of a decade, Jiryis returned in 1994 to his hometown of Fassuta, which he left in 1970.[63] Following the PLO's signing of the Oslo Accords, Jiryis's was one of a handful of families that Israel allowed to return to Israeli territory—rather than to the West Bank or the Gaza Strip, to which Arafat and other PLO leaders and activists moved in that period. In 2000, the Center attempted to revive its journal in Jerusalem, but, with the advent of the Second Intifada and Israel's crackdown on Palestinian institutions in Jerusalem in 2001, this attempt was shortlived. It would be a decade until the Center was given another lease on life; in August 2011, Palestinian president Mahmoud Abbas once again restarted the Center or, more precisely, revived the journal Shu'un Filastiniyya.[64]

FIGURE 7. Ibrahim al-Abid's book about the Israeli Mapai party, *al-Mabay*, published by the PLO Research Center. Stamped as belonging to the officers' library in the Syrian army base of Quneitra. Held by the National Library of Israel. Photograph by author.

In the early spring of 2018, a video was posted on the PLO Research Center's newly designed website announcing in dramatic fashion that the Center was finally being properly restored in Ramallah.[65] The promotional video included images of bookcases filled with books, suggesting the recreation of the Center's library. Photos from a conference held on the questions "Where were we mistaken? / Where were we right?" alluded to a revitalization of the atmosphere of vigorous debate that once characterized the Center in Beirut. In the video, Mohammad Shtayyeh (who was then president of the Center's executive committee and later became prime minister of the Palestinian Authority) claimed that a Palestinian delegation had traveled to Algeria and

FIGURE 8. The PLO Research Center office in Ramallah, 2018.
Photograph by author.

confirmed that the Algerian government had preserved the Center's library
and archive since they were sent to the North African country in the 1983
prisoner exchange. Shtayyeh assured viewers the Research Center's historic
documentary collection would soon be returned.

Naturally, I wanted to see the Center for myself. Thus, I scheduled a meeting with Samih Shabeeb (1948–2019), the then-director of the Center, and in
May 2018, the day before Palestinians would mark the seventieth anniversary
of the Nakba, I drove to Ramallah with Salah Ghanem, a professional guide
from Jerusalem. There we found a small sign hanging from a telephone pole
outside a nondescript building pointing, in Arabic, toward *Shu'un Filastiniyya*.
In even smaller Arabic print were the words "Palestine Liberation Organization
Research Center."

With much anticipation, I climbed up a stairwell lined with framed covers
of historic issues of *Shu'un*. As I opened the door to the Center, the staff
greeted me warmly and ushered me into Shabeeb's office.[66] I introduced myself and explained I had been eager to visit the Center after having learned of

its recent revival in Ramallah. Shabeeb, a frail man with eyeglasses taped together, sat me down and regaled me with memories of his years in the Research Center in Beirut beginning in 1978, then in Cyprus after 1983, and eventually in Jerusalem and Ramallah after the Oslo Accords.[67] He had been at the Center in February 1983 when the building was bombed and had written much about that day and about the victims of the bombing, the Center's martyrs, whose memory he sought to preserve.[68] Though I was interested in hearing about the Center's gloried past, I was mainly focused that day on learning about the Center's current mission and activities. I wanted to see the new library firsthand, to witness the debates, and to hear more details about when the archive would arrive from Algeria.

Disappointingly, none of this was possible. There was no new library, Shabeeb explained. He was unsure what I had seen in the video; perhaps, he suggested, those were images from a section of the Bir Zeit library that now holds Anis Sayegh's book collection? There were no spirited debates to observe, no scholars hard at work. The staff, Shabeeb counted aloud, amounted to six administrative positions dedicated to publishing the *Shu'un* journal. If *Shu'un* was once the Center's flagship journal, the journal and the Center were now one and the same. The sign that carried the words "PLO Research Center" seemed to be a relic of the past; perhaps it was also an expression of hope for the future. In any case, it was not a description of what lay behind the doors of the office in Ramallah.

But what about the promised return of the archive and library from Algeria? Shabeeb explained that these materials remained in Algeria. "We here [i.e., those in Ramallah] haven't seen anything—at all." Moreover, the significant documents in the Center during the Beirut days were on microfilm and microfiche; considering the poor physical conditions and the extreme heat in which the library and archive had been stored over the past three and a half decades, Shabeeb reasoned, they were now surely ruined.[69] Shabeeb's analysis could not have stood in greater contrast to the Center's promotional video.

Perplexed, I asked Shabeeb what was standing in the way of repatriation, if the location in Algeria of the Research Center's library and archive was known and the Algerian government was ready to return them to the PLO and ship them to Ramallah? After all, I had just devoted months of research to investigating the international efforts in 1982 and 1983 to pressure Israel to return the library and archive to the PLO. In one passionate voice, Palestinians and their supporters had proclaimed that these books and documents constituted crucial artifacts of Palestinian cultural heritage that needed to be restored to the

Palestinians. After fourteen months, Israel returned these artifacts (or most of them). If, for whatever reasons, the PLO chose not to have the collection sent to Cyprus during the decade that the Research Center was there, and if in the years following Oslo there were higher priorities or different obstacles that stood in the way of restoring these artifacts to the Palestinians in the West Bank or Gaza, or if the Algerians had temporarily lost track of the materials, one could understand why the library and archive had not been sent to Ramallah until now. But what were the obstacles today?

Shabeeb mentioned three considerations. First, in order to make the transfer, someone would need to go to Algeria to check the condition of the materials, an effort that would demand significant resources. Second, the books that had been in the library were now generally available in Palestinian libraries—at Bir Zeit University, the al-Bireh municipal library, and others—and many of these books had even been scanned and made available online. Third, and finally, the tens of thousands of books that had been housed in Beirut would not fit into the modest one-story office where the Research Center was now located.[70]

If Shabeeb was "not optimistic" about the return of the library and archive from Algeria, did he imagine a revival of the Research Center beyond the publication of *Shu'un Filastiniyya*? "Serious research requires a level of stability," he explained. "In Beirut, we were stable and happy." The Cairo Agreement of 1969 gave the PLO significant autonomy and flexibility in Beirut, Shabeeb recalled. The Center was able to establish close relationships with the various local universities, including the American University of Beirut and the Jesuit university of Saint Joseph. These partnerships were the fruit of the Research Center's secure position in Beirut. Now in Ramallah, by contrast, "our situation is not stable. Here there is much more volatility."[71] The day after my meeting with Shabeeb, the US embassy in Israel celebrated its official move from Tel Aviv to Jerusalem while sixty Palestinians were killed in the Gaza Strip as they participated in a mass protest march that quickly turned violent at the Israeli border.[72] The instability and volatility to which Shabeeb referred were plain to see.

Conclusion

EMPATHY, REALISM, AND THE EFFECTS
OF "KNOWING THE ENEMY"

DOES KNOWING our enemies change the way we relate to them? Does it change the way we relate to ourselves? These were some of the questions that motivated me as I began to study the work the PLO Research Center did to learn about those it deemed the enemy. Until this point in the book, such questions have remained in the background. In this conclusion, I bring them into clearer focus and inquire directly about the relationship between knowledge and perception in the case of the enemy.

The PLO's Path toward Political Compromise

The PLO's founding goal was to reclaim those parts of Palestine that Israel controlled by the end of the 1948 war. Its Covenant declared Palestine, in its British Mandate–era borders, an "indivisible territorial unit." The partition of Palestine and the establishment of Israel were considered a violation of the Palestinian people's right to self-determination, and thus invalid. Moreover, the Covenant insisted that the Jews "are not one people" and their "claims of historic and spiritual ties" to Palestine "are not in agreement with the facts of history." When, in 1968, Fateh and other Palestinian militant groups took over the PLO, they revised the Covenant, now emphasizing that "armed struggle is the only way to liberate Palestine." In the PLO's first years, then, its declared aim was taking control of all the territory ruled by Israel and doing so through violent guerrilla force.

By 1974, however, only a decade after the PLO was founded and a mere half-decade after the Fateh militant leader Yasser Arafat became chairman of the organization, the PLO was making subtle moves toward political accommodation with Israel. At its meeting in Cairo in June 1974, the Palestine National Council approved what became known as the "Ten Points Program." The second point began: "The Liberation Organization will employ all means, and first and foremost armed struggle, to liberate the Palestinian land and to establish the independent combatant national authority for the people over every part of Palestinian territory that is liberated." Here, the PLO set forth its agenda to pursue the liberation of any part of Palestine, if only so as to use that part as a base from which to pursue the rest of the homeland. This statement also effectively revised the organization's position on violence; "armed struggle" was no longer "the only way" (as it had been dubbed in the PLO Covenant) but rather "first and foremost" among the means to achieve liberation.

Although not everyone considered these to be major changes to PLO principles and policy, they were understood to be so by members of the organization. In fact, following the PLO endorsement of the Ten Points Program, the second-largest party within the organization, the PFLP, broke away. The opponents of the Ten Points formed the Rejectionist Front, which was committed to armed struggle and refused to accept, even temporarily, a solution to the conflict that would give the Palestinians anything less than all of Palestine.[1]

The Rejectionists' fear that the Ten Points Program signified a slippery slope toward accepting Israel proved to be warranted. In 1988, the PLO declared Palestinian independence and, in its declaration, it referenced the UN's 1947 partition plan, thereby implicitly recognizing Israel as distinct from Palestine. This gradual progression toward recognition of Israel culminated in 1993, when PLO chairman Arafat wrote to Israeli prime minister Yitzhak Rabin that "the PLO recognizes the right of the State of Israel to exist in peace and security."

During the first two decades of this halting and sometimes deadly progress toward accepting the enemy, a group of activist-scholars based in the PLO Research Center in Beirut were reading and writing about Israeli society and disseminating this knowledge among leaders and laypeople. Thus, the PLO moved toward political moderation during the same period in which one of its wings was studying and publishing about the enemy.[2] Of course, correlation is not causation. Below, we consider various possible factors behind the PLO's change of position.

The most obvious explanations have been studied extensively. After the 1973 Ramadan/Yom Kippur War, Egyptian president Sadat began to discuss a peace conference in Geneva. As scholar Yezid Sayigh noted, some factions of the Palestinian National Movement argued that if the Palestinians were to refuse to participate in the negotiations, they would effectively be ceding the West Bank to Jordan's King Hussein, who wanted to restore his rule to the territory he had lost to Israel in 1967. As Zuhayr Muhsin of Saʿiqa (a Palestinian pro-Syrian Baʿth group that joined the PLO in 1969) put it at the time, articulating the catch-22 in which the Palestinians found themselves, "if the PLO declares that it wishes to rule the Gaza Strip and West Bank, then it will seem to have abandoned the historic rights of the Palestinian people to the rest of Palestinian land . . . but if [the PLO] says that it is not concerned with UNSCR [242] and with this [peace] settlement, then it will have officially relinquished the [West] Bank and [Gaza] Strip to the Jordanian regime."[3] George Habash, leader of the Popular Front for the Liberation of Palestine (PFLP), opposed participation in the peace conference. Other Palestinian organizations, including Fateh, the Popular Democratic Front for the Liberation of Palestine (PDFLP), and Saʿiqa, thought it necessary to participate so as to have a voice in the process and to prevent Jordan from retaking the West Bank.

Like Yezid Sayigh, Matti Steinberg argued that the PLO desire to ensure that Jordan would not retake control over the West Bank was decisive. "The PLO feared that if it did not stake a claim compatible with an approach endorsed by all the Arab confrontation states," explained Steinberg, "Jordan, backed by the Arab collective, would usurp the PLO's place as the representative of the Palestinian people and as claimant of the territories, and the PLO would then be eliminated as a political force."[4]

For Steinberg, the "pioneering programmatic article" articulating this post-1973 war position was Salah Khalaf's "Clear Ideas before an Ambiguous Stage," published by the PLO Research Center's *Shuʾun Filastiniyya* in January 1974.[5] In this article, for the first time a senior Fateh leader called "openly on PLO organizations to readjust to the new reality in the wake of the October 1973 War" by focusing on the "interim aim" of the West Bank and the Gaza Strip. "His argument," wrote Steinberg, "was entirely based on the necessity to undermine Jordan's supposed intent to regain control over the West Bank."[6]

In his article, Fateh cofounder Khalaf (known as Abu Iyad) reported that the Central Council of the PLO, representing all the affiliated Palestinian fedayeen organizations, had met and agreed on the following principles: "(1) Maintaining the historic right of the Palestinian people to liberate all of its lands and soil; (2) The non-return of the [West] Bank and the [Gaza] Strip to the control of [Jordan's king] Hussein; and (3) The right of self-determination for the Palestinian people."[7] Abu Iyad insisted that these principles demanded that Palestinian leaders not simply reject any proposal or possibility they faced. "The absolute 'no' is not always the correct revolutionary position," he wrote, clearly arguing against the Rejectionist factions among the Palestinians. If a fundamental goal was to prevent the Hashemites' return to the West Bank and their rule over Gaza, true Palestinian revolutionaries needed to make choices and promote policies that would serve to prevent these outcomes rather than reflexively saying "no." "Absolute rejection," Abu Iyad contended, "is sometimes a kind of escape" from taking responsibility for difficult decisions.

To prevent Hussein from restoring his rule in the West Bank, argued Abu Iyad, Palestinians must ensure that the Hashemite king did not claim the right to represent the Palestinians in the proposed postwar peace conference. After the Hashemites' treatment of Palestinian militant forces in Jordan in the period that came to be known as Black September, "I do not understand," wrote Abu Iyad, "how the killer can represent the killed!"[8] The Palestinians would have to represent themselves, which would mean participating in the peace conference.

In addition, the Palestinian leadership was encouraged to engage in diplomacy by the Soviet Union, which simultaneously strengthened its military and political relations with Fateh and the PLO while encouraging the PLO to pursue a diplomatic front. According to Abu Iyad, who visited Moscow in late 1973, the Soviets told the Palestinian delegation that "there is no revolution in the world that does not have a program for each phase. You must phase your struggle."[9] In his *Shu'un Filastiniyya* article of the following January, Abu Iyad wrote that the PLO must keep in mind the interests and positions of its international allies. "The Soviet Union is our friend," he wrote, and it was therefore necessary to understand what the Soviets saw as the Palestinians' legitimate rights.[10] Soviet support for Palestinian political accommodation was articulated in militant logic. As another Fateh cofounder, Khalil al-Wazir (Abu Jihad) recounted, the Soviets asked the Palestinian delegation: "Would it not be better for you to fight from Tulkarm [in the West Bank], for example, than from outside?"[11] Thus, the PLO's desire not to permit Jordan to retake the West Bank (by claiming to represent the Palestinians at the peace conference) and the Soviet pressure on the PLO to engage in diplomacy were crucial in leading the PLO to embrace a "staged approach," even as Abu Iyad insisted that the PLO would never give up on the Palestinians' "historic right to complete liberation of the Palestinian soil."[12]

In line with Abu Iyad's position, PLO groups abandoned, with varying degrees of ambiguity and obfuscation, their previous refusal to negotiate on the basis of UN Security Council Resolution 242 and to legitimize the 1948 partition of Palestine. As scholar Yezid Sayigh has shown, Arafat argued that "what is called the West Bank and Gaza Strip . . . now faces two possibilities: one, to go to King Hussein . . . as to the second possibility, it is to set up a Palestinian authority on it, or to set up the Yigal Allon plan on it, that would transform our land and people into a reservoir that feeds Israel with laborers."[13] If the three options available for the Occupied Territories were to give them to Israel, to give them to Jordan, or to take those territories for the Palestinians, Arafat made the case that the Palestinians had to take the land under their own authority. When he made this argument in the PLO's *Filastin al-Thawra*, though, Arafat insisted that while the "fourth Arab-Israeli war [the 1973 war] will give us parts of Palestine," the next war "will give us Tel Aviv."[14] That is, even as Arafat was pushing the PLO to accept Palestinian control of only parts of Palestine, he kept alive the hope of returning Palestinians to all of historic Palestine, even those areas as demographically Jewish as Tel Aviv. Arafat's predilection for leaving all options on the table (or doubletalk) was famous. In the PLO itself, his approach to decisions was known by the Arabic portmanteau *la'am*—saying "no" (*la*) and "yes" (*na'am*) in one breath.[15]

In accounting for the shift in the PLO's position vis-à-vis a political settlement in 1974, Yezid Sayigh pointed to an additional factor; namely, the unintentional assistance Israel offered to those Palestinians who supported the more moderate position. "Israel unwittingly assisted the pragmatic trend," wrote Sayigh, "by deporting a number of prominent West Bank figures in spring 1974, all of whom [then] attended the crucial PNC debate in June."[16] By expelling more moderate proponents of diplomacy from the occupied West Bank (to which they would not have easily been able to return had they left voluntarily for a PLO meeting), Israel permitted those individuals to attend the fateful PNC meeting in Cairo in which the Ten Points Program was approved.

Notably, none of the above—Palestinian concern about being excluded from an Israeli settlement with Sadat's Egypt, fears of a separate Jordanian peace agreement with Israel and the Hashemites' return to ruling the West Bank, Soviet support and pressure for a "phased" program, Israel's deportation of advocates of the creation of a "Palestinian authority" in whatever territories the Palestinians managed to seize just in time for them to attend the 1974 PNC meeting—are in any apparent way connected to the PLO Research Center's studies of Zionism and Israel.

However, there may be more to the story than the conventional narrative conveys. Why, in response to their concerns and to the pressures placed upon them in 1974, were the PLO activists willing to entertain a political option that many of them had considered unimaginable a mere decade earlier? It is here, on the level of "why" and especially "why now," that we might tentatively tease out the influence of the PLO's efforts to learn about their enemy. It is here, perhaps, that we might better understand the significance of the fact that Abu Iyad's "pioneering programmatic article," as Steinberg dubbed it, arguing for a staged approach and engagement in diplomacy, was published in the PLO Research Center's journal.

Specifically, one may wonder if, as the PLO Research Center published content about Israel, the accumulation of knowledge among Palestinian intellectuals and leaders made the idea of reaching a compromise with Israel more palatable.[17] While we may not be able to answer this question clearly for the PLO as a whole, let us consider whether it was true for some who undertook such research efforts.

Sabri Jiryis, Mahmoud Darwish, and an Analogy

During our conversations about the PLO Research Center, I mentioned to Sabri Jiryis that I was interested in the relationship between perspectives on the enemy other and studying about that other. Do people become, for example, more sympathetic to their adversaries after studying them? Jiryis offered the following self-assessment: Studying Israel "made me, let me say, more realistic." "More sympathetic?" he asked himself aloud. "Certainly not. More hateful? Also, certainly not." In Jiryis's reckoning, learning about the enemy made him "more rational."[18]

Elaborating, Jiryis shared with me an anecdote. One day in the mid-1970s, after Jiryis had begun to advocate for a political settlement with Israel, he found himself speaking with his friend, the poet Mahmoud Darwish. It seems that Darwish had heard someone accuse Jiryis of harboring sympathies toward Zionism. "Somebody said that you are fond of Zionism, you love Zionism," the poet informed Jiryis. According to Jiryis, Darwish had responded that doctors and scientists can spend their entire careers studying cancer or other illnesses, but "that does not mean that they love sickness, or that they love cancer. It is the same with Sabri. He is just studying Zionism. That does not mean he likes Zionism."

Darwish was defending his friend. In hindsight, however, we might question his analogy. First, humans and microbes are different. It is at least plausible that one who researches a society would be more inclined to put oneself in the shoes of one who lives in that society. Second, and more definitively, Darwish was presenting a zero-sum game. Generally speaking, there was no getting along with cancer, of reaching an accommodation with the disease. *Accommodation*, however, is precisely what Jiryis was proposing after the 1973 war.

Sympathy, Pragmatism, and the "Dangers of Peace"

In his unpublished Hebrew memoirs, Jiryis wrote of the translations of the Israeli Hebrew press that he supervised in Beirut, initially for the Institute for Palestine Studies, and the lectures that he delivered about Israeli society. At the end of one such lecture, the wife of an Arab ambassador in Lebanon took him to task for what she considered his positive portrayal of Israeli society. Jiryis's response was consistent with what we have heard thus far: "whether one intends to fight, to negotiate with, or to come to a resolution with the enemy, one must first know the enemy." He noted that "the Arab world, since then, continued to translate Israel, and it apparently also enjoys reading it." Jiryis then reflected on the following question: "Did this reading of Israel have any impact, for good or for ill, on future developments of the Arab-Israeli conflict?" Jiryis was uncertain. "It is difficult for me to determine," he concluded, but the question is left for the reader to ponder throughout the remainder of Jiryis's book—and in this book as well.[19]

The question of the relationship between learning about the enemy and sympathy for the enemy resurfaces later on in Jiryis's memoirs. Though Jiryis was circumspect when thinking broadly about the impact of knowing the enemy on Palestinian politics, at various points in his memoirs he suggested that this knowledge proved to be highly effective in defending, justifying, or excusing—if not actually guiding—Palestinian policy. For instance, Jiryis wrote of an article he published in the Lebanese newspaper *al-Nahar*, "Israel vis-à-vis the Danger of Peace,"[20] and contended that this article played some role in persuading the PLO leadership to consider engaging in the proposed Geneva peace summit in the wake of the 1973 war (a key stage in the PLO move toward a negotiated settlement with Israel, discussed above).

In the two-part article published on November 7 and 8, 1973 (that is, less than two weeks after the conclusion of the Yom Kippur/Ramadan War), Jiryis offered a point-by-point response to what he saw as the main arguments offered by Arabs against direct negotiations with Israel. In each case, whether it concerned Israeli demographics and the motivations for Jewish immigration to Palestine, Israeli economics and the fears of Israel's economic dominance in the Middle East, or Israeli society's internal cohesion, Jiryis used his knowledge of the Israeli enemy to argue for Palestinian participation in a peace conference.

A key aspect of Jiryis's strategy was to demonstrate that, ultimately, Israel would be undermined by peace. "Over the course of a long period of time," wrote Jiryis, "Israel has been able to convince large portions of world public opinion of 'its love' for peace with the Arabs" and this apparent love garnered Israel "the sympathy of many of the world's countries." Now, though, in the wake of the 1973 war, Jiryis supposed that Israeli leaders regretted bluffing about their desire for peace. After all, in Jiryis's view, the Israelis were now compelled "to negotiate with the Arabs not from a position of strength—but rather, at best—from a position of equality with them and to talk openly about peace and to make concessions and guarantees for this; this is a situation that does not please Israel and does not serve its interests."

The first major risk that Israel faced from a peace accord, for Jiryis, was that it would have to withdraw from the territories it had occupied since 1967. From the Israeli point of view, explained Jiryis, "withdrawal from the occupied territories" means "restoring Israel to its real size, which is a size within which Zionist Israel cannot long live." Israel's continued rule over the West Bank, the Gaza Strip, the Golan Heights, and the Sinai Peninsula is critical for the long-term preservation of the country as a Jewish, Zionist state, argued Jiryis. Israel needs these territories because of the space they provide for expanded Jewish immigration and because of the natural resources they offer to maintain the high quality of life Jewish immigrants seek. "Contrary to Zionist claims of the Jews' attachment to 'the Land of Israel' and their unrelenting efforts to immigrate to it and to live in it," insisted Jiryis, "historical facts demonstrate the opposite." Even "a quick look at the history of Jewish immigration to Palestine over the last hundred years" since the rise of Zionism "reveals that the mass immigrations to the country," from which the majority of Israeli Jews originate, "came in the wake of a crisis that befell the Jews in their countries of origin." It was those crises, rather than a desire to live in the Holy Land, that drove those Jews to migrate to Palestine "with the hope of improving their economic conditions."

Jiryis then outlined the major waves of Jewish immigration to Palestine and Israel. The first two waves of immigration, in the 1880s and the early 1900s, were sparked by anti-Jewish violence in tsarist Russia. Another wave, at the end of the 1920s, consisted of Polish Jews who came "as a consequence of the economic decrees the Polish government made against the Jews." The largest wave of immigration that flowed into Palestine in the days of the Mandate, Jiryis noted, arrived in the 1930s as Jews fled Germany "after the rise of the Nazis and its extreme antisemitic measures." The same motivations (fleeing discrimination and violence and seeking improved conditions) stood behind "the largest Jewish group migration to Israel during the first years of its existence, most of whom came from the Arab countries (Iraq, Yemen, Morocco)." Aside from these mass waves of migration, wrote Jiryis, Jewish immigration to Palestine was minimal and, what is more, a significant proportion of those Jews who came "always returned," leaving Israel behind.

This recounting of late nineteenth- and twentieth-century Jewish migrations to Palestine and Israel served to support Jiryis's argument that giving up the occupied territories would diminish Israel's long-term viability. The state's Zionist nature depends on its attractiveness to Jewish immigrants and this attractiveness, Jiryis demonstrated through his historical narrative, was a function not of Jews' commitment to the "land of their forefathers" but rather of the economic opportunities that land promised them. Were Israel to contract to its original size, "given its smallness and the scantiness of its economic resources if measured by Zionist ambitions," it would be unable to "ensure a high standard of living for immigrants." Such a contraction would diminish Jewish immigration and "contribute to weakening the state in the long run." Israel's withdrawal from the occupied territories, asserted Jiryis, would ultimately lead to Israel's demise as a Jewish state.

This argument could have been articulated by a right-wing Israeli ideologue. And that is precisely the point. Jiryis used the knowledge of Judaism and Israel that he had acquired, starting in his exile to Safed, to persuade fellow Palestinians and Arabs that from a Zionist perspective, peace might lead to the end of Israel.

But that is not all. Peace with the Palestinians would weaken Israel, according to Jiryis, not only because of territorial issues, but also because it would remove Israeli society's main element of unification: the enemy. "Israel's move into the peace phase in its relations with the Arabs," wrote Jiryis, "is helpful in accentuating the latent internal tensions in Jewish Israeli society." In Jiryis's view, that society "can be divided—broadly—into two groups: the community of Western Jews who rule almost completely over Israel and who therefore live at a much higher level than do 'their brothers,' the Eastern Jews. The social chasm between these two groups is extremely wide and it does not seem to be shrinking but rather, on the contrary, it is widening."[21]

That fundamental gap between Ashkenazi Jews and Middle Eastern Jews was hidden, Jiryis explained, while Jewish Israeli society dealt with the challenges of conflict with the Palestinians and other neighboring Arabs. "For a fairly long period of time," wrote Jiryis, "the rulers of Israel have been able to conceal the differences between the groups in Israeli society under the guise of security requirements." Whenever the security situation improves and Israelis have the opportunity to turn their focus inward, though, the internal tensions come to the fore. Indeed, in Jiryis's assessment, this is precisely what happened, if briefly, just a few years earlier:

> It is no wonder that the social tensions became prominent, suddenly and severely, in 1971 and thereafter, that is, after the War of Attrition ended on the Egyptian front, and when there was a reduction in the *fedai* militant activities inside Israel, when the sense of security and confidence reigned and it was believed that there was a possibility to continue holding the occupied territories and, at the same time, to live in calm.[22]

Here, Jiryis probably had in mind the Black Panther movement that arose in Israel in 1971 with the protests of second-generation Israelis whose parents had immigrated from Arab countries. If such a movement could erupt in a period of relative quiet (but no peace agreements), the rifts in Israeli society could rend the fabric entirely in the face of peace.

And the Western-Eastern Jewish divide was hardly the only rift in Israeli society. Rather, wrote Jiryis, there were divisions within each of these camps. These tensions, too, would be expected to intensify "after the advent of peace and the disappearance of security tension factors that, in the past, overwhelmed" Israelis. The intensification of internal tensions would, in turn, "compel Israel to make serious attempts and to apportion major funds—difficult to imagine how they would be secured—to solve these problems."[23]

Jiryis argued that, in a state of peace and aggravated internal friction, Israel would face two options:

> Israel can either preserve calm in all its classes and strive to gain the approval of its Arab neighbors and therefore aim toward emptying the Zionist entity of its meaning, or ignore the internal conditions and leave them in their critical condition, which will lead ultimately to outmigration from Israel to any country that permits immigrants and permits them to work, including the Arab states if this becomes possible, with the dangers this situation poses to the Zionist entity.[24]

Either way, peace would ultimately bring about the dissolution of Israel as a Jewish, Zionist state.

In his memoirs, prepared decades after the 1973 war, Jiryis harked back to this argument, which provoked controversy—and, in Jiryis's mind, helped to spark a change—in the Palestinian and larger Arab political and intellectual world. Criticizing those Palestinians who opposed the idea of the Geneva peace summit, Jiryis argued that they were effectively playing into the hands of Israel, which he named "the primary rejectionist of peace." Israel, Jiryis insisted, was a deeply fragmented society. The state consisted of "groups, factions, and tribes—ideological and ethnic," for which "the tension with the Arabs, especially in the sphere of security, served in the past as effective glue." This "glue," Jiryis argued, would be necessary long into the future. Notwithstanding its existential need for the continuation of the conflict, Jiryis recalled writing, Israel managed deceptively to present itself as ever prepared and eager for peace. By refusing to engage in peace efforts, the Arabs "helped Israel to present them [the Arabs] negatively, as dangerous extremists who do not know what they want. The time had come," Jiryis wrote, "to change direction and to act in a new way," that is, for the Palestinians to take advantage of this opportunity.[25] Here, by employing his knowledge of Israeli society, and especially his assessment of its highly fragmented condition, holding together only due to its perceived common enemy, Jiryis made an argument for embracing a peace initiative. His study of the enemy led him to believe that making peace was the way to win the war.

Revealing the PLO's Evolution

After the Palestine National Council met for its thirteenth session in Cairo in March 1977, Jiryis continued to highlight the PLO's willingness to engage in a negotiated political settlement—a willingness that was not necessarily apparent to all readers of the Council's resolutions. As in 1974, the Council issued an aggressive, militant statement against Zionism (which it defined as "a form of racism") and Israel (against which it called for an escalation in "armed struggle" to "recover the inalienable national rights of the Palestinian Arab people, without peace [*sulh*] or recognition").[26] Buried within the Council's bellicose proclamation, however, were signs of a willingness to compromise.

Jiryis read the Council's resolutions as a major breakthrough in Palestinian political history, and he aimed to portray them as such to the wider public. In the fall 1977 issue of IPS's *Journal of Palestine Studies*, he wrote: "As expressed by the PLO, the Palestinian attitude to the efforts to reach a political settlement in the Middle East is now clearer than ever before."[27] "In brief," Jiryis continued, "the PLO is prepared to agree to, and to participate in, a political solution of the Middle East crisis in return for recognition of the Palestinian people's right to their homes and/or to be compensated for the loss of their property, and also their right to self-determination and to 'establish their independent national state on the soil of their homeland.'" This, asserted Jiryis, "is the gist of the political programme" of the recent session of the Palestine National Council. In Jiryis's mind, the Council was ultimately demanding "an independent Palestinian state in part of the territory of Palestine." And this demand "indicates that a considerable shift has taken place in the attitude of the Palestinian national movement in general and the PLO in particular." Indeed, wrote Jiryis, "since the first partition proposal was put forward forty years ago [the British Peel Commission Proposal of 1937], the Palestinian Arab attitude towards partition has been one of consistent rejection."[28] As Jiryis saw it, now that the Palestinians were declaring their willingness to accept the partition of Palestine, a radical political transformation had occurred.[29]

Jiryis relayed the history of firm Palestinian Arab opposition to partition from the first British proposal in 1937, through the UN partition plan in 1947, and then as expressed in numerous Palestine National Council resolutions. For instance, in 1970 the PNC declared that "the people of Palestine and their national liberation movement are struggling for total liberation and reject all peaceful, liquidationist and surrenderist solutions, including the reactionary-imperialist conspiracies to establish a Palestinian state in part of the territory of Palestine." The following year, the Council demanded "resolute opposition to those who advocate the establishment of a Palestinian state on part of Palestinian soil, inasmuch as efforts to establish such a state can be seen only in the context of the liquidation of the Palestine problem."[30] For decades, Jiryis asserted, the Palestinians were consistent and clear in their refusal to accept anything other than sovereignty over the entirety of historic Palestine.

Jiryis noted that the PLO's stance changed slightly in 1974, as discussed above, when the Council's Ten Points Program approved "establishment of the independent combatant national authority for the people . . . in the part of Palestinian territory that is liberated." But, Jiryis highlighted, the preamble of the Ten Points Program insisted that "it is impossible for a permanent and just peace to be established in the area unless our Palestinian people recover all their national rights and, first and foremost, their rights to return and to self-determination on the whole of the soil of their homeland." Just as Israeli critics had noted in 1974, Jiryis acknowledged in 1977 that "'whole' is the operative word" in the preamble; even in 1974, the PLO demanded all of Palestine.[31]

It appears that Jiryis was overstating his case when he claimed that "any comparison between the attitudes and phraseology of previous PLO political programmes, and those to be found in the new one, clearly demonstrates a fundamental change in the Palestinian position." Nonetheless, his close reading of the 1977 statement demonstrated significant differences between this statement and those the Council had issued at its previous sessions. "The new programme does not, like its predecessors, talk of a 'democratic state,' a 'national authority' or a 'Palestinian state over all of Palestine' with all that these expressions imply," wrote Jiryis. "On the contrary," he contended, "it is based on UN General Assembly resolutions (which, in principle, approve of the partition of Palestine and the establishment of two states in it, one Jewish and one Arab, and which are thus contradictory to the Palestinian National Charter). It calls for the establishment of an 'independent national state'—in short, an independent Palestinian state in part of the territory of Palestine." Jiryis also argued that the latest resolution included a subtle change in approach to "armed struggle." If, in the PLO Covenant, "armed struggle" was the "only way" to achieve the liberation of Palestine, the Council now considered it essential that it be "accompanied by all kinds of political and mass struggle."[32] For Jiryis, these changes were radical—"the Palestinians have adopted a new attitude, very different from all the previous attitudes"—and warranted discussion.

What led to this dramatic change in political approach?, Jiryis asked. First, the Palestinians came to recognize that earlier generations' refusal to compromise proved disastrous for them. "In fact," Jiryis wrote,

> modern Palestinian history can be summed up as a series of rejections of all the proposals and solutions suggested by every quarter for the solution of the Palestine problem. For example, the Palestinians rejected the Balfour Declaration in 1917, the British mandate over Palestine in 1920, the White Paper in 1922, which tried to meet some of their demands, the proposal for a Palestinian Legislative Council and the subsequent proposal for the establishment of an Arab Agency in 1923, the renewed proposal for a Legislative Council in 1931, the British proposal for the partition of Palestine in 1937, the United Nations partition resolution in 1947, the Arab-Israeli armistice agreements in 1949, the Bourguiba plan in 1965 and, finally, the Rogers Plan in 1970—half a century of continuous rejection.[33]

Following this approach, Jiryis argued, Palestinians believed that they "must get everything or nothing, with the result that they generally got nothing."[34] Palestinian leaders had convinced their constituencies that compromise with the

Zionists and Israelis was unconscionable, leading the Palestinians, according to Jiryis, to lose more and more of their homeland.

In contrast to the grandiloquent "declarations and speeches" of the Palestinian Arab leadership, the Zionists, according to Jiryis, "were far more realistic," pursuing "their aims with great flexibility, concentrating on actions, not just words." In comparing these two approaches, wrote Jiryis, "the majority of Palestinian have gradually learned . . . that realism, pragmatism and moderation are not to be despised as a means of achieving a people's goals."[35] The fact that Palestinians had studied Zionist history and thus seen how Zionists achieved their successes informed the Palestinians' subsequent political transformation. The Zionist values that Jiryis hailed in this 1977 essay—"realism, pragmatism and moderation"—are precisely the values Jiryis claimed he acquired from his years studying more about Zionism and Israel.

Of course, there were numerous other factors that led Palestinians to become more open to political compromise, Jiryis acknowledged. These included the Palestinian recognition that Arab states could not be relied upon to liberate Palestine and that violence in the name of complete victory had significant costs; the exceptional educational success of Palestinians; and the rise of a new generation of Palestinian leaders. These new leaders had generally earned, rather than inherited, their status and they were not implicated in the failures of earlier Palestinian generations. "On the contrary," wrote Jiryis, these contemporary leaders "feel that by being realistic, they are trying to correct the previous errors and to save what can be saved, for after all, Palestine was never in their pockets and it was not they who lost it." In addition, Palestinians have listened to their increasing numbers of supporters and allies in the international arena, most of whom have "advised moderation and realism." The most the Palestinians "can hope for," these sympathetic states have made clear, "is a Palestinian state in part of the territory of Palestine" whereas "not a single country of any importance is prepared to go along with them further than that." For all of these reasons, Jiryis contended, the majority of Palestinians, including many of their new leaders, have, since the 1973 war, slowly but surely come to accept the partition of Palestine.[36]

If the Palestinians were ready in 1977 to consider a compromise, "this does not mean that the Palestinians can agree to any political settlement at any cost and on any terms," Jiryis clarified. He then outlined those features of a solution that would be essential for Palestinians and the "'red lines' that Palestinian public opinion will not permit any Palestinian leadership to cross."[37] One such "red line," Jiryis contended, concerns "recognizing the legitimacy of Zionism."

While "realism may require recognition of the existence of a Jewish state in Palestine," wrote Jiryis, "no Palestinian Arab can ever accept as *legitimate* a doctrine that he should be excluded from most parts of his homeland, because he is a Christian or Muslim Arab, while anyone of the Jewish faith anywhere in the world is entitled to settle there."[38] Due to pragmatic, not ideological, considerations, Palestinians, explained Jiryis, were now coming around to accepting that Israel would continue to exist, resisting the compulsion to endlessly fight for the state's complete dissolution.

That the Palestinians were ready to accept a political settlement with Israel did not mean that such a settlement was likely soon, wrote Jiryis in 1977. But this time, according to Jiryis, the conflict was not the outcome of Palestinian intransigence. Israelis were now unwilling to consider a Palestinian state or even, for that matter, to accept the notion of a Palestinian nation. Meanwhile, Palestinians rejected the Israeli government's demand that, as a precondition for negotiations, the PLO recognize Israel. Palestinians and the Arab states believed that recognition of Israel should be "the culmination of, not the prelude to, efforts to reach a political solution."[39] Appealing to political pragmatism (rather than to ideology) to explain why the PLO refused to accept recognition of Israel as a precondition for negotiations, Jiryis wrote that "Palestinian recognition of Israel is a valuable and important card that will not be thrown away: it can only be played in the context of a definite and guaranteed solution for the Palestinian problem," namely, "the establishment of the Palestinian state, followed by the solution of the problem of the refugees living inside and outside that state."[40]

Jiryis added that "the Palestinians believe that if they withhold recognition from Israel in advance, the Arabs will automatically do the same, so that the Arab-Israeli conflict will be kept alive and along with it the pressures it gives rise to at the local and international levels, until such time as the Palestine problem is solved." Jiryis was confident of the Arab states' support of the Palestinian position because "the Arab governments have an inescapable commitment to the achievement of Palestinian national rights" and, in fact, "the very legitimacy of their rule may depend upon their ability to solve the problem satisfactorily." He explained further that "the underlying 'philosophy' of this attitude is that in no circumstances is it permissible to permit a settlement in the Middle East that safeguards the interests of anyone at all, unless it also, and to the same extent, safeguards the interests of the Palestinians." In its conflict with Israel, Jiryis claimed, the PLO "has the moral sympathy of the Arab people, which ties the hands of any Arab ruler who might be tempted to ignore the Palestinian cause."[41] It is difficult to know whether Jiryis believed he was describing the position of the Arab states or prescribing what he thought their position ought to be. In any case, just weeks after Jiryis published these lines, Egyptian president Anwar Sadat flew to Israel to address the Knesset. In this regard, it is clear, Jiryis had been wrong.

If the Palestinians had decided to pursue a peaceful path of negotiated settlement, according to Jiryis, why did the 1977 Palestine National Council not say so clearly? And why did the PLO governing body not explicitly renounce the "armed struggle"? Though they were ready to compromise, Jiryis argued, "the Arabs must systematically develop their strength so that it can be employed, should the need arise. The good intentions and sympathy of other parties alone cannot be relied on to make them respond to the Arab and Palestinian point of view." In addition, "the West," Jiryis contended, has "not generally shown much concern for the interests of the peoples or countries it has ruled or influenced, except when it has been obliged to do so in one way or another, such as when these peoples have exerted different kinds of pressure, including armed resistance."[42] In other words, the threat of armed resistance was a tool that the PLO needed to preserve and strengthen because, without it, Israel and the West (Jiryis had in mind especially the US) would have little incentive to compromise their own interests in solving the problem of the Palestinians.

Jiryis's 1977 article was an assessment of the Palestinians' contemporary political situation in light of a serious engagement with both Palestinian and Zionist history. These years of encounter and study led Jiryis to the conclusion that refusing to coexist with Zionism had been disastrous for the Palestinians. The time had come, therefore, to cut the Palestinians' losses and engage in a political settlement with Israel.[43]

We will never be able to measure the impact of the PLO Research Center's years-long effort to learn and educate about Zionism and Israel on the PLO's evolution toward political moderation. Certainly, the work of the Research Center was just one piece of a much broader array of geopolitical and other factors. And yet the connection between the Center and the move toward accepting a political settlement with Israel is not one of mere concurrence. Some of those studying and writing about Israel—notably Sabri Jiryis, the Center's Israel expert—were among the most outspoken advocates of a negotiated agreement with Israel and explicitly based their arguments on what they had learned about the enemy.

A "Moderating Impulse"?

An interesting parallel to our analysis here is the study of US Cold War–era Sovietologists. According to David Engerman, "the field of Russian Studies brought together scholars from a wide—though certainly not infinite— spectrum of political views." These included European Social Democrats, Eisenhower Republicans, and even some Communists. "Neither the field" of Sovietology "nor its founders were dominated by the fervent anti-Communists who appear in familiar depictions of postwar reactions." Engerman claimed that "it was instead a wide-ranging group determined to build expertise and to make itself useful in intellectual life, public debate, and foreign policy."[44]

As we have seen, the PLO Research Center scholars had similar qualities. First, the Center was staffed by people of diverse political perspectives and party affiliations.[45] Moreover, though the Center's researchers never expressed any affection toward Zionism or Israel, if one was searching for people in Beirut who were working to destroy Israel, there were better places to look than the PLO Research Center.

And now we come to the heart of the matter. Composed as the field was of scholars from a range of political perspectives, Sovietology, according to Engerman, was "often a moderating impulse, its exemplars clashing with ideologically driven experts; they saw to it that the Cold War stayed cold." Engerman explained that research funded by the US military and by the CIA actually "undermined public assumptions that the Soviet Union was an all-powerful state ruling over an atomized population that was waiting for an outside power to unshackle it." For instance, a joint army-CIA project "underscored the limits of the Kremlin's reach even within the USSR."[46]

Regarding his tenure at the PLO Research Center, Jiryis described himself as having a moderating effect. Previously, more ideologically driven Arab writers about Israel, Jiryis told me, "tended to accept the theory of conspiracy. And of the Israelis being naughty and strong and weak and being such devils." But Jiryis, having studied Jews and Israeli society, understood that there was no great conspiracy and there were no devils. Rather, as he put it, "they were just people. I knew their weak points and strong points. I could understand them better." This was the knowledge-based understanding of Israel that the PLO Research Center sought to disseminate.[47]

There is no question that the political principles and goals of the PLO informed the PLO Research Center's work. In other words, and unsurprisingly, politics guided knowledge production at the PLO Research Center. Importantly, though, the relationship between knowledge and politics was not unidirectional. There are hints that the relationship had gone in the other direction as well, with knowledge production having guided and informed politics. To be sure, learning about the enemy did not, and does not, always or ineluctably lead to political moderation, neither among Palestinians nor any other group; at times, the opposite is the case. But knowing more about Zionism and Israel led some Palestinians to believe, for a variety of reasons, that Palestinians would be best served by diplomatically pursuing the creation of their own state alongside Israel. Whether the knowledge yielded sympathy or pragmatism, the consequence was nonetheless a call for coexistence. And thus, in this way, the pursuit and acquisition of knowledge guided a politics that ultimately reached the very top of the PLO.

POSTSCRIPT

Mahmoud Abbas, Research, and the Gunman's Eyes

The thirtieth anniversary of the 1983 bombing of the PLO Research Center was an occasion for Palestinian leaders and intellectuals to reflect on the history of the Center and to contemplate its future. At a ceremony in February 2013 honoring the victims of the bombing, Palestinian president Mahmoud Abbas delivered a strange and rambling speech in which he mentioned other institutions, such as the Institute for Palestine Studies, other martyrs (in the parlance of the event organizers), and victims of other Israeli attacks.

At one point, Abbas questioned why Palestinian society waits to honor activists and heroes until after their deaths. "It is not enough to honor the man after his death," said Abbas. "Why not honor him while he is alive? We say to him—not to his descendants—thank you. We say to him: you have worked and acted and offered a great deal. You still think and you still live. We must honor him."[1] One has the sense that Abbas had himself in mind here; the then-seventy-seven-year-old leader was not feeling his people's love.

Notwithstanding his peculiar focus at the 2013 ceremony, the "know the enemy" mission of the PLO Research Center was one with which Abbas was intimately familiar. According to two of his biographers, Grant Rumley and Amir Tibon, Abbas was a key figure in acquiring and disseminating knowledge within the PLO about the Zionist enemy. "Away from the center of events," Rumley and Tibon wrote, "Abbas began carving a new role for himself as the PLO's in-house expert on Israel."[2]

In 1994, then in Tunis, Abbas looked back on the period in which he was living in Damascus while the main center of the PLO was in Beirut. He recalled that

> Unlike Beirut, the atmosphere in Damascus was relatively calm which allowed me to become engrossed in reading publications and information about Israel. I had dedicated a great deal of my time to becoming acquainted

with Israeli society. It had been a commonplace feature across the revolutionary ranks—both the leaders and the base—not to pay attention to knowing the Israeli composition [*al-tarkiba al-isra'iliyya*] that we intended to fight.[3]

The following year, Mahmoud Abbas wrote in his memoirs that those Palestinians who had criticized PLO officials in the late 1970s for their willingness to meet Israelis lacked any real understanding of Israel. "Their knowledge of Israel was limited to the simple fact that it was the enemy," wrote Abbas. He recalled aiming to rectify "this weakness within our ranks, to let my views on how to deal with enemies infiltrate and to suggest ways of attaining our goals" based on "seven years of reading and writing" about Zionism and Israel.[4]

Like Sabri Jiryis, Abbas not only dedicated himself to learning about Jews and Israel but also, in tandem with this study, began advocating for meeting with Israelis and exploring possible compromises. And just as some Palestinians questioned Jiryis's motivations for studying the enemy, "people began referring to him [Abbas] as a traitor and Zionist agent," according to Ahmad Tibi.[5] Suspicions about Abbas's studies of the enemy abounded.

Yet Abbas's experience was, in other ways, quite different from that of the PLO Research Center writers. Unlike many of those at the Beirut-based think tank who earned higher degrees from universities in Western countries, Abbas traveled to the Soviet Union to pursue his studies. Between 1980 and 1982, based at the Institute of Oriental Studies in Moscow, Abbas wrote a thesis on the relationship between the Nazis and the Zionists. Abbas's thesis gave credence to the theory that the typical figure given for Jewish victims of the Holocaust is grossly inflated.[6] This flirtation with Holocaust minimization was unacceptable to the PLO Research Center leadership, who, from the Center's earliest years, sought to distance Palestinian nationalism from antisemitism. Thus, according to Sabri Jiryis, when Abbas submitted a manuscript for a book he wished to publish on the history of Zionism (a version, presumably, of his doctoral thesis) to the PLO Research Center, Jiryis rejected it. As Jiryis recalled, he could not publish the manuscript because it "almost denied the Holocaust."[7] One wonders whether Abbas's cantankerous speech in 2013 reflected lingering feelings about the Center from days gone by.

Along with the odd tangents in this speech, Abbas reflected on the critical question of the relationship between research and fighting. Abbas explained:

> The Palestinian leadership that created the Liberation Organization and fired the first bullets remembered that it is necessary for the hand that fires

bullets to have eyes. And what are these eyes? They are studies, research, science, culture, so that it would be an educated rifle that knows when to shoot, at whom to shoot, and how to shoot. And from this was the importance of the Research Center.[8]

For Abbas, the Research Center served as the eyes of the Palestinian fighter. In this speech, Abbas played with the images not only of the rifle-carrier's hand and eyes, but also of the rifle and the pen. "The pen," asserted Abbas,

> is sometimes more dangerous than the rifle. Much more dangerous, because it instructs, it teaches. Because of this, these centers and these researchers were subjected to a series of assassination operations. All those who think faced them [such operations], because they [the Israelis] do not want the [Palestinian] rifle to think. They do not want anyone else to think for this rifle, for if it [the rifle] remains blind it is easy to uproot it, and it is easy to subdue it, and it is easy to strike it.[9]

For Abbas, the goal of this Palestinian research was not merely to "know the enemy" but to know how, when, and at whom to fire the rifle. In 2013, long after the PLO had officially renounced armed struggle, Abbas may have meant "the rifle" to be understood figuratively.

Notwithstanding the ambiguous imagery he used in this speech, and regardless of his ambivalence about the PLO Research Center as an institution, Abbas was unequivocal in his insistence that learning about the Jews and Israel was crucial for the success of the Palestinian national project. Thirty years after the PLO Research Center was forced to leave Beirut, Abbas asserted that one of its fundamental missions—to better understand Jewish and Zionist history—was not merely of academic interest but a political imperative for Palestinians.

On Not Finding the Center's Library and Archive

I spent a great deal of time over the past decade, as others have before and since, trying to locate the PLO Research Center's library and archives in Israel, Palestine, or Algeria. The inaccessibility of these documents, along with so many others from Palestinian history, has provoked significant frustration among scholars. Beshara Doumani has observed "an archive fever" that "has been coursing through the Palestinian body politic" for the past few decades.[10] Lila Abu-Lughod noted that "what archives are or should be in this case of a dispersed people with no state archive, no less a state, a majority of whom live in exile or under occupation and have had their 'proper' archive destroyed, seized, or sealed in inaccessible colonial archives belonging to those who dispossessed them and still rule over them with force, are tough questions."[11] Not least because of the absence of comprehensive, accessible Palestinian archives, the case of the missing PLO Research Center library and archive is a source of intense speculation and ongoing fascination.

I have not given up on finding the PLO Research Center's library and archive, and I trust others will not either. But to those who care to know and write Palestinian history, the PLO Research Center offers a treasure trove of source material in libraries around the world and, today, at the fingertips of everyone with an internet connection. We need not wait until those wooden crates are located in Algeria or elsewhere before we begin to study Palestinian history through the work of those scholars and activists who sat together in Beirut over the course of the Center's eighteen years there. Every issue of *Shu'un Filastiniyya* has been scanned and uploaded to the internet. The PLO Research Center's hundreds of books and pamphlets are available in university and national libraries; many have also been scanned and made accessible on the Center's website or elsewhere on the internet.[12] It is my hope that this book will encourage fellow scholars of Palestine and Palestinians, of Israel and Israelis, of Jews, Judaism, and Zionism, to turn to the Center's thousands of pages of publications to explore, to understand, and to share this troubled history.

ACKNOWLEDGMENTS

AFTER NEARLY a decade of work on this book, I am indebted to so many kind people that I had to divide the list between these acknowledgments and the preface. And still, no doubt, I am regretfully forgetting important people.

Rashid Khalidi and Derek Penslar, mentors since my graduate studies, remain inspirations for and generous champions of my work on Palestinian and Israeli history.

My years of research in Jerusalem were much more fulfilling owing to the friendship of Dima Azaiza-Dabbah, Orit Bashkin, Elisheva Baumgarten, Anwar Ben Badis, Johannes Becke, Michelle Campos, Efrat Cohen-Bar, Kamal Dabbah, Yaacov Deutsch, Edward Greenstein, Beverly Gribetz, Amit Gvaryahu, Ayman Hammad, Omar Hammad, Yusuf Hammad, Naama Hochstein, Fida Jiryis, Alexander Kaye, Yedidah Koren, Sari Kronish, Mahmoud al-Kurdiyyeh, Jonathan Price, Orit Rozin, Naomi Schacter, Noa Shein, Oded Steinberg, Scott Ury, and Joel Weinberg.

Joshua Abraham, Seth Anziska, Daniel Backenroth, Jessica Fechtor, Jessica Gribetz, Hanan Harif, Ethan Katz, Jesse Kellerman, Hagit Ofran, Eli Osheroff, David Rosen, Ari Roth, and the anonymous reviewers for the press read drafts of parts or all of the book and offered incisive suggestions.

Princeton's Near Eastern Studies department and Program in Judaic Studies were my professional homes as I wrote this book, and the NES department provided a generous grant to support it. I am grateful to my students Ladan Ahmadian Heravi, Adam Anabosi, Nadirah Mansour, Adam Sigelman, and Liora Tamir, who read drafts of this book, and to my many colleagues, including Leora Batnitzky, Michael Cook, Salam Fayyad, Behrooz Ghamari-Tabrizi, Şükrü Hanioğlu, Lara Harb, Bernard Haykel, Martha Himmelfarb, Eve Krakowski, AnneMarie Luijendijk, Hossein Modarressi, M'hamed Oualdi, Michael Reynolds, Marina Rustow, Cyrus Schayegh, Daniel Sheffield, Moulie Vidas, and Qasim Zaman. Deena Abdel-Latif, Angela Bryant, Ruchi Chaudhary, Karen Chirik, Tammy Fortson, James LaRegina, and Ginger Leonard ensured that everything in Jones Hall ran smoothly. My other home in Princeton for several years was that of Sheila and Daniel Kurtzer, who adopted me into their family and graciously hosted me countless nights.

Fred Appel of Princeton University Press has believed in this book from its inception and waited patiently as the project expanded in unexpected directions. James Collier assisted with key tasks and Terri O'Prey skillfully shepherded it through the final phases of production. Sara Tropper and Kim Hastings, truly extraordinary editors, helped me trim and clarify the manuscript in essential ways. Tobiah Waldron produced the index.

My in-laws, Esther, Shlomo, and Miriam; siblings Carin, Eric, Orit, Seth, Gabi, and Pavel; and nieces and nephews, have been a great source of strength and joy. My parents, Rhonda and Michael, have supported me proudly and read drafts of this book, lovingly, if impatiently, pushing me to finish. And without our dear friend Maria, I could never have made it to the finish line.

My children—Daniela, Sophie, and Max—grew up with the story of the PLO Research Center. They spent two years of childhood in Jerusalem, learning Hebrew and Arabic, as I worked on this book. They understand in a way most adults do not the complexities and human dimensions of the Palestinian-Israeli encounter. I pray they look back on these formative years fondly or, at least, forgivingly.

I met Sarit just days before I started learning the Arabic alphabet. Everything I have done since has been with her and thanks to her. Her love, kindness, integrity, beauty, and sheer brilliance leave me more awestruck with each passing day.

PLO Research Center Library Books Found in the National Library of Israel

1. Abrahams, Israel. *The Book of Delight, and Other Papers.* Philadelphia: 1912.
2. Alkalaʿi, Reʾuven. *Milon ʿIvri-Angli Shalem.* Tel Aviv: 1966.
3. Bell, Gertrude Lowthian. *Syria, the Desert & the Sown.* London: 1919.
4. Ben-Gurion, David. *The Jews in Their Land.* London: 1966.
5. Besant, Walter. *Jerusalem, the City of Herod and Saladin.* London: 1888.
6. Boddy, Alexander Alfred. *Days in Galilee and Scenes in Judaea.* London: 1900.
7. Browne, Henry. *A Handbook of Hebrew Antiquities.* London: 1852.
8. Buber, Martin. *Jiskor.* Berlin: 1920.
9. Colson, Percy. *The Strange History of Lord George Gordon.* London: 1937.
10. Copley, Frank Barkley. *The Impeachment of President Israels.* New York: 1913.
11. Desider, Balthazar. *Gefährdung des Christentums durch Rassenwahn und Judenverfolgung.* Luzern: 1935.
12. Edwardes, Allen. *Erotica Judaica.* New York: 1967.
13. Finn, James. *Stirring Times, or, Records from Jerusalem Consular Chronicles of 1853 to 1856.* London: 1878.
14. Forder, Archibald. *In and about Palestine, with Notebook and Camera.* London: 1919.
15. Gadsby, John. *My Wanderings.* London: 1871.

16. Goodrich-Freer, A. *Inner Jerusalem*. London: 1904.

17. Gordon, Charles George. *Reflections in Palestine*. London: 1884.

18. Graham, Stephen. *With the Russian Pilgrims to Jerusalem*. London: 1913.

19. Graves, Philip. *Palestine, the Land of Three Faiths*. London: 1923.

20. Hardy, E. J. *The Unvarying East*. London: 1912.

21. Harfield, Eugene. *An Oriental Constellation*. Richmond, Va.: 1891.

22. Henry, Michael. *Life Thoughts of Michael Henry*. London: 1876.

23. Hommel, Fritz. *The Ancient Hebrew Tradition as Illustrated by the Monuments*. London: 1897.

24. Hudson, Elizabeth Harriot. *A History of the Jews in Rome, B.C. 160–A.D. 604*. London: 1884.

25. Hurlbut, Jesse Lyman. *Traveling in the Holy Land through the Stereoscope*. New York: 1900.

26. [IDF Information Office]. *David and Goliath, Egyptian Version*. Tel Aviv: 1967.

27. Inchbold, A. Cunnick. *Under the Syrian Sun*. London: 1906.

28. Jacobs, Joseph. *As Others Saw Him*. London: 1895.

29. Jannaway, Frank George. *Palestine and the Jews*. Birmingham: 1914.

30. Kallen, Horace Meyer. *Zionism and World Politics*. London: 1921.

31. Lees, George Robinson. *Life and Adventure beyond Jordan*. London: 1909.

32. Levenston, Edward A. *The Megiddo Modern Dictionary, English-Hebrew*. Tel Aviv: 1966.

33. Levine, Shmaryahu. *In Milhome-Tsayten*. New York: 1915–1917.

34. Loewe, Heinrich. *Geschichten von jüdischen Namen*. Berlin: 1929.

35. Ludwig, Emil. *Genius and Character*. London: 1927.

36. Macartney, H. B., and Selim Kassab Mualim. *Two Stories from the Land of Promise*. London: 1906.

37. MacCoun, Townsend. *The Holy Land in Geography and in History*. New York: 1897.

38. Magnus, Laurie. *'Religio laici' Judaica: The Faith of a Jewish Layman*. London: 1907.

39. May, Herbert Gordon. *Oxford Bible Atlas*. London: 1962.

40. McCrackan, W. D. *The New Palestine*. London: 1922.

41. Meiers, Mildred and Jack Knapp. *Thesaurus of Humor*. New York: 1940.

42. Michener, James. *The Source*. New York: 1965.

43. Miller, William. *The Least of All Lands: Seven Chapters on the Topography of Palestine in Relation to Its History*. London: 1888.

44. Mitchell, Elizabeth Harcourt. *Forty Days in the Holy Land, Before and After*. London: 1890.

45. Mocatta, Isaac Lindo. *The Jewish Armoury*. Brighton: 1877.

46. Neil, C. Lang. *Rambles in Bible Lands*. London: 1905.

47. Newman, John Philip. *From Dan to Beersheba*. New York: 1864.

48. Palestine Exploration Fund. *Twenty-One Years' Work in the Holy-Land*. London: 1887.

49. Palmerston, Emily Lamb. *A Month in Palestine*. London: 1889.

50. Pearlson, Gustav. *Twelve Centuries of Jewish Persecution*. Hull: 1898.

51. Pines, Meir. *Di Geshikhte fun der Yudisher Literatur biz'n Yohr 1890*. Warsaw: 1920.

52. Prawer, Joshua. *Toldot mamlekhet ha-tsalbanim be-erets yisra'el*. Jerusalem: 1971.

53. Ravnitzky, Yehoshua. *Yidishe vitsen*. Berlin: 1923.

54. Réville, Albert. *Prolegomena of the History of Religions*. London: 1884.

55. Reynolds-Ball, Eustace A. *Jerusalem*. London: 1912.

56. Rivlin, Eliezer. *Horvot Yerushalayim*. Jerusalem: 1928.

57. Robinson, Agnes Mary Frances. *The Life of Ernest Renan*. London: 1898.

58. Sayce, Archibald Henry. *Patriarchal Palestine*. London: 1895.

59. Sayce, Archibald Henry. *The "Higher Criticism" and the Verdict of the Monuments*. London: 1895.

60. Schofield, Alfred Taylor. *Palestine Pictured*. London: 1913.

61. Serao, Matilde. *In the Country of Jesus*. London: 1919.

62. Simon, Leon. *Aspects of the Hebrew Genius*. London: 1910.

63. Simon, Rachel. *Beside the Still Waters*. London: 1899.

64. Simpson, William. *The Jonah Legend*. London: 1899.

65. Strack, Hermann Leberecht. *The Jew and Human Sacrifice*. London: 1909.

66. Sue, Eugène. *The Wandering Jew*. London: 1844–1845.

67. Thomson, William McClure. *The Land and the Book*. London: 1894.

68. Tidhar, David. *Intsayklopediya le-halutsay ha-yeshuv u-vonav*. Tel Aviv: 1947–1971.

69. Tieck, Heinrich. *Lebens Karawane*. Vienna: 1951.

70. Wedgwood, Julia. *The Message of Israel in the Light of Modern Criticism*. London: 1894.

71. [World Committee for the Victims of German Fascism]. *Sefer ha-Hum: 'al ha-Teror ha-Hitlera'i be-Germaniya.* Tel Aviv: 1933.

72. Zeitlin, William. *Taw-zikaron le-Zion. Bibliotheca sionistica: Hebräische schriften über zionismus (1852–1905).* Frankfurt a.M.: 1909.

73. *Al-Riwaya.* Cairo: 1936–1939.

NOTES

Preface

1. Early in my research for this book, scholars and activists I spoke with expected I might unearth in Israel secret copies of the materials Israeli forces seized from the PLO Research Center in September 1982. If I had, I would have faced an ethical dilemma in certain respects parallel to that which confronts scholars of Baʿthist Iraq: whether, and if so how, to use copies of the Baʿth Party archival materials the US seized during its invasions of Iraq, expatriated to the US, and since repatriated. See Walter 2022. I was, alas, spared this quandary, as discussed in chapter 13 of this book.

2. Regrettably, due to Lebanese policies, I was unable to visit the now-defunct site of the Research Center during its Beirut years. The US State Department warns: "Travelers who hold passports that contain visas or entry/exit stamps for Israel will be denied entry into Lebanon and may be subject to arrest or detention. Even if travel documents contain no Israeli stamps or visas, persons who have previously traveled to Israel may still face arrest and/or detention if prior travel is disclosed." "Lebanon International Travel Information" 2022.

Introduction

1. On the challenge of translating the phrase *al-qadiyya al-filastiniyya*, which was used to mean Palestine "question," "issue," "problem," or "cause," see below.

2. A. Sayegh 1970a; Razzouk 1968b; al-Kayyali 1966; al-Abid 1968; Kadi 1967; al-Abid 1966; Lamiyaʾ 1968; ʿAbd al-ʿAziz 1969; Halasa 1968; Razzouk 1970a; Shaʿban Sayegh 1971.

3. Amit 2014.

4. The complete Kahan Commission report is available at https://mfa.gov.il/mfa /foreignpolicy/mfadocuments/yearbook6/pages/104%20report%20of%20the%20commis-sion%20of%20inquiry%20into%20the%20e.aspx.

5. https://events.eventact.com/AIS/AIS/WebSite/AISBylaws2016c.pdf, accessed June 16, 2020.

6. To be sure, some of the Center's publications may be regarded as propagandistic or po-lemical, as we shall see.

7. This book joins recent scholarship in examining the PLO from the perspective of global history by considering the global elements of the PLO's intellectual attempt to understand its enemy. In *The Global Offensive*, Paul Thomas Chamberlin argues that "on the conceptual level, Palestinian fighters embraced the cause of revolutionary groups from around the Third World,

imagining their own movement as the spiritual successor to the Chinese, Algerian, Cuban, and Vietnamese examples. In their military capacity, Palestinian fighters built upon earlier models of guerrilla warfare, engineering a set of tactics designed to project their armed struggle into an increasingly interconnected world order." Chamberlin contends that "the PLO's greatest victories would come not on the battlefield, however, but in the political arena. As it continued this diplomatic campaign, the PLO emerged as the world's first globalized insurgency and became a seminal influence for rebellions in the post-Cold War era." Chamberlin 2012, 258. See also Fischbach 2018; Lubin 2014.

8. Husary 2018. I make use of the PLO Research Center publication list provided in appendix C of her important thesis.

9. Sleiman 2016, 50, 62. I examine later in this book Sleiman's claim that the PLO Research Center held the PLO archives.

10. R. Sela 2018, 201.

11. R. Sela 2017; Mandel 2021. Notwithstanding these documentaries, Sabri Jiryis insisted that Israel returned the films to the PLO in 1983 along with all of the other materials that the Israeli forces seized from the Center in 1982. S. Jiryis 2023.

Chapter One: Why Did the PLO Need a Research Center?

1. Yezid Sayigh 1997, 119, 139–40. Another helpful articulation of the policy and its logic is found in Filiu 2014, 117. See also A. Sela 2014, 271.

2. I am indebted here as elsewhere to the groundbreaking, comprehensive, and important work of Yezid Sayigh. On the rise of these movements, see Yezid Sayigh 1997, 71–94.

3. Fateh is also often rendered Fatah in English writing. Here, following Yezid Sayigh, I use Fateh as it more closely accords with Palestinian Arabic pronunciation of the organization's name.

4. Cited in Yezid Sayigh 1997, 84.

5. Yezid Sayigh 1997, 89.

6. Yezid Sayigh 1997, 89–90.

7. On Habash, see Galia 2017.

8. Cited in Yezid Sayigh 1997, 73.

9. Yezid Sayigh 1997, 78–80.

10. Yezid Sayigh 1997, 164–67; AbuKhalil 1987, 362.

11. Cited in Yezid Sayigh 1997, 96. For consistency, I have changed Sayigh's spelling of the name Shuqayri to Shukairy; the latter is the spelling the PLO Research Center used in a book it published by Shukairy.

12. Though the literal translation of the Arabic name of this institution is Palestinian National Council, it is more typically rendered Palestine National Council.

13. Yezid Sayigh 1997, 97–98. While in retrospect the founding of the PLO was an event of utmost importance in Middle Eastern and twentieth-century global history, it was not immediately recognized as such in the United States. The event earned a three-sentence article on the fifth page of the *New York Times*. By contrast, "Hasidim May Drop Roving Patrol Cars" was a front-page story that same day. *New York Times* 1964a; *New York Times* 1964b.

14. As Yehoshafat Harkabi noted, the PLO rendered the term *mithaq* as "Covenant" in its translation of the 1964 version and as "Charter" in its translation of the 1968 version. For an analysis of the document, see Harkabi 1979. Harkabi was a former chief of Israel's military intelligence,

director of strategic research for the Ministry of Defense, assistant for strategic policy for the Ministry of Defense, and intelligence advisor to Israel's prime minister. Though his introduction to the Covenant is overtly tendentious, his analysis and especially his comparisons of the 1964 and 1968 versions remain instructive. Israeli governments have demanded over the years that the PLO Covenant be amended to demonstrate Palestinians' acceptance of Israel's legitimate existence. The parties continue to contest whether such a change has officially been made.

15. For the 1964 version of the Arabic text, see Hourani 1980, 228–31. For an English translation, see appendix A in Harkabi 1979.

16. Harkabi 1979, 129. An Arabic version that matches Harkabi's is available at https://info .wafa.ps/ar_page.aspx?id=4923, accessed October 19, 2023. Archived at perma.cc/3VNF-RBV9. The Arabic version presented by Faisal Hourani, however, lists this as the department not for "research and specialized institutes" but rather for "public affairs and national advancement." See Hourani 1980, 232–35.

17. Strangely, years later, the PLO Research Center claimed that it was the "first research center on the Palestine question in the Middle East." See advertisement for Palestine Research Center (established 1965) in *Arab Palestinian Resistance* 4, no. 7 (July 1972): 95.

18. On Zurayk, see Kassab 2010, 65–74; Mattar 2000; H. A. Faris 1988; Atiyeh 1988. On Khalidi's life and work until the early 2000s, see Fischbach 2008; Mansour and Fawaz 2000, 349–52. Biographical details for Dajani are found at "Al-Dajani, Burhan (1921–2000)" 2021.

19. "Mu'assasat al-Dirasat al-Filastiniyya, 1963–2013" 2013, 7.

20. W. Khalidi 2016.

21. W. Khalidi 2016.

22. See "Mu'assasat al-Dirasat al-Filastiniyya, 1963–2013" 2013, 5.

23. On Sayegh in the years preceding the 1948 war, see Beshara 2019. See Levin 2023 for the most in-depth account of Sayegh's public activities in the 1950s.

24. Anis Sayegh lists the date of his brother's PhD as 1954. A. Sayegh 2006, 33. Thanks to Geoffrey Levin for catching this error.

25. Di-Capua 2018, 6–7.

26. F. Sayegh 1950; *New York Times* 1980. Sayegh, according to scholar Nina Fischer, was "probably the crucial catalyst to bring the term apartheid for the Palestinian situation into the UN and thus into broad circulation. Sayegh, though today less in the spotlight, was one of the most significant public intellectuals promoting the Palestinian cause before Edward Said." (Fischer later seems accidentally to conflate Fayez and his brother Anis when she writes that "as the director-general, Sayegh also founded the centre's paper *Shu'un Filastiniyya* [Palestinian Affairs] in 1971, which, under his influence, became one of the first vehicles to transport the apartheid analogy for the situation in Israel/Palestine to a popular level.") Fischer 2021, 1129. On Sayegh's influence in the debates about Zionism, racism, and apartheid, see also Baconi 2021. For a recorded interview of Sayegh (later in his life) with William F. Buckley on May 15, 1974, see https://youtu.be/04YQ8vMygrQ, accessed October 6, 2021.

27. Khalidi told me that Sayegh consulted IPS's statutes and modeled the PLO Research Center after IPS. W. Khalidi 2016.

28. Sayegh recognized his own reluctant attraction toward political activity. Just a few months earlier, on March 8, 1964, Sayegh told Khosrow Mostofi of the University of Utah that he preferred not to sign a long-term contract at the American University of Beirut because "the temptations (and pressures upon me) for involvement in practical, political affairs are too

strong" in the Middle East. "I would much prefer to teach about the Middle East than in the Middle East," he wrote, and thus Sayegh sought an academic position in Utah as early as the summer of 1965. F. Sayegh 1964.

29. In Sayegh's archives, held at the J. Willard Marriott Library at the University of Utah, we have the reports that he prepared in the founding period of the PLO Research Center. I am grateful to Geoffrey Levin for sharing with me several files from this archive. See Aldar 1965.

30. Shukairy 1965. The document includes the traditional formula "in the name of God, the most gracious the most merciful" above the Quranic phrase "help from God and speedy victory" (61:13).

31. The Arabic phrase *al-qadiyya al-filastiniyya* was translated into English by the PLO in multiple ways during this period, including as "the Palestinian cause," "the Palestine question," and "the Palestine problem." In this book, I try to translate the phrase in light of the context in which it is found in a particular text. As early as 1946, Fayez Sayegh used the phrase "Palestine Problem" as a parallel locution to "Jewish Problem." In his "Note on the Palestine Problem" submitted to the Anglo-American Inquiry Committee prepared on behalf of the National Party, Sayegh wrote of "the error of linking up the solution of the world-wide Jewish Problem with the solution of the Palestine Problem." See appendix 8 of Beshara 2019, 230. As Holly Case explains, "the formulation 'the x question' emerged slowly over the end of the eighteenth century and gathered momentum in the first decades of the nineteenth. Instead of being understood as questions to be answered, these were treated as problems to be solved." Case 2018, 3.

32. F. Sayegh 1965c.

33. Kadi 1966, 3.

34. F. Sayegh 1965c.

35. Note that Sayegh uses the same Arabic phrase here as Shukairy used in the PLO Covenant to describe the Jews' *lack* of an independent national identity.

36. F. Sayegh 1965c.

37. This cooperation indeed took place. For instance, in the foreword to Ibrahim al-Abid's 1969 *Israel and Human Rights*, Anis Sayigh notes that while "the information included in this study was primarily derived from sources available at the Research Center library, including files, documents, and clippings . . . some sources were acquired . . . from other institutes and centers, including . . . the Institute for Palestine Studies in Beirut." Al-Abid 1969a, 7.

38. Eventually, the PLO Research Center collected Israeli newspapers and analyzed news and opinions found in them. According to Brigadier General (ret.) Michael Herzog, Israel exchanged newspapers with its neighbors on a daily basis. Herzog 2018.

39. F. Sayegh 1965c, appendix 4.

40. W. Khalidi 2016.

41. On Anis Sayegh's earlier role as a consultant for the CIA-funded Congress for Cultural Freedom, see Holt 2021, 12–13.

42. A. Sayegh 2006, 20–22.

43. A. Sayegh 2006, 181–83.

44. A. Sayegh 2006, 185.

45. *Al-Mawsu'a al-Filastiniyya* 1984.

46. A list of IPS's publications in its first fifty years is found in *Qa'imat al-Manshurat, 1963–2013* 2013, which Walid Khalidi kindly shared with me.

47. Though Marjayoun came to be incorporated into the state of Lebanon, in the Ottoman period it was not meaningfully separated from Palestine, as Michael Hudson points out. "People who lived in Marjayoun," writes Hudson, "travelled easily southwards into what became Mandatory Palestine. They had picnics in Tiberias, bought land in Beisan, intermarried with cousins in Nazareth." Hudson 1997, 243.

48. During Jiryis's first years in Beirut, IPS published his work, including, e.g., S. Jiryis 1972.

49. When Khalidi described IPS in this way, I asked if he meant to imply the opposite concerning the PLO Research Center. He responded that I should draw my own conclusions. W. Khalidi 2016.

50. Sociologist Lewis Coser sees this tension as inherent to the "dual allegiance" of "bureaucratic intellectuals"—namely, "government professionals who, while striving to live up to the requirements of their bureaucratic positions, also attempt to maintain a voice in the goals of policy and to satisfy the standards prevailing in the wider professional and intellectual community." Coser 1965, 316. I am grateful to Gil Eyal for introducing me to Coser's scholarship.

51. The subsequent director general of the Research Center, Sabri Jiryis, dismissed Sayegh's complaint, telling me in an interview that Sayegh was a "snob" who never respected Arafat. Class and elitism are clearly part of this story.

52. "Markaz al-Abhath" 1984.

53. See Singh and Helou 1970.

54. I used https://fxtop.com/en/historical-currency-converter.php? and https://www .usinflationcalculator.com/ for this estimate.

55. F. Sayegh 1965c, 7.

56. Ironically, it is IPS that has survived and continues to thrive to this day while, as we shall see, the PLO Research Center is a mere shadow of its former self.

57. On Beirut as an educational and intellectual center in the mid-twentieth century, see Kassir 2011, 366–69. On the American University of Beirut, see B. S. Anderson 2012.

58. Hudson, citing Rosemary Sayigh, sets the initial number of Palestinian refugees in Lebanon at 104,000. Hudson 1997, 248; R. Sayigh 1979, 99; Bardawil 2020, 35.

59. Because few Palestinian refugees were granted work permits in Lebanon, Palestinian unemployment was high and exploitation of Palestinian labor rampant. As Abbas Shiblak writes, the poor treatment "of the majority of Palestinians in Lebanon explain[s] their enthusiastic reception of the Palestinian Revolutionary Movement." Shiblak claims that 50,000 Palestinians received Lebanese citizenship in the 1950s and '60s. Hudson renders the number as 40,000 in the three decades between 1948 and 1978. Shiblak 1997, 262–63; Hudson 1997, 249. With the exception of two small camps, the refugee camps were populated by Palestinian Muslims, explains anthropologist Julie Peteet, noting that Christian Palestinians generally "settled in urban areas and a large number received Lebanese citizenship." Peteet 1991, 25.

60. *Newsweek* 1970. I learned of this article from B. S. Anderson 2008, 262.

61. The term "confrontation states" was used widely in the period to refer to the four states surrounding Israel: Egypt, Jordan, Syria, and Israel. Shiblak notes of the years following the PLO leadership's move to Beirut from Jordan in 1970 that "although the Palestinians were liberated from the ruling hand of the Lebanese security agencies, the attitude of the official establishment remained the same. Laws, regulations and basic restrictions on Palestinian rights remained firmly in place—only the Lebanese state's power to enforce them had declined." Shiblak 1997,

264. Creswell argues that during the three decades between the end of World War II and the start of the Lebanese Civil War, "Lebanon established a unique role for itself in the region, becoming at once an intellectual center and a political outlier." Creswell 2018, 24.

62. Hudson 1997, 251–52. "The Cairo agreement," wrote Yezid Sayigh, "was to provide the formal basis for Palestinian-Lebanese relations for at least fifteen years, although it was to be observed more in the breach than the rule. Several of its 19 articles guaranteed the rights of residence, employment, and movement of Palestinian refugees in the country, although this proved to be a suspension, rather than a rewriting, of existing Lebanese regulations and legislation enacted since 1948. The PLO now won the right to manage the camps, working through popular committees and the PASC." Yezid Sayigh 1997, 191–92. See appendix by "participants in the activities" of the Center, in Rubenberg 1983. See also S. Jiryis and Qallab 1985.

63. The building was known as the Mukarim and Abu ʿIzz al-Din building. See *Shuʾun Filastiniyya* 1 (March 1971), title page.

64. The Institute for Palestine Studies was located in the Haddad building on Chile Street, off of Verdun, a kilometer-and-a-half walk from the PLO Research Center location on Colombani Street.

65. On Ras Beirut in this period, see Kassir 2011, 390–91.

Chapter Two: The PLO Research Center at Work

1. The Colombani Street location appears not to have been the first home of the Center. The address listed on the Center's earliest publications is 606 Sadat Street (Apt. 22). See, e.g., F. Sayegh 1965a.

2. Of these sixty employees, forty appear to have been researchers. A. Sayegh 2006, 215–16.

3. On the first decade of the Center's history, see A. Sayegh 2006, 215–16. On the Center's last years in Beirut, see Sabri Jiryis's unpublished memoirs. I rely as well on my interviews with Sabri Jiryis, here the one conducted on March 29, 2016. S. Jiryis 2016d.

4. A. Sayegh 2006, 215–16.

5. According to Rubenberg, there were 25,000 volumes in addition to microfilms, manuscripts, and documents. Rubenberg 2005.

6. *Al-Mawsuʿa al-Filastiniyya* 1984.

7. This list already appears on the back cover of F. Sayegh 1965a. Published in September 1965, this was the first in the Palestine Monographs series.

8. At the end of each newly published work, the Center typically listed many of the books previously published in the various series.

9. F. Sayegh 1965a; F. Sayegh 1965b.

10. F. Sayegh 1966. This is a nineteen-page pamphlet in the Facts and Figures series.

11. Shukairy 1966.

12. Different members of the Sayegh/Sayigh family rendered their family name into Latin letters differently. On Yusif Sayigh, see Yusif Sayigh and Sayigh 2015.

13. The Arabic title translates to *American and West German Aid to Israel*. Abdul-Rahman appears in a State Department list of "individuals admitted to the United States under waivers provided for under the McGovern Amendment," obtained by the Anti-Defamation League in 1981. He is described as a professor of political science at Kuwait University and was

granted two one-month visas in 1978 to attend academic conferences. ISA17–9344-שח digital page 222.

14. Initially the Center published these chronologies every six weeks or so in limited numbers and then combined them into a single volume covering six months. *Al-Yawmiyyat al-Filastiniyya: 1/1/1965–30/6/1965* 1966, 5–7. Beginning sometime in the 1970s, no later than 1979, the Center added the English title "Palestine Chronology" to the series.

15. *Al-Yawmiyyat al-Filastiniyya: 1/7/1965–31/12/1965* 1966.

16. Kanafani 1967 is a sharply critical analysis of proto-Zionist and Zionist literature. Recently translated into English: Kanafani 2022. Kanafani's introduction closes: "Know your enemy." See Holt 2021. According to Anis Sayegh's preface to the Histadrut volume, Kadi wrote it in English and then translated it into Arabic with the assistance of Asa'd Abdul-Rahman. Kadi 1967, 8. Helou 1967; Helou 1969; F. Sayegh 1967a; al-Abid 1967.

17. F. Sayegh 1967b; Abdul-Rahman 1967; Hashim and al-ʿAzm 1967.

18. S. Jiryis 1967a; Alloush 1967; al-Shaʿir 1967; Habibi 1970.

19. Shukairy 1967; H. A. Faris 1967; al-Tariqi 1967.

20. Emphasis in original. Saʿb 1968, 5.

21. Saʿb 1968, 9.

22. There is a typographical error in the text; it reads "one Turth." I have corrected it here.

23. Saʿb 1968, 33.

24. Saʿd 1968a; Saʿd 1968b; Shibl 1968; Shibl 1969; al-Abid 1968; A. Sayegh 1968a.

25. Shehadeh 1970; Darwish 1973; Darwish 1974; Darwish 1975.

26. The set appears to have been published in July 1973, the month in which ʿArif al-ʿArif died (though the fifth volume is dated July 1972 and the sixth and eleventh volumes are undated. The first five volumes consist of detailed lists and charts while the later volumes are notes, narratives, and diaries that al-ʿArif prepared in the late 1960s and early 1970s. The volume titles are as follows: (1) *Names of the Martyrs of the Palestine War of 1967*; (2) *The Palestinians in the Prisons of Israel, 1867–1972*; (3) *The Sons of Palestine Suffering in the Israeli Prisons, 1967–1972*; (4) *The Palestinians Deported from Their Country, 1967–1971*; (5) *The Palestinian Buildings that the Israelis Destroyed, 1967–1972*; (6) *Gaza: A Window into Hell*; (7) *The Events of Rafah and the Tragedy of Its Bedouins*; (8) *The Tragedy of the Bedouin in the Naqab and the Beer Sheba Strip*; (9) *My Objections to Israeli Rule in Jerusalem*; (10) *My Diary about the Activities of the Palestinian Resistance, 18 May 1970–27 December 1973*; (11) *My Diary about the Peace Efforts, 26 June 1970–31 December 1971*; (12) *Amman Is Burning: My Diary of the Year 1971*. Al-ʿArif 1973.

27. In his introduction to this volume, Anis Sayegh wrote, "Until now, there has not been an effort to assemble all of the political documents related to the Palestinian cause. There is no doubt that accessing, reading, and benefiting from the papers of the eminent Palestinian politicians who played a large role in the cause over several decades are important to all students who need to know about our cause and to study it objectively. Many of the books that study the Palestinian issue base their facts on foreign documents and correspondence, the pens of Palestine's men are silent despite their knowledge and experience. This is only because they did not record what happened at the time, or they neglected to collect their papers or publish them, or because these papers were lost, damaged or hidden because of the events to which Palestine was exposed over the years." ʿAbd al-Hadi 1974, 7. On ʿAbd al-Hadi, see "Awni Abd al-Hadi" 2023.

28. A. Sayegh 1971.

29. In a State Department list of "individuals admitted to the United States under waivers provided for under the McGovern Amendment," obtained by the Anti-Defamation League in 1981, Khoury (listed as the coeditor of "Palestine Monthly") and Darwish (described as "Poet, Editor, Director Institute for Palestinian Studies) entered the United States in October 1978 to attend the Association of Arab American University Graduates convention in Minneapolis. "McGovern Amendment Waiver Recommendations," ISA 17–9344-אח digital page 234. ʿAbd al-Fattah Qalqili, described as an employee of the PLO Research Center, received a visa to attend the same conference.

30. The following were double or triple issues: 41/42 in January/February 1975, 51/52 in October/November 1975, 53/54 in January/February 1976, 59 in July/August/September 1976 (with only 156 pages), 60 in October/November 1976, 63/64 in February/March 1977, 68/69 in July/August 1977, 72 in January/February 1978, 81/82 in August/September 1978, 87/88 in February/March 1979, 92/93 in July/August 1979, 122/123 in January/February 1982, 129/130/131 in August/September/October 1982, 132/133 in November/December 1982, and 136/137 in March/April 1983. Issue 138/139 in September/October 1983 was the first published in Nicosia, Cyprus.

31. Ameri 2020, 112–13.

32. The Center's final Beirut-era director general, Sabri Jiryis, to be discussed in detail, was educated at the Hebrew University, practiced law in Israel, and published a book in Hebrew, all before he left Israel for Beirut.

33. I rely here on my 2016 interview with Anan Ameri, to whom I am most grateful for her time, memories, and candor. Additional details are found in her two memoirs, Ameri 2017 and Ameri 2020.

34. B. S. Anderson 2008, 266.

35. Ameri 2017, 178.

36. Ameri 2020, 22. Ameri did not mention her precise salary at the Center but she noted that a side job she pursued as a freelance journalist for the *Orient Press* offered 500 Lebanese liras per celebrity interview, which was "more than half of my monthly salary at the Palestine Research Center." In other words, she was earning less than 1000 Lebanese liras per month.

37. Sayegh acknowledged and embraced his reputation as a stickler for punctuality in his memoirs. "Punctuality is a moral issue and a social virtue," he wrote. A. Sayegh 2006, 47–48.

38. Ameri 1974. She also wrote a section on the Palestinians in the Center's 1974 volume about the Arab-Israeli war the previous year. Abdul-Rahman 1974.

39. "Bilal al Hassan" 2018.

40. On the Nazareth-born Talhami, see http://passia.org/personalities/783, accessed November 17, 2021. On the Lydda native Qurah, see https://palarchive.org/index.php/Detail/objects/75597/lang/en_US, accessed October 5, 2023. Mandes is identified as a "Lebanese researcher" in the biographical line offered in Mandes 1993. Mandes also wrote and published poetry. See, e.g., Mandes 1982.

41. See, e.g., al-Azm 2011. Ameri added that if she was treated differently from her colleagues, it was not because she was a woman but rather because she was young and inexperienced. It is worth noting, though, that she was about the same age as her male colleagues.

42. S. al-Hout 2011, 109.

43. Brilliant 1972.

44. *New York Times* 1972a; *New York Times* 1972b; United Press International 1972.

45. Kanafani 1967; *Los Angeles Times* 1972. On Kanafani's assassination, see D. Rubinstein 2022, 303–15.

46. Reuters 1972; *Jerusalem Post* 1972; *Hartford Courant* 1973.

47. S. al-Hout 2007, 171; S. al-Hout 2011, 107. According to al-Hout, one of these letters was also sent to him, but it was detected beforehand and so it did not reach him. My translation from the Arabic.

48. Klein 2005; Reeve 2011; Bergman 2018a.

49. The 1972 letter bomb was not the first attack on the Center. Already in 1969, a small explosion shattered the glass of the entrance to the Center. See S. Jiryis 1983, 4.

50. Ameri 2016.

51. *Washington Post* 1974; S. al-Hout 2007, 189–90; S. al-Hout 2011, 131. Al-Hout wrote, "On the morning of December 14, 1974, I was awakened by the sounds of a massive explosion. The PLO office, less than 200 meters from my house had been the target. As soon as I arrived there, I learned the PLO-affiliated Palestine Research Center as well as one of Abu Jihad's units had been hit by similar attacks. The Israelis had rented cars and fitted missile launchers to their roofs, fired by remote control or pre-programmed timers."

52. A full reception history of the PLO Research Center's writings awaits future scholarship.

53. Sirhan 1969, 9.

54. Sirhan 1969, 10.

55. Sirhan 1969, 13–14.

56. Sirhan 1969, 14.

57. Rosemary Sayigh recounted that the Fifth of June Society was formed by a group of nationalist Palestinians in the wake of the 1967 war, which convinced these individuals that the Arab armies would not be able to liberate Palestine and that Palestinians "had to do something themselves." Believing that Western perception of the Palestinians mattered, the Fifth of June Society, led by, among others, Fuad Itayem, Antoine Zahlan, and Shafiq Kombarji, "started to disseminate information about Palestine," and, recalled Sayigh, who participated in the organization's efforts, "our work only increased after the emergence of the resistance movement, which brought an influx of journalists who wanted to write or make films about the revolutionaries. We welcomed journalists, took them on tours of the camps, and gave them educational kits on Palestine. We made a library and organized panels. The aim was also to build links with pro-Palestinian groups around the world." Soukarieh 2009, 13.

58. Rich 1969.

59. Al-Abid 1969b.

60. Hadawi 1968.

61. Arab Women's Information Committee 1969. This publication developed into a series, published annually, by the Institute for Palestine Studies. See, e.g., Arab Women's Information Committee 1970; Arab Women's Information Committee 1971. Note that the PLO Research Center published a book by the same name, also in 1969: *Arabs under Israeli Occupation* 1969.

62. Holladay 1968. Holladay, an American, taught at the Near East School of Theology in Beirut from 1963 until 1970. "William Lee Holladay, 1926–2016" 2017.

63. Rich 1969.

64. Rich 1969.

65. *New York Times* 1969.

66. J. A. Morris 1975.

67. The list also includes these PLO Research Center titles: *The Soviet Union and the Palestine Issue, Zionist Colonialism in Palestine, Zionism and Arab Human Rights, Israeli Aggression in the United Nations, Zionist Expansionist Ambitions* (the censor mistakenly transcribed this title as "Jewish Expansionist Ambitions"), *The Arab Boycott and International Law, The Legal Status of the Arab Resistance in the Occupied Land, Occupied Palestine, 1948–1967, Arab Media Planning, From Contemporary Zionist Thought,* and two of Mahmoud Darwish's works, *Goodbye War, Goodbye Peace* and *Diary of Ordinary Sadness.* Bar David 1982, 3–12.

68. *Prisoner Papers, The West Bank: Social and Economic Structure, 1948–1974, Six Years of the Open Bridges Policy, Palestinian Agricultural and Industrial Development, 1900–1970, 'Awni 'Abd al-Hadi: Private Papers.* Bar David 1982, 33. *The Popular Struggle in Palestine before 1948, The Second Displacement, Citrus Fruits in Occupied Palestine, Ignorance in the Palestinian Issue* (1970), *The Zionist Right* (1978), *The United Arab State Project, Arab Media and the Palestinian Issue, Studies on the Israeli Economy, Zionism, Israel, and Asia* (the English version of which was published by IPS), *The Palestine Issue in Lebanese Bourgeois Ideology* (1980), *Problems in the Education of Palestine's Children in Their Main Centers of Concentration, Arab Palestine in the Novel* (1975), *The Gaza Strip, 1948–1967: Economic, Political, and Social Developments, Education in Israel.* Bar David 1982, 36.

69. *The Histadrut, Students in Israel, The Distortion of Arab Education in Occupied Palestine* (1971), *Education and Modernization in Palestinian Arab Society: Part One, Education Curricula under Occupation, The History of the Palestinian Working Class, 1918–1948* (1980), *Canada and the Palestine Issue.* Bar David 1982, 38–39, 48.

70. *Palestinian Political Thought, 1964–1974, The Socio-Economic Composition of Transjordan, The Palestine Liberation Organization and the Arab-European Dialogue, Arms of the Israeli Military, Israeli Occupation and Palestinian Resistance* (1969), *Labor and Workers in the Palestinian Camp* (1974), *The Palestinians in Kuwait* (1979), *The Education of the Palestinians: The Reality and the Problems* (1975), *Palestine, Israel, and Peace, On Zionist Literature* (1967), *World Jewry, Zionism, and Israel* (1974). Bar David 1982, 50–55.

71. Bar David 1982, 57–58.

72. Shani 1985.

Chapter Three: From the Hebrew University to the PLO Research Center

1. S. al-Hout 2007, 486; S. al-Hout 2011, 285.

2. Some sources claim that Darwish was born in March 1942. See, e.g., Mattawa 2014. Darwish's life and literary works have been studied extensively in the English language in recent years. See, e.g., M. Nassar 2017; Abu Eid 2016; Mattawa 2014; Cohen-Mor 2019; H. K. Nassar and Rahman 2008.

3. Ameri 2016.

4. S. Jiryis 2015.

5. "Markaz al-Abhath" 1984, 32.

6. S. Jiryis 2016a, 11–14.

7. S. Jiryis 2016a, 18.

8. Al-Ard attracted the attention of Israeli Hebrew newspapers as early as the summer of 1959. "The editors of our newspaper in Haifa," noted *ha-Boker* in July 1959, "received an unsigned stencil-printed message that the commissioner of the Tel Aviv district received a request to publish a weekly political newspaper in Arabic called 'Al-Ard' (the land). The publisher is Mr. Mahmoud Faruji, a merchant from Acre, and the editor is Mr. Habib Qahwaji, an educator and poet from Haifa. About the aim of the new weekly, one can gather from the platform that the initiators proclaimed, including: the Arab nation in Israel is an inseparable part of the Arab nation. It supports the Arab National Movement. Recognizing the right of return of the Arab refugees to their homeland is the starting point for peace between Israel and the Arab states." *Ha-Boker* 1959. On the Ard movement, see, inter alia, Dallasheh 2010; J. M. Landau 1969a, 92–107; M. Nassar 2017, 98–152.

9. The Arab Front was quickly forced to change its name to the Popular Front due to Israeli government opposition.

10. S. Jiryis 1968, 127–30; Qahwaji 1971, 113. On the communist-nationalist tension, see also Vashitz 1960, 2.

11. This communiqué is cited in M. Nassar 2017, 100. Al-Ard's platform, according to the Israeli Arabist Yosef Vashitz's account from February 1960, included "abolishing the military rule, returning 'the stolen lands' to their owners, ending the 'theft of land' and the 'Judaization of the Galilee and the Triangle,' raising the level of education, effective equality, assistance to the farmer, returning the displaced to their villages." Vashitz 1960, 2. On Vashitz, see Beinin 1991.

12. S. Jiryis 1976, 185–88. According to Leena Dallasheh, who studied al-Ard's newspaper editions, "the movement applied for a license on July 10, 1959, and had not received an answer by October 1959, when it began publishing the newspaper . . . They finally received an answer in January 1960 in which the request for a license to publish a newspaper was rejected." Dallasheh 2010, 36 n. 7; M. Nassar 2017, 101.

13. S. Jiryis 2016a, 19.

14. Jiryis came in fifth place in the election, after Anis Qardush, Elias Muʿamar, Sami Nassar, and Elias Jabour. In sixth and seventh place were Ahmad Rinawi and ʿAli Jayousi. No member of either Mapai (the Labor party) or Maki (the Communist party) was elected. Amnon 1960.

15. *Ha-Boker* noted that the editors of this newspaper gave it numerous different names so as to avoid detection by the authorities. *Ha-Boker* explained that Israeli officials were concerned about the newspaper not only because of the way it sought to poison the views of Israel's minorities but also because of the contacts the editors appeared to have with foreign, especially Egyptian, sources. *Ha-Boker* 1960.

16. The title of one article on the subject was "On Nasser's Representatives in Jerusalem." Yoʾeli 1960.

17. Several of the movement's leaders were arrested, interrogated, and released pending trial. The same article named Jiryis as a key activist in the movement and author of an article in the December 21, 1959, issue of al-Ard's newspaper. "Anshei 'ha-Adama' Horshim Mezimot" 1960.

18. *Ha-Aretz* 1960. Earlier reports on this same case can be found in ʿAl ha-Mishmar 1960. The regional court as well as the Israeli Supreme Court approved the convictions. See R. Harris 2014, 117.

19. R. Harris 2014, 117–18.

20. Naqara 1985.

21. On this period of military rule in Israel, ending formally in 1966, see, inter alia, Robinson 2013; R. Harris 2014, 119–25.

22. S. Jiryis 2016a, 23–24.

23. S. Jiryis 2016a, 20–21. On Israel's perception of this effort as a provocation, see M. Nassar 2014, 82.

24. This decision caught international attention. See, e.g., *New York Times* 1964c.

25. For an excerpt of this memo, see J. M. Landau 1969a, appendix D. For the full text, see ISA 10–4326-צח.

26. The Arabic text of the 1964 PLO Covenant can be found at Hourani 1980, 228–31. An English translation is available in appendix A of Harkabi 1979.

27. In a very useful brief history of the Ard movement, Leena Dallasheh contends with al-Ard's decision not to question the legitimacy of Israel's existence. Citing Qahwaji's 1978 explanation that had al-Ard refused to recognize Israel, its members "would have faced persecution and imprisonment," Dallasheh writes that "it is understandable that the leaders of the movement would make such a strategic decision to allow them this space of activity that would be denied if they openly stated that they refused to recognize the state." Dallasheh cites a 2005 retrospective interview with Muhammad Meʿari of the Socialist List to assert that "al-Ard chose this strategy as a form of resistance, which allowed them some achievements and granted them more time and space for their activities," but she also adds that "adopting this strategy . . . implied recognition of the basic principles of the state." Dallasheh 2010, 24. My own view is that al-Ard's explicitly positive embrace of partition—at a time when the exact opposite was expressed by the PLO—is striking and leaves us reason to wonder whether it was based on something more than a merely "strategic decision."

28. S. Jiryis 2016a, 20.

29. *Jerusalem Post* 1964; *New York Times* 1964c.

30. See, e.g., *ha-Boker* 1964.

31. See *Kol ha-ʿAm* 1964.

32. September 18, 1964 in ISA 10–4326-צח digital pages 2–3.

33. The other two were Qardush and Qahwaji. See *La-Merhav* 1964.

34. His appeal challenged the Haifa district commissioner and the decision to ban al-Ard's registration as an organization under the then-still-enforced 1909 Ottoman associations law. See S. Jiryis 1981, 72.

35. "Sabri Jiryis n. ha-Memuneh ʿal Mehoz Hayfa" 1964, ISA 4–17032-גל digital pages 101–5. *Etgar* 1964.

36. "Sabri Jiryis n. ha-Memuneh ʿal Mehoz Hayfa," 677.

37. "Sabri Jiryis n. ha-Memuneh ʿal Mehoz Hayfa," 679.

38. "Sabri Jiryis n. ha-Memuneh ʿal Mehoz Hayfa," 681.

39. The article, "A Political Court Decision," November 13, 1964, appears in Hebrew translation in ISA 5–17032-גל digital pages 254–56.

40. The announcement was made on November 17, 1964. Draft copies of the announcement as well as the published version in *Yalkut ha-Pirsumim*, November 23, 1964, can be found in ISA 5–17032-גל digital pages 148–64.

41. An excerpt from the protocols of the Israeli government's meeting on July 26, 1964, is found in ISA 5–17032-גל digital page 238.

42. ISA 5–17032-גל digital pages 166–68. Many of the pages that follow in this folder remain classified and are blacked out in the electronic version that the archives released to me.

43. Prime Minister Eshkol received several letters and petitions from Arab citizens of Israel demanding the release of the four, whose only crime, wrote Ibrahim Farid Ghanaim of Baqa al-Gharbiyya in a letter to Eshkol on November 23, 1964, was "their just and persistent struggle to fulfill the rights of the Arab nation in Israel." ISA 5–17032-גל digital page 209. A very similar letter was sent to the prime minister by residents of the village of Qallansawe. ISA 5–17032-גל digital page 203.

44. Dor 1965a.

45. Wolf 1965. The article contends that, by his own admission, Jiryis continued to pursue ends that the Supreme Court ruled undermined the existence of the State of Israel and, consequently, the district commander's order against Jiryis was legitimate.

46. Dor 1965b.

47. See Pas 2020.

48. Sabri Geries [Jiryis] to Nathan Yellin-Mor, April 7, 1965, National Library of Israel Archives ARC. 4 * 1722 02 199.

49. The term *muwatin* might be rendered "citizen" or "compatriot." I suggest here "compatriot" because of the Arab League context of the book, linking the Arabs of Israel to Arabs beyond, but "citizen" is also a reasonable translation. The book's cover page does not mention Jiryis's name. His name appears only on the title page, which includes the following lines beneath the book's title: "a translation of the book 'The Arabs in Israel,' published in the occupied region in Hebrew, written by an Arab compatriot [*al-muwatin al-'arabi*] who lived the persecution and oppression in the Jews' state the lawyer 'Sabri Jiryis.'" S. Jiryis 1967b.

50. 'Al ha-Mishmar 1967.

51. Hirst 1968.

52. Ha-Tsofe 1968; La-Merhav 1968; 'Al ha-Mishmar 1969; ha-Tsofe 1969a; Priel 1969a. On the "Night of Grenades," see also Feron 1968.

53. Priel 1969b; ha-Tsofe 1969b.

54. See Davar 1969.

55. Reicher 1969.

56. Kedar 1970; La-Merhav 1970.

57. F. Jiryis 2022, 149–53.

58. S. Jiryis 1966; S. Jiryis 1967a; S. Jiryis 1968.

59. S. Jiryis 2016a, 1–2.

60. Ma'ariv 1971a.

61. Davar 1971.

62. Ma'ariv 1971b. The same three—Hussein, Darwish, and Jiryis—were cited a few days later in Davar, which noted that Jiryis had left Israel initially to Paris ostensibly to seek "therapy" (*ripuy*) but then went on to Beirut. Dor 1971.

63. Halabi 2017, 127 n. 1. After beginning the previous year as a volunteer, by 1970 Hussein was earning "a meager and irregular income doing odd jobs of translation for the PLO and for the Arab League offices in New York." Boullata and Ghossein 1979, 41–42.

64. The article noted that Jiryis's *The Arabs in Israel* had been translated "by terrorist organizations" into English and French and thus "used as propaganda against Israel." *Ma'ariv* also noted that Jiryis had recently published a series of articles in the newspaper *al-Ahram* about the situation of the Arabs in Israel "to prepare the ground" for his joining the PNC. *Ma'ariv* 1971c.

65. Waxman 1971.

66. F. Jiryis 2022, 133.

67. F. Jiryis 2022, 138, 147.

68. F. Jiryis 2022, 146–47.

69. The list of the four al-Ard figures to be "sent away" (*yurhaq*) to other cities—Saleh Baransa from Taybeh to Beit She'an, Jiryis from Haifa to Safed, Mansour Qardush from Nazareth to Arad, and Habib Qahwaji from Haifa to Tiberias—is found in ISA 5–17032-גל digital page 92. (Most of this file remains censored by the IDF.) Jiryis was caught in Nazareth, in violation of his Safed house arrest. See "Mahatsit ha-Tomhim 'al Reshimat 'al Ard' Bitlu Hatimoteyhem," *Davar*, found in ISA 17032 / 14—גל.

70. S. Jiryis 2016a, 21.

71. S. Jiryis 2016a, 21.

72. Jiryis would ultimately write two volumes of what was presumably meant to be a three-volume Arabic work on the history of Zionism: S. Jiryis 1977a; S. Jiryis 1986.

73. S. Jiryis 2016b, 12.

74. S. Jiryis 2016b, 12–13.

75. S. Jiryis 2016b, 39.

76. Elmessiri would later write an eight-volume Arabic encyclopedia on Jews, Judaism, and Zionism.

77. Elmessiri 1976.

78. Despite these many points of correspondence, Elmessiri noted that not all Hasidim supported Zionism as a result of Zionism's secularism. However, Elmessiri argued, Hasidim gradually changed their view, especially after the establishment of Israel. In fact, many Hasidim have even joined the political militant extreme, he contended.

79. Namely, Fateh, the Palestinian National Front, the Democratic Front for the Liberation of Palestine, al-Sa'iqa, the Palestinian Liberation Army, the Popular Front for the Liberation of Palestine, the Popular Front for the Liberation of Palestinian-General Command, the Arab Liberation Front, the Palestinian Popular Struggle Front, and the Abu Nidal Group.

80. ISA 6–1652-אח digital page 21. This list was replicated in a Dutch pamphlet, *De Grondslagen van de PLO*, published by Centrum voor Informatie en Documentatie Israel, June 1977. On page 28, "Dr. Sabri Jerays" is listed as "Lid van de Palestijnse Nationale Raad" (a member of the Palestine National Council). ISA 8–1652-אח digital page 130.

81. Gwertzman 1976a.

82. Gwertzman 1976c.

83. Kornberg 1978.

84. Waskow 1976.

85. Waskow 1976. I asked Jiryis if he remembered whether Waskow was quoting him or Sartawi. Jiryis responded: "No. I don't remember. But, most probably, it should be Sartawi. He used to talk too much [as I came to learn from conversations with Jiryis, he uses "too much" to mean "a lot"] about 'peace.' I didn't." Communication by WhatsApp, October 4, 2021.

86. Jiryis explained to the *New York Times* that because he could not use his Israeli passport as a PLO representative, Sudan had offered to provide him with a Sudanese passport. The Sudanese officials mistakenly recorded his place of birth as Sudan and Jiryis simply copied the details on the passport when he applied for his visa. See Gwertzman 1976b.

87. ISA 6–1652-חצ digital page 105. Benjamin Navon to Moshe Raviv, February 1, 1977. Navon notes in the memo that his unnamed source gathered this information from Norton Mezvinsky, a former executive director of the American Council for Judaism.

88. The Anti-Defamation League accused the Quaker-founded American Friends Service Committee of having become a "mouthpiece" for the PLO because of its invitation to Jiryis. *New York Times* 1977b. Zev Furst of the ADL penned a memorandum to Arnold Forster, the organization's general counsel, about these meetings, and the memo was shared with the ADL regional offices, community relations committees, and Jewish Federation offices. Furst wrote, "For us in the ADL, our position is clear. We are opposed to meetings with the Palestinian Liberation Organization, and we will refuse to attend any meetings in the future. The goal of the PLO in the meetings is propaganda—to lead Americans to believe the PLO is a moderate, peace-minded movement which is going to the extraordinary length of meeting with representative American Jews in an effort to connect finally to Israel. Its second purpose is to soften the American government refusal to meet with PLO representatives. We must not permit anyone to be deluded. The PLO peace campaign is a fraud—from beginning to end." ISA 5–1652-חצ digital page 217.

89. *New York Times* 1977a. At least initially Israeli officials feared that Jiryis would be permitted to return to the US. See the December 1, 1976, Israeli Foreign Ministry telegram warning that "Jiryis will return to Washington within a month in order to serve as head of the PLO office." ISA 5–1652-חצ digital page 238.

90. November 24, 1976, in ISA 4–1652-חצ digital pages 3–7. In a closed press conference on November 22, the State Department spokesman insisted that there was no "substantive contact" between the US officials and PLO representatives. The journalists at the conference noticed the spokesman's use of "substantive," which they regarded as a newly introduced qualifier of "contact" and suspected that this reflected a loosening of US policy refusing to engage with the PLO; the spokesman insisted it did not. See ISA 4–1652-חצ, pages 16–45.

91. *Time* 1976. A transcription of this article is found in ISA 5–1652-חצ digital page 218.

Part II: Studying the Enemy

1. Al-Abid 1966, 7.

2. Al-Abid 1966, 7.

Chapter Four: *Zionist Colonialism in Palestine:* Zionism and European Imperialism

1. This chapter is based on Gribetz 2018a.

2. Shukairy 1966, 31.

3. Harkabi 1979, 110, 116. In the original 1964 version, the Arabic phrase used was *waʿad Balfur* (Balfour's promise), while in 1968, when the Covenant was revised, the phrase was changed to *tasrih Balfur* (Balfour's declaration).

4. For a facsimile of the letter, see the opening page of Stein 1983.

5. See Yezid Sayigh 1997, 71–114.

6. Yezid Sayigh 1997, 141–42.

7. On whether to categorize the PLO-Jordanian conflict in 1970–71 as a "civil war," see Nevo 2008.

8. Sirriyeh 2000, 80.

9. Mishal writes, "The separation of the West Bank from Jordanian control thus undermined the temporary political arrangements that had been the basis for coexistence" between the Palestinians and the Hashemites. Mishal 1978, 116–17. On Jordan's initial ambivalence toward the PLO and the outbreak of political and ultimately violent tensions between them, see Massad 2001, 236–50.

10. On various Israeli conceptions and uses of the Balfour Declaration upon its jubilee, see Podeh 2017.

11. See, e.g., Bar-Siman-Tov 2014, 63; Maoz 2013, 31; Caplan 2011, 18; Tessler 2009, 437; Kimmerling 2008, 239; Dowty 2008, 122; Ben-Ami 2007, 1. In the past, I too have omitted this sentence. See, e.g., Gribetz 2013, 143; Gribetz 2017, 91–92.

12. Here I use Leila S. Kadi's translation of the 1968 Covenant. Kadi 1969, 140. For the different versions and translations, see Harkabi 1979, 107–18.

13. Shukairy took the task of composing the Covenant most seriously. He recalled in his memoirs that "more than once I spent two or three nights over one single word or phrase, as I was facing generations of Palestinians who read between the lines more than they read the lines themselves." Cited in Harkabi 1979, 9–10.

14. My emphasis.

15. Shukairy 1966, 31.

16. In this task Shukairy found allies in American Jewish anti-Zionists such as Rabbi Elmer Berger and the American Council for Judaism. See below.

17. The Arabic reads *nahnu al-shaʿb al-ʿArabi al-Filastini.* "Al-Mithaq al-Watani al-Filastini," 1964, 1, http://www.palestine-studies.org/sites/default/files/uploads/files/28-5-1964b.pdf, accessed February 19, 2018; Harkabi 1979, 107–8.

18. This book appears to have been written originally in English and only subsequently translated into Arabic by Abdul Wahhab al-Kayyali. F. Sayegh 1965b. Yoav Di-Capua offers an excellent reading of this book, though he seems accidentally to conflate IPS with the PLO Research Center. See Di-Capua 2018, 190–92.

19. F. Sayegh 1965a, 11–12.

20. F. Sayegh 1965a, 12–15. According to Charles Anderson, ʿIzzat Darwaza argued similarly that the primary concern of the British was to "shor[e] up the British regional position" and thus, when useful, as in 1939 when they issued another White Paper that limited Jewish immigration to Palestine, the British "strove to provide the public appearance of placating Palestinian demands rather than actually meeting them." C. W. Anderson 2013, 1125.

21. F. Sayegh 1965a, 40.

22. A. Sayegh 1966a, 34. My translation. The corresponding phrase in the later English edition refers to "this collaboration between the Zionists and imperialists." A. Sayegh 1970b, 26.

23. A. Sayegh 1970b, 26–27; A. Sayegh 1966a, 35.

24. Antonius 1938, 164–83.

25. Antonius 1938, 179.

26. Antonius 1938, 267.

27. Al-Abid 1971, 27–28. The Arabic is even stronger: *mufawadat Husayn-McMahon allati ta'ahhadat* [pledged, committed, or obligated itself] *Britaniya bi-natijatiha bi-l-i'tiraf rasmiyyan bi-l-istiqlal al-duwal al-'Arabiyya.* Al-Abid 1969c, 23–24.

28. Argument 2 is addressed below.

29. Al-Abid 1971, 27–29; al-Abid 1969c, 23–24. Argument 8 is a quote from Rizk 1968, 65. Argument 9 is that "the British Government, on several occasions, issued statements which indicate that its position regarding the Balfour promise was ambiguous." Al-Abid identified four such statements. As these do not bear directly on this chapter, they are not discussed here.

30. Recognizing this implication, Bligh argues that it "explains the PLO's frequent references to" the Balfour Declaration, "and [King] Hussein's infrequent ones." Bligh 2004, 21.

31. The correspondence remains part of Hashemite self-legitimization in Jordan. Abdullah II of Jordan 2012, ch. 1.

32. See Mishal 1978, 66–73; Braizat 1999, 123–30.

33. Institute for Palestine Studies, http://www.palestine-studies.org/sites/default/files /uploads/files/28-5-1964b.pdf, accessed March 21, 2018. My translation. The phrase is also translated as "regional sovereignty." See Sadat Hasan's rendering in Harkabi 1979, 111.

34. A. Sayegh 1966b. I am grateful to Yezid Sayigh for pointing me to this book, which, as he put it, made his uncle Anis a persona non grata in Jordan. I translate *qadiyya* as "question," following the Center's own translations of the term. Translations from this book are mine.

35. A. Sayegh 1966b, 8.

36. Sayegh cited Faisal's claim, during the Paris Peace Conference, that he asked his father for the text of the correspondence but that he did not receive a reply. A. Sayegh 1966b, 55.

37. A. Sayegh 1966b, 56.

38. A. Sayegh 1966b, 57.

39. A. Sayegh 1966b, 57.

40. Sayegh identified Kedourie as "the Zionist author, Iraqi in origin." A. Sayegh 1966b, 64.

41. A. Sayegh 1966b, 123. A future study might compare Sayegh's presentation of Abdullah to Shlaim's in his important later work on Zionist-Hashemite relations. See Shlaim 1988; Shlaim 1998.

42. A. Sayegh 1966b, 123.

43. A. Sayegh 1966b, 147–48.

44. A. Sayegh 1966b, 247–48.

45. A. Sayegh 1966b, 248–49.

46. A. Sayegh 1966b, 249–50. Use of the inverted commas surrounding Israel was a convention Sayegh followed, implying the artificial, illegitimate nature of the state. He continued using the convention when he took over the PLO Research Center. Sabri Jiryis told me that when he was later appointed director general of the Center, he issued a directive terminating its use. S. Jiryis 2015; Gribetz 2016, 264 n. 47.

47. In his memoirs, Sayegh acknowledged the anger that this book elicited among the Hashemite rulers of Jordan. According to Sayegh, this book (and all others Sayegh wrote) were banned in Jordan. Sayegh himself was personally banned from entering Jordan from 1966 through 1982. A. Sayegh 2006, 178.

48. Rizk 1968.

49. Al-Abid 1971, 28; al-Abid 1969c, 23.

50. See B. Morris 2003.

51. Clark 2004. Kanafani also published a book with the PLO Research Center during this period, on Zionist literature. See Kanafani 1967. Kanafani, as noted above, was assassinated two years later, in 1972.

52. Yahia 1970, 16–17.

53. Yahia 1970, 17–18. I continue to discuss the role of this assertion in PLO discourse in the chapters that follow.

54. Yahia 1970, 18–19.

55. Yahia 1970, 19–20.

56. On the waning years of pan-Arabism, see Ajami 1978. On debates over pan-Arabism within Fateh and the PLO during these years, see Steinberg 2016a, 197–201. At the third Fateh Congress in 1971, Steinberg notes, pan-Arabist circles "urged that the organization's ranks be opened not only to Palestinians but to any and all Arabs," but this effort was ultimately unsuccessful. Steinberg 2016a, 200. Rashid Khalidi argues that "while the demoralizing rout of 1967 seriously tarnished the prestige of Egypt and its charismatic president, the war did not sound the death knell of Arab nationalism as a political force." Rather, the war "simply reinforced and consecrated a preexisting, underlying trend among nominally Arab nationalist regimes," in which "narrow nation-state nationalism . . . increasingly became these regimes' primary guiding principle, seconded by powerful considerations of regime security." R. Khalidi 2012, 264–65. See also Gerges 2012.

57. F. Sayegh 1970, 25–26.

58. F. Sayegh 1970, 37. Emphasis in the original.

Chapter Five: *The Zionist Idea:* Judaism, Christianity, and the Arabic Translation of Zionism

1. This chapter is based on Gribetz 2016.

2. A. Sayegh 1970a.

3. Hertzberg 1959.

4. In a review of the book in the PLO's journal in 1972, Sadik al-Azm noted that "for some reason," neither the original English edition nor its compiler were mentioned in the Arabic. Sadik al-Azm, *Shu'un Filastiniyya* 9 (May 1972): 152.

5. See, e.g., references to the PLO's "secular nationalism" in Mishal and Sela 2006, 15; Cubert 1997, 167; Abu-Amr 1994, ix; Armajani 2012, ch. 3; Eisenberg and Caplan 2010, 171.

6. Steinberg 2008, 204.

7. Steinberg 2008, 207; Steinberg 1989, 41.

8. See, e.g., Zelkovitz 2012; Frisch 2005.

9. For examples of Palestinian Christian liberation theology, which has proliferated since the First Intifada, see Ateek 1989; Raheb 1995; Raheb 2014. For a helpful review of this literature, see Robson 2010. Scholars have also investigated the history of Palestine's Christians during the British Mandate period. Robson 2011; Haiduc-Dale 2013.

10. See, e.g., Frisch 2005, 326.

11. Owen 2010, 223.

12. A. Sayegh 1970a, 7.

13. Hertzberg later added an afterword.

14. On problems in the translation, see al-Azm's review in *Shu'un Filastiniyya* 9 (May 1972): 152–54.

15. In electronic correspondence with me, Sadik al-Azm noted that, in 1970, he had prepared an introduction for this volume but the PLO leadership did not permit its inclusion.

16. Killgore 1993. On the flight and later expulsion of the Arabs of Safuriyya, see B. Morris 2004, 417.

17. A. Sayegh 2006, 35. Herzl's diaries became a key source for the PLO Research Center's assessment of Zionism. A. Sayegh 1968a. See, e.g., Razzouk 1968, 19–28.

18. Al-Abid 1969c; al-Abid 1971.

19. See the As'ad Razzuq entry in Hamada 1985, 316–17. For obituaries, see *al-Watan al-'Arabi*, March 28, 2007: 56; and "al-Mahatta al-Akhira: As'ad Razzuq al-Mufakkir al-Istithna'i," January 11, 2008.

20. Hertzberg 1959, 104.

21. Hertzberg 1959, 109–10.

22. As Shlomo Avineri argues, the nationalist thought of "traditionalists" such as Alkalai and Kalischer was "imbued with ideas derived from the general European experience," not "merely from their religious background." Avineri 1999.

23. Hertzberg 1959, 46. Emphasis in the original.

24. Razzouk likely took this narrative from Alex Bein's biography of Herzl, which he cites in *Isra'il al-Kubra* of 1968. Cf. Bein 1970, 11, 13–14. Bein notes two Jewish religious-themed anecdotes concerning Herzl.

25. Razzouk 1970b, 16.

26. Hertzberg also highlighted the political context of the 1870s: the revolt against the Ottoman Empire by Bulgarians who were supported by Russians as "Slavic brothers." Though he did not provide all of the details Hertzberg did, Razzouk acknowledged that Ben-Yehuda "tried to copy the Russian nationalist idea and the Slavist movement in calling for a Jewish nationalism on a secular, political basis." A. Sayegh 1970a, 59. Cf. Hertzberg 1959, 159.

27. Hertzberg 1959, 443.

28. A. Sayegh 1970a, 317–18.

29. A. Sayegh 1970a, 429–31.

30. Hertzberg 1959, 562. Excerpted from "Evidence Submitted to the Palestine Royal Commission, House of Lords" 1937, 9–13.

31. A. Sayegh 1970a, 434. The translators also removed Jabotinsky's claim that Palestine's Arabs represent only a small "fraction" or "branch of that [Arab] race."

32. Cf. Hertzberg 1959, 562; A. Sayegh 1970a, 434. For "hold," the translators use the term *tastaw'ab*, a verb that can mean "to contain" or "to hold," but can also mean "to uproot" or "to exterminate." As this verb is applied here both to Arabs and to Jews, it seems that the translators intended the former sense.

33. See, e.g., the answer to "Did the Zionists plan to expel the Arabs from Palestine?" in al-Abid 1969c, 98–100; al-Abid 1971, 81–82. The answer begins: "From its inception Zionism has worked towards emptying Palestine of its original inhabitants."

34. Hertzberg 1959, 17.

35. Anis Sayegh, preface to Razzouk 1968b, 7. The apparently dismissive quotation marks appear in the original. Elsewhere, in the wake of the 1967 war, Razzouk contended that Zionism is "based on the principles of religious irredentism." Razzouk 1968b, 12.

36. Razzouk 1968b, 18. Quoting Herzl 1946, 54.

37. Razzouk 1968b, 18.

38. Razzouk 1968b, 19. Citing Herzl 1946, 60.

39. Razzouk 1968b, 19.

40. Razzouk 1968b, 19.

41. Elsewhere, concerning various forms of Zionism, the terms that Sayegh and Razzouk use are *istithmar*, *istighlal*, and *ikhtizal*. See, e.g., Razzouk 1968b, 7–9.

42. Talmon 1965, 228. Cited in Razzouk 1968b, 33.

43. Talmon 1965, 287–88. Cited in Razzouk 1968b, 33–34.

44. Razzouk 1968b, 34.

45. Compare Razzouk's assertion here to that of Rabbi Abraham Isaac Kook. On Kook, see Mirsky 2014.

46. A. Sayegh 2006, 37 On his parents' deep religious faith, see A. Sayegh 2006, 21.

47. Yusif Sayigh and Sayigh 2015, 25, 52, 161.

48. A. Sayegh 2006, 21. Sayegh wrote that once his father became a refugee in Beirut, "after 1950, he founded several churches, parishes, and schools in a number of towns, villages, and suburbs close to Beirut." Moreover, he was apparently widely recognized as a leading figure in the church as "he turned down more than one offer to take over major churches outside of Lebanon, such as in Damascus, Baghdad, and Kuwait." A. Sayegh 2006, 31.

49. A. Sayegh 2006, 20–38. Sayegh suggested that because of the harsh religious and prayer requirements in his childhood home, he did not pray the following fifty years (though his wife went every Sunday to her Orthodox church). Sayegh insisted that he received a dispensation from the Evangelical pastor Fouad Bahnan in Beirut in the 1970s that his work writing on behalf of Palestine on Sundays was an acceptable alternative to prayer in the eyes of God. A. Sayegh 2006, 37–38. Sayegh also insisted that the family's religiousness did not make it closed to those outside the Presbyterian community. As evidence, Sayegh highlighted the fact that many of his father's grandchildren married non-Presbyterian partners. A. Sayegh 2006, 36.

50. A. Sayegh 2006, 38.

51. A. Sayegh 2006, 175.

52. I thank Sadik al-Azm for sharing with me that he and Razzouk were classmates at the Gerard Institute.

53. On this period in Lebanese history, see El Khazen 2000; W. W. Harris 2015, 219–31; Traboulsi 2012, 139–89. On the lessons Palestinian Christians learned from "the disaster of sectarianism in Lebanon," see Lybarger 2007, 786.

54. A. Sayegh 1970b, 10. Sayegh originally published this book in Arabic: A. Sayegh 1966a.

55. A. Sayegh 1970b, 11. On Christian participation in the 1936–39 Revolt in Palestine, see, e.g., Haiduc-Dale 2013, 146–52.

56. A. Sayegh 1970b, 11–12.

57. A. Sayegh 1970b, 12. On Arab nationalism at AUB, where Anis Sayegh studied, see B. S. Anderson 2012, 129–38.

58. Cf. Antonius 1938.

59. F. Sayegh 1967a, 3.

60. In his memoirs, Anis Sayegh wrote that he stopped reading the Bible once he left his childhood home, but his brother Fayez continued. Anis also noted that his father "would reject the Zionist claims that God's promise of the land of Palestine to the Jews was an eternal promise regardless of what the Jews did to God." Anis further wrote that while his father taught him and his siblings to distinguish between Judaism and Zionism, the father also "held the Jews responsible for many of the world's evils and believed, like many other Evangelicals, that there is no salvation for the world without the conversion of the Jews to Christianity." The father looked suspiciously at European Jews who had converted to Christianity and served as missionaries. As Sayegh wrote, his father regarded every Jew who converted to Christianity to be "a deceiver" unless proven otherwise. A. Sayegh 2006, 37–39.

61. F. Sayegh 1967a, 4.

62. See Guillaume 1956. On Guillaume, see Smith 1966. Guillaume's study was reproduced in *Christians, Zionism and Palestine: A Selection of Articles and Statements on the Religion and Political Aspects of the Palestine Problem* 1970, 3–8.

63. F. Sayegh 1967a, 6. In an earlier volume by Sami Hadawi, the question "How does the 'Divine Promise' apply to present-day Israel?" is answered similarly, followed by: "The 'miracle of Israel's restoration' in 1948, was not 'God's will'—as the Zionists allege—but was an *unchristian* act of uprooting the Moslem and Christian inhabitants of the Holy Land." Emphasis mine. Hadawi 1961a, 11–12.

64. F. Sayegh 1967a, 6.

65. F. Sayegh 1967a, 7. Compare this claim to that of David Ben-Gurion, Yizhak Ben-Zvi, and other Zionists that Palestine's contemporary Arab masses (especially rural Muslims) were descendants of ancient Jews. See Zerubavel 2008; Gribetz 2014, 123–26. This theory has been repopularized in the work of Shlomo Sand and has been embraced by certain Palestinian Christian thinkers, including Mitri Raheb. Sand 2009; Raheb 2014, 11–14.

66. F. Sayegh 1967a, 7–8. See Joshua Starr, "Khazars," *Universal Jewish Encyclopedia*, vol. 6 (New York: Universal Jewish Encyclopedia Co., 1942), 375–78. The theory of Khazar conversion to Judaism as the ethnic source of significant portions of Ashkenazic Jewry has been the subject of scholarly and polemical debates for decades. See, e.g., Stampfer 2013. This theory emerged here and there in PLO Research Center publications. For instance, in recounting Israel's declaration of statehood, Bassam Bishuti wrote: "At one minute past midnight of 14 May 1948, Ben Gurion, the Kazar Jew, stood in a museum in Tel Aviv and declared the establishment of the Jewish State of Israel." Bishuti 1969, 108. On the role of the Khazar theory of Ashkenazic origins in Arab responses to Zionism, see Harkabi 1972.

67. F. Sayegh 1967a, 8.

68. F. Sayegh 1967a, 9.

69. F. Sayegh 1967a, 10. Cf. the June 18, 1967, memorandum of four Beirut-based Christian theologians who cite "the universal vocation of the Jews." "What Is Required of the Christian Faith Concerning the Palestine Problem," in *Christians, Zionism and Palestine* 1970, 75.

70. F. Sayegh 1967a, 11.

71. Razzouk was especially keen to distance Palestinian nationalism from antisemitism. See below in my assessment of 1970a.

72. F. Sayegh 1967a, 12.

73. F. Sayegh 1967a, 13. In accounting for the "outburst of anti-Semitic sentiment in the general Arab literature on the conflict" during this period, Nissim Rejwan argues that "we must take into account the impact of Christian religious teachings on the authors of these books." Rejwan 2000, 11.

74. I discuss the PLO's interest in such Jewish Reformers below.

75. Parkes 1947, 8.

76. Razzouk 1970c, 10.

77. Razzouk 1970c, 9.

78. Razzouk 1970c, 24.

79. Razzouk 1970c, 10–11. Elsewhere, Razzouk points to Parkes's successful pursuit of the financial support of other wealthy Jews as well, including the Warburg family and Simon Marks. See Razzouk 1970c, 18–19.

80. Razzouk 1970c, 28.

81. Razzouk 1970c, 32.

82. The charge that someone's ideology concerning Zionism is actually driven by that person's economic self-interest has a long and diverse history; indeed, it might be understood as a trope in debates concerning the Arab-Israeli conflict. For an early precedent, see Gribetz 2014, 231–32.

83. Razzouk 1970c, 31.

84. The problem of Evangelical Christian support for Zionism was one that continued to concern Anis Sayegh for decades to come. In his memoirs, published in 2006, Anis Sayegh contended that American Evangelical Christians who have embraced Zionism subscribe to a distorted and false conception of Christianity. True Evangelicals reject Zionism, insisted Sayegh, and he offered a list of departed Arab Evangelical opponents of Zionism, including Emil Habibi, Al-Faris Bawlus, Emil Aghabi, Ilya Khuri, Bawlus Shahadeh, Tawfiq Sayigh, Tawfiq Kan'an, Thiyufil (Theophil) Butaji, Habib Khuri, Hana ʿAsfur, Hana Salah, Hana Bulis, Hana Mikhail, Khalil Tawtah, Sami Hadawi, Shibli al-Jamal, Izzat Tannous, Fayez Sayegh, Fuʾad Bahnan, Fuʾad Saba, Karim Khuri, Kamal Nassar, Matilda and Mughanam Mughanam, Musa Nassar, Nabil Khuri, Nabiha Nassar, and Yusif Sayigh. A. Sayegh 2006, 43.

85. See, e.g., Almog, Reinharz, and Shapira 1999; Novak 2015.

Chapter Six: *The Talmud and Zionism:* Rejecting Antisemitism in the Name of Palestinian Liberation

1. This chapter is based on Gribetz 2018b.

2. For more on his background, see the "Asʿad Razzuq" entry in Hamada 1985, 316–17.

3. On Nuwayhid, see the biographical information about his daughter, Bayan Nuwayhed al-Hout, "Bayan Nuwayhed Al-Hout (1937–)" 2023.

4. Nuwayhid 1967, 106–7. Cited in Razzouk 1970a, 25.

5. Nuwayhid 1967, 106–7. Cited in Razzouk 1970a, 25.

6. Razzouk 1963.

7. The Soncino Press began publishing its first edition of an English translation of the Talmud between 1935 and 1948 (with an index published in 1952). The second edition, including the index, was published between 1952 and 1961. The publication history can be found in Razzouk 1970a, 12–13.

8. When he arrived in New York to promote the new edition in May 1961, S. M. Bloch, the managing director of the Soncino Press of London, explained that "we are presenting this new edition of the Talmud . . . at a time when the world thirsts for traditional values; when present-day members of the Jewish faith need to know and understand the basic philosophies of their forefathers. It is our modest hope that by scrupulously translating this revered repository of Hebraic knowledge and ideas into the language so many know best, we will help fill this void." See "Soncino Press Issues New 18-Volume Edition of English Translation of Talmud," *Jewish Telegraphic Agency Daily News Bulletin* 28:88, May 8, 1961, 6. This edition, as we see here, was of interest not only to "present-day members of the Jewish faith."

9. On the Damascus affair, see J. Frankel 1997; Florence 2004.

10. E.g., H. Faris 1890; H. Faris 1891.

11. On late nineteenth- and early twentieth-century Arabic writing about the Talmud, see Gribetz 2010. On blood libels in Egypt in the nineteenth century, see J. Landau 1961. On mid-twentieth-century Arab discussions of the Talmud, see also Harkabi 1972, 204, 243, 248, 271–76.

12. Achcar 2011, 90.

13. On al-Azm, see Kassab 2010, 74–81.

14. Al-Azm 2011, 62.

15. Al-Azm 2011, 63.

16. Al-Azm 2011, 63–64.

17. Razzouk also listed two books that he found on microfilm in the PLO Research Center's library: N. al-Khuri Nassar 1911 and Jabbour 1923. I have not found the latter book listed in library catalogues.

18. Having apparently relied on a note about this book found in the journal *al-Hilal*, Landau mistakenly deemed it "an apologia on the laws of the Talmud." J. M. Landau 1969b, 101. The title is sometimes translated *The Awaited Treasure* but I follow Stillman here, who renders it *The Guarded Treasure*. Stillman 2005, 104.

19. Ibn Hazm 1960; Ibn ʿAbbas n/d. On the latter, see Perlmann 1964.

20. Harb 1947.

21. Al-Tunisi 1951.

22. Some of these sources are Arabic translations from other languages, but others were originally written in Arabic. For example, Malul 1911. On this book, see Gribetz 2014, 221–32.

23. Razzouk 1970a, 111–23. On the composition of the Talmud, Razzouk followed Schechter in presenting the chain of transmission and development from Soferim to Zugot to Tannaim to Amoraim and finally to Saboraim. Razzouk 1970a, 125–48.

24. Razzouk 1970a, 149–76.

25. Razzouk 1970a, 177–207.

26. On "intellectual seriousness" as Fayez Sayegh's answer to the supposed "crisis of Arab thought" in the 1950s, see Di-Capua 2018, 77.

27. Razzouk 1970a, 15.

28. Razzouk 1970a, 15.

29. Barry Rubin has argued that "whereas Palestinians and other Arab, Soviet, and Third World audiences might not mind the expression of anti-Jewish sentiments, such attitudes would be costly among Western, Jewish, and Israeli listeners. Thus, while anti-Jewish arguments were discouraged in public and in English, they were less disadvantageous—and could even be useful—in Arabic and in private discussions of sentiment." B. M. Rubin 1993, 3. This PLO Research Center text, written in Arabic (and not translated into other languages), defies Rubin's generalization and suggests more complexity or diversity in PLO views. Rubin at times acknowledges the lack of PLO unanimity in this regard: "there was no one consistent line in the PLO about Jews but rather a set of often contradictory views. Those in PLO headquarters, the West Bank, Gaza, Jordan, and other Arab states all had different interests and somewhat different perspectives." B. M. Rubin 1993, 7.

30. Razzouk 1970a, 9–10.

31. Kanafani 1967, 28; Kanafani 2022, 17.

32. The Research Center was not alone in its interest in the question of the relationship between Judaism and Zionism. This was and remains a topic of interest and historical investigation in the fields of Jewish studies and Israel studies. The modern Jewish philosopher David Novak has recently argued that "Zionism needs to be thought of and formulated as a specific manifestation of Judaism in general in and for the modern world." Having found Herzl's political Zionism and Ahad Ha-'am's cultural Zionism (both purportedly "secular") to be problematic, Novak contends that "it would seem, the only cogent kind of Zionism to be developed is 'religious,' stemming from a [sic] some kind of theological-political Jewish worldview." See, inter alia, Almog, Reinharz, and Shapira 1999; Salmon 2002; Novak 2015, 84–85.

33. This article was printed in a journal called Issues, which was published by the American Council for Judaism (ACJ). As we will see in the following chapter, the PLO Research Center had a close relationship with the ACJ, though, as this instance demonstrates, PLO researchers did not always agree with what ACJ writers argued about Judaism.

34. Singer 1959, 43–44. Cited in Razzouk 1970a, 211.

35. Razzouk 1970a, 211.

36. Razzouk 1970a, 212.

37. It is clear that he was using the Soncino here because the page number cited, 427, is that of this English translation. The Zionist Idea was published in 1959, two years before the new edition of the Soncino.

38. Literally: making more descendants.

39. The Talmudic text uses the term osek bi-friya u-rviya, which might be rendered literally as "engaging in being fruitful and multiplying." The Soncino edition translates this phrase as "propagation of the race." Razzouk added the qualifier "Jewish" to the Soncino's phrase "the race."

40. Razzouk 1970a, 212–13.

41. Razzouk 1970a, 213.

42. Razzouk 1970a, 214.

43. Razzouk 1970a, 215.

44. Razzouk 1970a, 215.

45. Razzouk 1970a, 216. Here, Razzouk was translating from the English translation of Hess's Rome and Jerusalem. Razzouk did not provide the page from the Soncino edition of tractate

Sanhedrin. The Talmudic text reads: "Rab said: The world was created only on David's account. Samuel said: On Moses' account; R. Johanan said: For the sake of the Messiah." Sanhedrin 98a (Soncino translation).

46. Razzouk 1970a, 217.

47. It is clear that he turned to the Soncino again here because he cites the source in the Soncino pagination: "Ketubbot 110b, p. 712."

48. Razzouk 1970a, 218–19.

49. For an excellent recent study of Pinsker's nationalist pamphlet, see Volovici 2017.

50. As Leo Strauss wrote, "I remind you of the motto of the most impressive statement of political Zionism: Pinsker's *Autoemancipation*, written in the eighties of the last century. Pinsker's motto is: 'If I am not for myself, who will I be for? And if not now, when?' That is: do not expect help from others; and do not postpone your decision. This is a quotation from a well-known Jewish book, *The Sayings of the Fathers*; but in the original, something else is said which Pinsker omitted: 'But if I am only for myself, what am I?' The omission of these words constitutes the definition of pureblooded political Zionism." Strauss 1997a, 318. Three years later, Strauss repeated this observation, contending that what he called "strictly political Zionism" involved "a profound modification of the traditional Jewish hopes—a modification arrived at through a break with these hopes. For the motto of his pamphlet Pinsker chose these words of Hillel: 'If I am not for myself, who will be for me? And if not now, when?' He omitted the sentence which forms the center of Hillel's statement: 'And if I am only for myself, what am I?'" Strauss 1997b, 142.

51. Razzouk 1970a, 221.

52. Razzouk 1970a, 221.

53. Razzouk 1970a, 221–22.

54. Razzouk 1970a, 222.

55. Razzouk 1970a, 222.

56. Razzouk 1970a, 223–24; Bein 1970, 5.

57. Razzouk 1970a, 224; Bein 1970, 13–14.

58. Razzouk 1970a, 293–94.

59. Razzouk 1970a, 15. Compare to Ahmad Baha al-Din's 1965 *Isra'iliyyat*, in which the Egyptian author wrote that "if the Arabs nowadays find themselves the victims of a fanatical Zionist-Jewish aggression, they are thereby only paying the price of centuries of racial European bigotry that reached its peak with Hitler's crimes in the middle of the 20th century." Cited in Rejwan 2000, 61–62.

60. See, e.g., Youssef Zia al-Khalidi's 1899 letter to Rabbi Zadoc Kahn, who passed the letter on to Theodor Herzl. Al-Khalidi, challenging Zionist plans for Palestine on a variety of grounds, began his note by asserting his friendship toward the Jews and Judaism. "All those who know me well," wrote al-Khalidi, "know that I do not make a distinction between Jews, Christians and Muslims," citing "your prophet Malachi" that "we all have a common Father." It was al-Khalidi's sympathy with the Jews that, he explained, permitted him to write with candor against Zionism. Folder H197, Central Zionist Archives, Jerusalem.

61. Note that al-Khalidi also contended that his opposition to Zionism was in part motivated by his concern for Jews, especially those in the Ottoman Empire who, he feared, would be harmed by Zionism.

62. The full text of the English translation of Arafat's speech can be found in "Palestine at the United Nations" 1975.

63. The charge was recently revived in response to Palestinian president and PLO chairman Mahmoud Abbas's April 2018 speech before the Palestine National Council in Ramallah. See Aderet 2018. Barry Rubin challenged the assumptions of this debate, contending that "the conventional debate has been about finding the PLO guilty or innocent of antisemitism, while the real issue is to clarify the PLO's attitude toward the Zionism/Judaism, Israeli/Jewish dichotomies." B. M. Rubin 1993, 2–3.

64. Patterson 2011. Patterson is a prolific writer on antisemitism and the Holocaust; see Wiesel and Patterson 1991; Patterson 1992; Patterson 1999; Patterson 2006; and Patterson 2014, among other works.

65. Of the PLO chairman, Patterson also writes, "Like his Nazi-Mufti mentor, in the words of Efraim Karsh, Arafat was a 'bigoted megalomaniac . . . blinded by Jew hatred.'" Patterson 2011, 239, 243–44.

66. Fishman 2016, 98.

67. As Fishman puts it, "When we consider the rhetoric of the anti-Zionists, particularly of the Palestinian Arabs, it becomes evident that in their choice of terminology and language directed at the outside world they have endeavored to conceal their true purpose, which is not peace, but politicide." Fishman 2016, 99.

68. On the diversity within the PLO, see Yezid Sayigh 1997.

69. Compare to Di-Capua's assessment of Lutfi al-Khuli's insistence on "separating the Jewish question from Zionism." Di-Capua 2018, 41.

70. Already in 1961, Palestinian scholar and publicist Sami Hadawi (who would go on to publish works both with IPS and the PLO Research Center) argued that antisemitism benefits not Arabs nor individual Jews but the Zionist movement. See Hadawi 1961b.

71. This sort of work conducted by the PLO Research Center defies Barry Rubin's assertion, in 1993, that there has never "been—despite its importance for the organization—anything approaching a serious study of Judaism or Zionism [by the PLO], in part because these issues pose irreconcilable problems for the PLO's doctrine and goals." B. M. Rubin 1993, 7.

72. Yezid Sayigh wrote, "The decision in 1966 by the director of the PLO Research Centre, Anis Sayigh, to conduct academic research on Israeli society, economy, polity, and international relations and to disseminate the results in public, the first time an Arab institution had done so, represented a direct challenge to prevailing attitudes and broke an important psychological barrier." Yezid Sayigh 1997, 697 n. 43. The "psychological barrier" was perhaps even higher as it related to the twin terrors of Zionism and to the Talmud. The PLO Research Center's willingness, in these highly sensitive years, to engage with these subjects was all the more remarkable.

Chapter Seven: *The American Council for Judaism: American Jewish Anti-Zionism*

1. This chapter is based on Gribetz 2017.

2. The classic work on the history of Reform Judaism is Meyer 1995. The Pittsburgh Platform also appears in Meyer and Plaut 2000, 197–99.

3. In Gribetz 2017, I note a fascinating, if apparently unconnected, Late Ottoman precedent that may represent the starting point in the history of Palestinian Arab interest in Reform Judaism and a British Mandate–era Palestinian historiographical work that makes related, though somewhat different, arguments about the nonnational status of the Jews.

4. Of the process of crafting the Covenant, Shukairy recalled in his memoirs, "I wrote, altered, erased and changed the order of the articles until I formulated the 'National Covenant' and the 'Fundamental Law' of the Palestine Liberation Organization. I invested all of my experience of the Palestinian problem, both on the Arab and international planes, in their composition, taking into consideration the circumstances under which the Palestinian people were living." Cited in Harkabi 1979, 9–10.

5. The official English translation of the 1968 version renders the phrase *din samawi* simply as "religion," though "revealed religion" or "divine religion" are more precise. The PLO's translation is found in Kadi 1969, 137–42, and reproduced as appendix B(1) in Harkabi 1979, 113–18. Shukairy's original draft was modified before it was first adopted in 1964. Shukairy initially described Judaism as a revealed religion "worthy of esteem and respect"; this final phrase was removed in the adopted version. See Harkabi 1979, 78.

6. In a different context, I remarked on this similarity. Gribetz 2013, 143.

7. Shukairy 1966, 112. If Shukairy viewed the phrase "Rabbi Mrs." an oxymoron, he was not alone. At the time he gave this speech, in 1963, no major Jewish religious movement ordained women rabbis. See Nadell 2019. Shukairy's error, though, was in assuming that only rabbis—and therefore only men—were "people who know the Bible."

8. Adler 1878.

9. Shukairy 1966, 113.

10. "Unless," added Shukairy, "Mrs. Golda Meir comes here at the next session and presents herself as a Rabbi Mrs. Golda Meir, and we are prepared to accept her in that capacity." Shukairy 1966, 113.

11. Shukairy resigned in December 1967. He was initially replaced by Yahya Hammouda, who attempted to unite the PLO and the guerrilla groups, but these efforts were unsuccessful. By February 1969, Arafat was elected chairman of the new Executive Committee. See Rubenberg 1983, 6–7. On the post-1967 transformations in the balance of power between the Arab states (and their PLO) and the fedayeen association with the Palestinian resistance movement, see Farsoun and Aruri 2006, 180–87.

12. Al-Abid 1969c; al-Abid 1971.

13. The English version has 194 pages and a three-and-a-half-page "Selected Bibliography."

14. Al-Abid 1969c, 8. This line does not appear in Sayegh's foreword to the English edition.

15. Al-Abid 1969c, 7. This explanation appears in the English foreword as well, though there Sayegh writes simply of "Zionists" rather than "the Zionist enemy." Al-Abid 1971, 13.

16. Al-Abid 1969c, 7. Note that Sayegh's English foreword does not include this critical remark about Arabs' "sentimentality" in debates. Al-Abid 1971, 13.

17. Al-Abid 1969c, 8. Cf. al-Abid 1971, 13.

18. Al-Abid 1971, 37–38; al-Abid 1969c, 38. Note that the English renders *sha'b* as "a nation and a people," an acknowledgment of the difficulty in translating the Arabic term.

19. Al-Abid 1971, 38; al-Abid 1969c, 39. The mistaken year appears in both Arabic and English versions. Note that in the Arabic, the phrase "no longer" is not included. The quote is rendered: "We the Jews do not consider ourselves a nation (*umma*) but rather a religious sect (*ta'ifa diniyya*). But al-Abid did include the phrase "no longer" in the second instance (discussed below) and so I presume that the absence of the phrase here was not purposeful.

20. Al-Abid 1971, 41; al-Abid 1969c, 44.

21. I say "implied" here because the Zionist Organization as such had not yet been founded in 1885, though there were already a number of groups and thinkers identified in retrospect as "proto-Zionists" who were active in propaganda and colonization efforts by this time. On the notion of "proto-Zionists" or "forerunners to Zionism," see Katz 1996. For a more recent introductory work on these individuals and groups, see, e.g., Engel 2009, 1–52.

22. For the text of the Columbus Platform, see Meyer and Plaut 2000, 199–203.

23. On the Late Ottoman case of Muhammad Ruhi al-Khalidi, see Gribetz 2014, 39–92; Gribetz 2015, 48–64; al-Khalidi 2020. On the Mandate-era case of Sa'adi Bsisu, see Osheroff 2014, 85–87; Bsisu 1945.

24. For a study devoted to the early years of the ACJ, see Kolsky 1990.

25. For Berger's biographical details, I rely on the obituary composed by his friend and colleague Norton Mezvinsky. See Mezvinsky 1996, 25. See also Ross 2011.

26. Berger first served in Temple Beth Jacob in Pontiac (1932–36) and then in Temple Beth El in Flint (1936–42). See "Berger, Elmer" entry in Carmin Karpman 1978, 81.

27. Of course, by the 1930s, the faculty at HUC were not of one mind concerning Zionism, so Berger was certainly exposed as well to Zionist views during his studies there. See Sarna 1999. See also Meyer 1983.

28. Berger 1942.

29. On the defection of anti-Zionist Reform rabbis from the Central Conference of American Rabbis after the CCAR's vote to advocate for a Jewish army in Palestine in 1942 and on the founding of the ACJ, see Kolsky 1990, 42–62.

30. Berger anticipates the arguments Shlomo Sand would later publicize. Cf. Sand 2009. See Ross 2011, 182–83.

31. Berger 1945, 28.

32. Berger 1945, 40.

33. Berger 1957, 125.

34. Fischoff 1946.

35. Berger 1978, 28–29.

36. Berger 1978, 29–30. In 1975, when Sayegh was pushing the case for labeling Zionism a form of racism at the UN, he cited Berger as "an author of several profound books refuting the doctrines of Zionism." F. Sayegh 1976, 33.

37. Berger 1978, 29.

38. Berger 1978, 97.

39. Berger 1978, 117.

40. On Kombargi, see Killgore 1999. Killgore writes that the Fifth of June Society, "of which Shafiq Kombargi became the first president, developed information kits of articles and photographs, organized public lectures and invited American speakers to the Middle East, including a pioneer American anti-Zionist, the late Rabbi Elmer Berger. The Society coordinated with the Beirut-based Americans for Justice in the Middle East (AJME) and Friends of Jerusalem and the Arab Women's Information Committee in Washington, DC."

41. There were at this time two organizations by the name "Friends of Jerusalem." The other was an American branch of Neturei Karta, the ultra-Orthodox anti-Zionist movement. On confusion between the two, see *The Link: Published by Americans for Middle East Understanding* 1969.

42. Shukairy cited Berger on the absence of antisemitism in the Arab world. Shukairy's speech is reproduced in Shukairy 1966, 26. The article Shukairy mentioned immediately after he cited the Pittsburgh Platform was one published in the ACJ's journal *Issues*: Sigal 1961. See Shukairy 1966, 113.

43. See, e.g., Mallison 1964; Menuhin 1969.

44. Anis Sayegh, foreword to Razzouk 1970d, 9. Note that the American Council for Judaism is the only organization listed under "Anti-Zionist Jewish Organizations" in the index of the PLO Research Center's first volume of *al-Yawmiyyat al-Filastiniyya* (Beirut, September 1966), 273.

45. On the potential importance of the Christian background of the PLO Research Center staff, see Gribetz 2016.

46. Razzouk 1970d, 12.

47. Razzouk, quoting from the entry on "Rabbinical Conferences" from the early twentieth-century English-language *Jewish Encyclopedia*, cited the key passage from the Platform: "We consider ourselves no longer a nation, but a religious community, and, therefore, expect neither a return to Palestine nor a sacrificial worship under the sons of Aaron, nor the restoration of any of the laws concerning the Jewish state." Razzouk 1970d, 24. Note that this is the same encyclo-pedia that the Late Ottoman Palestinian opponents of Zionism Najib Nassar and Muhammad Ruhi al-Khalidi translated as they wrote their studies of Zionism. See Gribetz 2014, 90.

48. Razzouk 1970d, 25 n. 6; Berger 1951.

49. On Berger's resignation, see Ross 2011, 146–47; Berger 1978, 108–30.

50. Krebs 1967. Arthur Hays Sulzberger, editor of the *New York Times*, was an early supporter of the American Council for Judaism. In fact, he participated in the drafting of the ACJ's original official manifesto of 1943. That same year, Sulzberger's *Times* was accused by leading Zionist rabbi Abba Hillel Silver of reflecting Sulzberger's anti-Zionism. "Again and again," wrote Silver, "*The Times* has transformed itself into a transmission belt for anti-Zionist propaganda. It never misses an opportunity to focus attention on the anti-Zionist viewpoint." See Kolsky 1990, 69–70, 88.

51. Letter from Clarence Coleman to Norton Mezvinsky in Glickman 1990, 137–38. Cited in Ross 2011, 146.

52. Razzouk 1970d, 251–56.

53. Razzouk 1970d, 256.

54. 'Abd al-'Aziz 1969, 7–8.

55. 'Abd al-'Aziz 1969, 204.

56. 'Abd al-'Aziz 1969, 205.

57. 'Abd al-'Aziz 1969, 213–20.

58. The Arabic terms used here are *al-ruhaniyat* and *al-zamaniyat*, the latter of which may also be rendered "temporal" or "secular." 'Abd al-'Aziz 1969, 205.

59. As Constantine Zurayk wrote in his introduction to Berger's memoirs on behalf of IPS, "The Institute for Palestine Studies is proud to be associated in the publication of these *Memoirs* and takes this opportunity to pay tribute to its author—a remarkable Jew and US citizen, and a man who stands [quoting Berger] 'upon those great, monumental rocks of human values which, despite the parochialism of so much of life, are the genuine universalisms.'" Berger 1978, v. On IPS, see Michael R. Fischbach, "Institute for Palestine Studies," in Mattar 2005, 222–23. "Al-Mu'assasat al-Buhuth al-Filastiniyya" 1990.

60. Berger 1978, 30. Emphasis in original.

61. In a meeting he had with Egyptian president Anwar Sadat in 1975, Berger recalled in his memoirs, he discussed "Zionism's racist character as it is codified in Israel/Zionist law." Berger insisted that "many aspects of Israeli conduct . . . are genuine, organic manifestations of the central exclusivism or 'racism' of Israel's fundamental Zionist character." Berger 1978, 102–3.

62. Berger 1983.

63. Berger 1983, 304.

64. Wilford 2013, 185.

65. Berger 1978, 103; Wilford 2017. AFME's CIA sponsorship was exposed in 1967. In February 1967, the *New York Times* reported that "the American Friends of the Middle East, an organization mentioned in Congressional hearings in 1964 as receiving funds from the C.I.A.-connected J. M. Kaplan Fund of New York, obtained two grants of $20,000 and $15,000 from the J. Frederick Brown Foundation in 1964. The group sponsors travel to the Middle East and finances publications. It has usually taken a pro-Arab stand in its public policy pronouncements." See Sheehan 1967.

66. Elmer Berger to Wilbur Crane Eveland, March 24, 1978, box 4, Wilbur Crane Eveland Papers, Hoover Institution Library and Archives. Many thanks to Hugh Wilford for sharing this unpublished source with me.

67. Wilford 2013, 103.

68. Consider, for instance, Mufti 2007; Aydin 2007; Devji 2013; Manela 2009; Prashad 2008. On methodological issues in global intellectual history, see Moyn and Sartori 2013.

69. Consider, e.g., Campos 2011; Levy 2014.

70. Cf. Fischbach 2018; Yaqub 2016; Harrison 2016.

71. For a fascinating, revisionist reading of the Assembly of Notables and the Parisian Sanhedrin, where French Jews acknowledged and, in some cases, embraced these principles, see Berkovitz 2007.

72. These three disparate groups collaborated, for instance, in the effort to identify Zionism with racism. At a symposium on the topic in Sri Lanka in August 1976, figures such as Anis al-Qasem of the PLO, Alfred Lilienthal of the American Council for Judaism, and Gottfried Neuburger of Neturei Karta all participated. See The International Organization for the Elimination of All Forms of Racial Discrimination 1979 for their respective presentations.

Chapter Eight: *The Jewish Woman in Occupied Palestine:* The Promise of Gender Equality

1. Al-Azm 2011, 126; al-Azm 1969, 151.

2. Al-Azm 2011, 126–27; al-Azm 1969, 153. In criticizing his fellow Arab socialists, al-Azm cites Karl Marx in his footnote to this passage: "We are always able to determine the extent of the development of a particular historical era by the degree of the progress of women on the road to freedom." Al-Azm cites the Russian edition of Marx and Engels's writings. For the English translation, see Engels and Marx 1975, 196.

3. Al-Azm 2011, 129; al-Azm 1969, 155. Al-Azm cites a translation into Arabic provided by Fawwaz Tarboulsi in a May 1968 article in *Dirasat 'Arabiyya*. On Vietnamese women soldiers, see, e.g., Turner 2000.

4. The Vietnamese opposition to the US served as a frequent model and source of inspiration for the Palestinian resistance movement against Israel. In April 1970 in Central Hall Westminster, Yusif Sayigh defended Palestinian armed resistance as an essential part of the effort to achieve peace in a single, shared democratic, non-Zionist state in Palestine in an Arab environment. There, at an event sponsored by the Council for the Advancement of Arab-British Understanding, Sayigh contended that "the technological gap between the Israeli and the Arab war machines is not nearly as relevant in a war of liberation. Vietnam has provided the best illustration of the theory that an irregular war is the appropriate war for the underdeveloped society." Yusif Sayigh 1970, 28.

5. Al-Azm 2011, 128.

6. Qaʿwar 1968.

7. For an excellent study of de Beauvoir's visit, with Jean Paul Sartre and her long-time romantic partner Claude Lanzmann, and al-Azm's role, see Di-Capua 2018, 24–46.

8. Al-Azm 2011, 128; al-Azm 1969, 153.

9. Qaʿwar 1968, 9; Beauvoir 1967.

10. Al-Azm 2011, 128; al-Azm 1969, 153–54.

11. Al-Azm 2011, 48.

12. Al-Khalili 1977. On al-Khalili's place in the PFLP's expanded central committee, see Yezid Sayigh 1997, 272.

13. A. Sayegh 1968b, 7.

14. A. Sayegh 1968b, 7.

15. Qaʿwar 1968, 12.

16. Qaʿwar 1968, 13.

17. A. Sayegh 1968b, 8.

18. A. Sayegh 1968b, 8.

19. On Benno Jacob, see Wilhelm 1962.

20. Jacob 1934, 3.

21. Qaʿwar 1968, 15.

22. Qaʿwar 1968, 16–17. Compare to Jacob 1934, 17.

23. Qaʿwar 1968, 17.

24. Qaʿwar 1968, 16–17.

25. Jewish residential segregation in European "ghettos" was, generally, not self-imposed. On the history of the term "ghetto," see Schwartz 2019. On the phenomenon of the "mellah" or Jewish quarters in Morocco, and the extent to which they should be regarded as parallel to ghettos, see Gottreich 2006, 12–38.

26. Typical of this perspective is this line from the *American Journal of Orthopsychiatry*: "the kibbutz has achieved fundamental change in the social status of women; most of the goals of the Women's Liberation movement in the United States have been realized in the kibbutz." Gerson 1971.

27. Qaʿwar 1968, 18.

28. Herzl 1960, 55–56. Cited in Qaʿwar 1968, 18.

29. For a study of the image of women in Herzl's literary writings, see Mittelmann 2007.

30. Qaʿwar 1968, 18.

31. Herzl 1960, 67–68.

32. Qaʿwar 1968, 19.

33. Qaʿwar 1968, 19–20.

34. Qaʿwar 1968, 67.

35. Qaʿwar 1968, 78–81.

36. Qaʿwar 1968, 155.

37. Qaʿwar 1968, 156.

38. Qaʿwar 1968, 155.

39. Qaʿwar uses the term *thawrat*.

40. Qaʿwar 1968, 156–57.

41. Qaʿwar acknowledged that the precise "number of Zionist women terrorists in these gangs" was not available. Qaʿwar 1968, 169.

42. Qaʿwar 1968, 170.

43. Qaʿwar 1968, 171.

44. Von Horn 1966, 104.

45. Qaʿwar 1968, 191–92.

46. Von Horn 1966, 109–10; Qaʿwar 1968, 192–94. In the American edition of von Horn's book, published a year after the British one, Rachel and Ronnie are anonymized to B. and C. See von Horn 1967, 121.

47. Qaʿwar 1968, 200–201.

48. Qaʿwar 1968, 201–2; Badi 1961, 236–37. Note that while Qaʿwar was clearly relying heavily on Ada Maimon's account of the legislative history, he provided details that Maimon did not (e.g., about the revision to the 1936 British law). Cf. Maimon 1962, 244–46.

49. Badi 1961, 314.

50. For the Hebrew text, see https://www.nevo.co.il/law_html/law01/317_003.htm, accessed January 23, 2023.

51. Maimon 1962, 247.

52. Qaʿwar 1968, 202–3.

53. Maimon 1962, 248.

54. Qaʿwar 1968, 203.

55. Stern 2009, 150.

56. Maimon 1962, 248; Qaʿwar 1968, 203.

57. Maimon 1962, 248; Qaʿwar 1968, 203–4.

58. See, e.g., Abillama 2018; Zuhur 2002.

59. Maimon 1962, 249.

60. Maimon 1962, 252.

61. A typical passage in this chapter reads: "There is no rejoicing in the family when a girl is born. Although when she reaches marriageable age she becomes a valuable asset, soon after marriage she reverts to her lowly condition." Maimon 1962, 253.

62. Qaʿwar 1968, 207–9; Jacob 1934, 4; Roth 1966, 961; Badi 1961, 236–37. I use Badi's English translation of the Israeli law upon which Qaʿwar relies rather than translating Qaʿwar's translation back into English. Qaʿwar's Arabic translation is not substantively different.

63. Qaʿwar 1968, 246.

64. Qaʿwar 1968, 144–45, 246; Baki 1966, 305.

65. Qaʿwar 1968, 246–47.

66. Qaʿwar 1968, 246–53.

67. Qaʿwar 1968, 284.

68. Qaʿwar 1968, 284.

69. Qaʿwar 1968, 284.

Chapter Nine: *Jews of the Arab Countries:* The Question of Racism

1. The section's title nods to Abu-Lughod 2013. Qaʿwar 1968, 72–76; Maimon 1962, 141–43.

2. Qaʿwar 1968, 76–77 n. 1.

3. Qaʿwar 1968, 76–77 n. 1. Compare to Maimon 1962, 141.

4. Kasmieh (1936–2014), who was born in Haifa, fled during the 1948 war and eventually settled in Damascus. She earned a PhD in history from Cairo University in 1972, after which she taught in the history department at Damascus University until 2011. Tamari 2015.

5. Abdo and Kasmieh 1971a, 7 n. 1. In the Arabic, the authors explain that this study is not comprehensive but is rather meant to stimulate further research on other aspects of the history of Jews in the Arab world. Abdo and Kasmieh 1971b, 10, 15.

6. This term appears in the English but not in the Arabic. Later in the Arabic text, the terms that are used in parallel to "indigenous Jews" include *al-yahud al-sharqiyyin* (Eastern Jews) and *al-mustawtinin [al-yahud] al-qudama* (the ancient [Jewish] settlers). See, e.g., Abdo and Kasmieh 1971b, 11; Abdo and Kasmieh 1971a, 8.

7. Abdo and Kasmieh 1971a, 7; Abdo and Kasmieh 1971b, 7.

8. Abdo and Kasmieh 1971a, 7. Cf. Abdo and Kasmieh 1971b, 7–8.

9. Abdo and Kasmieh 1971a, 7.

10. Abdo and Kasmieh 1971b, 8.

11. Abdo and Kasmieh 1971b, 8.

12. Abdo and Kasmieh 1971b, 10. The authors cite Itzhak Ben-Zvi's work on the subject. Ben-Zvi 1958, 12.

13. Abdo and Kasmieh 1971a, 8; Abdo and Kasmieh 1971b, 10.

14. Abdo and Kasmieh 1971a, 8; Abdo and Kasmieh 1971b, 11.

15. Abdo and Kasmieh 1971b, 11.

16. Abdo and Kasmieh 1971a, 8; Abdo and Kasmieh 1971b, 11–12.

17. Abdo and Kasmieh 1971a, 10. The Arabic refers to their "shared origins." Abdo and Kasmieh 1971b, 15.

18. Abdo and Kasmieh 1971a, 10; Abdo and Kasmieh 1971b, 15–16.

19. Abdo and Kasmieh 1971a, 10.

20. Abdo and Kasmieh 1971b, 16.

21. Abdo and Kasmieh 1971b, 16–17. Cites Khadduri 1970, 10.

22. Abdo and Kasmieh 1971b, 17–18.

23. Abdo and Kasmieh 1971b, 18–19.

24. Abdo and Kasmieh 1971b, 25.

25. Abdo and Kasmieh 1971a, 11.

26. Abdo and Kasmieh 1971a, 12–13.

27. Cited in Abdo and Kasmieh 1971a, 14–15.

28. Abdo and Kasmieh 1971a, 12 n. 15.

29. Already in 1951, Joseph Gordon described Vladimir Lutsky as "the most prominent Soviet expert on Jewish questions." Gordon cites an account of an April 1950 meeting in Moscow of the Learned Council of the Pacific Institute and the Moscow Branch of the Oriental Institute of the Soviet Academy of Sciences at which Lutsky described Zionism as "the reactionary ideology of Jewish bourgeois nationalism" and as "one of the potent weapons of American and English imperialist policy in the Near East." Lutsky also contended that "Anglo-American war-mongers are utilizing Zionism as a disruptive weapon on a world-wide scale" and thus that "the immediate tasks of Soviet orientalists studying the Near East" were "to expose and smash the cosmopolitan ideology of the 'united Jewish nation.'" Gordon 1951, 331–32.

30. Abdo and Kasmieh 1971a, 15–16.

31. Until the end of the nineteenth century, the authors wrote, "Jews—whether they were coming from elsewhere in the empire or from beyond the empire—were permitted to enter and settle in Palestine, while Christians were permitted only to visit during pilgrimages." Abdo and Kasmieh 1971b, 25–26.

32. Abdo and Kasmieh 1971b, 26; Abdo and Kasmieh 1971a, 16–17; Ben-Zvi 1958, 3.

33. The PLO authors cite Ben-Zvi's *The Exiled and the Redeemed* to support this claim, noting that Ben-Zvi attributed "the lack of response on the part of Oriental Jews to the Zionist Movement" to these communities' small size and "the suspicions with which the Ottomans viewed the movement." Abdo and Kasmieh 1971a, 16–17; Ben-Zvi 1958, 3.

34. Abdo and Kasmieh 1971a, 17. Cf. Abdo and Kasmieh 1971b, 27–28.

35. Abdo and Kasmieh 1971a, 18.

36. Abdo and Kasmieh 1971b, 33.

37. Al-Abid 1969c, 214–15; al-Abid 1969b, 164–65.

38. Al-Abid 1969c, 247; al-Abid 1969b, 184–86.

39. Al-Abid 1969c, 239.

40. Al-Abid 1969c, 239–40; al-Abid 1971, 181–82.

41. Cited and translated in Miller 2016a, 6; Miller 2016b.

42. Anis met Hilda Jalil Sha'ban at the American University of Beirut, where they were both studying. Of Jordanian origin, Sha'ban was born in As-Salt. After marrying in Amman in 1959, the couple moved to Cambridge, where Sha'ban began pursuing a doctorate in Andalusian literature under the supervision of the British scholar A. J. Arberry at the University of Cambridge. While at Cambridge, she served as a teaching assistant in the Department of Oriental Studies. Upon the couple's return to Beirut, Sha'ban taught Arabic language and literature at the Beirut College for Women (which later became Beirut University College and now the Lebanese American University). According to her husband Anis's memoirs, Sha'ban's work at the Center was as a volunteer, presumably to avoid suspicions of nepotism. A. Sayegh 2006, 35.

43. Sha'ban Sayegh 1971, 7–8.

44. Selzer 1967.

45. Sha'ban Sayegh 1971, 50.

46. Sha'ban Sayegh 1971, 55.

47. Hillel Cohen dubs the notion of a Palestinian-Mizrahi alliance against Zionism as "a Palestinian fantasy." H. Cohen 2022, 161.

48. *Israeli Racism* 1975, 8.

49. *Israeli Racism* 1975, 12.

50. The PLO may have chosen to play the race card, as it were, because, in the 1970s, the term "racist" carried a great deal of moral weight. Hillel Cohen suggested, in private conversation, that "racist" was a socially acceptable term that approximated more colorful slurs that the PLO actually had in mind.

51. As public health scholar Michael Yudell puts it, "While we argue phasing out racial terminology in the biological sciences, we also acknowledge that using race as a political or social category to study racism, although filled with lots of challenges, remains necessary given our need to understand how structural inequities and discrimination produce health disparities between groups." Cited in Gannon 2016. As journalist Jenée Desmond-Harris writes, "although race isn't real, racism certainly is. The racial categories to which we're assigned, based on how we look to others or how we identify ourselves, can determine real-life experiences, inspire hate, drive political outcomes, and make the difference between life and death." Desmond-Harris 2014.

52. F. Sayegh 1976, 12.

53. F. Sayegh 1976, 12–13.

54. F. Sayegh 1976, 13.

55. F. Sayegh 1976, 24–25.

56. The contemporary parallel would be the use of the term "Apartheid" in describing Israel's policies and activities in the West Bank. See "A Regime of Jewish Supremacy from the Jordan River to the Mediterranean Sea: This Is Apartheid" 2022; "A Threshold Crossed: Israeli Authorities and the Crimes of Apartheid and Persecution" 2021; Goldstein 2021.

57. Arendt 1944.

58. F. Sayegh 1976, 17.

59. I am grateful to Ethan Katz for raising this possibility.

60. F. Sayegh 1976, 33.

61. F. Sayegh 1976, 15; *Times* 1963.

62. Toynbee 1969, 241.

63. F. Sayegh 1976, 26–27.

64. Interestingly, some Black Panthers referred to discrimination against Mizrahim in Israel as antisemitism. As Kokhavi Shemesh said in 1971, "in Israel today there is anti-Semitism. What happens to the Jews abroad happens to Sephardim here. It comes out in expressions such as 'Franks' and 'primitives' which come from the same racist way of thinking." S. Cohen and Shemesh 1976, 22. See also O. Frankel 2008.

65. On early Mizrahi protest movements, see Roby 2015. On the rise of the Black Panthers in Israel, see the interviews of Shalom Cohen (1976) and Kokhavi Shemesh (1971) in S. Cohen and Shemesh 1976.

66. H. Cohen 2022, 245–51. Cohen cites a Fateh activist who, in 1966, explained the logic of integrating into the struggle against Israel "the large sub-proletariat composed of Jews from Arab lands, the Sephardim, who are the Arabs of the Jews of central Europe, the Ashkenazim." On the Black Panthers, see H. Cohen 2022, 288–92.

67. Massad 1996, 64–65.

68. Massad 1996, 65. Cohen notes that the Toledo experiment quickly fell "from a mountain of hope to the abyss of reality" as, the day before the Israeli delegation returned home, Abd al-Hadi Ghanaim of Gaza overtook an Israeli bus and drove it off a cliff, killing sixteen passengers and injuring many more. H. Cohen 2022, 354–55.

69. By the 2000s, this solidarity had dissipated. Though there are exceptions, Israeli Mizrahim have not widely embraced a sense of camaraderie with Palestinians. See H. Cohen 2022; Habaz 2019.

Chapter Ten: *The Role of the Zionist Terror in the Creation of Israel: On the Necessity of Violence*

1. Abu Ghazala 1966; A. Sayegh 1967; al-Abid 1967; Bishuti 1969; Hadawi 1972; ʿAzmi 1973; ʿAzmi 1975; Muharib 1981.

2. I have not been able to find an Arabic version of this book. In 1973, the Arab League information office in Madrid published a version of it in Spanish. Bishuti 1973.

3. Bishuti 1969, 8.

4. Bishuti 1969, 9.

5. Though my chapter on race is separate from this chapter on violence, these topics were considered interconnected by the Center authors. This book on Zionist terrorism included, on the first page, an assertion that while Jewish nationalism led Jews to regard themselves as a single race, "anthropologically speaking, this is false, for the Jews belong to all the races of mankind." Bishuti 1969, 7.

6. Bishuti 1969, 7–9.

7. Bishuti 1969, 14–15.

8. Bishuti 1969, 19.

9. Bishuti 1969, 28.

10. Bishuti 1969, 32.

11. Bishuti 1969, 77–78.

12. Bishuti 1969, 29.

13. Bishuti 1969, 32.

14. Bishuti 1969, 7.

15. As noted above, Bishuti included a variety of actions, both violent and nonviolent, in his conception of "terror." Bishuti 1969, 8.

16. Bishuti later describes the Arab population of Palestine as "a people who had never persecuted the Jews." Bishuti 1969, 8.

17. Bishuti 1969, 94–95.

18. Bishuti 1969, 97.

19. Bishuti 1969, 20.

20. Bishuti 1969, 111.

21. Bishuti 1969, 125. Cites Sacher 1952, 193–94. The line that follows these words in Sacher's book (though not cited by Bishuti) is: "and for equally compelling reasons [Menahem] Begin [*sic*] has seized the opportunity to tell a story which is involved, inadequate and distorted, and indeed to a careful reader largely unintelligible."

22. Bishuti 1969, 139.

23. On the October 29 massacre and its aftermath, see Robinson 2003. In recently declassified transcripts from the 1957 Israeli trial, the colonel who oversaw the Kafr Qasim sector was quoted as having said, "It's desirable that there be some casualties." Aderet 2022.

24. Bishuti 1969, 195.

25. Bishuti 1969, 211.

26. Hadawi 1972, 7.

27. Hadawi 1972, 25.

28. Hadawi 1972, 12.

29. Nolan 2005, 1–2.

30. Abdallah 1974, 7.

31. Abdallah 1974, 7–8.

32. Abdallah 1974, 8.

33. Abdallah 1974, 8.

34. Howard 1976.

35. The Israeli intelligence expert Matti Steinberg described the PLO Research Center to me as a bona fide think tank, not a PLO unit engaged in violence. When I found this *Boston Globe* article, which offers a very different portrayal of the Center, I shared it with Steinberg and asked him how he accounted for this report. "This article seems to me as far-fetched," Steinberg wrote me by email. He continued: "It mentions a guy affiliated with the Red Army sitting in an office of the Center. The PLO, headed by Fatah, suspended in the wake of 1973 War all the external operations abroad. The Popular Front continued these operations but they were not part of the Center. Furthermore, the article mentions Said Hammami as a dangerous terrorist. The fact is that Hammami was targeted later because he managed close connections with Israeli doves talking about political settlement with Israel under the command of Arafat." When I asked Steinberg why he thought a journalist might have written this if the journalist had not himself witnessed it, he explained: "They only ate eagerly whatever they had been fed by the interested parties. They served, sometimes unwittingly, as a tool in their hands." Steinberg 2017c; Steinberg 2017d. On Hammami's contacts with Israeli peace activists, see Avnery 1986.

Chapter Eleven: The PLO Research Center in Tel Aviv

1. B. Morris 2000, 444–93.

2. B. Morris 2000, 499–501.

3. Hanf 2015, 228–30; Rabinovich 1985; Barak 2017, 192–95. Morris's estimates of the casualties are lower. On the Israeli side, Morris counts 18 Israeli troops killed and 113 wounded and on the Palestinian side 300 fighters killed, "several hundred wounded, and several dozen captured," with "hundreds of Lebanese homes" destroyed and "tens of thousands of villagers" forced to flee. B. Morris 2000, 501.

4. This narrative follows closely, and is indebted to the excellent work of, Hanf 2015, 252.

5. While the conventional view is that Ariel Sharon covertly had more expansive aims than Menachem Begin, and deceived Begin in order to carry them out, Dan Naor argues that Begin played an active, conscious role in these decisions from the start. See Naor 2023.

6. Relying on Charles Hill's contemporaneous notebooks, Seth Anziska shows that on May 25, 1982, US secretary of state Alexander Haig gave Ariel Sharon a "green light" to undertake an invasion as long as there was "a recognizable provocation." Anziska 2018, 201–2.

7. Rashid Khalidi helpfully periodizes the war into four phases. See R. Khalidi 1986, 47–50.

8. "D. Ha-Hitpathuyot ha-Tsvaʾiyot ve-ha-Mediniyot ʿal Rekaʿ ha-Mitrahesh be-Levanon ba-Yamim ha-Ahronim" 1982. The English version of the government decision read: "to place all the civilian population of the Galilee beyond the range of the terrorists' fire from Lebanon where they, their bases, and their headquarters are concentrated." *New York Times* 1982a; Rabinovich 1985, 121.

9. In an assessment of the war published first in 1986, Rashid Khalidi argued that the Israeli leadership's "aim was not simply to drive back the P.L.O. from the border region, thereby making Galilee 'safe' for its Israeli inhabitants. It was rather to destroy utterly the P.L.O., thus making the West Bank and Gaza Strip 'safe' for annexation." R. Khalidi 1986, 46.

10. C. Campbell 1982a.

11. Anziska 2018, 215–21.

12. A protest in Tel Aviv on Saturday night, September 25, 1982, against the invasion and calling upon Begin and Sharon to resign in light of the Sabra and Shatila massacres, drew over 300,000 Israeli citizens at a time when Israel's entire population was about four million. Farrell 1982c.

13. *New York Times* 1982b.

14. Farrell 1982a.

15. Gwertzman 1982.

16. *New York Times* 1982c.

17. Nossiter 1982.

18. C. Campbell 1982b; C. Campbell 1982c. On the massacres, see also B. N. al-Hout 2004.

19. Farrell 1982b; Schmemann 1982; *New York Times* 1982d; Brilliant 1982; Walsh 1982.

20. Spiegel 2018.

21. Spiegel 2018. I am grateful to Itamar Radai and Mike Herzog for information about AMShaT.

22. Herzog 2018; Spiegel 2018; Gilead 2018.

23. Safire 1982; C. Campbell 1982d; Shipler 1982b.

24. *Philadelphia Inquirer* 1982.

25. Steinberg eventually taught at the Hebrew University, and as a visitor in Princeton and Heidelberg, and between 1996 and 2003 he served as senior advisor to the heads of various Israeli intelligence branches.

26. Steinberg 2017b.

27. Steinberg's conclusion was that "The problem with the Palestinians is essentially a political problem, not a military one. From a military perspective even they know that they are a marginal factor. Therefore, it is necessary to fight them with appropriate tools, in a political fashion." Steinberg 1975, 11–12.

28. Steinberg 2017a.

29. Steinberg 2017b.

30. Steinberg 2017a.

31. Though Steinberg recalls having handwritten a fifteen-to-twenty-page report, the document I was shown consisted of only four pages. "Homer Shalal me-Arkhiyonei Asha"f be-Beirut—Bedikat Matzai ve-Afyon Rishoniyim" 1982. I am grateful to the IDF Archives staff, especially Avi Zadok and Yovav Ben-Gat, for their efforts in locating this document. I also appreciate the assistance of Professor Yigal Sheffy in this regard. When I showed the document to Steinberg, he determined it to be a summary of his report with some additional commentary that he believed was written by the then-head of the Palestinian section of the IDF's intelligence division. (He declined to name this individual.) In a meeting in May 2022, Steinberg characterized this report as a "diluted version" of his original report, which he insisted was "very clear cut" and "straightforward" in its determination that, despite the few violent texts produced by the PLO Research Center, the materials in its library were of no "operational value from the point of view of intelligence." Steinberg 2022.

32. Hatsav is the name of the Israeli intelligence unit responsible for analyzing open sources, or OSINT. According to Ephraim Lapid, this unit "tracked that which was written and heard in Arab lands," especially in Arabic newspapers and radio broadcasts. Lapid 2008, 65. For English, see Gilboa 2012, 69. In 2012, Shay Shabtai noted that the Hatsav unit had been disbanded in the preceding decade. See Shabtai 2012. However, in 2016 *ha-Aretz* reported that the unit still existed. See G. Cohen 2016.

33. "Homer Shalal me-Arkhiyonei Asha"f be-Beirut" 1982, 1.

34. Emphasis in the original.

35. "Homer Shalal me-Arkhiyonei Asha"f be-Beirut" 1982, 1. On the Western Sector's role, Yezid Sayigh 1997, 207, 349–53.

36. S. Jiryis and Qallab 1985.

37. S. Jiryis 2015.

38. "Homer Shalal me-Arkhiyonei Asha"f be-Beirut" 1982, 1.

39. "Homer Shalal me-Arkhiyonei Asha"f be-Beirut" 1982, 2.

40. "Homer Shalal me-Arkhiyonei Asha"f be-Beirut" 1982.

41. "Homer Shalal me-Arkhiyonei Asha"f be-Beirut" 1982, 2–3.

42. It seems that the report's author may not have been certain whether one of these "archives of pictures" belonged to the Research Center. The report noted that "prominent in this was the archive of *Al-Hadaf*." "Homer Shalal me-Arkhiyonei Asha"f be-Beirut" 1982, 3–4.

43. "Homer Shalal me-Arkhiyonei Asha"f be-Beirut" 1982, 4.

44. "Homer Shalal me-Arkhiyonei Asha"f be-Beirut" 1982, 4.

45. In contrast to the PLO Research Center publications I analyzed in part 2 of this book, the *Handbook for the Palestinian Fighter* is difficult to find—even in the largest university libraries. My search eventually led me to the catalogue of the University of Jordan library, which holds a copy. I am most grateful to Amanda (Mandy) Swenson for her efforts in scanning and sharing the book with me. Later, I also found the book listed in the catalogue of the Institute for Palestine Studies Constantine Zurayk Library in Beirut.

46. I have not found the other three in the series.

47. *Dalil al-Muqatil al-Filastini* 1972, 1:60.

48. *Dalil al-Muqatil al-Filastini* 1972, 1:60–61.

49. *Dalil al-Muqatil al-Filastini* 1972, 1:61.

Chapter Twelve: A Global Debate about the PLO Research Center

1. T. Rubin 1982.

2. Jenkins 1982; Trounson 1982. According to Trounson's report, one pilfered vehicle was a bulldozer owned by the Oger Liban Company. The president of the company, Rafik Hariri, "watched as the bulldozer was loaded onto a flatbed truck near the port of west Beirut by a group of Israeli logistics engineers." Hariri would later serve as prime minister of Lebanon from 1992 until 1998 and again from 2000 until 2004. He was assassinated, allegedly by Hezbollah, on February 14, 2005.

3. Loren Jenkins reported on allegations by Beirut residents who returned to their homes to find "feces deliberately deposited around the room, including on [the] dining room table." Jenkins 1982.

4. Said erroneously alleged that the same fate befell the Institute for Palestine Studies. Israeli forces apparently entered the Institute for Palestine Studies but, according to IPS officials at the time, "the Israelis took a few publications and looked into the computer room and opened some filing cabinets, but did not loot the place." Hijazi 1982. In an interview with me, Walid Khalidi confirmed that the Israelis entered and searched IPS in mid-September 1982 but did not seize the full collection as they did in the PLO Research Center. W. Khalidi 2016.

5. Said 1982. Two days earlier, the *Los Angeles Times* had reported that an apartment in the same building as the PLO Research Center had been ransacked but that article claimed that the Research Center itself "was not damaged nearly as badly" as the neighboring apartment. Kennedy 1982. In his memoirs, Shafiq al-Hout recounted how Israeli officials seized personal and historical documents, including his wife's British Mandate–era Palestinian passport, from his home during the siege of West Beirut. "The erasure of Palestinian national identity," wrote al-Hout, "is a strategic goal of the Zionists from which they have not and will not deviate." The Zionists seek both "the physical and the spiritual eradication of the Palestinian person. As long as there remains anything that points to Palestinian existence, even if it just a painting or a poem or a sculpture, Israel will not be confident of its continued existence." S. al-Hout 2007, 278–84; S. al-Hout 2011, 167–71. I offer my own translation of the Arabic here and provide the corresponding pages in the English translation.

6. Hijazi 1982.

7. "Decisions Adopted by the Executive Board at Its 115th Session" 1982, 73.

8. "Decisions Adopted by the Executive Board at Its 115th Session" 1982, 73.

9. "Decisions Adopted by the Executive Board at Its 115th Session" 1982, 74.

10. Golan 1982a. See also Golan 1982b.

11. "Records of the General Conference, 4th Extraordinary Session" 1983, 481–82. I am grateful to Eng Sengsavang, UNESCO Reference Archivist, for her assistance in locating this speech.

12. Childs 2010.

13. E. Rubinstein 1982.

14. E. Rubinstein 1982.

15. A. M. Campbell 1983a, 230–33.

16. A. M. Campbell 1983b, 229.

17. "Arkhiyon Asha"f" 1982.

18. "Arkhiyon Asha"f" 1982.

19. Granot 1982. The Foreign Broadcast Information Service's translation of the article's title was "Two Aspects of the 'Center for Palestinian Studies' in Beirut: Assisting the PLO with Terrorist Attacks behind a Facade of Academic Work in Beirut." The translation here generally follows the FBIS version, though I note at times certain differences. I discuss the apparent reach of the English translation below.

20. The FBIS report translates *ha-merkaz le-mahkarim palastiniyim* as "the Center for Palestinian Studies." I render it here "the Palestinian Research Center" both to avoid confusion with the Institute for Palestine Studies (though as we see the two institutes were indeed confused even in this article) and because the more literal translation, "the Center for Palestinian Researches," reads awkwardly.

21. The FBIS translation renders *hokrim* as "investigators"; in the context, "researchers" seems preferable.

22. The FBIS translation notes only the "Jewish objectives for terrorist acts," not the "Israeli and Jewish objectives."

23. The Hebrew translation of the title is more precisely rendered "A Guide [*moreh derekh*] for the Palestinian Fighter," but I use *Handbook* here so that it is clear that this is the same text referred to in the October 13, 1982, intelligence report.

24. R. Khalidi 2013.

25. A. Sayegh 1969. The Jewish National and University Library in Jerusalem acquired a copy of this book on August 4, 1975. It is catalogued as 75 B 1911 in the library. I thank the National Library of Israel's Yaniv Levi-Korem for his help in finding the original handwritten document in which the acquisition of the book was registered.

26. Granot 1983.

27. Sinai was unwilling to speak with me about this matter. In an email, he wrote simply: "During the war I served as a young officer at the office of the IDF Intelligence branch in Tel Aviv. I don't remember anything concerning the issue you mention." Sinai 2018.

28. Sinai 1982. This letter cites earlier correspondence with the Defense Ministry from November 18 and December 19, so the matter was already under discussion between the Defense Ministry bureau and Military Intelligence a few weeks before Granot acquired his information.

29. Alsberg quoted this February 6, 1983, letter in another he addressed to Canada's dominion archivist, Wilfred Smith, on June 19. Alsberg 1983.

30. "Records of the General Conference, 4th Extraordinary Session" 1983, 482.

31. Lambert-Finkler 1983.

32. One of these victims was a neighbor of the Center. Her grandson, Stefan Tarnowski, reflected on the event in Tarnowski 2021.

33. In the first issue of *Shu'un* published after the attack, Sabri Jiryis wrote that there were few doubts that the bombing was planned by "the Zionist gangs, also known as Israel" and conducted by Israel's "agents in Lebanon, who are not few in number." S. Jiryis 1983, 4.

34. Bergman 2018a, 638.

35. Bergman 2018b.

36. Bergman 2018b.

37. PLO Research Center 1982.

38. PLO Research Center 1982.

39. Litani 1982a; Litani 1982b.

40. Kuwait KUNA 1982.

41. Ottaway 1982.

42. Faramarzi 1983; *Atlanta Constitution* 1983.

43. Friedman 1983a; Friedman 1983b.

44. *Newsview* 1983a.

45. Granot 1982; Granot 1983.

46. *Newsview* 1983b.

47. *Newsview* 1983b.

48. The quotations in this sentence are Shipler's paraphrases from his interview with Benvenisti.

49. The quotation in this sentence was attributed by Shipler to Benvenisti. Shipler 1983a.

50. Benvenisti alluded to this claim when he wrote that the PLO's "provocation in southern Lebanon offered Begin and Sharon an excuse to attack the national center in Beirut, to scatter its activists to the four winds, and then to destroy their centers of research and thought." Benvenisti 1983.

51. Ozick 1974.

52. The letter was published on March 3, 1983.

53. Here Ozick refers to the institution as "the Center for Palestine Studies" but it is clear she is referring to the PLO Research Center, even as she (following Granot) conflates aspects of it with the Institute for Palestine Studies. More on this confusion below. Ozick 1983a.

54. Stuart Schaar sent the original letter to the *Times*. Schaar 1983a.

55. In email correspondence, Schaar recalled that the initiators of the scholars' effort were Edward Said and Eqbal Ahmad. Schaar said that he had "worked closely with Eqbal and did some of the leg work, getting others to sign." Schaar 2017a. Schaar reasoned that Said was not one of the signatories because "it would have been obvious where he stood on the issue." Judging from Schaar's recollections, it seems that it was of significance from the perspective of the letter organizers that a number of the signers were Jewish. As Schaar noted, "Besides myself, Irene [Gendzier], Don Peretz, and Miriam [Rosen] were Jewish. I got their signatures as well as Richard Bulliet's, Edmund [Burke III]'s, and Don Will's. Eqbal [Ahmad] or Edward [Said] got the signatures of Masao [Mioshi] (a good friend of both of them), Alan [Richards], and George [Saliba]."

56. One of the signatories retrospectively noted to me in an email, "Ozick, besides being a notable novelist, was a propagandist for the Israelis and signed letters that we imagined they probably asked her to publish under her name." Given the immediacy of Ozick's responses, and her long history of engaging in these polemics, I have no evidence that this scholar's assumption was correct, but it does reveal that, in his mind, he and his fellow signatories were engaged in a sort of proxy battle on the other end of which was ultimately not Ozick but the State of Israel.

57. Ahmad et al. 1983.

58. Partington 1983.

59. Schaar 1983b. I have not found such a letter.

60. Partington served as the association's vice president in 1985–86 and as its president in 1986–87. See "Middle East Librarians Association: Past Officers" 2017.

61. In a private note to Stuart Schaar, Peretz lamented: "I don't know why she picked me as the butt of her attack." Peretz n/d. The handwritten note appears on a paper with a copy of Peretz's April 11 note to David Partington and a copy of Schaar's April 20 note to Peretz.

62. Ozick 1983b.

63. That Ozick had actually met Peretz may explain why she chose to name him in her letter to the *New York Times*.

64. Ozick 1983c.

65. That the scholars did not specify that it was a Lebanese militia that claimed responsibility for the bombing led Ozick to accuse the scholars of intentionally falsely implying that Israel was behind the attack. Of course, if this had been their intention, according to Ronen Bergman they would not have been entirely wrong to do so.

66. Ozick 1983c.

67. In an undated, handwritten letter (apparently a draft) to Ozick, Peretz, having lost his patience for Ozick, asserted his greater knowledge of the conflict: "I actually know, not only Israelis, but real live Palestinians . . . I have actually been, not only to Jerusalem, but to Beirut, and actually *saw* the materials at the Research Center I mentioned." Peretz undated, 3. I am grateful to Geoffrey Levin for reviewing Peretz's passport and other materials and for informing me of Peretz's visits to Lebanon in 1967 and 1969. It is unclear which of the signatories had conducted research there. In email correspondence, Schaar and Bulliet separately noted that they had never been to the Center. Schaar was uncertain if any of the signatories had been. Schaar 2017b; Bulliet 2017.

68. "Jeanette" 1983; Ekin 1983. I suspect "Jeanette" was scholar Jeanette Wakin. On the AAUG, see Levin 2017; Bardawil 2020, 91.

69. Peretz 1983.

70. Ozick 1983d. In a subsequent letter to Peretz, Ozick mentioned that the newspaper article had been shared with her "by a friend at the State Department." Ozick 1983e. In an email, Ozick told me that that friend "could only have been, and surely was, Eugene Rostow." Ozick 2017. At the State Department, Rostow (1913–2002) served as under secretary of state for political affairs from October 1966 until January 1969 and as director of the US Arms Control and Disarmament Agency from June 1981 until January 1983. "Eugene Victor Debs Rostow" 2017. A scholar of international law, Rostow, it may be noted, defended Jewish settlement in the West Bank and Gaza. "The Jewish right of settlement in the area," he wrote in 1990, "is equivalent in every way to the right of the existing population to live there." Rostow 1990, 720. On November 30, 2015, the Israeli Ministry of Foreign Affairs cited this article in its statement on "Israeli Settlements and International Law." Israeli Ministry of Foreign Affairs 2015. On Rostow's argument for the legality of Israeli control of the West Bank and the Gaza Strip, see Anziska 2018, 142–45.

71. Denton 1983.

72. Associated Press 1983. Peretz sent a clipping of this *Times* article to Ozick on July 7, 1983.

73. Ozick 1983e, 1.

74. Ozick 1983f, 2. In her family memoirs, Fida Jiryis claims that her father "joined the resistance" shortly after the 1967 war and that "their first task was transporting half a ton of arms from the Lebanese border to the West Bank." F. Jiryis 2022, 127.

75. Ozick 1983e, 4.

76. Interestingly, thirty-six years earlier, Peretz wrote a letter to his parents, remarking that "American Jews suffer from the horrible disease of self-hatred and self-misunderstanding." Now Ozick accused him of the same. Don Peretz to Parents, February 5, 1947. Geoffrey Levin shared this letter with me. Peretz Papers, GL PDF 2/42. For an excellent study of Peretz, see Levin 2023.

77. Peretz's archive includes another note from Ozick, sent half a decade later. Typed on a postcard, it is an "Ode Concerning Another Middle Eastern Injustice." Apparently a response to Peretz's then-recent article in *Foreign Affairs* about the Palestinian intifada, in which he mentioned a conference he attended at the Palestinian university in Bir Zeit, as well as to Jerome Segal's meeting with Arafat in Tunis, the poem reads: "Jerome Segal / (in all his Jewness) / flied like an eagle / to Tunis, / eye to eye / with Arafat's sty. / But Don Peretz / (who knows *aleph* from *beyt*) / merits / only the local Bir Zeit. / O pity poor Peretz, consider his woes! / He gets Foreign Affairs to publish his prose / with scarcely a PLO thanks, / A bow from Said / won't fill the need / while Segal ascends to the PLO's / highest Yevsektsia ranks!"

78. Hommel, Frusciano, and Swanson 1983.

79. In 2015, Mattar kindly spoke with me about his experience in Beirut in 1979 when he was conducting research for his book on the Mufti Hajj Amin al-Husseini. In an email to me, Mattar wrote, "Even though I spent a month in Beirut, I did not find the material very helpful since there were few useful documents on either subject [the Mufti during the Mandate and the Mufti's relationship with Yasser Arafat]. After spending four months at the PRO [the Public Record Office in London] and two months at the ISA [the Israel State Archives in Jerusalem], the documents on the Mandate at the PLO [Research Center] did not add much. And the PLO had little on the relationship between the Arab Higher Committee and the PLO." Mattar 2015.

80. On the Shiloah Institute and the Dayan Center, see Eyal 2006.

81. Bashan 1983. On April 6, 2022, Hebrew University librarian Avishag Gross and PhD candidate Yogev Elbaz permitted me to dig through the Truman Institute library, which was being dissembled and distributed to other campus libraries. In the boxes I examined, I found many books published by the PLO Research Center and also several books that had been the property of various Arab libraries, but none that had been the property of the PLO Research Center. In this collection, I found Arabic books bearing the stamps of the following Arab libraries: the PLO Executive Committee in Jerusalem (Naji Alloush's 1964 *The March to Palestine*); al-Bira's public library (a 1978 translation of Jack Woddis's *New Theories of Revolution* and a 1970 translation of Jean Lacouture's biography of Ho Chi Minh); the al-Salahiyyeh Charitable Society (the second volume of the 1929 *History of the Nationalist Movement and the Development of the Governing Regime in Egypt*); the Arab Higher Committee for Palestine's Jeddah office (a 1964 book about the theft of Arab water); the Zaynabiyya School library (a translation of a book by Elmer Berger); Asira al-Shamaliyya secondary school library (a book on Zionism's past and present); Silwan girls' school library (Qadri Hafiz Tuqan's *After the Nakba*); Jenin elementary school library (Muhammad Izza Darwaza's *The Modern Arab Movement*); and so on.

82. The earlier report did not use the term "proper," *mehugan*. In addition, it simply referred to "the sphere of operations," whereas here the report is more specific in rendering it "the sphere of executing acts of terror." "Merkaz le-Mehkarim Filastiniyyim" 1983.

83. See ch. 1 above.

Chapter Thirteen: Exchanging Prisoners, a Library, and an Archive

1. For archival documents related to the prisoner exchange, see "Shele"g Shevuyim/ 'Atsurim" 1983.

2. The six Israeli prisoners released in the exchange were Sergeant Reuven Cohen and privates Eliyahi Abutbol, Dani Gilboa, Rafael Hazan, Avraham Mintbalski, and Avraham Kronenfeld. "Shele"g Shevuyim/'Atsurim" 1983.

3. "Shele"g Shevuyim/'Atsurim" 1983.

4. In Shafiq al-Hout's memoirs, he says that Israel released 5,900 Lebanese and Palestinian prisoners. He seems to be conflating the 1983 deal with the prisoner exchange of 1985 known as the "Jibril Agreement." S. l-Hout 2007, 355; S. al-Hout 2011, 207.

5. Another retired Israeli brigadier general in military intelligence, Gadi Zohar, told me in an interview that, though he was not involved in the decision to confiscate the PLO Research Center's library and archive, he believed "no deep thought" stood behind this act. Rather, the Center was swept up along with anything connected to the PLO, which, in the Israelis' minds, was equivalent to terrorism. Zohar did acknowledge, however, that shipping such a large collection of materials to Israel by truck in the midst of the war was a major undertaking that a senior official would have had to approve. He said that he was not sure who that was. "It is always difficult to ascertain exactly who issued a particular command during a war," he explained. Zohar 2022.

6. Gilead 2018.

7. "Annual Report 1983" 1984, 62–63; Sheffy 2018.

8. One wonders what role Shipler's use of the phrase "the P.L.O.'s archives" in this article had on the subsequent speculation about its contents. See below.

9. Shipler 1983b.

10. S. Jiryis and Qallab 1985.

11. S. Jiryis 2015.

12. The entry continues: "The Center places the acquisitions and documents of its library at the service of its researchers and visiting scholars and researchers who can benefit from the acquisitions during the Center's work hours, or photocopies of references that they need, and this is almost free of charge. Also, the Center offers similar services to those who request assistance by mail, and offers them advice for studies, and assists them in learning what references are available that they lack in their studies." *Al-Mawsu'a al-Filastiniyya* 1984, 33.

13. A. Sayegh 2006, 218. Sayegh renders Newton's private names Emily Frances rather than Frances Emily.

14. On the CID, see Harouvi 2016.

15. I. Khalaf 1991, 40; Lockman 1996, 205.

16. A. Sayegh 2006, 218.

17. A. Sayegh 2006, 218–19.

18. A. Sayegh 2006, 219.

19. A. Sayegh 2006, 219.

20. Sleiman 2016, 64 n. 8.

21. Sleiman 2016, 46.

22. S. Jiryis 2015.

23. S. Jiryis 2016c.

24. Shipler 1983b.

25. Shipler 1983b.

26. In October 1982, the month after Israel had seized the library, Shipler visited the Research Center and met with Jiryis. Apparently, Jiryis hinted then that "much of the material had been microfilmed and placed in safekeeping somewhere in the United States. But some old books had been lost, he said, and they were irreplaceable." This interview took place before Israel returned the library the following year. In 1986, when he published his book *Arab and Jew: Wounded Spirits in a Promised Land,* Shipler wrote in language that sounded much like what Benvenisti had told him in February 1983: "It was as if Israel had tried to steal the Palestinians' past and identity, as if the Israelis could not stand to see the Palestinians have a historical archive." Shipler 1986, 75–76.

27. S. Jiryis 2015; Rabinovich 1985, 174.

28. S. Jiryis 2015.

29. S. Jiryis 2015.

30. Shabeeb 2005.

31. S. Jiryis 2015.

32. S. Jiryis 2015.

33. S. Jiryis 2015.

34. Parks 2016.

35. Sleiman 2016, 47.

36. "Annual Report 1983" 1984, 62–63.

37. Red Cross documents from the period say that one hundred prisoners were meant to be released; by contrast, Israeli documents say sixty-three.

38. *New York Times* 1984. Abu Ayn was eventually released as part of a later prisoner exchange in 1985 and ultimately served as an official in the Palestinian Authority government. He died during a protest in the West Bank in 2014 in circumstances that remain disputed. Friedman 1985; Booth and Eglash 2014. See ISA 1–4361-א for the correspondence and reports on this episode.

39. Interestingly, in al-Hout's memoirs he does not say that "all" of the Center's materials were meant to be returned—only "most." "This deal also included the return of most of the documents confiscated by Israeli troops from the PLO Research Center in West Beirut." The original Arabic memoirs read: "the return of most of the documents of the PLO-affiliated Research Center, which were confiscated during the enemy's—treacherous—destruction of West Beirut." S. al-Hout 2007, 355; S. al-Hout 2011, 207.

40. Alon 2015.

41. Zohar 2022. He said he was not certain where one might find the materials that Israel kept.

42. When I asked the late Professor Shaked (1933–2021) about this manuscript, he wrote: "I have a dim recollection of the episode to which you (or rather Matti Steinberg) refer. . . . The manuscript in question may have been part of the library of the PLO centre in Beirut, which was seized (and eventually largely returned), but I may be wrong. I cannot recall another occasion on which I might have been involved in examining books or manuscripts from a PLO library." Shaked 2016.

43. Steinberg 2016b. Responding to my inquiry about this manuscript, the National Library has not been able to identify it.

44. Eyal 2006, 198–200.

45. "Homer Shalal me-Arkhiyonei Asha"f be-Beirut" 1982, 1.

46. "Homer Shalal me-Arkhiyonei Asha"f be-Beirut" 1982, 3.

47. Rabi 2016.

48. Rabinovich 2018.

49. Eyal 2006, 205. Eyal cites works based on the Jordanian police archive captured in 1967 as well as books that rely on Syrian, Egyptian, and Iraqi documents. See Eyal 2006, 283 n. 33. Rabinovich acknowledges his use of captured documents in his own scholarship. As Rabinovich told journalist Nora Boustany, when he was a soldier in the 1967 war, he entered the abandoned Ba'th Party office in Quneitra and found a filing cabinet. "I realized it was a treasure," Rabinovich recalled. "He stored the papers in the trunk of his car," Boustany wrote, "and later was able to reconstruct the inner workings of the Baath Party from the files, research that ended up in his dissertation." Boustany 1996. In reference to his use of these archives, Rabinovich explained that "this was an entirely different matter and [his doctoral] supervisor Malcolm Kerr had no problem with it." Rabinovich 2018.

50. "Haim Gal" 2018. The colleague who shared this story with me requested not to be identified.

51. See Dayah 1978.

52. *Yedi'ot Aharonot* 1983.

53. In interviews I have conducted, the same has been consistently asserted—namely, that the offer was extended by the military and refused by the universities and the Dayan Center, on the grounds that universities should not build their libraries through military conquest. Rabinovich 2016. To be sure, in earlier periods in Israeli history, this principle was not observed. See Amit 2014.

54. This person asked that he not be identified by name.

55. B 2018.

56. Dan 1981. This book appears to have been purchased in London in November 1981 from the bookstore Woolston's and Blunt's (on the transformation of this historic bookstore, see https://www.ornaverum.org/family/blunt/and-sons.html, accessed March 2, 2022). During the 1982 invasion of Beirut, Dan was serving as Defense Minister Ariel Sharon's spokesman. Shipler 1982a, A1.

57. Brunner 2007.

58. Jacir 2012.

59. Amit 2014.

60. Israeli institutions have been known to make inaccessible previously accessible materials once they are recognized to be politically sensitive. See, e.g., Anziska 2019; Hazkani 2019; Pappe 2020.

61. In the library catalogue, it is unclear how many volumes of Tidhar's encyclopedia and of the Arabic periodical *al-Riwaya* entered the system with this package. I count each of these as one item but each may in fact constitute several volumes.

62. A. Sayegh 2006, 221.

63. F. Jiryis 2022, 259–67.

64. "Thalathun ʿaman ʿala istishhadihim" n/d; "Markaz al-Abhath (pamphlet)" 2018.

65. *Ihyaʾ Markaz Al-Abhath* 2018.

66. Shabeeb passed away in Damascus in 2019. See his obituaries: "Rahal baʿidan ʿan Yafa: Samih Shabib Yudafin bi-Mukhayim al-Yarmuk" 2021; Hourani 2021.

67. Shabeeb 2018.

68. Shabeeb 2005; "Thalathun ʿaman ʿala istishhadihim" n/d.

69. Shabeeb 2018.

70. Shabeeb 2018.

71. Shabeeb 2018.

72. Halbfinger, Kershner, and Walsh 2018.

Conclusion: Empathy, Realism, and the Effects of "Knowing the Enemy"

1. Muslih 1976.

2. Here, I use "moderation" in the sense that Salim Yaqub uses "moderate," that is, as a description, rather than as a judgment, of a political position. See Yaqub 2016, 16.

3. Cited in Yezid Sayigh 1997, 337.

4. Steinberg 2016a, 28–29.

5. S. Khalaf 1974. The title in the issue's table of contents reads "New Ideas before an Ambiguous Stage." On Khalaf (Abu Iyad), see the excellent chapter dedicated to him in Thompson 2013.

6. Steinberg 2016a, 29. Already in 1976, scholar Muhammad Muslih noted that a significant motivation in the PLO's embrace of the interim territorial goal of the West Bank and Gaza was to "block their possible takeover by the Hashimite [*sic*] regime." Muslih 1976, 131.

7. S. Khalaf 1974, 6.

8. S. Khalaf 1974, 7–8.

9. S. Khalaf 1974, 10. Cited also in Yezid Sayigh 1997, 342.

10. S. Khalaf 1974, 7.

11. Cited in Yezid Sayigh 1997, 342.

12. S. Khalaf 1974, 10.

13. Cited in Yezid Sayigh 1997, 338–39.

14. Cited in Yezid Sayigh 1997, 338.

15. S. Jiryis 2016b, 27.

16. Yezid Sayigh 1997, 342.

17. To be sure, the Center's publications were far from unanimous on the matter of coexistence with Israel. After Uri Avnery wrote *Israel without Zionists* (1967), in which he advocated for a Palestinian state alongside Israel, the PLO Research Center published Camille Mansour's *Uri Avnery or Neo-Zionism*, arguing that his was "a Zionist plot to end the Palestinian revolution and induce the Palestinians to settle down in a state of their own and recognize Israel." Avnery argued that he was not the ultimate target of this polemic but rather those Palestinian intellectuals who shared his views. Mansour 1971; Avnery 1986, 35.

18. Note the similarities, in timing and logic, between the PLO's Israel expert Jiryis's post-1973 acceptance of a two-state solution and Israel's PLO expert Yehoshafat Harkabi's push for Israel to negotiate with the PLO and to pull out of the West Bank. In April 1974, Harkabi wrote: "We certainly have historic links to Judea and Samaria but I believe that realistic considerations

should make it clear to us that we cannot maintain the present borders and refuse to withdraw or refuse to abandon settlements. If only I were wrong." The published English translation, which I largely follow here, does not include the last remark I have cited. Harkabi 1974b, 18; Harkabi 1974a, 256.

19. S. Jiryis 2016a, 4–5.

20. S. Jiryis 1973a; S. Jiryis 1973b.

21. S. Jiryis 1973a.

22. S. Jiryis 1973a.

23. S. Jiryis 1973a.

24. S. Jiryis 1973a.

25. S. Jiryis 2016b, 12.

26. See https://info.wafa.ps/ar_page.aspx?id=3982, archived at perma.cc/FL34-W82R, and the entry on the March 1977 PNC session on www.palquest.org, archived at perma.cc/S2CB-WUQ7.

27. If the 1974 Ten Points Program set the bar for clarity of such expression, it was not set high.

28. In fact, as Eli Osheroff has shown, Palestinians did propose alternatives other than "consistent rejection." Osheroff 2021.

29. S. Jiryis 1977b, 3–4.

30. S. Jiryis 1977b, 4.

31. S. Jiryis 1977b, 5.

32. S. Jiryis 1977b, 6.

33. S. Jiryis 1977b, 7.

34. S. Jiryis 1977b, 8.

35. S. Jiryis 1977b, 8.

36. S. Jiryis 1977b, 8–10.

37. S. Jiryis 1977b, 11.

38. S. Jiryis 1977b, 13.

39. S. Jiryis 1977b, 18.

40. S. Jiryis 1977b, 21.

41. S. Jiryis 1977b, 21–22.

42. S. Jiryis 1977b, 24.

43. Sadik al-Azm cited Jiryis's article in *The Nation* in December 1981. Al-Azm argued that "the moderate Palestinians, who advocate the territorial solution, are inverse Zionists." Al-Azm named two examples: Walid Khalidi's 1978 article in *Foreign Affairs* and this article by Sabri Jiryis. Jiryis, according to al-Azm, "praised the PLO leadership's realism in adopting a limited territorial solution to the Palestinian question. Jiryis wrote that this welcome development signified that the leadership had studied and profited from the pragmatism of the Zionists." Al-Azm 1981.

44. Engerman 2011, 4.

45. Ameri 2016.

46. Engerman 2011, 4–5.

47. The parallels do not end there. Engerman notes that "while the government agencies and foundations that supported Russian Studies had created the field to learn more about the Politburo, they also created experts on Pushkin. Though they sought insights into Brezhnev, they

also boosted the study of Bulgakov and, eventually, Bakhtin." Engerman 2011, 6. Similarly, while the Arab League and other funders of the PLO Research Center presumably sent their grants for books like *Zionist Colonization in Palestine, The Balance of Military Power between the Arab States and Israel*, or *Israeli Belligerent Occupation and Palestinian Armed Resistance in International Law*, those funds were also used to support the publication of books on the kibbutz and the moshav, research on classic rabbinic texts, and studies of Hebrew literature. If the impulse to found the PLO Research Center and to study about Israel was obviously driven by politics, those who participated in the efforts had their own intellectual interests.

Postscript

1. "Thalathun ʿaman ʿala istishhadihim" n/d, 7.

2. Rumley and Tibon 2017, 32.

3. This recollection is found on Mahmoud Abbas's official website. The translation here follows the English version except in the last sentence where I provide a more literal translation of the Arabic. In particular, the Arabic refers to the "Israeli composition" while the English renders this "the composition of the enemy." Abbas 1994b; Abbas 1994a. Cited in Rumley and Tibon 2017, 32.

4. Abbas 1995, 13–14. Cited in Rumley and Tibon 2017, 35.

5. Interview cited in Rumley and Tibon 2017, 35. Tibi, a Palestinian citizen of Israel, is a longtime member of Israel's Knesset.

6. Rumley and Tibon 2017, 35–36. For a fascinating analysis of the evolution of Abbas's perspective on Zionism, see Miller 2016a; Miller 2016b.

7. S. Jiryis 2018.

8. "Thalathun ʿaman ʿala istishhadihim" n/d, 5.

9. "Thalathun ʿaman ʿala istishhadihim" n/d, 6.

10. Cited in Abu-Lughod 2018, 3.

11. Abu-Lughod 2018, 3. Abu-Lughod's father, Ibrahim, edited *The Judaization of Palestine* for the PLO Research Center in 1972. Cf. Weld 2014; Elkins 2015.

12. Many are now found on Internet Archive at archive.org.

WORKS CITED

Don Peretz Papers
Fayez A. Sayegh Collection, University of Utah Archives
Israel Defense Forces and Defense Establishment Archives (IDF Archives)
Israel State Archives (ISA)
National Library of Israel Archives
Shuʾun Filastiniyya Digital Archive

Abbas, Mahmoud. 1994a. "*Mahattat fi Hayat al-Raʾis*." At http://president.ps/Stage.aspx, accessed February 19, 2018.
———. 1994b. "Stages in the Life of the President." At http://president.ps/eng/general.aspx?id=99, accessed February 19, 2018.
———. 1995. *Through Secret Channels: The Road to Oslo: Senior PLO Leader Abu Mazen's Revealing Story of the Negotiations with Israel*. Reading: Garnet Pub.
ʿAbd al-ʿAziz, Mustafa. 1969. *Israʾil wa-Yahud al-ʿAlam: Dirasa Siyasiyya wa-Qanuniyya*. Dirasat Filastiniyya 59. Beirut: PLO Research Center.
ʿAbd al-Hadi, ʿAwni. 1974. *ʿAwni ʿAbd al-Hadi: Awraq Khassa*. Edited by Khairieh Kasmieh. Kutub Filastiniyya 54. Beirut: PLO Research Center.
———, ed. 1974. *Al-Harb al-ʿArabi al-Israʾili al-Rabiʿa: Waqaʾiʿ wa-Tafaʿulat*. Kutub Filastiniyya 59. Beirut: PLO Research Center.
Abdallah, Hisham. 1974. *Aslihat al-Jaysh al-Israʾili*. Haqaʾiq wa-Arqam 48. Beirut: PLO Research Center.
Abdo, Ali Ibrahim, and Khairieh Kasmieh. 1971a. *Jews of the Arab Countries*. Palestine Monographs 82. Beirut: PLO Research Center.
———. 1971b. *Yahud al-Bilad al-ʿArabiyya*. Dirasat Filastiniyya 82. Beirut: PLO Research Center.
Abdullah II of Jordan. 2012. *Our Last Best Chance: A Story of War and Peace*. London: Penguin.
Abdul-Rahman, Asaʾd. 1967. *Al-Tasallul al-Israʾili fi Asya: Al-Hind wa-Israʾil*. Dirasat Filastiniyya 11. Beirut: PLO Research Center.
al-Abid, Ibrahim. 1966. *Al-Mabay: al-Hizb al-Hakim fi Israʾil*. Dirasat Filastiniyya 7. Beirut: PLO Research Center.
———. 1967. *Al-ʿUnf wa-l-Salam: Dirasa fi al-Istratijiya al-Sahyuniyya*. Dirasat Filastiniyya 10. Beirut: PLO Research Center.

———. 1968. *Al-Mushaf: al-Qura al-Taʿawuniyya fi Israʾil*. Dirasat Filastiniyya 26. Beirut: PLO Research Center.

———. 1969a. *Israel and Human Rights*. Palestine Books 24. Beirut: PLO Research Center.

———. 1969b. *A Handbook to the Palestine Question: Questions and Answers*. Palestine Books 17. Beirut: PLO Research Center.

———. 1969c. *Dalil al-Qadiyya al-Filastiniyya: Asʾila wa-Ajwiba*. Kutub Filastiniyya 17. Beirut: PLO Research Center.

———. 1971. *A Handbook to the Palestine Question: Questions and Answers*. 2nd ed. Beirut: Palestine Books 17. PLO Research Center.

Abillama, Raja. 2018. "Contesting Secularism: Civil Marriage and Those Who Do Not Belong to a Religious Community in Lebanon." *PoLAR: Political and Legal Anthropology Review* 41, no. S1: 148–62.

Abu-Amr, Ziad. 1994. *Islamic Fundamentalism in the West Bank and Gaza: Muslim Brotherhood and Islamic Jihad*. Bloomington: Indiana University Press.

Abu Eid, Muna. 2016. *Mahmoud Darwish: Literature and the Politics of Palestinian Identity*. London: I. B. Tauris.

Abu Ghazala, Bassam. 1966. *Al-Judhur al-Irhabiyya li-Hizb Herut al-Israʾili*. Dirasat Filastiniyya 5. Beirut: PLO Research Center.

AbuKhalil, Asʿad. 1987. "Internal Contradictions in the PFLP: Decision Making and Policy Orientation." *Middle East Journal* 41, no. 3: 361–78.

Abu-Lughod, Lila. 2013. *Do Muslim Women Need Saving?* Cambridge: Harvard University Press.

———. 2018. "Palestine: Doing Things with Archives." *Comparative Studies of South Asia, Africa and the Middle East* 38, no. 1: 3–5.

Achcar, Gilbert. 2011. "Assessing Holocaust Denial in Western and Arab Contexts." *Journal of Palestine Studies* 41, no. 1: 82–95.

Aderet, Ofer. 2018. "Joining Chorus of Criticism, Yad Vashem Slams Abbas Speech as 'Fundamentally' Anti-Semitic." *Haaretz*, May 3. At https://www.haaretz.com/israel-news/yad-vashem-slams-abbas-speech-as-fundamentally-anti-semitic-1.6052336, accessed November 20, 2023. Archived at perma.cc/N9R4-79BW.

———. 2022. "Transcripts of Kafr Qasem Massacre Trial Revealed: 'The Commander Said Fatalities Were Desirable.'" *Haaretz*, July 29. At http://www.haaretz.com/israel-news/2022-07-29/ty-article/.highlight/kafr-qasem-massacre-trial-transcripts-the-commander-said-fatalities-were-desirable/00000182-49f2-d2c3-a5a3-5df201a50000, accessed September 1, 2022. Archived at perma.cc/4F95-SHNJ.

Adler, Hermann. 1878. "Jews and Judaism: A Rejoinder." *The Nineteenth Century: A Monthly Review* 4, no. 17: 133–50.

Ahmad, Eqbal, Richard Bulliet, Irene Gendzier, Don Peretz, George Saliba, and Stuart Schaar. 1983. "Bona Fide Archives of Palestinian History." *New York Times*, March 16: A26.

Ajami, Fouad. 1978. "The End of Pan-Arabism." *Foreign Affairs* 57, no. 2: 355–73.

Aldar, Nicolas. 1965. Letter to Fayez Sayegh. January 20. Bx 281 Fd3 It 49. Fayez A. Sayegh Collection.

ʿAl ha-Mishmar. 1960. "Mishpat ha-Neʿeshamim be-Pirsum ʿal-Ard'—be-16 May." April 25: 3.

———. 1967. "Sifro shel Ish ʿal-Ard' Yufats ba-ʿOlam ʿal-yedei ha-Liga ha-ʿAravit." May 4: 1.

———. 1969. "Hugshu Sikumim be-Mishpat ha-Ne'eshamim be-Hanahat Mit'anei-ha-Habala be-Yerushalayim." January 9: 5.

Alloush, Naji. 1967. *Al-Muqawama al-'Arabiyya fi Filastin, 1917–1948*. Kutub Filastiniyya 6. Beirut: PLO Research Center.

Almog, Shmuel, Jehuda Reinharz, and Anita Shapira, eds. 1999. *Zionism and Religion*. Hanover: University Press of New England.

Alon, Ilana. 2015. Correspondence with Jonathan Marc Gribetz. July 21.

Alsberg, Paul Abraham. 1983. Letter to Wilfred Smith. June 19. 824/2003–114. IDF Archives.

Ameri, Anan. 1974. *Al-Tatawwur al-Zira'i wa-l-Sina'i al-Filastini, 1900–1970: Bahath Ihsa'i.* Haqa'iq wa-Arqam 47. Beirut: PLO Research Center.

———. 2016. Interview by Jonathan Marc Gribetz. May.

———. 2017. *The Scent of Jasmine: Coming of Age in Jerusalem and Damascus*. Northampton, MA: Olive Branch Press.

———. 2020. *The Wandering Palestinian: A Memoir*. Plymouth, MI: BHC Press.

Amit, Gish. 2014. *Eks Libris: Historiya shel Gezel, Shimur ve-Nikus ba-Sifriya ha-Le'umit bi-Yerushalayim*. Jerusalem: Ha-Kibbutz ha-Me'uhad.

Amnon, K. 1960. "Tevusa le-Mak"i u-Mapa"i bein Studentim 'Araviyim." *'Al ha-Mishmar,* February 14: 1.

Anderson, Betty S. 2008. "September 1970 and the Palestinian Issue: A Case Study of Student Politicization at the American University of Beirut (AUB)." *Civil Wars* 10, no. 3: 261–80.

———. 2012. *The American University of Beirut: Arab Nationalism and Liberal Education*. Austin: University of Texas Press.

Anderson, Charles W. 2013. "From Petition to Confrontation: The Palestinian National Movement and the Rise of Mass Politics, 1929–1939." PhD dissertation, New York University.

"Annual Report 1983." 1984. Geneva: International Committee of the Red Cross.

"Anshei 'ha-Adama' Horshim Mezimot." 1960. *Davar ha-Shavu'a,* March 4: 3, 6.

Antonius, George. 1938. *The Arab Awakening: The Story of the Arab National Movement*. London: H. Hamilton.

Anziska, Seth. 2018. *Preventing Palestine: A Political History from Camp David to Oslo*. Princeton: Princeton University Press.

———. 2019. "The Erasure of The Nakba in Israel's Archives." *Journal of Palestine Studies* 49 no. 1: 64–76.

Arab Women's Information Committee. 1969. *The Arabs under Israeli Occupation: Memorandum*. Beirut: Institute for Palestine Studies.

———. 1970. *The Arabs under Israeli Occupation 1969*. No. 2. Beirut: Institute for Palestine Studies.

———. 1971. *The Arabs under Israeli Occupation 1970*. No. 3. Beirut: Institute for Palestine Studies.

Arabs under Israeli Occupation. 1969. Palestine Monographs 55. Beirut: PLO Research Center.

Arendt, Hannah. 1944. "Race-Thinking before Racism." *The Review of Politics* 6, no. 1: 36–73.

al-'Arif, 'Arif. 1973. *Awraq 'Arif Al- 'Arif*. 12 vols. Beirut: PLO Research Center.

"Arkhiyon Asha"f." 1982. Lebanon/104.1/PLO Stockholm: Foreign Ministry—Communication Department. 8367/6-צח. ISA.

Armajani, Jon. 2012. *Modern Islamist Movements: History, Religion, and Politics.* Malden, MA: Wiley-Blackwell.

Associated Press. 1983. "Beirut Issues Report on Massacre." *New York Times,* June 21: A4.

Ateek, Naim Stifan. 1989. *Justice, and Only Justice: A Palestinian Theology of Liberation.* Maryknoll, NY: Orbis Books.

Atiyeh, George N. 1988. "Humanism and Secularism in the Modern Arab Heritage: The Ideas of al-Kawakibi and Zurayk." In *Arab Civilization: Challenges and Responses: Studies in Honor of Constantine K. Zurayk,* edited by George N. Atiyeh and Ibrahim M. Oweiss, 42–62. Albany: State University of New York Press.

Atlanta Constitution. 1983. "20 Killed in Beirut Explosion." February 6: 1A, 15A.

Avineri, Shlomo. 1999. "Zionism and the Jewish Religious Tradition: The Dialectics of Redemption and Secularization." In *Zionism and Religion,* edited by Shmuel Almog, Jehuda Reinharz, and Anita Shapira, 1–9. Hanover: University Press of New England.

Avnery, Uri. 1986. *My Friend, the Enemy.* Westport, CT: Lawrence Hill.

"Awni Abd Al-Hadi." 2023. *Interactive Encyclopedia of the Palestine Question.* At https://www.palquest.org/en/biography/9835/awni-abd-al-hadi, accessed November 17, 2023. Archived at perma.cc/PS53-Q4J9.

Aydin, Cemil. 2007. *The Politics of Anti-Westernism in Asia: Visions of World Order in Pan-Islamic and Pan-Asian Thought.* New York: Columbia University Press.

al-Azm, Sadik. 1969. *Al-Naqd al-Dhati Baʿda al-Hazima.* Acre: Dar al-Jalil li-l-Tibaʿa wa-l-Nashr.

———. 1981. "Palestinian Parallels: The Zionist Analogy." *The Nation,* December 5: 611–12.

———. 2011. *Self-Criticism after the Defeat.* Translated by George Stergios. London: Saqi.

ʿAzmi, Mahmud. 1973. *Al-Quwat al-Israʾiliyya al-Mahmula Jawwan.* Dirasat Filastiniyya 96. Beirut: PLO Research Center.

———. 1975. *Al-Quwat al-Mudarraʿa al-Israʾiliyya ʿabra Arbaʿ Hurub.* Dirasat Filastiniyya 101. Beirut: PLO Research Center.

B, S. 2018. Interview by Jonathan Marc Gribetz. May.

Baconi, Tareq. 2021. "What Apartheid Means for Israel." *New York Review of Books,* November 5.

Badi, Joseph, ed. 1961. *Fundamental Laws of the State of Israel.* New York: Twayne Publishers.

Baki, Roberto. 1966. *Shnaton Statisti le-Yisrael.* Jerusalem: Government. At https://www.cbs.gov.il/he/publications/DocLib/shnaton_saruk/shnaton1966_num17.pdf, accessed January 19, 2021. Archived at perma.cc/2T5A-2HQK.

Barak, Oren. 2017. *State Expansion and Conflict: In and between Israel/Palestine and Lebanon.* Cambridge: Cambridge University Press.

Bar David, Yehoshuʿa. 1982. "Tsav bi-dvar Pirsumim Asurim/Amr bi-shaʾni al-Matbuʿat al-Mahdhura." *Minsharim, Tsavim, u-Minuyim shel Ezor Yehuda ve-Shomron* 50. Israel Defense Forces.

Bardawil, Fadi A. 2020. *Revolution and Disenchantment: Arab Marxism and the Binds of Emancipation.* Theory in Forms. Durham: Duke University Press.

Bar-Siman-Tov, Yaacov. 2014. *Justice and Peace in the Israeli-Palestinian Conflict.* Edited by Arie M. Kacowicz. London: Routledge.

Bashan, Raphael. 1983. "Shomer ha-Hotam shel ha-Historiya ha-Yisraʾelit." *Yediʿot Aharonot,* June 10: 12–14.

"Bayan Nuwayhed Al-Hout (1937–)." 2023. *Interactive Encyclopedia of the Palestine Question*. At https://www.palquest.org/en/biography/34679/bayan-nuwayhed-al-hout, accessed July 16, 2023. Archived at perma.cc/W97S-4VA4.

Beauvoir, Simone de. 1967. "On Israeli Women." *New Outlook* 10, no. 4 (88): 27–28.

Bein, Alex. 1970. *Theodore Herzl: A Biography*. Translated by Maurice Samuel. New York: Atheneum.

Beinin, Joel. 1991. "Knowing Your Enemy, Knowing Your Ally: The Arabists of Hashomer Hatza'ir (MAPAM)." *Social Text* no. 28: 100–121.

Ben-Ami, Shlomo. 2007. *Scars of War, Wounds of Peace: The Israeli-Arab Tragedy*. Oxford: Oxford University Press.

Benvenisti, Meron. 1983. "The Turning Point in Israel." *New York Review of Books*, October 13.

Ben-Zvi, Itzhak. 1958. *The Exiled and the Redeemed; the Strange Jewish "Tribes" of the Orient*. Translated by Isaac Abraham Abbady. London: Vallentine, Mitchell.

Berger, Elmer. 1942. "Why I Am a Non-Zionist." Flint, MI.

———. 1945. *The Jewish Dilemma*. New York: Devin-Adair.

———. 1951. *A Partisan History of Judaism*. New York: Devin-Adair.

———. 1957. *Judaism or Jewish Nationalism: The Alternative to Zionism*. New York: Bookman.

———. 1978. *Memoirs of an Anti-Zionist Jew*. Beirut: Institute for Palestine Studies.

———. 1983. "Review of The Palestine Liberation Organization/Its Institutional Infrastructure." *Arab Studies Quarterly* 5, no. 3: 301–5.

Bergman, Ronen. 2018a. *Rise and Kill First: The Secret History of Israel's Targeted Assassinations*. New York: Random House.

———. 2018b. "How Arafat Eluded Israel's Assassination Machine." *New York Times Magazine*, January 23.

Berkovitz, Jay R. 2007. "The Napoleonic Sanhedrin: Halachic Foundations and Rabbinic Legacy." *CCAR Journal: A Reform Jewish Quarterly* 54, no. 1: 11–34.

Beshara, Adel. 2019. *Fayez Sayegh: The Party Years 1938–1947*. London: Black House Publishing.

"Bilal al Hassan—Who Is Bilal al Hassan?" 2018. At http://www.webgaza.net/palestine/people_profiles/Hassan_Bilal.htm, accessed July 5, 2018. Archived at perma.cc/QQ4Q-CAZQ.

Bishuti, Bassam. 1969. *The Role of the Zionist Terror in the Creation of Israel*. Palestine Monographs 58. Beirut: PLO Research Center.

———. 1973. *Terrorismo: Factor principal en la creación del Estado de Israel*. Madrid: Oficina de Información de la Liga de los Estados Árabes.

Bligh, Alexander. 2004. "Palestinian and Jordanian Views of the Balfour Declaration." In *Views from the Edge: Essays in Honor of Richard W. Bulliet*, edited by Neguin Yavari, Lawrence G. Potter, and Jean-Marc Ran Oppenheim, 19–26. New York: Columbia University Press.

Booth, William, and Ruth Eglash. 2014. "Senior Palestinian Official Dies after Clash with Israeli Forces in the West Bank." *Washington Post*, December 10, sec. Middle East.

Boullata, Kamal, and Mirène Ghossein, eds. 1979. *The World of Rashid Hussein, a Palestinian Poet in Exile*. AAUG Monograph Series 12. Detroit: Association of Arab-American University Graduates.

Boustany, Nora. 1996. "Sitting with the Enemy." *Washington Post*, May 29: F1, F11.

Braizat, Musa S. 1999. *The Jordanian Palestinian Relationship: The Bankruptcy of the Confederal Idea*. London: British Academic Press.

Brilliant, Moshe. 1972. "Israelis Kill 2 Hijackers and Free 100 on Airliner." *New York Times*, May 10: A1–A2.

———. 1982. "Some Israeli Politicians Urge Begin and Sharon to Resign." *New York Times*, September 20: A10.

Brunner, Benny, dir. 2007. *The Great Book Robbery: Chronicles of a Cultural Destruction*. Documentary. 2911 Foundation and Xena Films in association with Al-Jazeera English. At https:// bbrunner.eu/movie/the-great-book-robbery/, accessed March 3, 2022.

Bsisu, Saʿadi. 1945. *Al-Sahyuniyya: Naqd wa-Tahlil-*. Jerusalem: Dar al-Muʿarif.

Bulliet, Richard. 2017. Correspondence with Jonathan Marc Gribetz. September 14.

Campbell, Ann Morgan. 1983a. "The Society of American Archivists, Minutes: Annual Business Meeting, 20 October 1982." *The American Archivist* 46, no. 2: 230–33.

———. 1983b. "The Society of American Archivists, Minutes: Council Meeting, 22 October 1982." *The American Archivist* 46, no. 2: 228–30.

Campbell, Colin. 1982a. "Gemayel of Lebanon Is Killed in Bomb Blast at Party Offices." *New York Times*, September 15: A1, A8.

———. 1982b. "Israel Increases Its Grip on Beirut." *New York Times*, September 18: 1, 4.

———. 1982c. "Raids on Camps Started Day after Gemayel Died." *New York Times*, September 19: A14.

———. 1982d. "Survivors of Massacre Tell of Reign of Terror." *New York Times*, September 21: A18.

Campos, Michelle U. 2011. *Ottoman Brothers: Muslims, Christians, and Jews in Early Twentieth-Century Palestine*. Stanford, CA: Stanford University Press.

Caplan, Neil. 2011. *The Israel-Palestine Conflict: Contested Histories*. West Sussex: Wiley-Blackwell.

Carmin Karpman, Itzhak J., ed. 1978. *Who's Who in World Jewry: A Biographical Dictionary of Outstanding Jews*. 4th ed. Tel Aviv: Olive Books.

Case, Holly. 2018. *The Age of Questions*. Princeton: Princeton University Press.

Chamberlin, Paul Thomas. 2012. *The Global Offensive: The United States, the Palestine Liberation Organization, and the Making of the Post-Cold War Order*. Oxford: Oxford University Press.

Childs, Martin. 2010. "David Kimche: Spymaster Who Established Mossad as a Force in International Espionage." *The Independent*, April 29: 8.

Christians, Zionism and Palestine: A Selection of Articles and Statements on the Religion and Political Aspects of the Palestine Problem. 1970. Anthology Series 4. Beirut: Institute for Palestine Studies.

Clark, Peter. 2004. "Faris Glubb: Journalist, Poet, and Political Activist with a Deep Islamic Faith." *Guardian*, May 17.

Cohen, Gili. 2016. "Tsaha"l Shakal lisgor et Yehidat ha-Modi'in 'Hatsav,' akh Histapek be-Horadat Daragat Mefakdah." *Ha-Aretz*, October 29.

Cohen, Hillel. 2022. *Son'im Sipur Ahavah: ʿAl Mizrahim ve-ʿArvim (ve-Ashkenazim gam) me-Reshit ha-Tsiyonut ve-ʿad Meʾoraʿot 2021*. Tel Aviv: Ivrit.

Cohen, Shalom, and Kokhavi Shemesh. 1976. "The Origin and Development of the Israeli Black Panther Movement." *MERIP Reports* no. 49 : 19–22.

Cohen-Mor, Dalya. 2019. *Mahmoud Darwish: Palestine's Poet and the Other as the Beloved*. Cham, Switzerland: Palgrave Macmillan.

Coser, Lewis A. 1965. *Men of Ideas: A Sociologist's View*. New York: Free Press.

Creswell, Robyn. 2018. *City of Beginnings: Poetic Modernism in Beirut*. Princeton: Princeton University Press.

Cubert, Harold M. 1997. *The PFLP's Changing Role in the Middle East*. London: F. Cass.

"D. Ha-Hitpathuyot ha-Tsvaʾiyot ve-ha-Mediniyot ʿal Rekaʿ ha-Mitrahesh be-Levanon ba-Yamim ha-Ahronim." 1982. At https://knesset.gov.il/tql/knesset_new/knesset10/HTML_27_03_2012_05-50-30-PM/19820812@19820812004@004.html, accessed October 24, 2021.

"Al-Dajani, Burhan (1921–2000)." 2021. At http://passia.org/personalities/468, accessed October 7, 2021. Archived at perma.cc/ZH2A-MRCQ.

Dalil al-Muqatil al-Filastini. 1972. Part 1: Al-Jalil wa-l-Murtafaʿat al-Suriyya. Nasharat Khasa. Haqaʾiq wa-Arqam 40. PLO Research Center.

Dallasheh, Leena. 2010. "Political Mobilization of Palestinians in Israel: The al-ʾArd Movement." In *Displaced at Home: Ethnicity and Gender among Palestinians in Israel*, edited by Rhoda Kanaaneh and Isis Nusair, 21–38. Albany: State University of New York Press.

Dan, Uri. 1981. *Mivtsaʿ Gome*. Tel Aviv: Maʿariv.

Darwish, Mahmoud. 1973. *Yawmiyat al-Huzn al-ʿAdi*. Beirut: PLO Research Center.

———. 1974. *Wadaʿan ayyatuha al-Harb, wadaʿan ayyuha al-Salam*. Beirut: PLO Research Center.

———. 1975. *Tilka Suratuha wa-hadha Intihar al-ʿAshiq*. Beirut: PLO Research Center.

Davar. 1969. "Neʾesham mi-ʿal-Ard': Hitnagadti le-hitstarfut ʿArviyei Yisraʾel le-Irgunei ha-Habala." October 13: 14.

———. 1971. "ʿOʾd Sabri Jiryis Hishtakeʿa Bi-Levanon." January 12: 4.

Dayah, Jan. 1978. "Majallat ʿal-ʿAlam al-Israʾili' al-Bayrutiyya." *Shuʾun Filastiniyya* 74–75: 113–34.

"Decisions Adopted by the Executive Board at Its 115th Session." 1982. Paris: United Nations Educational, Scientific and Cultural Organization. At https://unesdoc.unesco.org/ark:/48223/pf0000050991?posInSet=1&queryId=b90969fe-d66c-4621-b7ef-b51282789417http://unesdoc.unesco.org/images/0005/000509/050991E.pdf, accessed October 17, 2023.

Denton, Herbert H. 1983. "Arafat Returns to Damascus, Has Talks with Soviet Envoy." *Washington Post*, June 24: A22.

Desmond-Harris, Jenée. 2014. "11 Ways Race Isn't Real." *Vox*. At https://www.vox.com/2014/10/10/6943461/race-social-construct-origins-census, accessed October 21, 2021.

Devji, Faisal. 2013. *Muslim Zion: Pakistan as a Political Idea*. Cambridge, MA: Harvard University Press.

Di-Capua, Yoav. 2018. *No Exit: Arab Existentialism, Jean-Paul Sartre, and Decolonization*. Chicago: University of Chicago Press.

Dor, Yoʾel. 1965a. "Huʾarakh Tokef Tsavei-ha-Rituk Neged Anshei 'al-Ard.'" *Davar*, March 8: 4.

———. 1965b. "Mahatsit ha-Hotmim ʿal Reshimat 'al Ard' bitlu Hatimotehem." *Davar*, September 14: 2.

———. 1971. "Ha-Meshorer she-Yatsa likhfor." *Davar*, February 14: 7.

Dowty, Alan. 2008. *Israel/Palestine*. 2nd ed. Walden, MA: Polity.

Eisenberg, Laura Zittrain, and Neil Caplan. 2010. *Negotiating Arab-Israeli Peace: Patterns, Problems, Possibilities*. Bloomington: Indiana University Press.

Ekin, Larry. 1983. Letter to Don Peretz. June 13. A16 Ozick. Don Peretz Papers.

Elkins, Caroline. 2015. "Looking beyond Mau Mau: Archiving Violence in the Era of Decolonization." *American Historical Review* 120, no. 3: 852–68.

Elmessiri, Abdelwahab M. 1976. "Al-Hasidiyya: Ihda Rawafid al-Ghaybiyya al-Sahyuniyya." *Shu'un Filastiniyya* 53–54: 140–56.

Engel, David. 2009. *Zionism*. Short Histories of Big Ideas Series. New York: Pearson/ Longman.

Engels, Friedrich, and Karl Marx. 1975. *Collected Works*. Vol. 4. London: Lawrence & Wishart.

Engerman, David C. 2011. *Know Your Enemy: The Rise and Fall of America's Soviet Experts*. New York: Oxford University Press.

Etgar. 1964. "'Al Ard' Mefareshet Matateroteha." November 26: 7.

"Eugene Victor Debs Rostow—People—Department History—Office of the Historian." 2017. At https://history.state.gov/departmenthistory/people/rostow-eugene-victor-debs, accessed October 24, 2017. Archived at perma.cc/72DL-HNZ8.

"Evidence Submitted to the Palestine Royal Commission, House of Lords." 1937. London: New Zionist Press.

Eyal, Gil. 2006. *The Disenchantment of the Orient: Expertise in Arab Affairs and the Israeli State*. Stanford, CA: Stanford University Press.

Faramarzi, Scheherezade. 1983. "20 Killed, 136 Hurt in Beirut Explosion: Libyan and PLO Centers Destroyed by Car Bomb." *Boston Globe*, February 6: 1, 9.

Faris, Habib. 1890. *Al-Dhaba'ih al-Bashariyya al-Talmudiyya*. Cairo: Kutub Qawmiyya.

———. 1891. *Surakh al-Bari' fi Buq al-Hurriyya wa-l-Dhaba'ih al-Talmudiyya*. Cairo: Al-Matba'a al-Jami'a.

Faris, Hani A. 1967. *Al-Tamthil al-Diblumasi al-'Arabi*. Haqa'iq wa-Arqam 11. Beirut: PLO Research Center.

———. 1988. "Constantine K. Zurayk: Advocate of Rationalism in Modern Arab Thought." In *Arab Civilization: Challenges and Responses: Studies in Honor of Constantine K. Zurayk,* edited by George N. Atiyeh and Ibrahim M. Oweiss, 1–41. Albany: State University of New York Press.

Farrell, William E. 1982a. "Egypt Assails Israeli Move into West Beirut." *New York Times*, September 16: A13.

———. 1982b. "Egypt Calls Home Its Envoy to Show Anger with Israel." *New York Times*, September 21: A16.

———. 1982c. "Israelis, at Huge Rally in Tel Aviv, Demand Begin and Sharon Resign." *New York Times*, September 26: A1.

Farsoun, Samih K., and Naseer H. Aruri. 2006. *Palestine and the Palestinians: A Social and Political History*. 2nd ed. Boulder: Westview Press.

Feron, James. 1968. "Israel's 'Night of Grenades.'" *New York Times,* August 25: E5.

Filiu, Jean-Pierre. 2014. *Gaza: A History*. London: Hurst.

Fischbach, Michael R. 2008. "Khalidi, Walid (1925–)." In *Biographical Encyclopedia of the Modern Middle East and North Africa*, edited by Michael R. Fischbach, 1: 423–27. Detroit: Gale.

———. 2018. *Black Power and Palestine: Transnational Countries of Color*. Stanford, CA: Stanford University Press.

Fischer, Nina. 2021. "Palestinian Non-Violent Resistance and the Apartheid Analogy." *Interventions* 23, no. 8: 1124–39.

Fischoff, Ephraim. 1946. "Berger, Elmer. The Jewish Dilemma (Book Review)." *American Sociological Review* 11, no. 6: 495.

Fishman, Joel. 2016. "Anti-Zionism as a Form of Political Warfare." In *Anti-Judaism, Antisemitism, and Delegitimizing Israel*, edited by Robert S. Wistrich, 92–105. Lincoln: University of Nebraska Press.

Florence, Ronald. 2004. *Blood Libel: The Damascus Affair of 1840*. Madison: University of Wisconsin Press.

Frankel, Jonathan. 1997. *The Damascus Affair: "Ritual Murder," Politics, and the Jews in 1840*. New York: Cambridge University Press.

Frankel, Oz. 2008. "What's in a Name? The Black Panthers in Israel." *The Sixties* 1, no. 1: 9–26.

Friedman, Thomas L. 1983a. "Lebanon's Massacre Inquiry: Few Answers after 4 Months." *New York Times*, January 30: A1, 14.

———. 1983b. "Lebanese Probe of Massacre Is in Chaos." *Courier-Journal*, January 30: A10.

———. 1985. "Israeli Coalition Seems Imperiled." *New York Times*, May 21: A5.

Frisch, Hillel. 2005. "Nationalizing a Universal Text: The Quran in Arafat's Rhetoric." *Middle Eastern Studies* 41, no. 3: 321–36.

Galia, Eli. 2017. *Jurj Habash: Biyografiya Politit: Idi'ologiya u-Politika ba-Ma'avak 'al-Falastin*. Tel Aviv: Resling.

Gannon, Megan. 2016. "Race Is a Social Construct, Scientists Argue." *Scientific American*. At https://www.scientificamerican.com/article/race-is-a-social-construct-scientists-argue/, accessed October 21, 2021.

Gerges, Fawaz A. 2012. "The Transformation of Arab Politics: Disentangling Myth from Reality." In *The 1967 Arab-Israeli War: Origins and Consequences*, edited by Avi Shlaim and Wm Roger Louis, 285–314. Cambridge Middle East Studies. Cambridge: Cambridge University Press.

Gerson, Menachem. 1971. "Women in the Kibbutz." *American Journal of Orthopsychiatry* 41, no. 4: 566–73.

Gilboa, Amos. 2012. "Collecting Information in Preparation for the Six-Day War (1967)." In *Israel's Silent Defender: An Inside Look at Sixty Years of Israeli Intelligence*, edited by Amos Gilboa, Ephraim Lapid, and Yochi Erlich, 65–70. Jerusalem: Gefen Books.

Gilead, Amos. 2018. Interview by Jonathan Marc Gribetz. June.

Glickman, Mark. 1990. "One Voice against Many: A Biographical Study of Elmer Berger, 1948–1968." Rabbinical dissertation, Hebrew Union College.

Golan, Tamar. 1982a. "UNESCO: Be-Levanon Hafra Yisra'el et Megillat Zekhuyot ha-Adam." *Ma'ariv*, October 5: 6.

———. 1982b. "Tsorfat lo Hidsha Heskem ha-Tarbut 'im Yisra'el: UNESCO Megana et Yisra'el 'al 'Hafarat Zekhuyot ha-Adam.'" *Ma'ariv*, October 8: 2.

Goldstein, Warren. 2021. "Appropriating 'Apartheid' to Bash Israel." *Wall Street Journal*, May 10, sec. Opinion: A15.

Gordon, Joseph. 1951. "Soviet Union." *The American Jewish Year Book* 52: 328–36.

Gottreich, Emily Benichou. 2006. *Mellah of Marrakesh: Jewish and Muslim Space in Morocco's Red City*. Bloomington: Indiana University Press.

Granot, Oded. 1982. "Shtey Panim la-'Merkaz le-Mehkarim Filistiniyyim' be-Birat Levanon: Siyu'a le-Asha"f be-Pigu'im ve-Habala—me'ahorei Mikhse Akademit be-Beyrut." *Ma'ariv*, December 2: 21.

———. 1983. "Activities of Palestinian Research Center Discussed." Near East/South Asia Report—Foreign Broadcast Information Service Joint Publications Research Service Reports. 2701.

Gribetz, Jonathan Marc. 2010. "An Arabic-Zionist Talmud: Shimon Moyal's At-Talmud." *Jewish Social Studies* 17, no. 1: 1–30.

———. 2013. "'Their Blood Is Eastern': Shahin Makaryus and Fin de Siècle Arab Pride in the Jewish 'Race.'" *Middle Eastern Studies* 49, no. 2: 143–61.

———. 2014. *Defining Neighbors: Religion, Race, and the Early Zionist-Arab Encounter*. Princeton: Princeton University Press.

———. 2015. "Reading Mendelssohn in Late Ottoman Palestine: An Islamic Theory of Jewish Secularism." In *Secularism in Question: Jews and Judaism in Modern Times*, edited by Ari Joskowicz and Ethan Katz, 48–64. Philadelphia: University of Pennsylvania Press.

———. 2016. "When the Zionist Idea Came to Beirut: Judaism, Christianity, and the Palestine Liberation Organization's Translation of Zionism." *International Journal of Middle East Studies* 48, no. 2: 243–66.

———. 2017. "The PLO's Rabbi: Palestinian Nationalism and Reform Judaism." *Jewish Quarterly Review* 107, no. 1: 90–112.

———. 2018a. "'This Shameful Document': Early PLO Intellectuals on the Balfour Declaration and the Hussein-McMahon Correspondence." *Journal of Levantine Studies* 8, no. 1: 35–58.

———. 2018b. "The PLO's Defense of the Talmud." *AJS Review* 42, no. 2: 293–314.

Guillaume, Alfred. 1956. "Zionists and the Bible: A Criticism of the Claim That the Establishment of an Independent Jewish State in Palestine Is Prophesied in Holy Scripture." New York: Palestine Arab Refugee Office.

Gwertzman, Bernard. 1976a. "Palestinians Preparing to Open Office in Washington." *New York Times*, November 20: 6.

———. 1976b. "U.S. Orders P.L.O. Representative to Leave Country." *New York Times*, November 24: 3.

———. 1976c. "American Jewish Leaders Are Split Over Issue of Meeting with P.L.O." *New York Times*, December 30: 1, 6.

———. 1982. "U.S. Calls Israeli Act a 'Violation' and Demands Immediate Pullout." *New York Times*, September 17: A1, A8.

Ha-Aretz. 1960. "Kenas u-Ma'asar 'a"t le-Anshei 'al Ard.'" June 12: 6.

Habaz, Moran. 2019. "'Our Boys' Exposes the Mizrahi-Palestinian Fault Line." +972 *Magazine*, October 11. At https://www.972mag.com/our-boys-mizrahi-palestinian-racism/, accessed July 10, 2023. Archived at perma.cc/Y3M5-XT5Z.

Habibi, Amira. 1970. *Al-Nuzuh al-Thani: Dirasa Midaniyya Tahliliyya li-Nuzuh 1967*. Dirasat Filastiniyya 75. Beirut: PLO Research Center.

Ha-Boker. 1959. "Al-Ard" in "Mi-Boker 'ad Boker." July 15: 2.

———. 1960. "'Orkhei 'al-Ard'" in "Mi-Boker 'ad Boker." February 24.

———. 1964. "Ne'esra Hakamat 'Tenuat al-Ard'." July 27: 1.

Hadawi, Sami. 1961a. *Palestine: Questions and Answers*. New York: Arab Information Center.

———. 1961b. *Who Benefits from Anti-Semitism.* New York: Arab Information Center.

———. 1968. *Palestine in Focus.* Palestine Essays 7. Beirut: PLO Research Center.

———. 1972. *Crime and No Punishment: Zionist-Israeli Terrorism, 1939–1972.* Palestine Essays 30. Beirut: PLO Research Center.

Haiduc-Dale, Noah. 2013. *Arab Christians in British Mandate Palestine Communalism and Nationalism, 1917–1948.* Edinburgh: Edinburgh University Press.

"Haim Gal." 2018. *Moshe Dayan Center for Middle Eastern and African Studies.* At https://dayan .org/author/haim-gal, accessed October 18, 2023.

Halabi, Zeina G. 2017. *The Unmaking of the Arab Intellectual: Prophecy, Exile and the Nation.* Edinburgh Studies in Modern Arabic Literature. Edinburgh: Edinburgh University Press.

Halasa, Tahani. 1968. *David Bin Juryun.* Dirasat Filastiniyya 44. Beirut: PLO Research Center.

Halbfinger, David M., Isabel Kershner, and Declan Walsh. 2018. "Israel Kills Dozens at Gaza Border as U.S. Embassy Opens in Jerusalem." *New York Times,* May 14, sec. World.

Hamada, Muhammad ʿUmar. 1985. *Aʿlam Filastin: Min al-Qarn al-Awwal hatta l-Khamis ʿAshara Hijri, min al-Qarn al-Sabiʿ hatta al- ʿIshrin Miladi.* Vol. 1. Damascus: Dar al-Qutaiba.

Hanf, Theodor. 2015. *Coexistence in Wartime Lebanon: Decline of a State and Rise of a Nation.* London: I. B. Tauris.

Harb, Amil al-Khuri. 1947. *Muʾamarat al-Yahud ʿala al-Masihiyya: Tabhathu fi Haqiqat Ahdaf al-Haraka al-Sahyuniyya wa-ma Yughla fiha min Shahwat al-Intiqam mina al-Nasraniyya wa-l-Raghbah fi-l-Qadaʾ ʿalayha wa-ʿala Saʾir al-Shuʿub.* Beirut: Dar al-ʿIlm li-l-Malayin.

Harkabi, Yehoshafat. 1972. *Arab Attitudes to Israel.* New York: Hart.

———. 1974a. *Palestinians and Israel.* Jerusalem: Keter Publishing House.

———. 1974b. "Le-Heshbon ha-Nefesh ha-Leʾumi." *Maʿariv,* April 19: 18.

———. 1979. *The Palestinian Covenant and Its Meaning.* London: Vallentine, Mitchell.

Harouvi, Eldad. 2016. *Palestine Investigated: The Criminal Investigation Department of the Palestine Police Force, 1920–1948.* Chicago: Sussex Academic Press.

Harris, Ron. 2014. *Ha-Mishpat ha-Yisraʾeli—Ha-Shanim ha-Meʾatsvot: 1948–1977.* Bnei Brak: Ha-Kibbuts ha-Meʾuhad.

Harris, William W. 2015. *Lebanon: A History, 600–2011.* New York: Oxford University Press.

Harrison, Olivia C. 2016. *Transcolonial Maghreb: Imagining Palestine in the Era of Decolonization.* Stanford, CA: Stanford University Press.

Hartford Courant. 1973. "Israeli, Arab Killers Fight Shadowy Mideast Battle." August 5: 9A.

Hashim, ʿAqil, and Saʿid al-ʿAzm. 1967. *Israʾil fi Urubba al-Gharbiyya.* Dirasat Filastiniyya 23. Beirut: PLO Research Center.

Ha-Tsofe. 1968. "Nistayma Shmiʿat ha-ʿEduyot be-Mishpat ʿYom ha-Rimonim.'" December 9: 3.

———. 1969a. "Nistaymu ha-Sikumim be-Mishpat ha-Neʾeshamim shel ʿLeil ha-Rimonim.'" January 9: 3.

———. 1969b. "Hablanei ʿQawmiyun al ʿArab' Tikhnenu Pitsuts ha-Kotel ha-Maʿaravi." January 22: 3.

Hazkani, Shay. 2019. "Israel's Vanishing Files, Archival Deception and Paper Trails." *Middle East Report* 291.

Helou, Angelina. 1967. *ʿAwamil Takwin Israʾil al-Siyasiyya wa-l-ʿAskariyya wa-l-Iqtisadiyya.* Dirasat Filastiniyya 16. Beirut: PLO Research Center.

———. 1969. *Interaction of Political, Military and Economic Factors in Israel*. Palestine Mono-graphs 16. Beirut: Palestine Research Center.

Hertzberg, Arthur. 1959. *The Zionist Idea: A Historical Analysis and Reader*. Garden City, NY: Doubleday.

Herzl, Theodor. 1946. *The Jewish State*. Edited by Jacob M Alkow. Translated by Sylvie D'Avigdor. New York: American Zionist Emergency Council.

———. 1960. *The Complete Diaries of Theodor Herzl*. Edited by Raphael Patai. Translated by Harry Zohn. Vol. 1. 5 vols. New York: Herzl Press.

Herzog, Michael. 2018. Interview by Jonathan Marc Gribetz. February.

Hijazi, Ihsan A. 1982. "Israelis Looted Archives of P.L.O., Officials Say." *New York Times*, Octo-ber 1: A8.

Hirst, David. 1968. "Arabs' New Approach to the War of Words." *Guardian*, December 12: 9.

Holladay, William Lee. 1968. "Is the Old Testament Zionist?" Beirut: University Christian Cen-ter Forum.

Holt, Elizabeth M. 2021. "Resistance Literature and Occupied Palestine in Cold War Beirut." *Journal of Palestine Studies* 50, no. 1: 3–18.

"Homer Shalal me-Arkhiyonei Asha"f be-Beirut—Bedikat Matsaʾi ve-Afyon Rishoniyim." 1982. Secret 699/0049. IDF Archives.

Hommel, Claudia, Thomas Frusciano, and Dorothy Swanson. 1983. Letter to Ann Morgan Campbell. June 2. 824/2003–114. IDF Archives.

Hourani, Faisal. 1980. *Al-Fikr al-Siyasi al-Filastini 1964–1974*. Beirut: PLO Research Center.

———. 2021. "Sadiq al-ʿumr Samih Shbib fi Dhikra Rahilihi al-Sanawiyya al-Ula." At http://www.al-ayyam.ps/ar_page.php?id=13f9f9cey335149518Y13f9f9ce, accessed October 25, 2021. Archived at perma.cc/ZM98-EJ5D.

al-Hout, Bayan Nuwayhed. 2004. *Sabra and Shatila: September 1982*. London: Pluto Press.

al-Hout, Shafiq. 2007. *Bayna al-Watan wa-l-Manfa: Min Yafa badaʾa al-mishwar*. Beirut: Riad El-Rayyes Books.

———. 2011. *My Life in the PLO: The Inside Story of the Palestinian Struggle*. Translated by Jean Said Makdisi. New York: Pluto Press.

Howard, Walter. 1976. "Terrorists: How They Operate a Worldwide Network." *Boston Globe*, January 18: I14–15.

Hudson, Michael C. 1997. "Palestinians and Lebanon: The Common Story." *Journal of Refugee Studies* 10, no. 3: 243–60.

Husary, Jacqueline Bader. 2018. "Recovering the PLO Research Center: Limits and Potential for Digital Methods to Retrieve Dispersed Archives." MSc dissertation, University College London.

Ibn ʿAbbas, al-Samawʾal bin Yahya (al-Maghribi). n/d. *Badhl al-Majhud fi Ifham al-Yahud*. In-troduced by Muhammad Ahmad al-Shami. Cairo: al-Fajjala al-Jadida.

Ibn Hazm, ʿAli ibn Ahmad. 1960. *Al-Radd ʿala Ibn al-Nighrila al-Yahudi wa-Rasaʾil Ukhra*. Edited by Ihsan ʿAbbas. Cairo: Maktabat Dar al-ʿUruba.

Ihyaʾ Markaz Al-Abhath. 2018. At https://www.youtube.com/watch?v=mfEnMPbZ7-8&feature=youtu.be, accessed May 15, 2018.

International Organization for the Elimination of All Forms of Racial Discrimination. 1979. *Zionism & Racism: Proceedings of an International Symposium*. New Brunswick, NJ: North American.

Israeli Ministry of Foreign Affairs. 2015. "Israeli Settlements and International Law." At http://www.mfa.gov.il/mfa/foreignpolicy/peace/guide/pages/israeli%20settlements%20and%20international%20law.aspx, accessed October 24, 2017.

Israeli Racism. 1975. Beirut: Palestine National Assembly and PLO Research Center.

Jabbour, Rafiq. 1923. *Al-Ruh al-Sahyuniyya Qadiman wa-Hadithan.* Jaridat al-Mahrusa.

Jacir, Emily. 2012. *Ex Libris.* Cologne: Verlag der Buchhandlung Walther König.

Jacob, Benno. 1934. "The Jewish Woman in the Bible." In *The Jewish Library,* edited by Leo Jung, 3–26. New York: Jewish Library Publishing.

"Jeanette." 1983. Letter to Don Peretz. May 8. A16 Ozick. Don Peretz Papers.

Jenkins, Loren. 1982. "Israeli Soldiers Accused of Looting in West Beirut." *Washington Post,* September 29: A15.

Jerusalem Post. 1964. "'El Ard' Vilifies Authorities." July 14: 6.

———. 1972. "Terrorist Official Wounded by Bomb in Beirut Office." July 20: 2.

Jiryis, Fida. 2022. *Stranger in My Own Land: Palestine, Israel and One Family's Story of Home.* London: Hurst.

Jiryis, Sabri. 1966. *Ha-ʿAravim bi-Yisraʾel.* Haifa: Al-Ittihad.

———. 1967a. *Al-ʿArab fi Israʾil.* Dirasat Filastiniyya 14. Beirut: PLO Research Center.

———. 1967b. *Al-Muwatinun al-ʿArab fi Jahim Israʾil.* Jerusalem: League of Arab States.

———. 1968. *The Arabs in Israel 1948–1966.* Beirut: Institute for Palestine Studies.

———. 1972. *Democratic Freedoms in Israel.* Beirut: Institute for Palestine Studies and University of Libya.

———. 1973a. "Israʾil fi Muwajahat Khatar al-Salam: 1." *Al-Nahar,* November 7: 9.

———. 1973b. "Israʾil fi Muwajahat Khatar al-Salam: 2." *Al-Nahar,* November 8: 9.

———. 1976. *The Arabs in Israel.* New York: Monthly Review Press.

———. 1977a. *Tarikh al-Sahyuniyya, 1862–1948.* Vol. 1: 1862–1917. Beirut: PLO Research Center.

———. 1977b. "On Political Settlement in the Middle East: The Palestinian Dimension." *Journal of Palestine Studies* 7, no. 1: 3–25.

———. 1981. "Domination by the Law." *Journal of Palestine Studies* 11, no. 1: 67–92.

———. 1983. "Maʿa Tafjir Maqarr Markaz al-Abhath bi-Sayyara Malghuma: Kalima ila al-Muʿtadin." *Shuʾun Filastiniyya* 136–137: 3–6.

———. 1986. *Tarikh al-Sahyuniyya, 1862–1948.* Vol. 2: 1918–1939. Nicosia, Cyprus: PLO Research Center.

———. 2015. Interviews by Jonathan Marc Gribetz. January, July, and August.

———. 2016a. "Sihei ha-Tsabar." Fassuta, Israel.

———. 2016b. "Karov la-Moked." Fassuta, Israel.

———. 2016c. Correspondence with Jonathan Marc Gribetz. July 9.

———. 2016d. Interviews by Jonathan Marc Gribetz. February and March.

———. 2018. Interview by Jonathan Marc Gribetz. January.

———. 2023. Interview by Jonathan Marc Gribetz. May.

Jiryis, Sabri, and Salah Qallab. 1985. "The Palestine Research Center." *Journal of Palestine Studies* 14, no. 4: 185–87.

Kadi, Leila Salim, ed. 1966. *Israʾil fi al-Maydan al-Dawli.* Haqaʾiq wa-Arqam 4. Beirut: PLO Research Center.

———. 1967. *Al-Histadrut.* Dirasat Filastiniyya 9. Beirut: PLO Research Center.

————, ed. 1969. *Basic Political Documents of the Armed Palestinian Resistance Movement.* Palestine Books 27. Beirut: PLO Research Center.

Kanafani, Ghassan. 1967. *Fi al-Adab al-Sahyuni.* Dirasat Filastiniyya 22. Beirut: PLO Research Center.

————. 2022. *On Zionist Literature.* Translated by Mahmoud Najib. Oxford: Ebb Books.

Kassab, Elizabeth Suzanne. 2010. *Contemporary Arab Thought: Cultural Critique in Comparative Perspective.* New York: Columbia University Press.

Kassir, Samir. 2011. *Beirut.* Berkeley: University of California Press.

Katz, Jacob. 1996. "The Forerunners of Zionism." In *Essential Papers on Zionism,* edited by Jehuda Reinharz and Anita Shapira, 33–45. New York: New York University Press.

al-Kayyali, Abdul Wahhab. 1966. *Al-Kibutz, aw al-Mazari' al-Jama'iyya fi Isra'il.* Dirasat Filastiniyya 4. Beirut: PLO Research Center.

Kedar, Sham'aya. 1970. "Rov ha-'Atsirim ha-'Aravim Hifsiku Shevitat ha-Ra'av." *Yedi'ot Aharonot,* April 30: 23.

Kennedy, J. Michael. 1982. "Lebanese Blame Looting on Israeli Units." *Los Angeles Times,* September 27: 15.

Khadduri, Walid. 1970. "The Jews of Iraq during the Nineteenth Century." *The Arab World* 16, no. 5/6: 10–12.

Khalaf, Issa. 1991. *Politics in Palestine: Arab Factionalism and Social Disintegration, 1939–1948.* Albany: State University of New York Press.

Khalaf, Salah. 1974. "Afkar Wadiha amama Marhala Ghamida." *Shu'un Filastiniyya* 29: 5–10.

al-Khalidi, Muhammad Ruhi. 2020. *Al-Sayunizm ay al-Mas'ala al-Sahyuniyya: Awwal Dirasa 'Ilmiyya bi-l-'Arabiyya 'an as-Sahyuniyya.* Edited by Walid al-Khalidi. Institute for Palestine Studies and Khalidi Library.

Khalidi, Rashid. 1986. *Under Siege: P.L.O. Decisionmaking during the 1982 War.* New York: Columbia University Press.

————. 2012. "The 1967 War and the Demise of Arab Nationalism: Chronicle of a Death Foretold." In *The 1967 Arab-Israeli War: Origins and Consequences,* edited by Avi Shlaim and Wm Roger Louis, 264–84. Cambridge Middle East Studies. Cambridge: Cambridge University Press.

————. 2013. "In Remembrance: Elias Shoufani." *Journal of Palestine Studies* 42, no. 3: 7–9.

Khalidi, Walid. 2016. Interview by Jonathan Marc Gribetz. February.

al-Khalili, Ghazi. 1977. *Al-Mar'a al-Filastiniyya wa-l-Thawra: Dirasa Ijtima'iyya Maydaniyya Tahliliyya.* Beirut: PLO Research Center.

El Khazen, Farid. 2000. *The Breakdown of the State in Lebanon, 1967–1976.* Cambridge, MA: Harvard University Press.

Killgore, Andrew I. 1993. "In Memoriam: Lutfi Abdul Rahman al-Abed." *Washington Report on Middle East Affairs,* June: 55.

————. 1999. "Shafiq W. Kombargi." *Washington Report on Middle East Affairs,* September: 33–34.

Kimmerling, Baruch. 2008. *Clash of Identities: Explorations in Israeli and Palestinian Societies.* New York: Columbia University Press.

Klein, Aaron J. 2005. *Striking Back: The 1972 Munich Olympics Massacre and Israel's Deadly Response.* New York: Random House.

Kol ha-ʿAm. 1964. "Mishpat Tsiburi la-Memshal ha-Tsevaʾi." August 12: 4.

Kolsky, Thomas A. 1990. *Jews against Zionism: The American Council for Judaism, 1942–1948.* Philadelphia: Temple University Press.

Kornberg, Jacques. 1978. "Zionism and Ideology: The Breira Controversy." *Judaism* 27, no. 1: 103–14.

Krebs, Albin. 1967. "U.S. Jews Split on Mideast War; Some See Response in Nation as 'Hysteria.'" *New York Times,* July 16: 48.

Kuwait KUNA. 1982. "PLO Journal Reappears after 3-Month Absence." November 16. Translated into English and published in Foreign Broadcast Information Service Daily Report: Middle East & Africa. FBIS-MEA-82-822: A6.

Lambert-Finkler, Anne-Marie. 1983. Secret to Shmuel Divon. "Merkaz ha-Mehkarim shel Ashaʾf." January 23. 8367/6-חצ. ISA.

La-Merhav. 1964. "Pekudat Maʿatsar Neged ʿAtsurei ʿal-Ard.'" November 16: 1.

———. 1968. "Beit ha-Mishpat Isher Kabalat Hodaʿot ha-Neʾeshamim be-ʿLeil ha-Rimonim' ba-Mishtara." December 30: 5.

———. 1970. "Huʾarakh Maʿatsaro shel ʿoʾd Jiryis." May 3: 6.

Lamiyaʾ, Jamil Mujaʿis. 1968. *Al-Mabam: Hizb al-ʿUmal al-Muwahhad fi Isra'il.* Dirasat Filastiniyya 41. Beirut: PLO Research Center.

Landau, Jacob. 1961. "ʿAlilot Dam u-Redifot Yehudim be-Mitsrayim be-Sof ha-Meʾah ha-19." *Sefunot: Sefer Shanah le-Heker Kehilot Yisraʿel ba-Mizrah* 5: 417–60.

———. 1969a. *The Arabs in Israel: A Political Study.* New York: Oxford University Press.

———. 1969b. *Jews in Nineteenth-Century Egypt.* New York: New York University Press.

Lapid, Ephraim. 2008. "Hag ha-Asif: Maʿarekh ha-Isuf likrat Milhemet Sheshet ha-Yamim." In *Melʾekhet Mahshevet: 60 Shana la-Modiʿin ha-Yisraʿeli—Mabat mi-Bifnim,* edited by Amos Gilboa, Ephraim Lapid, and Yochi Erlich, 62–65. Tel Aviv: Ha-Merkaz le-Moreshet ha-Modiʿin.

"Lebanon International Travel Information." 2022. At https://travel.state.gov/content/travel/en/international-travel/International-Travel-Country-Information-Pages/Lebanon.html, accessed August 31, 2022.

Levin, Geoffrey. 2017. "Arab Students, American Jewish Insecurities, and the End of Pro-Arab Politics in Mainstream America, 1952–1973." *Arab Studies Journal* 25, no. 1: 30–58.

———. 2023. *Our Palestine Question: Israel and American Jewish Dissent, 1948–1978.* New Haven: Yale University Press.

Levy, Lital. 2014. *Poetic Trespass: Writing between Hebrew and Arabic in Israel/Palestine.* Princeton: Princeton University Press.

The Link: Published by Americans for Middle East Understanding. 1969. "Confusion Cleared on 2 'Friends of Jerusalem." January: 6.

Litani, Yehuda. 1982a. "Gormim Mediniyim bi-Yerushalayim: Hashʾarat Misradim shel Ashaʾf be-Bayrut Hafara Hamura shel Heskem ha-Pinuy." *Ha-Aretz,* October 14: 1, 2.

———. 1982b. "PLO Offices in Beirut Breach of Agreement." *Ha-Aretz,* October 14, Foreign Broadcast Information Service edition: I6, I7.

Lockman, Zachary. 1996. *Comrades and Enemies: Arab and Jewish Workers in Palestine, 1906–1948.* Berkeley: University of California Press.

Los Angeles Times. 1972. "Bomb Kills Arab Linked to Lod Massacre." July 9, sec. A: 2.

Lubin, Alex. 2014. *Geographies of Liberation: The Making of an Afro-Arab Political Imaginary*. Chapel Hill: University of North Carolina Press.

Lybarger, Loren D. 2007. "For Church or Nation? Islamism, Secular-Nationalism, and the Transformation of Christian Identities in Palestine." *Journal of the American Academy of Religion* 75, no. 4: 777–813.

Maʿariv. 1971a. "ʿAravi-Yisraʾeli Yaʿarokh be-Beirut Shevuʿon Filastini." January 4: 3.

———. 1971b. "Meshorer ʿAravi Yisraʾeli (Rakaʾh) Higiʿa mi-Moskva le-Kahir." February 10: 3.

———. 1971c. "ʿArafat Hitpayes ʿim Brigadir Yahye ahar she-Hivtiah Kesef la-ʿTsava ha-Filastini.'" March 4: 2.

Maimon, Ada. 1962. *Women Build a Land*. Translated by Shulamith Schwarz-Nardi. New York: Herzl Press.

Mallison, W. T., Jr. 1964. "The Zionist-Israel Juridical Claims to Constitute 'the Jewish People' Nationality Entity and to Confer Membership in It: Appraisal in Public International Law." *George Washington Law Review* 32, no. 5: 983–1075.

Malul, Nissim. 1911. *Kitab Asrar al-Yahud*. Cairo.

Mandel, Karnit, dir. 2021. *Shalal—A Reel War*. Documentary. Haifa Films.

Mandes, Hani. 1982. "Al-Mawluda Akthar min Mara." *Al-Karmil*, January: 69–76.

———. 1993. "Itifaq al-Intidab al-Sahyuni." *Al-Adab*, September 1: 44–46.

Manela, Erez. 2009. *The Wilsonian Moment: Self-Determination and the International Origins of Anticolonial Nationalism*. New York: Oxford University Press.

Mansour, Camille. 1971. *Uri Afniri aw al-Sahyuniyya al-Mustahaditha*. Dirasat Filastiniyya 80. Beirut: PLO Research Center.

Mansour, Camille, and Leila Fawaz, eds. 2000. *Transformed Landscapes: Essays on Palestine and the Middle East in Honor of Walid Khalidi*. Cairo: American University in Cairo Press.

Maoz, Moshe. 2013. "The Zionist/Jewish and Palestinian/Arab National Movements: The Question of Legitimacy—A Comparative Observation." *Israel Studies* 18, no. 2: 30–40.

"Markaz al-Abhath." 1984. *Al-Mawsuʿa al-Filastiniyya*. Damascus: Hayʾat al-Mawsuʿa al-Filastiniyya.

"Markaz al-Abhath." 2018. PLO Research Center.

Massad, Joseph. 1996. "Zionism's Internal Others: Israel and the Oriental Jews." *Journal of Palestine Studies* 25, no. 4: 53–68.

———. 2001. *Colonial Effects: The Making of National Identity in Jordan*. Chichester: Columbia University Press.

Mattar, Philip. 2000. "Constantine Zurayk." *Review of Middle East Studies* 34, no. 2: 303–4.

———, ed. 2005. *Encyclopedia of the Palestinians*. Rev. ed. New York: Facts on File.

———. 2015. Correspondence with Jonathan Marc Gribetz. June 9.

Mattawa, Khaled. 2014. *Mahmoud Darwish: The Poet's Art and His Nation*. Syracuse, NY: Syracuse University Press.

Al-Mawsuʿa al-Filastiniyya. 1984. Damascus: Hayʾat al-Mawsuʿa al-Filastiniyya.

"McGovern Amendment Waiver Recommendations." 17–9344-זח. ISA.

Menuhin, Moshe. 1969. *The Decadence of Judaism in Our Time*. Beirut: Institute for Palestine Studies.

"Merkaz le-Mehkarim Filastiniyyim." 1983. Secret 699/0148 Military Intelligence—Research Division. 824/2003–114. IDF Archives.

Meyer, Michael A. 1983. "American Reform Judaism and Zionism: Early Efforts at Ideological Rapprochement." *Studies in Zionism* 4, no. 1 (7): 49–64.

———. 1995. *Response to Modernity: A History of the Reform Movement in Judaism*. Detroit: Wayne State University.

Meyer, Michael A., and W. Gunther Plaut, eds. 2000. *The Reform Judaism Reader: North American Documents*. New York: UAHC Press.

Mezvinsky, Norton. 1996. "In Memoriam: Rabbi Elmer Berger." *Washington Report on Middle Eastern Affairs*.

"Middle East Librarians Association: Past Officers." 2017. At https://www.mela.us/about/officers/past-officers/, accessed September 14, 2017.

Miller, Elhanan. 2016a. "Mahmud ʿAbbas ve-ha-Tsiyonut: Mi-Maʾavak le-Hashlama." Forum for Regional Thinking. At https://www.regthink.org/images/upload/files/Miller-September-2016.pdf, accessed November 1, 2021. Archived at perma.cc/322E-VALP.

———. 2016b. "Mahmoud Abbas and Zionism: From Struggle to Acceptance." Forum for Regional Thinking. At https://www.regthink.org/en/articles/mahmoud-abbas-and-zionism-from-struggle-to-acceptance, accessed November 1, 2021.

Mirsky, Yehudah. 2014. *Rav Kook: Mystic in a Time of Revolution*. New Haven: Yale University Press.

Mishal, Shaul. 1978. *West Bank/East Bank: The Palestinians in Jordan, 1949–1967*. New Haven: Yale University Press.

Mishal, Shaul, and Avraham Sela. 2006. *The Palestinian Hamas: Vision, Violence, and Coexistence*. New York: Columbia University Press.

Mittelmann, Hanni. 2007. "Threatened Masculinity and the Ambivalence of Being a Jew: The Image of Women in Theodor Herzl's Literary Writings." *Seminar: A Journal of Germanic Studies* 43, no. 3: 301–17.

Morris, Benny. 2000. *Righteous Victims: A History of the Zionist-Arab Conflict, 1881–1999*. London: John Murray.

———. 2003. *The Road to Jerusalem: Glubb Pasha, Palestine and the Jews*. London: I. B. Tauris.

———. 2004. *The Birth of the Palestinian Refugee Problem Revisited*. Cambridge: Cambridge University Press.

Morris, Joe Alex. 1975. "Arab Scholars Press 'Racist' Zionism Point: Zionism." *Los Angeles Times*, November 30, sec. part X: 3.

Moyn, Samuel, and Andrew Sartori. 2013. "Approaches to Global Intellectual History." In *Global Intellectual History*, edited by Samuel Moyn and Andrew Sartori, 3–30. New York: Columbia University Press.

"Al-Muʾassasat al-Buhuth al-Filastiniyya: Muʾassasat al-Dirasat al-Filastiniyya." 1990. *Al-Mawsuʿa al-Filastiniyya: al-Dirasat al-Khassa*. Beirut: Hayʾat al-Mawsuʿa al-Filastiniyya.

"Muʾassasat al-Dirasat al-Filastiniyya, 1963–2013." 2013. Beirut: Institute for Palestine Studies.

Mufti, Aamir. 2007. *Enlightenment in the Colony: The Jewish Question and the Crisis of Postcolonial Culture*. Princeton: Princeton University Press.

Muharib, ʿAbd al-Hafiz. 1981. *Haghanah, Itsil, Lihi: al-ʿAlaqat bayna al-Tanzimat al-Sahyuniyya al-Musallaha, 1937–1948*. Beirut: PLO Research Center.

Muslih, Muhammad Y. 1976. "Moderates and Rejectionists within the Palestine Liberation Organization." *Middle East Journal* 30, no. 2: 127–40.

Nadell, Pamela S. 2019. "Paving the Road to Women Rabbis, 1889–2015." In *Gender and Religious Leadership: Women Rabbis, Pastors, and Ministers*, edited by Hartmut Bomhoff, Denise L Eger, Kathy Ehrensperger, and Walter Homolka, 89–112. New York: Lexington Books.

Naor, Dan. 2023. "A War Waiting to Happen: How Menachem Begin and His Administrations Paved the Way to the 1982 Lebanon War." *Middle Eastern Studies* 59, no. 4: 625–39.

Naqara, Hanna. 1985. *Muhami al-Ard wa-l-Sha'ab*. Acre: Al-Aswar.

Nassar, Hala Khamis, and Najat Rahman, eds. 2008. *Mahmoud Darwish, Exile's Poet: Critical Essays*. Northampton, MA: Olive Branch Press/Interlink Books.

Nassar, Maha. 2014. "'My Struggle Embraces Every Struggle': Palestinians in Israel and Solidarity with Afro-Asian Liberation Movements." *Arab Studies Journal* 22, no. 1: 74–101.

———. 2017. *Brothers Apart: Palestinian Citizens of Israel and the Arab World*. Stanford, CA: Stanford University Press.

Nassar, Najib al-Khuri. 1911. *Al-Sahyuniyya: Tarikhuhu Gharaduhu Ahammiyyatuhu (Mulakh-khasan 'an al-Insaykulubidiyya al-Yahudiyya)*. Haifa: Al-Karmil.

Nevo, Joseph. 2008. "September 1970 in Jordan: A Civil War?" *Civil Wars* 10, no. 3: 217–30.

New York Times. 1964a. "Arabs Create Organization for Recovery of Palestine." May 29: 5.

———. 1964b. "Hasidim May Drop Roving Patrol Cars." May 29: 1, 11.

———. 1964c. "Israeli Arab Party Ordered to Disband." July 27: 3.

———. 1969. "U.N. Panel Is Told Israel Used Torture on Some Prisoners." August 12: 3.

———. 1972a. "Gunmen Linked to Group of Ultraleftists in Japan." May 31: 27.

———. 1972b. "Arab Group Claims Credit." May 31: 27.

———. 1977a. "Vance Rejects a Visa for P.L.O. Official." February 9: 4.

———. 1977b. "World News Briefs." February 11: A4.

———. 1980. "Fayez A. Sayegh, 58, Palestinian Adviser: Consultant to Kuwaiti Mission at U.N. Had Heart Attack—Was a Spokesman for Arabs." December 11: D19.

———. 1982a. "Begin Orders Israelis to Push Palestinians 25 Miles to North." June 7: 1, A12.

———. 1982b. "West Europeans Voice Concern Over Lebanon." September 16: A12.

———. 1982c. "U.N. Council Meets on Beirut." September 17: A8.

———. 1982d. "Texts of American Statements on the Killing of Palestinians." September 19: 14.

———. 1984. "Israel Criticized on P.L.O. Exchange." January 26: A8.

Newsview: The Israeli Weekly News Magazine. 1983a. "PLO Back in Beirut." February 8: 32.

———. 1983b. "Terrorist Academic." February 22: 32–33.

Newsweek. 1970. "Guerrilla U." October 5: 68,70.

Nolan, Michael E. 2005. *The Inverted Mirror: Mythologizing the Enemy in France and Germany, 1898–1914*. New York: Berghahn Books.

Nossiter, Bernard D. 1982. "Security Council Condemns Latest Israeli Incursion." *New York Times*, September 18, sec. 1: 4.

Novak, David. 2015. *Zionism and Judaism: A New Theory*. New York: Cambridge University Press.

Nuwayhid, 'Ajaj. 1967. *Brutukulat Hukama' Sahyun*. Vol. 2. 2 vols. Beirut.

Osheroff, Eli. 2014. "Me-Ayin Ba'tem? Toldot 'Am Yisra'el be-Historiyografiya ha-Falastinit ha-Mukdemet (1920–1948)." MA thesis, Hebrew University of Jerusalem.

———. 2021. "Ba'ayat Filastin, ha-She'elah ha-Yehudit u-Fitronot Politiyim Neshkahim: Neku-dat ha-Mabat ha-'Aravit 1908–1948." PhD dissertation, Hebrew University of Jerusalem.

Ottaway, David B. 1982. "Fearful Refugees Face New Turmoil: Minus Protectors, Refugees Grapple with Harsh 'New Lebanon.'" *Washington Post*, December 28: A1, A8.

Owen, John M., IV. 2010. *The Clash of Ideas in World Politics: Transnational Networks, States, and Regime Change, 1510–2010*. Princeton: Princeton University Press.

Ozick, Cynthia. 1974. "All the World Wants the Jews Dead." *Esquire*, November: 103–7, 207–10.

———. 1983a. "What the PLO Calls a Cultural Archive." *New York Times*, March 3: A26.

———. 1983b. "Ill-Conceived Defense of a PLO Center." *New York Times*, April 9, sec. 1: 22.

———. 1983c. Letter to Don Peretz. April 15. A16 Ozick. Don Peretz Papers.

———. 1983d. Letter to Don Peretz. June 30. A16 Ozick. Don Peretz Papers.

———. 1983e. Letter to Don Peretz. July 11. A16 Ozick. Don Peretz Papers.

———. 1983f. Letter to Don Peretz. July 20. A16 Ozick. Don Peretz Papers.

———. 2017. Correspondence with Jonathan Marc Gribetz. October 22.

"Palestine at the United Nations." 1975. *Journal of Palestine Studies* 4, no. 2: 181–94.

Pappe, Ilan. 2020. "An Indicative Archive: Salvaging Nakba Documents." *Institute for Palestine Studies* 49, no. 3: 22–40.

Parkes, James. 1947. "Judaism and Zionism: A Christian View." In *Some Religious Aspects of Zionism: A Symposium*, edited by Leo Baeck, 7–12. London: Palestine House.

Parks, Robert Patrick. 2016. Correspondence with Jonathan Marc Gribetz. April 13.

Partington, David H. 1983. Letter to Don Peretz. March 16. A16 Ozick. Don Peretz Papers.

Pas, Itzik. 2020. "Hidat Natan Yellin-Mor: Tamid Mi-huts la-Kontsenzus." *Ha-Uma*: 95–103.

Patterson, David. 1992. *The Shriek of Silence: A Phenomenology of the Holocaust Novel*. Lexington: University Press of Kentucky.

———. 1999. *Along the Edge of Annihilation: The Collapse and Recovery of Life in the Holocaust Diary*. Seattle: University of Washington Press.

———. 2006. *Open Wounds: The Crisis of Jewish Thought in the Aftermath of Auschwitz*. Seattle: University of Washington Press.

———. 2011. *A Genealogy of Evil: Anti-Semitism from Nazism to Islamic Jihad*. New York: Cambridge University Press.

———. 2014. *Genocide in Jewish Thought*. Cambridge: Cambridge University Press.

Peretz, Don. 1983. Letter to Cynthia Ozick. June 28. A16 Ozick. Don Peretz Papers.

———. n/d. Letter to Stuart Schaar. A16 Ozick. Don Peretz Papers.

———. Undated. Handwritten to Cynthia Ozick. A16 Ozick. Don Peretz Papers.

Perlmann, Moshe. 1964. "Samau'al al-Maghribī Ifḥām Al-Yahūd: Silencing the Jews." *Proceedings of the American Academy for Jewish Research* 32: 5–136.

Peteet, Julie Marie. 1991. *Gender in Crisis: Women and the Palestinian Resistance Movement*. New York: Columbia University Press.

Philadelphia Inquirer. 1982. "Israelis Seize Leftists, Search Houses in W. Beirut, Lebanese Police Say." September 19: 24A.

PLO Research Center. 1982. "Hadha al-'Adad." *Shu'un Filastiniyya* 129–131: 4.

Podeh, Elie. 2017. "Diversity within a Show of Unity: Commemorating the Balfour Declaration in Israel (1917–2017)." *Israel Studies* 22, no. 3: 1–30.

Prashad, Vijay. 2008. *The Darker Nations: A People's History of the Third World*. New York: New Press.

Priel, Aharon. 1969a. "Hurshe'u Shiv'a Menihei ha-Petsatsot be-'Leil ha-Rimonim' bi-Yerushalayim." *Ma'ariv*, January 30: 4.

———. 1969b. "Irgunei ha-Habala Me'unyanim ba-'Aravim mi-Yisra'el." *Ma'ariv*, January 21: 4.

Qahwaji, Habib. 1971. "Al-Qissa al-Kamila li-Harakat al-Ard." *Shu'un Filastiniyya* 1: 112–25.

Qa'imat al-Manshurat, 1963–2013. 2013. Beirut: Institute for Palestine Studies.

Qa'war, Adib. 1968. *Al-Mar'a al-Yahudiyya fi Filastin al-Muhtalla.* Dirasat Filastiniyya 29. Beirut: PLO Research Center.

Rabi, Uzi. 2016. Correspondence with Jonathan Marc Gribetz. July 21.

Rabinovich, Itamar. 1985. *The War for Lebanon, 1970–1985.* Ithaca: Cornell University Press.

———. 2016. Correspondence with Jonathan Marc Gribetz. July 20.

———. 2018. Correspondence with Jonathan Marc Gribetz. March 12.

"Rahal ba'idan 'an Yafa: Samih Shabib Yudafin bi-Mukhayim al-Yarmuk." 2021. Archived at perma.cc/DR3N-NFUB.

Raheb, Mitri. 1995. *I Am a Palestinian Christian.* Minneapolis: Fortress Press.

———. 2014. *Faith in the Face of Empire: The Bible through Palestinian Eyes.* Maryknoll, NY: Orbis Books.

Razzouk, Ass'ad. 1963. "Die Ansätze zu einer Kulturanthropologie in der gegenwärtigen deutschen Philosophie." Tübingen: Eberhard-Karls-Universität zu Tübingen.

———. 1968a. *Isra'il al-Kubra: Dirasa fi al-Fikr al-Tawassu'i al-Sahyuni.* Kutub Filastiniyya 13. Beirut: PLO Research Center.

———. 1968b. *Al-Dawla wa-l-Din fi Isra'il.* Dirasat Filastiniyya 37. Beirut: PLO Research Center.

———. 1970a. *Al-Talmud wa-l-Sahyuniyya.* Kutub Filastiniyya 31. Beirut: PLO Research Center.

———. 1970b. *Greater Israel: A Study in Zionist Expansionist Thought.* Palestine Books 13. Beirut: PLO Research Center.

———. 1970c. *The Partisan Views of Reverend James Parkes.* Palestine Essays 22. Beirut: PLO Research Center.

———. 1970d. *Al-Majlis al-Amriki li-l-Yahudiyya: Dirasa fi al-Badil al-Yahudi li-l-Sahyuniyya.* Dirasat Filastiniyya 68. Beirut: PLO Research Center.

"Records of the General Conference, 4th Extraordinary Session, Paris 1982, Volume 3: Proceedings." 1983. 12th plenary meeting, November 30, 1982. Paris: UNESCO.

Reeve, Simon. 2011. *One Day in September: The Full Story of the 1972 Munich Olympics Massacre and the Israeli Revenge Operation "Wrath of God."* New York: Arcade.

"A Regime of Jewish Supremacy from the Jordan River to the Mediterranean Sea: This Is Apartheid." 2022. At https://www.btselem.org/publications/fulltext/202101_this_is_apartheid, accessed September 1, 2022. Archived at perma.cc/9P5U-VA4K.

Reicher, Gid'on. 1969. "Nidhitah Peniyah le-Baga"ts shel Toshavei Reh' ha-Gay'." *Yedi'ot Aharonot*, July 7: 26.

Rejwan, Nissim. 2000. *Arab Aims and Israeli Attitudes: A Critique of Yehoshafat Harkabi's Prognosis of the Arab-Israeli Conflict.* Davis Occasional Papers 77. Jerusalem: Leonard Davis Institute for International Relations, Hebrew University of Jerusalem.

Reuters. 1972. "2 Hurt in Beirut by Letter Bombs." *Boston Globe*, July 20: 8.

Rich, Spencer. 1969. "Anti-Israel Diatribes Bombard Congress." *Philadelphia Inquirer Public Ledger*, July 29: 15.

Rizk, Edward, trans. 1968. *The Palestine Question: Seminar of Arab Jurists on Palestine, Algiers, 22–27 July, 1967*. Beirut: Institute for Palestine Studies.

Robinson, Shira. 2003. "Local Struggle, National Struggle: Palestinian Responses to the Kafr Qasim Massacre and Its Aftermath, 1956–66." *International Journal of Middle East Studies* 35, no. 3: 393–416.

———. 2013. *Citizen Strangers: Palestinians and the Birth of Israel's Liberal Settler State*. Stanford, CA: Stanford University Press.

Robson, Laura. 2010. "Palestinian Liberation Theology, Muslim-Christian Relations and the Arab-Israeli Conflict." *Islam and Christian-Muslim Relations* 21, no. 1: 39–50.

———. 2011. *Colonialism and Christianity in Mandate Palestine*. Austin: University of Texas Press.

Roby, Bryan K. 2015. *The Mizrahi Era of Rebellion: Israel's Forgotten Civil Rights Struggle, 1948–1966*. Syracuse, NY: Syracuse University Press.

Ross, Jack. 2011. *Rabbi Outcast: Elmer Berger and American Jewish Anti-Zionism*. Washington, DC: Potomac Books.

Rostow, Eugene V. 1990. "Correspondence." *American Journal of International Law* 84, no. 3: 717–23.

Roth, Cecil, ed. 1966. *The Standard Jewish Encyclopedia*. London: W.H. Allen.

Rubenberg, Cheryl. 1983. *The Palestine Liberation Organization, Its Institutional Infrastructure*. Belmont, MA: Institute of Arab Studies.

———. 2005. "Palestine Research Center." In *Encyclopedia of the Palestinians*, rev. ed., edited by Philip Mattar, 371. New York: Facts on File.

Rubin, Barry M. 1993. *The PLO—between Anti-Zionism and Antisemitism: Background and Recent Developments*. Analysis of Current Trends in Antisemitism 1. Jerusalem: Hebrew University of Jerusalem, Vidal Sassoon International Center for the Study of Antisemitism.

Rubin, Trudy. 1982. "Israelis Unsure What Achieved by Beirut Stay: International Force Begins to Replace Perplexed Israeli Troops." *Christian Science Monitor*, September 24: 1, 13.

Rubinstein, Danny. 2022. *Madu'a lo Dafaktem 'al Dafnot ha-Mekhalit? 'A'san Kanafani, Sofer ha-Galut*. Rishon le-Tsiyon: Yedi'ot Aharonot.

Rubinstein, Elyakim. 1982. "Homer Asha"f she-Nitpas be-Beyrut." Lebanon/104.1/PLO Jerusalem: Foreign Ministry. 8367/6-אח. ISA.

Rumley, Grant, and Amir Tibon. 2017. *The Last Palestinian: The Rise and Reign of Mahmoud Abbas*. Amherst, NY: Prometheus Books.

Sa'b, Hasan. 1968. *Zionism and Racism*. Palestine Essays 2. Beirut: PLO Research Center.

"Sabri Jiryis n. ha-Memuneh 'al Mehoz Hayfa." November 11, 1964. High Court of Justice 253/64. https://www.takdin.co.il/Document/index/2237387, accessed July 27, 2021.

Sacher, Harry. 1952. *Israel: The Establishment of a State*. London: Weidenfels & Nicolson.

Safire, William. 1982. "All Hell Breaks Loose." *New York Times*, September 20: A15.

Sa'd, Ilyas. 1968a. *Isra'il wa-l-Siyaha*. Dirasat Filastiniyya 32. Beirut: PLO Research Center.

———. 1968b. *Isra'il wa-l-Batala*. Dirasat Filastiniyya 39. Beirut: PLO Research Center.

Said, Edward W. 1982. "'Purifying,' Israelis Called It." *New York Times*, September 29: A27.

Salmon, Yosef. 2002. *Religion and Zionism: First Encounters.* Jerusalem: The Hebrew University Magnes Press.

Sand, Shlomo. 2009. *The Invention of the Jewish People.* Translated by Yael Lotan. New York: Verso.

Sarna, Jonathan D. 1999. "Converts to Zionism in the American Reform Movement." In *Zionism and Religion,* edited by Shmuel Almog, Jehuda Reinharz, and Anita Shapira, 188–203. Hanover: University Press of New England.

Sayegh, Anis. 1966a. *Filastin wa-l-Qawmiyya al-'Arabiyya.* Abhath Filastiniyya 3. Beirut: PLO Research Center.

———. 1966b. *Al-Hashimiyyun wa-Qadiyat Filastin.* Sidon: Jaridat al-Muharrir wa-l-Maktaba al-'Asriyya.

———. 1967. *Mizan al-Quwa al-'Askariyya bayna al-Duwal al-'Arabiyya wa-Isra'il.* Dirasat Filastiniyya 12. Beirut: PLO Research Center.

———, ed. 1968a. *Yawmiyyat Hartzil.* Translated by Hilda Sha'ban Sayegh. Kutub Filastiniyya 10. Beirut: PLO Research Center.

———. 1968b. Preface to *Al-Mar'a al-Yahudiyya fi Filastin al-Muhtalla,* by Adib Qa'war, 7–8. Dirasat Filastiniyya 29. Beirut: PLO Research Center.

———, ed. 1969. *Khara'it Turuq al-Muwasalat fi Filastin al-Muhtalla.* Khara'it wa-Suwwar Filastiniyya 3. PLO Research Center.

———, ed. 1970a. *Al-Fikra al-Sahyuniyya: al-Nusus al-Asasiyya.* Kutub Filastiniyya 21. Beirut: PLO Research Center.

———. 1970b. *Palestine and Arab Nationalism.* Palestine Essays 3. Beirut: PLO Research Center.

———. 1971. "Shu'un Filastiniyya." *Shu'un Filastiniyya* 1: 4.

———. 2006. *Anis Sayigh 'an Anis Sayigh.* Beirut: Riad El-Rayyes Books.

Sayegh, Fayez. 1950. "Existential Philosophy: A Formal Examination." PhD dissertation, Georgetown University.

———. 1964. Letter to Khosrow Mostafi. Correspondence for Teaching Positions 1962–1964. Mid001 Bx 189 Fd 1 (Stapled set 1/4). Fayez A. Sayegh Collection.

———. 1965a. *Zionist Colonialism in Palestine.* Palestine Monographs 1. Beirut: PLO Research Center.

———. 1965b. *Al-Isti'mar al-Sahyuni fi Filastin.* Translated by Abdul Wahhab al-Kayyali. Dirasat Filastiniyya 1. Beirut: PLO Research Center.

———. 1965c. "General Report on the Founding Period beginning 1 February and ending 30 April 1965." Bx 281 Fd 1 It 9. Fayez A. Sayegh Collection.

———. 1966. *The United Nations and the Palestine Question: April 1947–April 1965.* Facts and Figures 2. Beirut: PLO Research Center.

———. 1967a. "Do Jews Have a 'Divine Right' to Palestine?" Palestine Essays 4. Beirut: PLO Research Center.

———. 1967b. *Al-Diblumasiyya al-Sahyuniyya.* Dirasat Filastiniyya 13. Beirut: PLO Research Center.

———. 1970. *Palestine, Israel and Peace.* Palestine Essays 17. Beirut: PLO Research Center.

———. 1976. *Zionism: "A Form of Racism and Racial Discrimination": Four Statements Made at the U.N. General Assembly.* New York: Office of the Permanent Observer of the Palestine Liberation Organization to the United Nations.

Sayigh, Rosemary. 1979. *Palestinians: From Peasants to Revolutionaries: A People's History*. London: Zed Press.

Sayigh, Yezid. 1997. *Armed Struggle and the Search for State: The Palestinian National Movement, 1949–1993*. Oxford: Oxford University Press.

Sayigh, Yusif. 1970. *Towards Peace in Palestine*. Beirut: Fifth of June Society.

Sayigh, Yusif, and Rosemary Sayigh. 2015. *Yusif Sayigh: Arab Economist and Palestinian Patriot: A Fractured Life Story*. Cairo: The American University in Cairo Press.

Schaar, Stuart. 1983a. Letter to the Editor, *New York Times*. March 8. A16 Ozick. Don Peretz Papers.

———. 1983b. Letter to David H. Partington. March 22. A16 Ozick. Don Peretz Papers.

———. 2017a. Correspondence with Jonathan Marc Gribetz. September 14.

———. 2017b. Correspondence with Jonathan Marc Gribetz. September 15.

Schmemann, Serge. 1982. "Brezhnev Bids Reagan Join in U.N. in 'Bridling' Israelis." *New York Times*, September 21: A16.

Schwartz, Daniel B. 2019. *Ghetto: The History of a Word*. Cambridge, MA: Harvard University Press.

Sela, Avraham. 2014. "The PLO at Fifty: A Historical Perspective." *Contemporary Review of the Middle East* 1, no. 3: 269–333.

Sela, Rona, dir. 2017. *Looted and Hidden: Palestinian Archives in Israel*. Documentary.

———. 2018. "The Genealogy of Colonial Plunder and Erasure—Israel's Control over Palestinian Archives." *Social Semiotics* 28, no. 2: 201–29.

Selzer, Michael. 1967. *The Aryanization of the Jewish State*. New York: Black Star.

Sha'ban Sayegh, Hilda. 1971. *Al-Tamyiz didda al-Yahud al-Sharqiyyin fi Isra'il*. Dirasat Filastiniyya 85. Beirut: PLO Research Center.

Shabeeb, Samih. 2005. *Al-Dhakira al-Da'i'a: Qissat al-Masir al-Ma'sawi li-Markaz al-Abhath al-Filastini*. Ramallah: Muwatin.

———. 2018. Interview by Jonathan Marc Gribetz. May.

Shabeeb, Samih, and Bayan Nuwayhid Hut. 2010. *Anis Sayigh wa-l-Mu'assasa al-Filastiniyya: al-Siyasat, al-Mumarasat, al-Intaj*. Ramallah: Muwatin.

Shabtai, Shay. 2012. "OSINT in the Service of Intelligence." In *Israel's Silent Defender: An Inside Look at Sixty Years of Israeli Intelligence*, edited by Amos Gilboa, Ephraim Lapid, and Yochi Erlich, 217–35. Jerusalem: Gefen Books.

al-Sha'ir, Muhammad. 1967. *Al-Harb al-Fida'iyya fi Filastin 'ala Daw' Tajarib al-Shu'ub fi Qital al-'Isabat*. Kutub Filastiniyya 7. Beirut: PLO Research Center.

Shaked, Shaul. 2016. Correspondence with Jonathan Marc Gribetz. July 19.

Shani, Yitzhak. 1985. "Tsav bi-dvar Pirsumim Asurim/Amr bi-sha'ni al-Matbu'at al-Mahdhura." *Minsharim, Tsavim, u-Minuyim shel Ezor Yehuda ve-Shomron* 71. Israel Defense Forces.

Sheehan, Neil. 1967. "5 New Groups Tied to C.I.A. Conduits." *New York Times*, February 17: 1, 16.

Sheffy, Yigal. 2018. Interview by Jonathan Marc Gribetz. February.

Shehadeh, Imad. 1970. *David and Goliath, in Nine Easy Lessons*. Beirut: PLO Research Center.

"Shele"g Shevuyim/'Atsurim." 1983. 9332-7-צה. ISA.

Shibl, Yusuf. 1968. *Al-Siyasa al-Maliyya fi Isra'il*. Dirasat Filastiniyya 36. Beirut: PLO Research Center.

————. 1969. *Tijarat Isra'il al-Kharijiyya*. Dirasat Filastiniyya 60. Beirut: PLO Research Center.

Shiblak, Abbas. 1997. "Palestinians in Lebanon and the PLO." *Journal of Refugee Studies* 10, no. 3: 261–74.

Shipler, David K. 1982a. "Israelis Pressing for Peace Treaty with the Lebanese." *New York Times*, September 8: A10.

————. 1982b. "Evidence Suggests Israelis Were Aware of Killings." *New York Times*, September 21: A1.

————. 1983a. "A Blind Spot Shows in the Jewish State." *New York Times*, February 20: 4E.

————. 1983b. "Palestinians and Israelis Welcome Their Prisoners Freed in Exchange." *New York Times*, November 25: A1, A11.

————. 1986. *Arab and Jew: Wounded Spirits in a Promised Land*. New York: Times Books.

Shlaim, Avi. 1988. *Collusion across the Jordan: King Abdullah, the Zionist Movement, and the Partition of Palestine*. New York: Columbia University Press.

————. 1998. *The Politics of Partition: King Abdullah, the Zionists, and Palestine, 1921–1951*. New York: Oxford University Press.

Shukairy, Ahmad. 1965. Letter to Fayez Sayegh. 12 February. Bx 281 Fd 3 It 49. Fayez A. Sayegh Collection.

————. 1966. *Liberation—Not Negotiation*. Palestine Books 3. Beirut: PLO Research Center.

————. 1967. *Mashru' al-Dawla al-'Arabiyya al-Muttahida*. Abhath Filastiniyya 5. Beirut: PLO Research Center.

Sigal, Phillip. 1961. "Reflections on Jewish Nationalism." *Issues* 15, no. 5: 20–29.

Sinai, Moshe. 1982. Letter to Haim Israeli. "The Archive of the PLO Center in Beirut." December 21. 824/2003–114. IDF Archives.

————. 2018. Correspondence with Jonathan Marc Gribetz. January 30.

Singer, Richard. 1959. "Excerpts from 'The Role of the Minority in Jewish Experience.'" *Issues* 13, no. 2: 41–45.

Singh, Bhim, and Angelina Helou. 1970. *An Examination of Documents on Which the State of Israel Is Based*. Palestine Monographs 76. Beirut: PLO Research Center.

Sirhan, Bassem. 1969. *The American Community in Lebanon and the Palestine Problem: A Study in Changing Attitudes*. Facts and Figures 27. Beirut: PLO Research Center.

Sirriyeh, Hussein. 2000. "Jordan and the Legacies of the Civil War of 1970–71." *Civil Wars* 3, no. 3: 74–86.

Sleiman, Hana. 2016. "The Paper Trail of a Liberation Movement." *Arab Studies Journal* 24, no. 1: 42–67.

Smith, Sidney. 1966. "Obituary: Alfred Guillaume." *Bulletin of the School of Oriental and African Studies, University of London* 29: 478–81.

Soukarieh, Mayssun. 2009. "Speaking Palestinian: An Interview with Rosemary Sayigh." *Journal of Palestine Studies* 38, no. 4: 12–28.

Spiegel, Baruch. 2018. Interview by Jonathan Marc Gribetz. May.

Stampfer, Shaul. 2013. "Did the Khazars Convert to Judaism?" *Jewish Social Studies* 19, no. 3: 1–72.

Stein, Leonard. 1983. *The Balfour Declaration*. London: Jewish Chronicle Publications.

Steinberg, Matti. 1975. "Ha-Irgunim ha-Falastiniyim be-Asha"f." Kenasim Merkaz ha-Hasbarah—Sherut ha-Pirsumim.

———. 1989. "The PLO and Palestinian Islamic Fundamentalism." *Jewish Quarterly* 52: 37–54.

———. 2008. *'Omdim le-Goralam: ha-Toda'ah ha-Le'umit ha-Falastinit 1967–2007*. Tel Aviv: Yedi'ot Aharonot.

———. 2016a. *In Search of Modern Palestinian Nationhood*. Tel Aviv: Moshe Dayan Center for Middle Eastern and African Studies, Tel Aviv University.

———. 2016b. Correspondence with Jonathan Marc Gribetz. July 19.

———. 2017a. Interview by Jonathan Marc Gribetz. September.

———. 2017b. Correspondence with Jonathan Marc Gribetz. October 25.

———. 2017c. Correspondence with Jonathan Marc Gribetz. November 9.

———. 2017d. Correspondence with Jonathan Marc Gribetz. November 10.

———. 2022. Interview by Jonathan Marc Gribetz. May.

Stern, Bat-Sheva Margalit. 2009. "'She's Got a Man's Head on Her Shoulders': Ada Fishman (Maimon) as a Test Case for Private, Public and Gendered Aspects of Women's Political Activity." *Nashim: A Journal of Jewish Women's Studies & Gender Issues* no. 17: 141–75.

Stillman, Norman. 2005. "Islamic Anti-Semitism." In *New Dictionary of the History of Ideas*, edited by Maryanne Cline Horowitz, 6 vols., 1:103–5. Detroit: Charles Scribner's Sons.

Strauss, Leo. 1997a. "Why We Remain Jews: Can Jewish Faith and History Still Speak to Us?" In *Jewish Philosophy and the Crisis of Modernity: Essays and Lectures in Modern Jewish Thought*, edited by Kenneth Hart Green, 311–56. Albany: State University of New York Press.

———. 1997b. "Preface to *Spinoza's Critique of Religion*." In *Jewish Philosophy and the Crisis of Modernity: Essays and Lectures in Modern Jewish Thought*, edited by Kenneth Hart Green, 137–77. Albany: State University of New York Press.

Talmon, J. L. 1965. *The Unique and the Universal: Some Historical Reflections*. New York: Braziller.

Tamari, Steve. 2015. "Khairieh Kasmieh (1936–2014)." *International Journal of Middle East Studies* 47, no. 3: 655–57.

al-Tariqi, 'Abd Allah. 1967. *Al-Bitrul al-'Arabi: Silah fi al-Ma'raka*. Dirasat Filastiniyya 20. Beirut: PLO Research Center.

Tarnowski, Stefan. 2021. "Confirming the Already Confirmed." *London Review of Books Blog*, February 10. At https://www.lrb.co.uk/blog/2021/february/confirming-the-already-confirmed, accessed July 16, 2023. Archived at perma.cc/92L7-WYUF.

Tessler, Mark. 2009. *A History of the Israeli-Palestinian Conflict*. 2nd ed. Bloomington: Indiana University Press.

"Thalathun 'Aman 'ala Istishhadihim." n/d. PLO Research Center.

Thompson, Elizabeth. 2013. *Justice Interrupted: The Struggle for Constitutional Government in the Middle East*. Cambridge, MA: Harvard University Press.

"A Threshold Crossed: Israeli Authorities and the Crimes of Apartheid and Persecution." 2021. Human Rights Watch. At https://www.hrw.org/report/2021/04/27/threshold-crossed/israeli-authorities-and-crimes-apartheid-and-persecution, accessed October 21, 2021. Archived at perma.cc/JG8K-SB7Z.

Time. 1976. "The World: Reality and a Right to Dream." December 13.

The Times (UK). 1963. "Who Is a Jew?" July 25: 8.

Toynbee, Arnold Joseph. 1969. *Experiences*. New York: Oxford University Press.

Traboulsi, Fawwaz. 2012. *A History of Modern Lebanon*. London: Pluto Press.

Trounson, Rebecca. 1982. "In Beirut's Aftermath, Looting Laid to Israelis." *Boston Globe*, October 19: 1, 8.

al-Tunisi, Muhammad Khalifa. 1951. *Al-Khatar al-Yahudi: Brutukulat Hukama' Sahyun: Awwal Tarjama 'Arabiyya Amina Kamila*. Cairo: Matba'at Dar al-Kitab al-'Arabi.

Turner, Karen. 2000. "Soldiers and Symbols: North Vietnamese Women and the American War." In *A Soldier and a Woman: Sexual Integration in the Military,* edited by Gerard J. DeGroot and C. M. Peniston-Bird, 185–204. New York: Longman.

United Press International. 1972. "25 Die at Israeli Airport as 3 Gunmen from Plane Fire on 250 in a Terminal." May 31: 1, 27.

Vashitz, Yosef. 1960. "Kevutsat 'al Ard' ve-Sevivah." *'Al ha-Mishmar*, February 3: 2, 5.

Volovici, Marc. 2017. "Leon Pinsker's Autoemancipation! And the Emergence of German as a Language of Jewish Nationalism." *Central European History* 50, no. 1: 34–58.

von Horn, Carl. 1966. *Soldiering for Peace*. London: Cassell.

———. 1967. *Soldiering for Peace*. New York: David McKay.

Walsh, Edward. 1982. "Israeli Newspapers, Protesters Criticize Begin and Sharon Over Beirut Killings." *Washington Post*, September 24: A18.

Walter, Alissa. 2022. "The Repatriation of Iraqi Ba'th Party Archives: Ethical and Practical Considerations." *Journal of Contemporary Iraq & the Arab World* 16, no. 1–2: 117–36.

Washington Post. 1974. "Automated Rockets Damage 3 PLO Offices in Beirut." December 11: A14.

Waskow, Arthur I. 1976. "Talking with the P.L.O." *New York Times*, December 16: 47.

Waxman, Yosef. 1971. "Nehsefa Reshet ha-Hashuda be-Haf 'alat Mekhonit-ha-Tofet be-Sederot Kaka"l." *Ma'ariv*, July 25: 9.

Weld, Kirsten. 2014. *Paper Cadavers: The Archives of Dictatorship in Guatemala*. Durham: Duke University Press.

Wiesel, Elie, and David Patterson. 1991. *In Dialogue and Dilemma with Elie Wiesel*. Wakefield, NH: Longwood Academic.

Wilford, Hugh. 2013. *America's Great Game: The CIA's Secret Arabists and the Shaping of the Modern Middle East*. New York: Basic Books.

———. 2017. "American Friends of the Middle East: The CIA, US Citizens, and the Secret Battle for American Public Opinion in the Arab–Israeli Conflict, 1947–1967." *Journal of American Studies* 51, no. 1: 93–116.

Wilhelm, Kurt. 1962. "Benno Jacob, a Militant Rabbi." *The Leo Baeck Institute Year Book* 7, no. 1: 75–94.

"William Lee Holladay, 1926–2016." 2017. At http://www.duxburysystems.org/downloads /holladay/bill/obit.htm, accessed November 22, 2017. Archived at perma.cc/6YHB-M4EN.

Wolf, Arye, ed. 1965. "Piskei Din: Hashgaha Mishtarit." *La-Merhav*, July 22: 4.

Yahia, F[aris]. 1970. *The Palestine Question and International Law*. Palestine Books 28. Beirut: PLO Research Center.

Yaqub, Salim. 2016. *Imperfect Strangers: Americans, Arabs, and U.S.-Middle East Relations in the 1970s*. United States in the World. Ithaca: Cornell University Press.

Al-Yawmiyyat al-Filastiniyya: 1/1/1965–30/6/1965. 1966. Vol. 1. PLO Research Center.

Al-Yawmiyyat al-Filastiniyya: 1/7/1965–31/12/1965. 1966. Vol. 2. PLO Research Center.

Yediʿot Aharonot. 1983. "Ha-ʿZikaron' Hozer ha-Bayta." December 11: 13.

Yoʾeli, Z. 1960. "ʿAl Shlihei Natsar bi-Yerushalayim." *Davar,* February 29: 2.

Zelkovitz, Ido. 2012. *Tenuʿat ha-Fataʾʾh: Islam, Leʾumiyut u-Folitika shel Maʾavak Mezuyan.* Tel Aviv: Resling.

Zerubavel, Yael. 2008. "Memory, the Rebirth of the Native, and the 'Hebrew Bedouin' Identity." *Social Research* 75, no. 1: 315–52.

Zohar, Gadi. 2022. Interview by Jonathan Marc Gribetz. March.

Zuhur, Sherifa. 2002. "Empowering Women or Dislodging Sectarianism: Civil Marriage in Lebanon." *Yale Journal of Law and Feminism* 14, no. 1: 177–209.

INDEX

Aaron, 143

abandoned property (AP), 50, 245

Abaza, Ibrahim, 246, 250

Abbas, Mahmoud: antisemitism and, 276; Beirut and, 275–77; Damascus and, 275; Institute for Palestine Studies (IPS) and, 275; Jiryis and, 276; Nazis and, 276; Palestine National Council (PNC) and, 310n63; race and, 163; restarting Center by, 251; Washington, DC, and, 60

ʿAbd al-ʿAziz, Mustafa, 131–32

ʿAbd al-Hadi, ʿAwni, 31, 233

Abdallah, Hisham, 179–81

Abd al-Nasir, Shawqi, 109

Abdo, Ali Ibrahim, 157–61, 317n5

Abdul-Rahman, Asaʾd, 28–29

Abed, Lutfi al-, xi, 89, 94

Abid, Ibrahim al-, xi; American Council for Judaism and, 126–27, 311nn12–19; Balfour Declaration and, 74–75; European imperialism and, 74–75, 80, 301n27–29; *Handbook to the Palestine Question*, 39–40, 74, 89, 125–27, 162; *Israel and Human Rights*, 288n37; *The Moshav: The Cooperative Village in Israel*, 30; prisoner exchange and, 251, 252; racism and, 162–63; translation and, 89; work of PLO Research Center and, 28–30, 39–40

Abraham, 101–2

Abu Asba, Naif Awad Hassan, 239

Abu Ayn, Ziad, 239, 330n38

Abu Ghazala, Bassam, 28

Abu-Lughod, Lila, 277–78

Abu Nidal, 187

Agmon, David, 211

Agranat Commission, 182

Ahmad, Eqbal, 216–17, 326n55

Aiken, George D., 39

Air France, 2, 230, 237, 245, 250

Algeria, 2, 285n7; archives and, 230–31, 236–39, 245, 250–55, 277–78; race and, 157, 160

Alkalai, Yehuda, xii; antisemitism and, 114–16, 119; Kalischer and, 90–91, 116, 303n22; translation and, 86, 90–91

Allis, Oswald, T., 102

Alloush, Naji, 29

All-Palestine Government, 233

Alon, Ilana, 239, 240, 245

Alsberg, Paul Abraham, 208, 210, 223–24

AMaN, 208, 210

Ameri, Anan, xv; Jiryis and, 43; *Palestinian Agricultural Industrial Development, 1900–70*, 34; work of PLO Research Center and, 32–36, 292nn33–36

American Community in Lebanon and the Palestine Problem, The: A Study in Changing Attitudes (Facts and Figures series), 38

American Council for Judaism, 124–36; Abid and, 126–27, 311nn12–19; Anis Sayegh and, 125, 129, 131, 133, 310n72, 313n44; antisemitism and, 132, 313n42; anti-Zionism and, 123–36; Arab League and, 125, 130, 133; Arab states and, 311n11; Arafat and, 125; Berger and, 124, 127–35, 312nn25–27, 312n40, 313n42, 313n59, 314n61;

363

Old Testament, 40, 101–2

On Zionist Literature (Kanafani), 29, 36, 112–13

operational intelligence, 194–97

Operation Hiram, 44

Operation Litani, 186

Operation Peace for Galilee, 187

Organization of Arab Students, 129

Oriental (Eastern/Mizrahi) Jews, 159, 161, 164–65, 168–70, 264,317n6, 318n33, 319n64, 320n69

OSINT, 323n32

Oslo Accords, 49, 237–38, 251, 254

Other, the, xiii, 129

Ottaway, David, 212

Ottomans, xii, 232; antisemitism and, 120; European imperialism and, 72, 74–77, 81, 83; gender equality and, 147; Hudson and, 289n47; racism and, 159–60

Owen, John M., IV, 88

Ozick, Cynthia, xv; accusations of, 216–21; *Esquire* article of, 216; global debate and, xv, 216–22, 226, 326n53, 326n56, 327nn63–67, 327n70, 328n77; Granot and, 226; Jiryis and, 216–21, 226, 327n74; *New York Times* and, 215–19; Peretz and, 215–22, 226, 327n63, 327n67, 327n70, 327n75, 328n77; Quakers and, 218–20; scholars' objection to, 216–18

Palestine and Arab Nationalism (Anis Sayegh), 98–100

Palestine and the Jews (Jannaway), 246

Palestine Arab Delegation, 124

Palestine Chronology series, 26–29, 31, 291n14

Palestine in Focus (Hadawi), 39–40

Palestine Liberation Organization, The (Rubenberg), 133

Palestine Mandate System, 67

Palestine Monographs series, 27, 71, 290n7

Palestine National Council (PNC): Abbas and, 310n63; European imperialism and, 69; Executive Committee of, 14; Jiryis

and, 55; "knowing the enemy" and, 257, 266–71; need for PLO Research Center and, 12, 14, 286n12; political compromise and, 256–61; Ramallah and, 310n63; revealing evolution of, 266–71; Ten Points Program and, 49, 256–61, 267, 333n27

Palestine National Fund, 4, 14, 22

"Palestine question": American Council for Judaism and, 125; archives and, 232; European imperialism and, 74, 77, 79, 81; *Handbook to the Palestine Question* and, 39–40, 74, 89, 125, 162; need for PLO Research Center and, 1, 13, 15, 21, 287n17, 288n31; racism and, 161–62; translation of, 1, 285n1; work of PLO Research Center and, 1, 16, 19, 39–40

Palestine Question, The (seminar collection), 79–80

Palestine Question and International Law, The (Yahia), 81

Palestinian Affairs: archives and, 230, 243, 251–55, 278; Darwish and, 43; global debate and, 206, 224, 227; Jiryis and, 43, 49, 58–60; "knowing the enemy" and, 258–59; Tel Aviv and, 189; work of PLO Research Center and, 21–22, 26, 31, 37, 39, 287n26

Palestinian Christians, 11, 21, 88, 98–99, 177, 289n59, 302n9, 304n53

Palestinian Encyclopedia, 20, 27, 232

"Palestinian Liberation Organization and the Arabs of Israel, The" (memo), 49

Palestinian National Liberation Movement (Fateh): Ameri and, 34; American Council for Judaism and, 125; Arab states and, 10, 87, 125, 226, 267; Battle of Karameh and, 69; Cohen and, 319n66; European imperialism and, 69; founding of, 10–11; global debate and, 225; Jiryis and, 55, 58, 60; "knowing the enemy" and, 256–59; pan-Arabism and, 302n56; publications of, 87; terrorism and, 182; translation and, 286n3

Palestinian National Movement (PNM): American Council for Judaism and, 126,

Sayegh, Hilda Sha'ban, xi, 30, 35, 89, 164, 318n42

Sayigh, Rosemary, 289n58, 293n57

Sayigh, Yezid, 10, 258, 260, 286nn1–3, 290n62, 310n72

Sayigh, Yusif, 27, 315n4

Schaar, Stuart, xv, 216–17

Schechter, Solomon, xii

Schlesinger Library, 203

Schmidt, Helmut, 187

Schwarz-Nardi, Shulamith, 150

secularism, 87–88, 97, 109, 298n78

Segal, Jerome, 327n75

Sela, Rona, 5

Self-Criticism after the Defeat (al-Azm), 109, 137

Selzer, Michael, 164

Sephardim, 169, 319n64, 319n66

Shabeeb, Samih, xv, 253–55

Sha'ir, Muhammad al-, 29

Shaked, Shaul, 239–40

Shakur, Imad, 225

Shamir, Shimon, 240

Sharon, Ariel, 187

Shatila: global debate and, 199–200, 213, 221; massacre in, 2, 199–200, 213, 221, 322n12; refugees and, 2, 33, 188, 200, 213, 221; Tel Aviv and, 188, 322n12

Shefer, Dov, 239

Sheffy, Yigal, xiv–xvi, 230, 250, 323n31

Shehadeh, Imad, 30

Shemesh, Kokhavi, 169–70, 319n64

Shibl, Yusuf Ahmad, 30

Shiblak, Abbas, 289n59, 289n61

Shiite Muslims, 211

Shiloah Institute, 223, 240–43, 245

Shipler, David, 215, 218, 231, 330n26

Shomer, Ha-, 146

Shoufani, Elias, 216–17, 225

Shtayyeh, Mohammad, 252–53

Shukairy, Ahmad, 288n30; American Council for Judaism and, 124–29, 311n4; Anis Sayegh and, 20, 43; Arab states and, 12, 29; Balfour Declaration and, 67, 70–73;

Beirut and, 16, 22–23, 126; Berger and, 300n16, 313n42; Bible and, 124–25; Covenant and, 12–14, 67–71, 124–25, 300n13, 311nn4–11; European imperialism and, 67–73; Fayez Sayegh and, 15–16, 18, 20, 27, 43, 73, 288n35; Institute for Palestine Studies (IPS) and, 15, 18; Khalidi and, 22; Palestine Arab Delegation and, 124; work of PLO Research Center and, 27, 29

Simon, Ernst, 220

Sinai, Moshe, 209, 325nn27–28

Sinai Peninsula, 9, 68, 72, 100, 187, 263

Singer, Richard, 113–14

Sirriyeh, Hussein, 69

Six-Day War, 29, 69, 80, 109, 129–30, 180

Sleiman, Hana, 5, 234–35, 238

Sneh, Moshe, 88

socialism: al-Ard and, 48, 50, 296n27; European imperialism and, 79; gender equality and, 137, 314n2; Jumblatt and, 35; Palestinian nationalism and, 13; Progressive Socialist Party and, 35; Razzouk and, 92, 117

Society of American Archivists (SAA), 202–4, 222–23

Society of Friends, 218–20, 299n88

Sofer, Naim, 49

Soldiering for Peace (von Horn), 148

Soncino Press, 108–11, 115, 117, 307nn7–8, 308n37, 308n45

Sovietology, 272–73

Soviet Union, 9, 43, 203, 259, 272

Spain, 157–58, 170

Spiegel, Baruch, xvi, 188

spies, 50

Standard Jewish Encyclopedia, 157

State and Religion in Israel (PLO Research Center), 1, 41

State of Israel: American Council for Judaism and, 130–33; establishment of, 9; European imperialism and, 68; gender equality and, 142, 147, 149; global debate and, 226, 326n56; Jiryis and, 43–44, 50–52, 297n45; "knowing the enemy" and, 257;

State of Israel (*continued*)
    need for PLO Research Center and, 23;
    Ozick and, 326n56; racism and, 162, 168;
    Razzouk and, 104, 108, 305n66; terrorism
    and, 173, 175; work of PLO research cen-
    ter and, 40
Statistical Abstract of Israel, The, 145
Steinberg, Matti, xvi, 49; archives and, 229,
    239–41, 246, 330n42, 331n43; background
    of, 189; European imperialism and,
    302n56; global debate and, 202, 207, 226;
    as Israeli intelligence expert, 321n35;
    "knowing the enemy" and, 258, 261; mili-
    tary and, 322n27; National Library of
    Israel and, 246; Tel Aviv and, 189–92,
    195–96, 321n35, 322nn25–27, 323n31
Stranger in My Own Land (F. Jiryis), 56
Strauss, Leo, 309n50
Sudan, 60, 63, 299n86
Suez Canal, 72
Sukkot, 190
Suleiman, Muhammad, 53
Sunni Muslims, 15
Supreme Court: al-Ard and, 46, 50–54; Ard,
    Jiryis and, 46, 50–54, 295n18, 297n45;
    racism and, 168
surveillance, 50, 52, 56, 209, 224–25
Sweden, 204–5
Sykes-Picot agreement, 72
Symington, Stuart, 39
Syria: antisemitism and, 108, 116; Damascus,
    11, 32, 55, 64, 90, 108, 163, 275, 317n4,
    332n66; European imperialism and, 78–79;
    gender equality and, 137; global debate
    and, 198, 211; Jiryis and, 50; "knowing
    the enemy" and, 258; need for PLO
    Research Center and, 9, 11–15, 20–21,
    289n61; prisoner exchange and, 241–42,
    331n49; racism and, 156–57; Tel Aviv
    and, 195; work of PLO Research Center
    and, 32

Talhami, Daoud, 34
Talmon, Jacob, 96–97

Talmud: antisemitism and, 107–21; Babylo-
    nian, 159; Bloch and, 307n8; Herzl and,
    118–19; Landau on, 307n18; psychological
    barrier and, 310n72; Razzouk and, 95, 106,
    307n23, 308n39; translation of, 307n7;
    Zionism and, 107–21
Talmud and Zionism, The (Razzouk), 1;
    antisemitism and, 106–8, 112–20; global
    debate and, 227; translation and, 95
Tamir, Shmuel, 229
Tannaim (mishnaic rabbis), 114–15
Tariqi, ʿAbd Allah al-, 29
Tel Aviv University, xvi, 240
Ten Points Program, 49, 247, 256–61, 267,
    333n27
Terra Santa, 44
terrorism: Abdallah on, 179–81; American
    Council for Judaism and, 133; Anis Sayegh
    and, 36; antipathy and, 178–79; Arab states
    and, 171, 179; Arafat and, 216, 221, 321n35;
    Beirut and, 105, 171, 181–82; Bishuti on,
    171–76, 320nn15–16; bombing and, 36 (*see
    also* bombs); British Mandate and, 172,
    175–76, 178; Christians and, 177; colonial-
    ism and, 177; common association of, 2;
    Counter-Terrorism Act, 170; Deir Yassin
    and, 176; Egypt and, 101; fear and, 178–79;
    France and, 178–81; Gaza Strip and,
    319n68; gender equality and, 140, 316n41;
    global debate and, 205–21, 225–27, 325n19,
    325n22; guerrilla groups and, 176; Hadawi
    on, 39; Hammami and, 321n35; Herut
    party and, 28, 65, 94, 171; hijackings and, 2,
    24, 36; immigration and, 172; Institute for
    Palestine Studies (IPS) and, 177; Israel
    Defense Forces (IDF) and, 176; Jerusalem
    and, 173, 177; Jiryis on, 54–55, 298n64;
    Jordan and, 318n42; Kafr Qasim and, 176;
    Lebanon and, 55, 133, 182, 187, 205, 211, 215,
    227, 231, 322n8; massacres and, 173, 176, 178,
    321n23; military and, 171–74, 179–81,
    320n15; Munich Olympics and, 36, 176–78;
    murder and, 172, 176, 178, 320n15; Muslims
    and, 87, 90, 98–101; necessity of, 171–73;